SURVIVOR

A Story About Facing Adversity and Coming Out on Top

Richard René Silvin

Silvin Books and Productions

 All persons and events in this book are real, although some names have been changed.

ISBN: 9798375499253
Graphics and Design: Robert Versteeg

Cover photo's:
René as a young boy, 1954
René at Le Rosey, 1965
René aboard the QM2, 1987
René in Palm Beach, 2019
www.rrsilvin.com

FOREWORD

By Dr. Robert Versteeg

When I met René in 2013, he was 65 and I was 45. Our obvious age difference never mattered to either one of us. What I didn't know in the beginning was that he had been single for 15 years after his last partner died. I was only single for 15 days before I decided, with full conviction, that René was my soulmate and that I would "fight for him" to become his partner for the rest of our lives.

When you start dating someone, you normally slowly reveal your history to one another. Initially, one probably tries to paint a rosy picture of themselves, and then slowly add some sordid details, if any exist. With René this was different, because he had written two books, one about his childhood (*I Survived Swiss Boarding Schools*) and one about his adult life (*Walking the Rainbow*). I must admit, it was an odd experience to get to know someone's past so quickly by reading about it, instead of exploring a new partner's history over dinner. What was mostly striking to me was all the trauma he had endured growing up and living through the AIDS crisis, when he lost two long-term partners. I was impressed that the man I saw before me, despite all these setbacks in life, had kept his sense of humor, his positive outlook on life, and his upbeat personality intact. What most endeared me was that he allowed the little boy inside to come out and continued to look at life with a sense of wonder and exploration. One of the first things he said to me, when we embarked on our journey through life together was, "We will experience 20 years in five years," and we certainly have…and them some!

Furthermore, both books included in this anniversary edition, although completely based on real-life, read like novels. The number of celebrities he met through his education at a prestigious Swiss boarding school is astounding.

He had also written a book about his relationship with Wallis Simpson, the Duchess of Windsor, *Noblesse Oblige – The Duchess of Windsor as I knew her.* As a hobby, he was sporadically giving lectures about Wallis, and he asked me if I would be interested in expanding these activities. He didn't have to ask me twice. After watching him speak to an audience in Palm Beach, I knew that here was an untapped talent that should be seen by larger audiences. We started our own company, Silvin Books & Productions.

With our little company, we use his multi-faceted life to find stories that are close to his heart. As a child, with his parents living on both sides of the Atlantic, he developed a love for ocean liners that crossed the Atlantic; we created several lectures about that topic. Through his work he flew all over the world and was a frequent flyer on the supersonic Concorde; we developed a lecture about that. And like I mentioned, through Swiss boarding schools he befriended the grandsons of Marlene Dietrich, the children of Aristotle Onassis, and met famous people like Jacqueline Kennedy-Onassis, Audrey Hepburn, Elizabeth Taylor, and many others. So, it made sense to have lectures on their lives. By now we have over 25 topics, and René is a sought-after lecturer. In the last 10 years we have grown René's speaking engagements from two to almost 40 a year.

If you are one of the lucky ones who knows René personally, you know that what I am talking about is true: he is a kind, generous, funny and classy gentleman. If you don't know him, after reading his life story you will agree that he must be a special man to remain such an optimist and come out on top as a survivor.

I am proud and honored that he chose me to walk through life beside him, after having two previous partners die in his arms. It was a big step for him to open up to one more person in his life, and I am glad he did. Here's to many more years together.

TABLE OF CONTENTS

BOOK ONE
I SURVIVED SWISS BOARDING SCHOOLS

"Give me a child for the first seven years, and I'll give you the man."
Saint Ignatius of Loyola, founder of the Jesuits

PART 3: VICTOR page 113

AFTERMATH page 189

"You may weather the storm, but will you weather the aftermath?"
Anthony T. Hincks

BOOK TWO
WALKING THE RAINBOW

FOREWORD page 207

PART 1: INNOCENCE page 207

PART 2: TIM Page 251

BOOK ONE

I SURVIVED SWISS BOARDING SCHOOLS

All That Glitters Is Not Gold

P

PREFACE

Previous page:
René at his parental house, 2018

"Give me a child for the first seven years, and I'll give you the man."

Saint Ignatius of Loyola, founder of the Jesuits

My grandfather, Léon Silvin, a wealthy, entrepreneurial Lyonese who, sadly, died at the early age of 52 from a minor infection, left too much money to his six children. My father, John Léon Silvin, and his siblings preferred to enjoy the lives of the French haute bourgeoisie, rather than maximize their father's considerable achievements. Among the most valuable assets my grandfather left them were several important patents and rights, which were all quickly sold or given away by them without much thought about their true value.

Léon Silvin, 1876-1928

My grandfather developed or directed the development of significant inventions at his paper manufacturing plant in Lyon, France.

René's grandfather's paper factory
Lyon, France, 1920

Upon his untimely death, he left his children the paper factory in Lyon, aluminum plants in New Jersey and Kentucky, and all the patents to his inventions. This included aluminum foil, and the patents to the processes necessary to complete the development of cellophane and color film. These patents were sold to the first bidders:

Reynolds Metals, E.I. DuPont, and Kodak, respectively. Additionally, the French government had recently awarded the family all mineral rights to French Equatorial Africa. This region now includes the countries of Chad, the Central African Republic, Cameroon, the Republic of the Congo, and Gabon. The heirs promptly returned these rights to the French government.

John Léon Silvin, 1909-1990

In my father's words: "I certainly did not want to spend the rest of my days dealing with savages."

Shortly before my grandfather's death, he sent my father to America to oversee his emerging empire's US operations. The corporate headquarters were in a new Manhattan skyscraper, and the President's secretary was a beautiful, Italian-American linguist from Brooklyn. When my father arrived in New York at the eve of the Great Depression aboard the French Line's flag ship *The Paris,* my mother was dispatched to the pier with a Stutz Bearcat automobile. This gift, from her boss to my father, was intended to amuse my father, and to send him off on a lengthy American visit, in an effort to divert his attention away from the company. Instead, my father and the president's secretary began their on-again, off-again, life-long romance, giving my father a reason to spend the next several years traveling back and forth from France to New York.

My mother was entranced with this suave, young version of Maurice Chevalier, who spoke English with a thick French accent. He had 50 suits set up in closets by seasons of the year, and he always wore white spats on his shoes. His future bride was putty in his hands. Before long, she would have to learn to mortgage her personality in order to keep the peace with her domineering, old-fashioned husband.

During the first years of their marriage, they split their time between Bay Shore, Long Island and Lyon, France, traveling back and forth on the great luxury liners of the period. They bought an old mansion on the Great South Bay where my father kept the latest and best-equipped fishing boats. He enjoyed these throughout the depression and even during the fuel-limited war years. The property had its own three-hole golf course across a small harbor from the main house. Five waterfront homes now stand on that property.

The Frank Guldens, close friends and neighbors in Bay Shore, traveled to Europe with my parents for many years, until a feud developed between them. In the early years, however, they were very close and became my brother's godparents, while my mother became their daughter's godmother. Frank Gulden, who introduced mass produced mustard and olives to the United States, had financed the construction of the Southside Hospital in Bay Shore where I was born.

A lady by the name of Mary Lee worked in the new "sterile supply" department of what was then a modern hospital. For me, she was a miracle. My father made an arrangement with "Nonnie" to house my brother and me during the majority of the year, while our parents were in France. She accepted the mission because her husband was chronically ill, and the Lee family could use the extra money. Duty soon turned into love as Nonnie and her husband became the best parental figures any child could want.

René with Nonnie, 1950

The Lees, my brother and I lived in a very small and leaky house in Islip, New York. Nonnie bathed me in two inches of hot water to conserve energy. In spite of an advanced case of emphysema, Mr. Lee brought me down to the basement several times a day to "help" him shovel coal into an old-fashioned coal burner. He kept a tiny shovel there for me to amuse myself and feel useful. Nonnie made a big deal out of preparing my favorite meal of macaroni and cheese, and she protected me better than any lioness ever guarded her cub.

One day when I had chicken pox, Nonnie exhibited just how far she was willing to go to assure my well-being. I was running the typical high fever small children with the illness experience. The Lees had put me on the couch in the living room, as Nonnie anxiously awaited Doctor Garbin, the hospital's Chief of Staff. His arrival for the then-customary house call took longer than she believed reasonable. In fact, it was after dark when he arrived and, apparently, I was frightened and disoriented when he awoke me. From stories I heard over the next decades from both Garbin, the Guldens and Nonnie, I was not as frightened as the doctor when Nonnie, who was a low-level employee in the hospital, seriously bawled out the chief of staff for being late and scaring her pup.

Although my brother did spend some time with us at Nonnie's, he did not form the same attachment, perhaps because he was five years older than I. During these first five years of my life, I was innocently and peacefully happy. When my parents were in the States, I would return to my parents' house on the point in Bay Shore, where I ate with a severe, German cook in the kitchen. This was anguishing and I eagerly waited to see the preparations for my parents' next trip abroad when I knew I would soon be safely back in Islip.

The old Jesuit educators said, "give me a child for the first six years and I have him for life." I am convinced that any good that exists in me, was generously infused in me by "my" Nonnie, to whom I remained loyal and stayed in frequent touch with for the rest of her long life.

My normal childhood ended abruptly when my father decided that I needed to be "Europeanized" and learn French. The last time I left Nonnie's loving and simple house in 1954, was the first time I saw her cry. I discovered over the next few years she intuitively sensed that my happy childhood was going to come to an abrupt end.

René at Nonnie's house, 2018

PART 1

VICTIM

Previous page:
René and his mother boarding the French Line *SS Liberté*

Chapter 1: La Clairière

September 1955

At the age of seven, I was dropped off at a boarding school in Switzerland that my parents had never seen. Being a traditional Frenchman, my father was distressed that my older brother and I did not have perfect command of the French language. A prior attempt to educate us during a six-month residency with a French nanny in Cannes, France had been aborted because the governess's daughter, Danielle, had contracted viral meningitis.

Because I did not understand the gravity of the illness, I was naively excited about all the special attention we received as a result of Danielle's illness. We were lodged in a suite at the Gallia Hotel in Cannes. Suddenly, the waiters left our food trays at the door, and we received many phone calls inquiring about our welfare. Even my mother started phoning with regularity and was clearly upset. If it took meningitis to spark motherly love, I was all for it! As soon as the quarantine was lifted, my father made plans for the next phase in our Europeanization.

The Gallia Hotel in 1950

The Gallia, now luxury condominiums, preserves its beautiful gardens to this day. I was standing on a balcony overlooking these gardens with a tropical koi pond, when my parents arrived. My father was obviously angry and frustrated with the situation. He was an avid shooter and resented that his hunting season had been interrupted by this unexpected and unwelcome annoyance. Even at that early age, I could detect a severe strain between my parents and the governess. That was my first realization that, if my father's plans were altered in any way, his reaction was to express anger at anyone, including innocent bystanders. Madame Lainier and her daughter Danielle's crisis had unexpectedly interfered with his plans, so everyone - especially my mother - would have to tolerate his ill temper.

Our father announced that he had arranged a much better situation for us. He clearly expected our gratitude in return for the sacrifice and expense our near-term future realignment would cost him. My brother, John Jacques, who was five years my senior, and I were to attend boarding schools in Switzerland. To plan our future, my father had consulted his banker who had recommended the most expensive school in the world: Le Rosey with campuses in Rolle and Gstaad. "Jackie," as the family called my brother, had been accepted there, but the school did not take children younger than nine years old. When my perplexed father had inquired what other parents did with younger children, the headmistress at Le Rosey had recommended La Clairière, and that was where I was headed until I was old enough to attend Le Rosey. I did not understand what this meant, and no one explained it to me. I also knew that my autocratic father would not tolerate questions.

Excited and happy to be on a grand excursion with my parents as we drove from the South of France to Switzerland, I was even more delighted because my mother had bought me another toy. I spent a lot of the trip playing with my old, much-loved Smokey the Bear, and my new wooden horse and carriage. Not having developed any affection for the frigid Madame Lainier and her daughter, I soon forgot them both.

Our first stop was at Le Rosey. I do not remember leaving Jackie there, nor of any good-byes we might have said, even though the previous six months in Cannes were probably the closest we had been in all my life.

My parents and I spent our last night together at the elegant Beau Rivage Palace in Lausanne's lakeside section of Ouchy, Switzerland. There, while a porter was loading luggage into the car, my new horse and buggy gift was caught between two bags and broken. Of course, I knew we did not express emotions for such silliness, and I tried my best to hide my sadness and disappointment while I tried to mend the broken carriage myself.

"Don't worry, René," my father said, "this wonderful school you are to attend has a workshop and they will fix the carriage as soon as we leave. Imagine, you'll make friends with the fellow in charge and can work with him regularly."

It sounded pretty good to me, as I conjured up visions of a kind, gentle man, similar to Mr. Lee, surrounded by broken toys and equipped with the necessary tools to repair them all. Reassured by my daydreams, I began to believe that this Swiss experience might be a fun adventure with lots of great distractions.

Our pre-highway route from Rolle followed the shoreline of Lake Geneva, around to Montreux and into the Rhone Valley, through Aigle and finally, up a mountain to the ski resort town of Villars-sur-Ollon. At the far end of the village, in a clearing on a wooded hillside, was an old, dark chalet with a sign on the lawn that read "La Clairière – pension pour jeunes garcons," which translates as La Clairière, boarding school for young boys. Barren and austere-looking, without trees near the building, and with a soaked and dirty lawn, the sight of the school did not make me feel welcome.

La Clairière

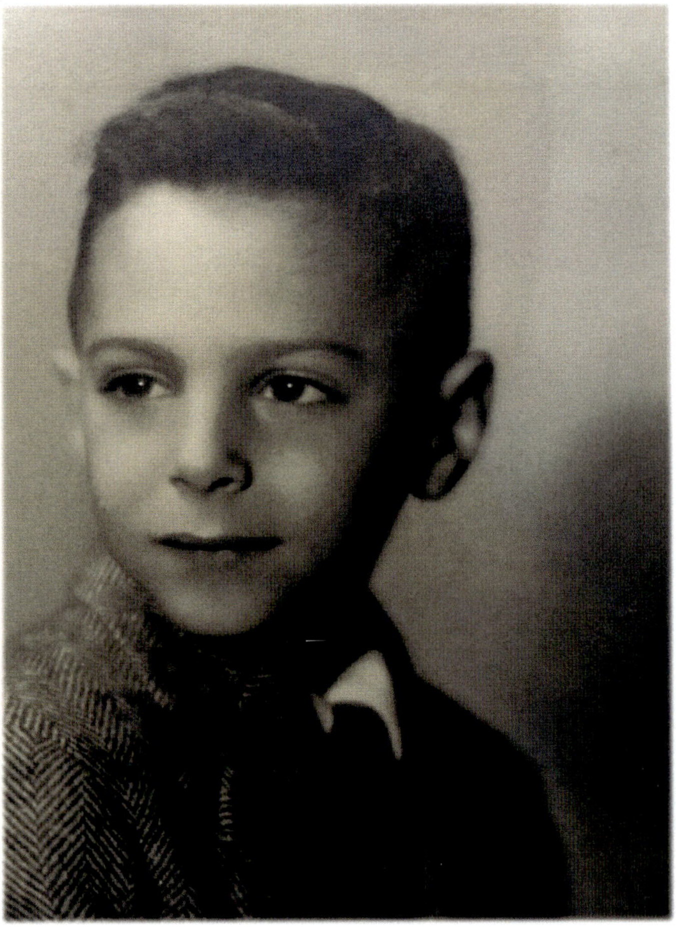

René at age 6

My father had to put the car into low gear to climb the steep driveway, leaving our tire tracks in the mud. At the front door, my father rang the bell. It was an old-fashioned iron handle connected to a rod that ran through the wall, to a small bell just inside the building. I soon heard unusually hard footsteps approaching, and through the opaque glass in the door I saw a menacing female figure loom toward us to open the door.

"Monsieur et Madame Silvin, je présume."

Madame Beauverre did not greet me and barely glanced at me. Her harshness increased my fear of her and this strange situation. From the words and tones they used in speaking, I became aware that my parents and she had probably never even spoken before. With her jet-black hair severely pulled back into a bun, her strong, frigid facial features and her ice-cold voice, Madame Beauverre seemed quite masculine and very commanding. She would be my surrogate mother for nearly three years.

We were escorted a few meters into the building to a small, narrow room, which was the headmaster's living room, where Monsieur Beauverre awaited us. He was tall, abnormally thin, with an aquiline nose and a protruding Adam's apple. He smelled odd. I soon learned that this was the odor of chain smokers with poor oral hygiene. The Beauverres spoke little English, which delighted my father because his goal was for me to achieve native fluency in French. My father had already explained to me how important speaking proper French was, and I was warned not to take on a "peasant Swiss accent."

I did not know how I would learn the difference between proper French and peasant Swiss French.

After a brief introduction to this strange, ungainly couple, and without ever viewing the school's facilities, my father announced that they were leaving immediately. By now I had become accustomed to being with my family and was already worried about them leaving me in this strange, dark building. A lead bowling ball seemed to have lodged itself in my stomach, a new feeling that would continue to plague me all my life and become a constant challenge for me to keep under control. But boys were not supposed to cry, and I was maintaining my composure, until my mother's sobbing released my tears. I wept and choked as my father hurriedly rushed my mother outside and into the car. I recall her 1950s style fur coat flopping in the wind as she left the chalet. I watched through a window as the car maneuvered around and crept down the hill leaving new tire tracks in the mud. I looked for those tracks, my link to my family, until new rains washed them away.

My steamer trunk, standing alone in the front hall, appeared to be the only connection to my past. Its colorful stickers from the *Andrea Doria*, the *Ile de France*, and the *Flandre*, ocean liners that we had traveled on, reminded me of happier moments. I had already developed a life-long love for luxury liners and shipping history. But, for now, I decided to take my father's advice and cheer myself up by bringing my broken toy to the workshop.

"Sir, may I please go to the workshop and have my toy fixed?" I asked Monsieur Beauverre, as I opened my trunk on the floor to show him the broken horse and carriage.

With the speed of summer lightning, Beauverre swung his long arm in a wide arc that landed on the side of my face, propelling me across the narrow hallway and slamming me into the wall. Stunned, I slid to the cold, grey, stone floor. Through the shock, I felt a stinging pain on my face and back, as well as the icy coldness of the floor. Cold still brings me pain and fear, which, in turn, creates the dreaded, weighty pain in my stomach.

"I'll teach you about workshops and toys, you little brat!" were the first words Monsieur Beauverre ever directed to me.

"Take the trunk up the stairs to the 'Teeth of the South' and unpack at once. Put all your belongings out on the bed, and Madame Beauverre will decide what you may keep. And take off your shoes. If you scratch the stairs you'll meet with me again!" he growled, as he glared at me. His steel grey eyes would cause me fear every time I saw him, so that I tried to avoid his eyes, just as I tried to avoid his hand, his wrath and the sound of his wife's footsteps.

I dragged the trunk up the stairs, paying extra attention not to damage the old, well-worn wooden stairs. On the first landing were three rooms along one wall and a shower room opposite them. The bedrooms had names of mountains and my room was called "Les Dents du Midi," the "Teeth of the South." I was relieved that I had discovered what Monsieur Beauverre meant and where I had to unpack. Five beds had been shoved into a tiny, dark room. Clearly, mine was the one with linens placed on top, ready to be made up. Within a few minutes I heard those harsh, determined steps echoing up the stairs. Madame Beauverre entered the room to inspect my possessions.

"This is all together too much," she said, as she started to divide pants, shirts and underwear in half. "And stuffed animals are not allowed!" I heard in horror as she grabbed Smokey.

She made two trips up and down the stairs with my excess belongings, most of which I never saw again. When her pillaging was complete, she coldly said, "Put your things on that shelf and go to the basement for tea in five minutes. There will be no shoes worn in the chalet." Her stark figure stomped out.

I sat on the bed and wept until I feared I was approaching the five-minute deadline. Already apprehensive, I could not imagine the consequences of being late. So, feeling the cold floor through my socks, I cautiously followed the stairs down to the basement for tea where about ten other young boys were gathered, each inmate eating a piece of bread and drinking tea.

Chapter 2: The Boys and Our Routine

The stark grey concrete basement with bare windows and a door on one wall was our tearoom, our group meeting room, our coat and muck room, as well as the only entrance and exit from the chalet that we were permitted to use. Our shoes were stored here on wooden shelves below pegs for jackets. There were no lights to brighten the dark, dingy space with its plain wooden table in the center. On the table were a pewter-like pot and a plate of sliced bread, from which each child was served.

As I stole glances at the boys, they neither welcomed nor rejected me. Their passive expressions showed the self-absorbed trance in which, I found out, we all had to live in order to survive. Each one sipped tea and chewed dry bread. None of the boys spoke. No one introduced us. I simply sat down where someone who handed me the tea and dry bread had indicated. The only adult in the room, Mademoiselle Demars, who was a tall woman also dressed in grey with dark hair also tied in a bun, seemed to match the basement. She had beckoned me over to the table, handed me a piece of bread and poured some dark tea. I was now one of the group, like an animal being released into a holding pen awaiting adoption.

I tried to see what my companions in this deadly silence looked like, and I sometimes saw their eyes stray in my direction. I saw differences without any knowledge of race or nationality - blue eyes in a fair skinned face, dark eyes in darker skinned faces, a varied group. A few boys stood out: an angelic-looking, clean-cut American with blue eyes and blonde hair named Chuck sat next to a darker-skinned, older boy with piercing yet kind eyes. Faisal, a Saudi, much bigger than I, was always kind and pleasant to me. Another boy, close to my age, looked doll-like with his porcelain skin, black eyes, and jet-black, straight hair. Miguel, a South American whose father was ambassador to one of Switzerland's neighboring countries, was one of my new roommates.

At least three of us had one thing in common: we were waiting to go to Le Rosey. The school was perceived by the Beauverre's to be for spoiled, rich brats whose parents used La Clairière as a holding corral for their offspring. Therefore, Klaus, Ron and I suffered the scorn of the Beauverres. The American Ron, one of the oldest boys at La Clairière, would play an important and disastrous role in my life during the next five years. Klaus, son of a Danish count, was a strikingly good-looking boy three years my senior.

All boys gathered four times a day: three times for meals in the dining room in the recently added shed, and once for afternoon tea in the basement. We ate our meals seated at one of three tables, each headed by either a Beauverre or Mademoiselle Demars. The Beauverre's two children, a girl my age named Rose Marie and her younger brother Claude always sat with one of their parents. Other than at meals, we were usually kept quite separate from Rose Marie and Claude, much like crew are separated from officers and passengers on the luxury ocean liners or freighters.

The maid, Leticia, usually served the loaded plates with food before we had heard the bell, after which we rushed into the room to be seated. Leticia was a hairy, Spanish lady who had a big heart and, I soon learned, was sympathetic to us vis-à-vis the Beauverre's overreaction to discipline.

The bland, unappetizing food was very different from that served at The Gallia, or the macaroni and cheese my Nonnie had spoiled me with. Gradually, I adjusted to eating boiled potatoes, chicken or horsemeat, and a vegetable, most often steamed fennel. Each boy was required to eat his entire meal. If the plate at one's assigned seat was not cleaned, the maid had been instructed to leave the dish there, so that it awaited us at the following meal. I quickly learned that choking down fennel at night beat a cold, crusty dish of it for breakfast.

We were not allowed to touch food with our fingers, other than the bread that sat on a large plate in the center of each table. If we did use our fingers, the teacher at the table's head took out a ruler from his or her lap and gave us a strong whack across the knuckles. As a result, I still can clean meat off a chicken bone without touching it better than if it were soaked overnight in acid.

I fearfully sat in the classes, especially those taught by the Beauverres. I did not learn much as my entire body and mind were focused on avoiding disciplinary slaps and insults. Our classes were divided into three groups by age. Monsieur Beauverre taught handwriting, Madame Beauverre geography that consisted of tracing and drawing maps. The headmaster couple clearly had a penchant for disciplined precision, but not education. Mademoiselle Demars taught the rest of the classes to the best of her ability: some basic mathematics and French grammar with dictation. These lessons took place in three different rooms: one in the main building adjacent to the owner's private drawing room where I had last seen my parents; the second upstairs next to the dorm rooms; and the third in the wing next to the dining room.

We all had to perform most of the housekeeping in the old chalet and the new wing. Leticia, the only housekeeper, taught us what to do. We washed our clothes and sheets using a primitive, hand-operated washer. We used mops and brooms to keep the chalet as polished as the Beauverres demanded. We were careful to meet their standards. I was much happier cleaning with Leticia than being in classes with any of the other adults, because Leticia was compassionate and kind to all the boys. Also, I associated these chores with my "Nonnie" who had lovingly taught me to do many of them.

And so, I settled into that routine. I ate what was presented to me, went to my classes, which were mostly handwriting and map drawing, and cried myself to sleep most nights. The children spoke little and laughed even less. We attended an exercise class in the afternoon: either gymnastics in the dining room that also housed a ping-pong table, or we jogged around the property depending on the season. Once a week, for exercise, we walked single file into the village, which was two kilometers away, holding onto a rope with knots to keep us in line and at regular intervals from each other.

Chapter 3: Rose Marie

Sometime during my first year at the school, Rose Marie and I became friends. Looking back, I realize just how unusual this was. Our days were regimented without much time for contact with the Beauverre children. No other students played with us.

Rose Marie had a two-wheel, un-motorized scooter. It had a small platform between the wheels, so the rider could place one foot on the pad while pushing him or herself along with the other foot. The handlebar was long enough to permit a child to stand erect while scooting along. During a few of the afternoon outdoor periods, Rose Marie would talk to me while riding her scooter, and she finally asked me if I'd like to try it myself.

A scooter to a seven or eight-year-old who has no toys is like a Ferrari to a young adult without a car. I was delighted and loved racing along on this brilliant contraption. Within no time we had turned our rides into a game. One of us would pretend to be a tourist traveling around Europe, while the other was a concierge at a fine hotel who greeted and assisted the guest on arrival. "Europe" was a barn that sat off to one side of the property away from the hill on a relatively flat plateau.

The barn had a resident: an unusually muscular, older, grey-haired man with a messy beard and the usual bad teeth. He smoked an odd-looking pipe, which I later learned was an alpine pipe that many farmers and shepherds still smoke. His job was to chop wood for the two wood stoves in the chalet, one in the dining room, the other at the far end of the hall on the building's main level. He also performed some maintenance and yard cleaning tasks. I wondered if this fellow was the chap who manned the imaginary workshop my father had mentioned on my first trip up to Villars. The man watched us as we played international traveler.

"Welcome to the Palace hotel, Madame," I would greet Rose Marie as she "arrived." "Have you had a pleasant trip? No? Oh, I am so sorry you are tired. Perhaps a hot bath and some room service would help?"

We invented many different arrival and departure scenarios, such as having the "car" washed, running errands, and loading suitcases. Since my father hunted constantly, many of our stories centered on guns and hunting. "Yes, Madame, I'll be extra careful with the guns. An armurier? Certainly, Madame, we will send for a gun specialist."

By the second year of our games, I had attended my father's favorite sport during one of the school's recesses: live pigeon shoots. Rose Marie listened while I explained this so-called sport, so our games involved many pigeon shoot stories. "Don't play with these new electric windows when you park my car, make sure it is not in the sun and take my guns and the shell boxes to the locker room," we shouted at each other from the scooter.

While we played, the woodchopper watched from "Europe's" door saying nothing, while drawing puffs of smoke from his pipe. He had an odd smile, one that I would now call sarcastic or sardonic. He seemed to know more about me than I did. It would not be long before I would learn more about what his odd gaze and smile meant.

Rose Marie's brother, Claude, also wanted to play, but was rejected by his sister as being too young and inexperienced in worldly travel. The older Beauverre child was quite happy keeping our fantasy game private. Claude pouted at our rejection; this would cost me in the future.

Chapter 4: The Nash Rambler

We inmates played our own version of hide and seek Saturdays on the steep hills behind the chalet. Our mostly unsupervised game entertained and freed us for a while from the stress of living within the Beauverre's punishing discipline. In our version of the game, two teams built low rock walls we called forts. We joyfully penalized the opposing team if they "attacked" an empty fort, so these walls had to be high enough to conceal a small boy.

The woods we played in were reached by walking past the forbidden front door, Monsieur Beauverre's office window and, in the driveway, his pride and joy: a tiny, blue and white Nash Rambler. He washed and waxed it without fail every Sunday, which was the closest we came to any religious observance. Since we performed many other utilitarian chores around the school, I thought it odd that Beauverre did not have us wash the car. Clearly, he did not trust us to give it the attention and care he believed it merited.

1950s Nash Rambler

One early spring day, after the snow had melted, we paired off into teams for the game. Faisal, being one of the largest boys in the school, was one of the two captains. To be on his team was a sure win because Faisal was older, faster and smarter than all of the boys, including Ron, the opposing team's captain. I admired Faisal and looked up to this 12-year-old as if he were a hero. He had a gentle smile and was obviously fond of me since he had chosen me, a younger kid, as the first to be on his team. I proudly walked out of the group of gathered boys waiting to be selected and stood next to "my" captain.

Several hours later, just as we were completing the fort, Faisal lifted a well-rounded rock into place. It rolled off the wall and began to roll down the hill toward the driveway. Amused, we watched the rock gain momentum. We suddenly realized that the Nash was directly below the rock, which seemed to be aiming for it. Faisal ran down the hill in an attempt to stop or deter the projectile. But, before he reached it, the rock bounced off a small retaining wall and landed squarely onto the Nash's hood, leaving a large dent. When I reached the wall, Faisal and I stared at each other in total panic, which only deepened when Monsieur Beauverre emerged from the chalet's front door.

With his steel blue-grey eyes squinting filled with rage and fury, Beauverre looked at the car, then at us. He walked over to the Nash, briefly appraised the damage, and then walked deliberately to where we were standing, shivering from the fear of unimaginable retribution. Beauverre's long left arm swatted me like a professional tennis player's back hand, sending me flying to the ground as he grabbed Faisal by the hair and dragged him through the front door into his office.

By this time a few other boys had arrived. We fearfully stood together listening to the terrible sounds of Faisal being thrown around Beauverre's office for what seemed like an eternity. Faisal never screamed. Beauverre's screeching made his words indecipherable. Helplessly, we sensed that Monsieur Beauverre had totally lost control of himself. I ran around the building, into the basement and up the stairs. As I reached the first floor near Monsieur Beauverre's office door, Faisal flew past me into the corridor. I instantly feared that my smack had been only the opening salvo, that I would also be dragged into the office to be given the same treatment Faisal had suffered. Beauverre slammed the door, shutting himself back into his room.

As I knelt down next to Faisal, I saw his bruised face and his bloody left eye. Beauverre had also punched Faisal in the abdomen. By evening, Faisal's face had swollen up so much that his injured eye was nearly shut. Not a word was said at dinner, not by Beauverre, nor the teacher, nor anyone. No medical attention or even first aid was offered. We spent the remainder of the day in silence, the only indication that something horrible had occurred.

After dinner, I saw Faisal in the shower room as we all washed prior to bed. What a hero! How silently he had sustained that beating! Our eyes met and in one split second his expression seemed to say: "I'm OK René, please don't say anything or there will be more pain. Just go to bed." When he turned to walk down the narrow hall to "Mont Blanc," a room I had been transferred to, I saw a large bruise on his back. In total silence Madame Beauverre shut off the lights, our room first, then the other two and she closed the doors. Our silence soon turned into the sounds of stifled crying and sniffling.

We usually whispered to each other after lights were out, but not this night. We had learned that slaps were not the only weapon in Beauverre's arsenal. Eventually, the three other boys in my room sniffled themselves to sleep. I stayed awake with my fear and stared out the window adjacent to my bed. How could anyone sleep now? At eight years old, that night was my introduction to the curse of insomnia.

Chapter 5: A Bad Day Traveling Around Europe

Days dragged into months, months into seasons. Sometime after my first year, Claude reappeared asking to play with us while Rose Marie and I were "traveling." Being at least three years his senior, Rose Marie was much stronger than her brother. Not a dainty child, Rose Marie strongly resembled a farmer and fought ferociously. The two scuffled. Rose Marie pushed Claude down, his knee bruising as he fell on gravel. Crying loudly, he ran into the chalet followed by his sister.

The woodchopper had witnessed this struggle. With his all-knowing gaze, he took my arm leading me into the barn. He sat me on his lap. Then he began fondling me. I was confused. What was happening? I had hoped he would comfort me. I tried to leave, but he yanked me back down and continued. His dirty beard felt like sandpaper on my face, his teeth smelled as badly as they looked. He squeezed me into his chest so hard that I could barely breathe.

This abuse became routine, even though from then on I would avoid the barn. He would find me as he loaded wood bins near the stoves, or when we returned from town and hung around the chalet waiting for tea. He was able to complete his thrill in less than a minute.

This first time established the pattern that he would follow, and which I could not change. When he was done masturbating, he pushed me aside. Troubled and not understanding what had been done to me, I ran out of the barn. My heart was pounding so hard, so fast that I feared it would pop right out of my mouth.

I ran toward the chalet's basement door where I wanted to find safety from the beast. There stood Beauverre looking right and left, his ugly Adam's apple bobbing up and down. When he saw me, he grabbed me by the collar and took me up the stairs into his office.

"Do you think you can get away with it?" he asked. Now I was totally bewildered. Had Beauverre seen what had happened inside the barn? What was going on?

"I'll show you what it's like to be hit by someone stronger than you. Take off your pants," he barked.

Again, I wondered if there was some connection to what the wood chopper had done, because Beauverre had never ordered me to strip before. Totally confused, I could barely remember the struggle between Rose Marie and Claude, while I took down my pants as the headmaster removed his belt from his waist band.

"Turn around and put your hands against the wall," barked Beauverre.

I complied, still not knowing the reason for this punishment. Soon, I felt an amazing, painful sting on my bottom, accompanied by a sharp crack. Crack! Sting! Crack! Sting! After several rounds, he opened the door saying, "Get dressed, get out and never touch Claude again." His nostrils flared like a horse after a hard ride. I realized that this, my worst beating yet, had nothing to do with the barn. Even worse, I had done nothing to deserve it.

I never again played with Rose Marie. From then on, I hated the sight of Claude almost as much as the smell of the black-clad, silent, dirty wood chopper.

I did not associate the first time I was molested with the beating immediately thereafter. The entire encounter felt humiliating, forced and wrong. Various confusing emotions and fears twirled around in my immature head. Who would believe this had happened? And what exactly did happen? Had I caused it in any way? I had no one I could ask for advice or help, and no one to confide in.

In retrospect, I am not surprised to hear of previously unreported child molestation and abuse at La Clairière. Not uncharacteristically, I never mentioned this abuse to anyone for some 25 years; certainly not to my parents, not to my friends, teachers or peers, and not even to my wife. After all, even if they believed the story, what would they think of me? Equally as telling, I have never been able to utter the word "sperm." Even now, when I hear it, I shudder and when I smell it, I want to throw up.

Chapter 6: Charlie and Charles

Uncle Charles and
Aunt Charlie
Cannes, France, 1954

"Aunt Charlie" which is the French diminutive for the name Charlotte, visited me at La Clairière. The first time, she noticed that I did not have a pillow on my bed. When she returned the next day, she brought me one and a candy "care package." Both were confiscated upon her departure.

My father's brother, Uncle Charles, and Aunt Charlie lived in both Lyon and Cannes, France. Uncle Charles and my father shared ownership of a hunting preserve in the small town of Dompierre, near Vichy. My father and his brother were close, albeit in a formal way and, as such, I saw my uncle nearly as much as I saw my father. Uncle Charles looked very much like my dad, but contrary to my father he encouraged communication with us, as he also did with his two children, who were more or less Jackie and my age. His wife, Charlotte, was generous, kind and fun to be around. I had gotten to know her at pigeon shoots and at the shared hunting preserve in France.

I truly never had any idea when I would be removed from La Clairière, even for vacations or breaks. Monsieur Beauverre would tell me when and if he saw fit. My parents did not often communicate with me while I was there. For Christmas vacations I would be with my family on Cap Ferrat, a peninsula near Monte Carlo. I traveled alone by train to meet my parents for these visits.

For summer vacations, I would usually return to New York with my mother aboard an ocean liner. During the week-long crossing, I would be left with other children in playrooms for most of the day, and I would eat earlier than the adults in a supervised, children's dining room. The French Line's kindergarten supervisor taught the children one French song each day. That night we would sing it in the children's dining room. Obviously, I recall learning "Frère Jacques" (Brother Jack) with some irony. My favorite song was "Au Claire de la Lune" (in the brightness of the moon) because it conjured up freedom.

Around eight o'clock, after a ship's employee had prepared me for bed, my mother would kiss me good-night. She would always be wearing a formal evening gown and be headed to the first-class dining room to sit at the captain's table. That was when I saw her longest during the entire voyage.

René's mother seated at the right of the Captain, *SS Liberté*, 1955

The most exciting event during these trips was a 'mid-Atlantic rendezvous.' Throughout the 1950's both the Cunard Line and the French Line had two luxury ships dedicated to the North Atlantic route. Cunard had the two great Queens: *Mary* and *Elizabeth*. The French line had the *Ile de France* and the *Liberté*. One ship, from each company would leave Europe (England or France) at the same time as the sister ship left New York. This custom had been created in the 1920s when control of North Atlantic travel was as big a concern as controlling an Internet service provider is today. The most powerful steamship companies boasted that one could book passage through their company from each continent every week.

Since there were no public-address systems on these grand floating palaces, a little boy dressed in a blue and red uniform, wearing a red child's beret, would walk through the public rooms with announcements. These pages might have been looking for a specific passenger to deliver a telegram or announce the beginning of a meal. Once a week, they would tell us when we would rendezvous with the company's other ship, which was headed in the opposite direction. This was a very festive event. If allowed, I always attended these mid-Atlantic encounters, sometimes almost alone because I enjoyed being on deck during storms at sea. On a clear day, however, most passengers would be on deck, watching the little speck on the horizon turn into a huge liner, mirroring our own ship. You could hear cheers from the other passengers, and even the sound of the sister ship cutting through the waves. Then, like all special treats, the ships would separate and eventually disappear over the horizon.

***Queen Mary* and *Queen Elizabeth* mid-Atlantic rendezvous**

Chapter 7: Breaks from La Clairière

I would occasionally see my father when he would send for me to accompany him at his live pigeon shoots. The forefather of clay pigeon shooting, this perverted sport was practiced by the rich and famous. Many resort cities such as Monte Carlo, Vichy, Paris and Arcachon, had pigeon shooting clubs. Monte Carlo's club was on the site currently occupied by Lowe's Hotel and Casino overlooking the yacht harbor. Cliffs were an especially desirable location for a pigeon shoot club, to give the birds lift from the updraft as they flew. The pigeon shooting club in Paris was in the Bois de Boulogne and is now a museum.

Monte Carlo, pigeon shoot club lower right corner

Behind the club house, a one-meter-high semi-circular fence enclosed the area where the pigeons would be released. The club house contained a restaurant, a gun shop and changing rooms.

Families, reporters and spectators gathered on the terrace as each shooter emerged into the shooting field and stood facing the five pigeon boxes. A loudspeaker would announce the sequence of the next three shooters: "Count Antoine de Chavagnac, Ann Woodward next, Mr. John Silvin ready yourself."

As a marksman took his position on the path, an employee stood by to echo his "Pret" (ready). At the sportsman's "Pull" command, one of the five boxes opened as a ball dropped onto the bird's back, scaring it into flight. The object was to kill the bird before it reached the fence. If successful, the shooter went on to the next round until all other contestants had been eliminated by getting "a zero" meaning a missed bird, or one that died beyond the fence. A large board with the shooter's name was in the clubhouse. Red chips were added to the line of the shooter's name indicating a "kill," or a white chip for a "zero," a miss. If my father performed well in a tournament, I felt relief rather than jubilation. If he believed that he would lose, there was a blanket of silence and tension. While he did not hit me, it was clear he paid other people to do so. Therefore, I was very silent when he was angry.

Pigeon shooting competition in Monte Carlo, 1950s

There was no child play at pigeon shoots. I had to be very silent so as to not disturb my father or any other marksman. I would sit erect in a chair in the club house all day. I looked forward to the times that my Aunt Charlie would be at the shoots, because she always took time to talk to me and to make me laugh. Instead of hissing an annoyed "shhhhhhhhh" as a shooter approached the pad, she would whisper things like "this one will probably miss. He's an old drunk. Let's hope he knows what end of the gun to put against his shoulder." Although she too shot, she made it clear to me that she understood my aversion to the killing. Most importantly, she was the first adult to treat me as an equal and as an interesting person.

The pigeons were prepared to be difficult targets by the removal of their tail feathers to create erratic flight. Sometimes my father offered my services to perform this task and place them in a large cage awaiting their loading into one of the five death boxes. Although I wanted to only pretend I performed the job, I knew that a bird with a torn tail had a better chance of survival, so I chose the middle road and only removed some tail feathers. I identified with certain pigeons more than others and I'd watch a few in particular, hoping that the runner would not choose them to load into one of the five death traps. I would stare into their tiny, red eyes and believed that they were asking for my help. Invariably, however, my "pet" pigeons would be selected and brought out to be shot.

I had learned how to tell where a bird had been wounded. One whose wing had been broken fluttered to the ground, its injured wing dragging along as a runner raced after it to break its neck. Sometimes a bird would drop out of the sky like a lump of lead, which meant multiple pellets had penetrated vital parts of the body. What I feared the most for my "adopted birds" was a head injury, as these poor creatures would rapidly roll around on the ground like a ball being pulled by conflicting magnets from many directions.

About a quarter of the birds would escape a hit, and I'd joyfully watch them fly away while the spectators moaned in sympathy for the embarrassed shooter. If the topography allowed, local children would hide on the other side of the fence, hoping to collect birds that fell beyond the semi-circle to feed their families. Not infrequently, one of these youngsters' over-zealousness would lead him into the line of fire and he would lose an eye to a pellet. While such a tragic accident might be mentioned in the club house, it was of less consequence than if the champagne were not served sufficiently chilled.

After a week's shoot in one town, the entire group traveled to the next club and started another round. French, Spanish, European and world championship competitions throughout Europe occupied the group's time for several months every year.

In 1955, my first year at La Clairière, the world championship was held in Cairo, Egypt. Several years earlier, my father inaugurated a reward called the Silvin cup. This much coveted prize was given to the shooter who had the longest string of "kills" without any misses and up until this time was always presented by my mother.

René's mother presenting the Silvin Cup in Cairo, Egypt, 1955

The last Easter break I had while at La Clairière, I met my father in Spain where he was competing in the world championships. He picked me up in Madrid, driving a recently delivered four-seater Thunderbird, and he took us south to Seville. That day he was eliminated in the finals for the title. He was angry and, consequently, I was frightened. He was so engrossed in his ill humor that, as we reached the front door of Seville's then great hotel the Alfonso XIII, he put the car in reverse rather than in park. My father entered the lobby mumbling ahead of me, when I saw the Thunderbird sliding backwards towards a pond. I ran to the car, applied the brake and put it into park. My father emerged from the hotel furious and yelling. When I explained what had happened he called me a liar. He said that I must have gotten into the driver's seat and played with the gears behind his back. If that was his story on a day he lost at pigeon shooting, I was not about to contradict him.

Chapter 8: A Parental Visit

One afternoon after exercise class, I was summoned by Madame Beauverre to her husband's office. *What had I done that could possibly justify going to THE office?* The only times I had been there were either to get a beating, speak to a parent on the only phone in the building, or be handed one candy bar, my entire share of a care package my aunt Charlie would send. When we got to the office, Madame Beauverre uncharacteristically came in with me and sat in the only other chair. I stood between the two tyrants as my interrogation began.

"Let me tell you a story," Beauverre started. "There were two schools. One was a serious place, the other had few rules and lax discipline. That school also had several vacations during which the boys went all over the world. The serious school had none of this, just Christmas and Easter. Now, there were two brothers, one in each school, which meant than one brother had vacation when the other did not."

Could this be good? Would I be released because Jackie had a holiday? I thought.

"So, René," continued Madame Beauverre, "do you think it is responsible for the boy in the good school to go away with his brother from the bad school, while his classmates have no such vacation?"

When do I get out of here? I wanted to shout! Instead I said nothing, just feigned a dumb look as I glanced at one inquisitor, then at the other.

Then Beauverre spoke again. "Well, Le Rosey has a holiday, and your parents are taking you out of school at the same time as your brother. You will miss school and you'll have to make it up." Then, Beauverre opened the door which meant "beat it."

Wow! I was leaving! When? It had to be shortly. Today? I so wished I had asked that during our cozy, little chat in the office. To bring it up later required more intestinal fortitude than I had, plus the physical strength to withstand a slap or a beating, if Beauverre felt like giving me one.

That evening before dinner I sat near a window while we were supposed to be practicing our handwriting. I kept looking outside, watching the car headlights drive toward La Clairière. One after another passed the driveway. When a larger set of headlights appeared, belonging to a wider automobile, my heart would race, thinking that my parents were about to arrive. They did not. Not that night, the next day or even the next.

I began to think this was a ruse, another one of the Beauverre's cruelties. I kept looking at all the passing cars and wanting my parents to come. The hope of leaving boarding school was fading, being replaced by disappointment. A few evenings later I did not finish dinner. Perhaps this was some sort of silent rebellion, an expression of my misery. I'd face the cold fennel in the morning. After lights-out that night, I whispered to Chuck, my American roommate, for several minutes, until I heard the heavy stomping of Madame Beauverre bursting into the room.

"René, you are getting out of hand. You did not eat dinner and now you are talking after lights are out. TO SLEEP!" she bellowed and walked out.

The next day, during late morning classes with Mademoiselle Demars, Madame Beauverre interrupted class by ordering me to follow her. I wondered how badly I would be disciplined for my disobedience of the previous day. As we approached the Beauverre sitting room, Beauverre opened the door and raised his arm. Immediately I fell to the floor in a fetal position, trying to protect my face with my hands, and my abdomen with my legs and feet.

"Come here, René," an atypically kind Beauverre's voice said. "Come on," as he helped me up.

Beyond the skinny giant, I saw my parents sitting at the far end of the room. Between us stood a small bag. My father, smiling, stood and picked up the bag. He motioned me to the door. I followed him and my mother down the hall, out the forbidden front door and into the car. I had an odd feeling: both thrilled to be leaving, as well as confused and concerned at what my father's reaction would be to my efforts at self-protection.

As we drove past the village, my father broke the silence saying, "I hear that you cannot spell even the simplest of words, and that you fail at dictation."

I can still remember how horrible I felt. I instantly knew that trying to explain what life was like in that chalet was pointless. Later on, as I would sometimes overhear my father's conversations with his friends, I realized that he had found my fervent attempt at self-defense hilarious. He had never recognized my fear or seen it as a sign of trouble. Instead, he mimicked what he had witnessed with great amusement.

We went to Rosey to pick up my brother and then, as a family, traveled to Monte Carlo for a long weekend to attend Grace Kelly's marriage to Prince Rainier.

Principality of Monaco, 1950s

Chapter 9: Monte Carlo

The short distance from Lake Geneva to Monaco was a long day's drive for us without today's highways. "Monaco" is the name of the principality, while Monte Carlo refers to the city. Since Monaco is a city-state, the names are essentially interchangeable.

My father loved cars, especially what the French called "La Belle Americaine" (the pretty American gal.) Post-war Europe had few large cars, so they stood out. Once a year my mother would travel by ship to Europe from New York with "a pretty American gal." One year with an Oldsmobile for my uncle in Lyon, and the following year with a Cadillac for my father to use in Europe as he travelled to his frequent pigeon shoots and hunting preserves.

For now, we were working our way south in not one, but two Cadillacs. My father's white Cadillac was followed by a baby blue convertible, belonging to friends of my parents. This unusual procession in post-war Europe attracted countless looks and comments, many referring to the French names: "Cadillac," a French village, and the model name "Coupe de Ville" or town car, as the old carriages were called. At one stop, where numerous people had gathered to see the cars, I laughed when one man pointed to the large, protruding chrome bumpers and said: "Gina Lollobrigida!"

One would think that leaving La Clairière would create a sense of euphoria in me, but it did not. The overall message the Beauverres and life at the "school" had imprinted on me was to have fear, and no fear could be stronger, none. The loneliness coupled with the cold and fear created a permanent 'blanket' over me, a total repression of any child-like behavior or creativity.

My parents' presence could not begin to thaw this ice cube of fear. Even if they had been inquisitive and forthcoming, I doubt I could have spoken about my life. That opportunity was lost forever when my father laughed at the sight of me trying to protect myself from Beauverre, and then admonished me immediately afterwards for having failed at dictation. The total silence that followed his remarks reinforced my fears, and encouraged me to include my father in the same category as the Beauverres. I began to treat my parents as I reacted to the Beauverres: fearfully, politely and silently.

I could no more have imagined asking my parents questions about *anything*, than I would have queried an adult at school. If I spoke, it was because I was asked to or because I knew that I could remain invisible, hidden behind superficial chatter. It was a safe way to exist.

One short glimpse of re-becoming a child took place on the drive to Monte Carlo in 1956 for the royal wedding. Mari and Ben Schwindt, driving behind us in the blue convertible, were neighbors of my parents on Long Island. On a number of occasions, they would travel to France by ship accompanied by a car with which to tour Europe. Somehow, that day I ended up in their Cadillac, sitting between them, which was in stark contrast to being seated in my parent's car at near attention in the back seat. The Schwindts and I played a game called: "I spy with my little eye…" where one repeats that phrase and finishes with '….beginning with the letter 'C'." Then the others would guess what you saw that started with 'C'. We laughed and played for what I thought, perhaps hoped, was an eternity. But the silly, fun game and the drive ended, as did this fleeting moment of being allowed to be a child, when we reached Monte Carlo.

In my parents' presence I had to be polite and proper in the extreme, regardless of my age. In that respect, sending me to La Clairière had been a success in my father's eyes, because it made me look well-bred. Nonnie Lee's education would have been much too normal and, naturally, would have encouraged childlike behavior from a child. While in my father's car, I would sit quietly, look out the windows and occasionally listen to my parents' conversation. Their mention of the royal wedding between the future Princess Grace and Monaco's benevolent dictator and gaming entrepreneur, Prince Rainier, brought a negative assertion from my father.

"It will never last. She is just an actress and will never learn how to be the symbol Monaco needs. I give it three years," he said, confidently.

Ironically, over the next three decades, until her tragic death in an automobile accident in 1982, Princess Grace was a much-revered symbol, a great patron of many worthy charities, and a central figure in Monte Carlo's rise in popularity and wealth. The dashing, young couple had met the previous year during the filming of *To Catch a Thief*, which starred Grace Kelly and Cary Grant. The prince had invited the cast to his palace. A romance had emerged, after which a royal wedding followed.

Prince Rainier had managed to obtain tax free status for Monaco from France, which hastened the construction of luxury condominiums. At the same time, the famed Hotel de Paris, on the town square adjacent to the opulent, rococo casino, was renovated and modernized. The pigeon shooting club was located slightly to the east below the casino overlooking the harbor where Aristotle Onassis' yacht, the 325-foot converted Canadian frigate "The Christina" was usually moored.

My father was very friendly with a "player" in the principality's rise to fame in the gambling world. René Polard had installed all the city's "one armed bandits," or slot machines, and was active in the casino's affairs. At this time, he commanded great respect in town and occupied the top floor of one of the new, modern condominium buildings. Along with my parents, Polard and his wife were to attend the royal wedding and compete in the "Grand Prix de Monte Carlo." This was a major event in the pigeon shoot season, not to be confused with the world-renowned car race bearing the same name.

Commemorative card for Princess Grace and Prince Rainier's wedding

Little did they know then that Princess Grace would find pigeon shooting to be overly cruel, and within a few years would have Monaco's club permanently shut down. Naturally, this did not endear her to the shooters, who witnessed town after town throughout Europe following Monaco's lead over the subsequent decade. A great first for the "actress who would never live up to being a Princess" I'd say. My father won the last Grand Prix prior to Monte Carlo's club's closing, and never stopped ridiculing Princess Grace's decision.

My brother Jackie and I stayed at the Polard's huge apartment during the day of the wedding. I have no memory of any special toys or any games that we might have played together during the day, nor of any other children being present. That night, a governess and Mr. Polard's kind, aging mother brought us up to their tropical roof top garden to watch the fireworks.

April 19, 1956

Monaco sits in a bowl surrounded by hills, where firework launching sites had been erected. More launching pads had been placed on barges in the Mediterranean. The resulting display of color, light and sound covered the entire sky in a magnificent, overwhelming show. I was completely mesmerized. Only two days before, I had feared beatings for little or no apparent reason and had eaten disgusting food in a frigid environment. Now, I was witnessing the greatest show I could ever have imagined in the company of two attentive, affectionate women who lovingly gave me delicious food.

Unfortunately, within a few days, joy turned to fear and sorrow. My brother and I returned by train to boarding school or, as I later referred to it, prison camp. The night before we were to leave, I cried for hours. My head throbbed, I choked, my pillow case was soaked with tears. The entire next day on the sad train ride, my ribs hurt from sobbing as I approached La Clairière and my worst fears.

Chapter 10: Leticia

Leticia was the one bright spot at La Clairière. The housekeeper who, seemingly, worked 24-7, scrubbed floors, cleaned the two bathrooms and the group shower room, and served us our boiled vegetables and horsemeat. She was simple, kind and good. A religious Spaniard, Leticia showed her compassion for us by crossing herself and kissing the crucifix she always wore when she witnessed some of our harsher punishments.

Since I was on the Beauverre's blacklist for being headed to Le Rosey, Leticia paid special additional attention to me. A genuine smile accompanied by her rough hand on my shoulder was like medicine. When we walked up to the lunch table to get our previously served plate, she would discretely point to a particular plate for me to take. Invariably, it contained less fennel, which she knew I dreaded, and some finer cuts of the horsemeat. Her assistance was a huge part of my well-being.

Leticia also took risks to protect us. We all knew she thinned out the leftover food, which we had to eat at the following meal when our plates were not cleaned. Breakfast presented no problem since we served ourselves bread and jams, no butter. Lunch, the main meal of the day, was a different story, and Leticia's guidance was helpful. Dinner was always "souper swiss," the Swiss supper: boiled potatoes, cheese, bread and yogurt. An occasional "souper swiss" is amusing but, when consumed every night, it becomes maddeningly repetitious. The worst dinners were re-runs of unfinished lunch, dried out meat, and fennel.

Our best bedtimes were when Leticia turned off our lights because the Beauverres were dining out. Her nighttime parting words now remind me of the headmaster at the orphanage in *Cider House Rules* saying: "Good night, you princes of New England." She would say gentle things in Spanish like "sleep well" or "cover up, it's cold," accompanied by a visit to each cot and a touch. Being touched affectionately was rare, therefore her hand on my forehead took on great meaning. The few sentences I heard of hers have stayed with me and formed the basis of my ability to speak Spanish.

One of Beauverre's favorite punishments was to send a boy to his room for a specified number of hours. That period might well run through a meal time, which did not bother us because Leticia invariably came up with some bread and cheese for the punished child, each ingredient well hidden in her apron.

Sometime in 1958, Miguel, the angelic looking South American lad, had accidentally broken a window for which he was sent off to his room for much of the day. Shortly after lunch time, while we were in class with Monsieur Beauverre, we heard screams coming from a dorm room directly above the classroom, which was Miguel's room. Beauverre rushed out and up the stairs. A less frightened group might have tried to find out what was going on, especially when we subsequently saw the Nash Rambler tear down the driveway and head off toward the village with both Beauverres. We rigidly sat in our seats, too terrorized to move.

Shortly afterwards, Mademoiselle Demars came in and told us all to go to the largest classroom, the one adjacent to the dining room without a view of the front of the property or the driveway. We stayed there through two long class periods, two hours each, marked by an automatic bell. We had to do homework in silence, under her supervision. Nothing like this had happened previously and we stole questioning, furtive looks at each other.

Late in the afternoon, an obviously upset Beauverre opened the classroom door and beckoned Mademoiselle Demars out onto a small landing in front of the room's door. We all strained to hear what was going on, to no avail. Eventually she returned saying, "OK, boys, there will be no more classes today. Go outside and play." This was really strange. We looked at each other with curious stares, believing that we would suffer for some reason because of whatever had happened. Outside, we saw Beauverre by himself head back toward town, while Miguel, the punished child, joined us.

"You won't believe what happened!" Miguel said, as we crowded around him. "Leticia snuck food up in her dress and was cutting off a hunk of cheese when the witch caught her, knocked her down and kicked her. Then took the knife and stabbed her."

"Is Leticia dead?" I screamed.

"She's fine! She only got kicked," Miguel explained. Suddenly it was clear: Leticia, our heroine, had stabbed Madame Beauverre! Through my daze, I was disappointed that "the witch" had not left on a stretcher or, better yet, under a sheet.

"There was blood!" continued Miguel. "And she yelled a lot, until Beauverre ran in and took her down the stairs."

"What did you do?" I asked, as if expecting the sequel to a great novel.

"I tried to hide in the corner of my bed. Beauverre didn't hit me or anything like that. When they left, I got on the floor with Leticia."

We never saw Leticia again. That night, the cook's wife put out our "Swiss supper." Mademoiselle Demars watched us shower, put shampoo in our open hands and, once we were in bed, turned off the lights. The entire night, because my bed was directly above his office, I heard Beauverre's voice answering the constantly ringing phone. I couldn't sleep. I knew that something important had happened but did not know what it might mean to me.

Villars-sur-Ollon, Switzerland today

Chapter 11: Leaving La Clairière

The following day, shortly after breakfast, two new faces appeared at the chalet. One man wore a suit and tie, the other was dressed in the grey-green Swiss police uniform. They interviewed Mademoiselle Demars, Miguel and his roommates in the small classroom on the main floor. When they had finished, we once again were told to assemble in the large classroom near the dining room. There, Beauverre told us that Leticia had injured his wife, but that we were not to worry because Madame Beauverre would be back in a few days. *Worry?* I thought…

The two men nodded as if to dismiss Monsieur Beauverre, who obediently left. *Wow!* The all-powerful giant obeyed orders! These men must be more powerful still. The fellow in the suit then asked us what we thought of Leticia. Silence followed for an uncomfortable period until I cautiously lifted my hand in the air.

"Yes, Mon Petit (little one)," he acknowledged me.

"She is very nice to us and helps us a lot," I offered.

"Has she ever hit you?"

"No, sir," I spoke emphatically, while other children murmured in agreement.

"Have you been beaten by anyone? I don't mean a normal spanking, but really hit?" he asked the group.

I wondered who would have the nerve to answer. What exactly was the difference? Many little heads bobbed around looking at each other, until finally Miguel started the dialogue and several boys followed with their tales. Faisal's beating was related by one boy, then another story and another and another.

He concluded the meeting with: "Well, my children, these things will never happen again, I can assure you of that. For now, you will continue your classes as before. There will be a man and a lady moving in to assume Leticia's work and to look after you." His sentences were constructed in simple words for young children to understand, but his tone was determined, final and believable. The two people he had referred to, began working immediately. I never learned their names.

Late that afternoon Miguel's mother arrived in a black Bentley with foreign, diplomatic plates. She was a strikingly elegant lady, whose coat lining and blouse were of the same beautiful floral print. She walked self-assuredly into the chalet to find her son. She did not ring the bell. She simply threw open the door and entered, a hint of anger in her demeanor. As she knelt down to hug Miguel, she wiped tears away from her face. Miguel knew he was leaving because his bags had been packed by the mysterious new couple. Several of us watched through windows in the day's diminishing light. A uniformed driver loaded two suitcases into the car, as Miguel and his mother got into the back seats. I was amazed that this huge event had occurred so quickly, seamlessly, and most importantly, in the presence of neither Beauverre.

My turn to leave was to be the subsequent day. Beauverre told me that I was leaving school, and that my French Uncle and Aunt would be coming to get me. Like the mysteriously timed parental visit for my weekend in Monte Carlo, I wondered when this happy event might occur. I was very eager to see my Aunt Charlie and Uncle Charles again!

The last day I was to wake up at La Clairière was a bright, brisk, clear morning. After breakfast, I saw a black Citroën in the driveway. I looked around eagerly for my aunt, but saw only Pierre, their driver, standing beside the car. The mystery man brought down the same steamer trunk I had arrived with three years earlier and, with Pierre's help, secured it to the roof of the car. As taught, I shook hands with Pierre and, reminiscent of Miguel's departure the previous day, my departure was speedy and with no involvement of either Beauverre. Pierre had backed the car in beside the chalet, so when I entered the front passenger door (which opened backwards), I was facing away from the school. As Pierre maneuvered down the steep driveway, I did not look back at the building. I sat speechless in a blank stupor, wearing a white shirt and tie. Instinctively, I knew I was in good hands. I inhaled deep breaths all day as we drove back down to Lake Geneva and on to Lyon, France.

Chapter 12: Lyon, France

My beloved Aunt Charlie and Uncle Charles lived on Place Bellecour in the center of Lyon. The porte-cochère leading into a small courtyard had been altered so that wider American cars could pass through. Their home was bright and full of antiques, which were Aunt Charlie's passion.

Pierre had stopped to call ahead to alert Aunt Charlie as to our expected arrival time. She greeted me at the front door with open arms, a big smile and a welcoming hug. She explained that my father and her husband were hunting, and they would be back in 48 hours. The next day she spent time explaining the differences between Louis XIV, XV and XVI style furniture, and how to differentiate a reproduction from an original. For lunch, she took me to Paul Bocuse, one of Lyon's celebrated Michelin-rated three-star restaurants. This almost unbelievably different life overwhelmed me.

My father and his brother arrived on schedule. Their conversation focused on the condition of the hunting preserve, particularly on how much game was being raised and released for shooting. They discussed their game keeper, Déforges, whom they referred to by his surname only, reminiscent of centuries past when butlers and key employees were called by their surnames. During hunting season, several land owners would host five-day shoots on their respective properties. The following week another preserve would be the venue and so on, until both the season and the game were exhausted.

Hunting days consisted of a large breakfast and a review of which fields would be hunted and in what sequence. The shooters would then drive to a hedge at the allotted field and sit on hunting seats which doubled as walking sticks, invented by Hermès, while a bus drove local children to a location several fields away. The children, dressed in white shirts and pants with a red sash, carried noise makers. Their job was to "beat the game" in the shooter's direction by walking in a line towards the shooters while making as much racket as possible. Each shooter had two loaded, 12-gauge shotguns, one held in his or her arms, the second held by a servant standing at their side. As the game started flying over or running through the hedge, the shooters would begin firing constantly and rapidly. As each double-barreled shotgun was discharged, the shooter handed that gun to his servant who passed him the second loaded gun, so that the hunter need not interrupt his firing to reload. When the children reached the hedge and all game had been beaten forward, everyone was loaded into cars and busses and taken to the next set of fields where a similar scenario took place. At mid-day, a beautifully prepared, catered lunch was served, usually under tents set up in a field. Large dinner parties celebrated the end of each day's sport.

I had been to these hunts when released from La Clairière, because Le Rosey had an annual, long weekend vacation over All Saint's Day, which was the time my father's preserve was on the shooting tour.

Game displayed in a "tableau"

I dreaded the killing nearly as much as the return to Villars. Each evening the shooters gathered in a courtyard, either at the game keeper's farm or the property owner's manor home. There, all the game killed that day was laid out in neat lines called the "tableau" – the painting. The bigger the tableau, the better the owner's hunt was rated, and the more successful the shoot. I looked at all these animals thinking that, only hours before, they were alive and free. I admired a deer's large, open eye or the beautiful colors of a pheasant's feathers as I cried in the darkness. My father's friends would shrug their shoulders, confused by my reaction. Only Aunt Charlie comforted me by putting her arm around me.

The most upsetting event that could happen was an injury to one of the child game-beaters. As the children approached the hedges where the hunters waited, they were in the direct line of fire. At least once a year, at one hunt or another, a careless or inebriated shooter would wound a child, occasionally in the eye. As at pigeon shoots, these accidents did not alter the schedule nor interfere with the evening's party and gayety.

One particular evening, while surveying the tableau, a memorable event took place. It was telling of both the disparity between the wealthy shooters and their lack of sensitivity regarding the servants who ably attended to their employers. The tableau had been set up in the courtyard of Déforges' old farmhouse, which had no electricity or running water. In the darkness of this damp autumn evening, I could see a candle burning on a window ledge and noticed Déforges' 20-year-old son was reading at a small table.

I asked my aunt Charlie what the young man was doing, and she explained he was taking a correspondence course to obtain a college degree in political science. She then explained what a correspondence course and political science were. The young man switched his gaze from his poorly lit books to the scene below, which was flanked by the latest cars from America and England.

Years afterwards, to my father's bewilderment, the young man became a prominent member of the French Communist Party. It has always struck me that Déforges' son's political affiliation was inevitable and, as with his later political allies, could have been avoided had more inclusive behavior and better communication been practiced by this and similar groups of wealthy Europeans in the 1950's, when the French Communist Party became more powerful.

By this time my father was spending a great deal of time with Ann Woodward, and they shot or hunted together constantly. When Ann watched me cry seeing the tableau, she would say to my father:

"John, he's going to always give you trouble."

After dinner that night in Lyon, I listened to discussions about specific preparations for the week of hunting planned at Dompierre. Eventually, Aunt

Charlie told me to go to bed, and as I shut the living room door behind me, I overheard her admonish my father:

"Jean," she began, "I have been telling you that sending the children to boarding school at their ages is ridiculous. Do these recent events not convince you of that?"

"It's all highly exaggerated," replied my father. "Anyway, René is now old enough to go to Le Rosey."

"Do you seriously mean to tell me that, after what happened, he is going there immediately?" she inquired.

"Of course," he replied. "It'll be good for him."

"I must tell you, Jean," she insisted, "I protest. As you know I have told Nancy that she should not allow you to get away with this. I would never let Charles do something so idiotic."

From that day on, I felt a kindred spirit with my aunt. Over the next decades, my mother told many friends how often and clearly Aunt Charlie, amongst others, voiced her concern about early attendance at Swiss boarding schools. She would add that she regretted not having had her French sister-in-law's strength to stand up to her husband.

I tiptoed up the stairs to the bedroom and wondered what my life at Le Rosey would be like. I had to make it different. I'd start, I thought, by changing my name. I would use my first name, Richard. After all, the previous day, Aunt Charlie had referred to me as "Richard the Lion Hearted." I did not know that Richard the First, the son of Eleanor of Aquitaine, was one of Medieval Europe's fiercest warriors, but it sounded convincing and robust. I would be Richard and I soon developed a love for French history.

Chapter 13: Returning to La Clairière

When I thought about writing this disturbing story, I was able to find out more about the ownership and management of La Clairière. I discovered the building at the time belonged to a well-established and respected family from the French speaking, Swiss "canton" of Vaud, named Clerc. Gaston Clerc, who had an honest interest in education, purchased the building not long before I was sent there, and had rented it to the Beauverre family on a long-term lease in order to run a school for very young boys.

It was not too difficult to track down the Clerc family. The senior Monsieur Olivier Clerc had passed away, but his son André-Olivier was not only willing to speak openly about the experience, but seemed genuinely relieved that a former, young student was planning on telling the story.

"When we discovered that Beauverre was running the institution with an iron fist and a cleaver, we were horrified," said Monsieur André-Olivier Clerc. "We knew the building had been neglected, but we were ignorant of the child abuse."

The chalet was eventually sold to an intermediary, who in turn sold it to the village of La Chaux-de-Fonds, which runs it to this day as a ski and hiking camp for local children. It is a common tradition in Switzerland, that a town not in the mountains purchases a chalet in a skiing village where children can go for a few weeks to ski in the winter and hike in summertime.

I have returned to La Clairière only once as an adult when I was in my late-30s, some 30 years after leaving the school. I was urged to visit the scene of this hideous period in my life by my well-meaning, late partner, Tim. At that time, Tim and I lived in Lausanne, Switzerland where I was building a network of private hospitals for American Medical International, and we kept a weekend apartment in Gstaad.

There are two ways to reach Gstaad from Lausanne and, whenever we went to Gstaad, we took the route via Château d'Oex, consciously avoiding driving through Villars. On several occasions Tim insisted I "confront my daemons," and he urged we take the alternate way and stop in at La Clairière. In a moment of weakness, I reluctantly agreed to go visit the dark chalet.

"Be sensible René," Tim had said, "you're a successful adult. This will put all of that story in perspective." On this last point Tim was right.

The chalet sits atop a hill and can be seen from a considerable distance down the road. As I turned into the long, steep driveway, I had visions, more like hallucinations, of being seated behind my parents more than a quarter century earlier, as my father put the car in low gear to climb the hill. Upon entering the unaltered front hall, the same place where I had been thrown around on several occasions, I experienced the first real panic attack of my life. In fact, it began *before* I entered the building when I saw the unchanged primitive metal bell, which served as the doorbell.

Once I crossed the earlier-forbidden doorway and stood by what had been Beauverre's office, visions and sensations of humiliation, pain and cold permeated my body and I started to hyperventilate. Tim told me to take deep breaths and calm down, as innocent and curious children watched this curious adult couple. Some raced outside to look at our car. Another vision popped into my mind: that of Beauverre's precious Nash Rambler.

Within seconds, Tim and I both knew the visit was not a good idea. Even if I did not pass out during a tour of the building, I either did not possess the courage to face what Tim called "daemons," or I instinctively had adopted the Swiss mantra of never digging up past unpleasant thoughts or events. The fact that the building now housed seemingly happy, vacationing children made no difference for me at that moment. The unaltered chalet triggered visions too unpleasant for me to want to explore any further.

In much the same way as my father had rushed my mother to the car when I was first dropped off, Tim almost carried me to our car. Although he avoided driving on the Swiss mountain roads, he shoved me into the passenger seat, turned the car around in the same mud that I, as a child, had stared at for three years, and tore down the hill onto the main road. Upon reaching Gstaad, I had to have the car washed immediately, as the thought of bringing *that* mud into our garage was quite literally nauseating.

I never had any further urge or desire to see La Clairière again, nor will I.

PART 2

SURVIVOR

Previous page: Le Rosey coat of arms

Chapter 1: Arriving at Le Rosey

September 1958

During the drive from Lyon to Rolle, my father and I spoke little. Putting his new Thunderbird, the first four-seater model, through its paces, and driving as fast as possible over the mountains he had maneuvered through his entire life, occupied his attention.

"Father?" I asked reluctantly.

"Mmmmm?"

"I'd like to be called Richard"

"That's silly. Why?"

"Just because it is different, father"

"It will be shortened to Dick or Rick. One **is** a prick, the other sounds like it."

John Jacques Silvin
1943-2013

He spoke categorically, thereby ending the conversation.

That does it, I thought. Rick sounded more "jock-like" and seemed to displease my father the most. I decided to introduce myself as Rick at this new school.

As my father drove, I had plenty of time to consider what I had learned about Le Rosey from my brother, who had already spent three years there. I had listened with particular attention when he described the most severe teachers, Madame Stickel and Monsieur Mastelli. I believed all his information and began to put it into the only school framework I had: La Clairière.

The Stickels ran the "Junior section" at Le Rosey. I would be assigned to this small group of 33 boys aged nine to 12. Our dormitory, classes and dining room tables would be isolated from the older boys and, as such, the Junior section was like a school within a school, run by the Stickels. This seemed eerily similar to La Clairière and the Beauverres, which added to my apprehension. I knew the Stickels lived in their own apartment with their two children, which was in the Junior dorm, from where they managed every detail of the young boys' lives.

Mireille, their daughter, and her younger brother Giles were about the ages of Rose Marie and Claude. Another similarity that frightened me. Worst of all, Madame Stickel was known as a quick-tempered, unreasonably strict disciplinarian. Since I had only known La Clairière, these apparent similarities created a heightened tension in me as we inched our way closer and closer to Rolle. Consequently, I assumed my new life would be no different than the previous three years. Because of the similarities of the Stickel family to the Beauverres, and the size of the section they ran with an allegedly iron fist, I deeply feared that I would face the same treatment that I had experienced at La Clairière. I concluded that the only change in my life might be the location.

Rolle, Canton de Vaud, Switzerland

Gates to Le Rosey, Rolle

We eventually reached Rolle, a charming, typical Swiss, lake-side village 30 kilometers east of Geneva. In the middle of town, we took the road heading north, up toward the low-lying Jura mountains. About one kilometer up the hill, we turned into a driveway between an imposing set of gates engraved with the words "Château du Rosey." We drove down the long, tree-lined, paved driveway, past the original "Château" and into the central courtyard flanked by a fountain and two buildings, each containing classrooms with dorm rooms above them.

The Château du Rosey, the heart of Rosey's Rolle campus

Upon our arrival, my father took me to meet the two headmasters: Monsieur Johannot and Mr. Hughes. We walked through a double sized wooden door, which I noticed had no bell, into a well-designed hall and into the headmaster's office through its open door. These were the first noticeable details which differed from La Clairière. All three occupants of the office were at their desks when we stepped onto the old, well-polished, creaking wooden floor.

Louis Johannot

"Louis, how are you?" my father asked the headmaster, using his charming social manner. He continued, "This is René, errr, Richard René." My father seemed to have a cordial relationship with the senior staff of Le Rosey, which was another difference I observed as compared to the terrifying introduction to La Clairière three year earlier.

Monsieur Louis Johannot, the headmaster, was one of the only two Swiss army's colonels, the highest attainable rank in peacetime. This huge man, I would soon learn, had a sweet wife, but the colonel demanded absolute order and adherence to all rules. At the second desk in this office sat Mr. Cyril Hughes, a "Mr. Chips" sort of gentleman. He and his charming wife, Enid, headed up the English side of the school, so we referred to him as "Mr." not "Monsieur."

Cyril Hughes

The third desk in the office belonged to Mademoiselle Schaub, one of the school's largest shareholders. Her role was to communicate with the parents. It was she who, out of ignorance I believe, had recommended La Clairière to my parents; a decision, which would always make me resentful of her.

"Hello Richard," said the headmaster "welcome to Le Rosey." He extended a large hand. I cautiously took it. *More differences*, I thought… Then I shook hands with Mademoiselle Schaub and Mr. Hughes.

Hélène Schaub

"How is Nancy?" inquired Mademoiselle Schaub. I was amazed she knew my mother's name. After a few more pleasantries, she spoke kindly to me: "Now let me take you to meet Madame Stickel."

Out we went, my father, Mademoiselle Schaub and I, across the courtyard through a classroom building into the Junior's dorm. It all looked so large to me. We went up a flight of stairs to the Junior's floor and knocked on a door in the middle of the long hall. As the door opened, my heart raced. But then I saw a rather kind looking lady, wearing a colorful dress and sporting a broad smile! I quickly searched for more clues indicating what she might be like. This lady appeared to be nothing like what I feared. Then a handsome, tall man appeared behind her and introduced himself as "Monsieur Stickel." He was gentle-mannered with a soft voice. He didn't smell like Beauverre! Other than the fact he was bald, there were no apparent similarities with the man I had been terrified of.

Antoinette and Charlie Stickel

"Antoinette, this is Silvin 2. Richard René," said Schaub. At Rosey we were all called by our surnames. Since my older brother was "Silvin" I would be known as Silvin 2. Again, we all shook hands, after which Madame Stickel walked us down the long hall with bedrooms on each side. It was clean and looked more like a Swiss hotel than a dark chalet. Close to the end of the hallway, we all entered a room which contained three beds in the same space where La Clairière held five.

"You have two roommates," Madame Stickel said, "Gellhorn and Brancovan. You'll meet them later because they are doing sports now." The room was bright and attractive. I saw that the other occupants had put pictures on side tables. The rules obviously allowed for some personalizing of the décor; another encouraging difference. Gellhorn had also tacked posters of British theater debuts near his bed, while Brancovan had added some pictures of beautiful, green rolling hills near his bed.

Unlike my first sight of the crowded, drab room at La Clairière, my initial impressions were much more cheerful. My bed was made up and I was assigned my own night table for personal items. It was clear that Smokey The Bear would not have been confiscated in this environment. The shared closet had ample space for my clothes, each piece of which was labeled with "Silvin 2" sewn into it, so that the laundry could readily return them all after washing. My days working the antiquated washing contraption in Villars were clearly over!

"Well, I'll be off!" said my father, who then walked down the hall with Mademoiselle Schaub. I thought I caught a surprised look on Madame Stickel's face at his cold departure and lack of uttering any words of encouragement. It was already beginning to feel comfortable for me to sense that I was in the care of someone who identified such subtleties.

Martha and Sandy Gellhorn

That afternoon I met my roommates. Sandy Gellhorn was the adopted son of Ernest Hemingway's third wife, Martha Gellhorn who was married to Hemmingway from 1940 to 1945. She was working for Collier's Magazine and met Hemingway in Spain while they were both covering the Spanish Civil War in late 1937. Sandy had been adopted from an Italian orphanage in 1949 and, like many of the children who entered boarding school at a young age, had a formal, often distant relationship with his parents.

Gellhorn was a chubby child, which was an oddity for me since we were all nearly starved at La Clairière. Had he stayed at Le Rosey for years, I am sure we would have become long-term, close friends. His round face was as warm and friendly as was his personality, and I have regretted not staying in touch with him over the decades.

Brancovan would turn out to be a totally different, but equally fascinating story. His father was a Romanian prince who had escaped with his family to Switzerland when the communists took over his country. The family's full name is Bassaraba de Brancovan and is known as one of the families considered to be "the Heirs of Europe."

Brancovan was sullen and distant. Perhaps the exile his relatives had experienced had added a sense of defeat and betrayal to the entire family. My relationship with him was cold, almost formal, in an adult fashion. While our relationship was emotionless, it was not at all hostile.

Prince Brancovan

Madame Stickel took some time to explain what classes I would attend, where they were located and how to get to each classroom. Her instructions were clear and stated factually, not threateningly. She would teach me French and history, while her husband taught mathematics and geography. I had never heard of history classes and was curious to see what this was all about. As it turned out, I loved the subject and have remembered the teachings of this dedicated couple forever.

Madame Stickel's riveting descriptions of the Roman Empire, the Punic Wars and ancient Greek history were like going to the movies. It was the basic subjects of French and mathematics that were the problem for me, although some of Monsieur Stickel's instruction have served me well, even throughout studying college mathematics. Since I had learned nothing at La Clairière except how to survive, my lack of academic ability soon became alarmingly apparent to the Stickels.

After lights were out that first night, my two roommates immediately went to sleep, and I cried until there were no more tears. Although my introduction to Le Rosey was nothing like it had been at La Clairière three years previously, the confusing unknown made me feel that weighty, bowling ball pain in my stomach. It would take some time to grow into the understanding that Le Rosey would be better, much better. At least right now, I knew that my brother's definition of harsh discipline was not consistent with my experience.

Chapter 2: A Day at Le Rosey

Rosey's motto then, as now, is "Actis Virtus." The medieval Latin phrase has two appropriate meanings. The simple translation being "virtuous action." The more descriptive and profound translation is "only your actions show what you are." Both explanations are perfect euphemisms for Louis Johannot's philosophy.

"Rosey" (as it is often called in English, without the male pronoun "le") had earned a reputation over the previous hundred years as a boarding school for the privileged and was often referred to "as the school of princes and kings." However, Rosey did not spoil the students while in attendance. Its goal was to form, not "just" to educate, multi-lingual, sports-oriented boys, destined for universities in numerous countries before beginning lives of "haute bourgeoisie" or royalty in their respective countries. One of the immediate benefits of the philosophy and international mix of students was an environment where cultural differences did not surprise any of the young "Rosey boys." The primary focus along with sports was the mastering of languages, as well as being completely comfortable with foreign travel. However, most parents quickly understood that subjects of music, religion and art history were omitted from the curriculum, and some parents assumed that part of their sons' education during summer vacations.

My first full day on campus began, as all our days did, with breakfast at 7AM. Classes started at eight and lasted until noon, with a short break for hot chocolate mid-morning. After lunch, we played two hours of mandatory sports. Afternoon classes began again at four, after tea, and ended just before a seven o'clock dinner. We ate our perfectly adequate meals all together in one large dining room, dressed in a jacket and tie. The twelve tables of ten, with a teacher at each end of the table, easily fit in the bright, walnut paneled room. After dinner, we were required to do our homework and to study in "La Grande Salle" (The Great Room) before bed.

In those days Le Rosey was a school for boys only, and it offered three levels of education over nine years: Junior for 9 to 11-year olds, "Moyen" for ages 12 through 14, and "Senior" for age 15 through graduation. Students could choose between a French curriculum and an English one. The former prepared students for the French Baccalaureate or the Swiss "Maturité" and eventual acceptance at a university in one of those countries. The English curriculum readied the student for the British GCE exams or the American College Boards, and acceptance at universities in the UK or the US. Consequently, 18 grades were offered, nine in each of the languages. With only 120 boys enrolled, our class sizes were very small, from two to 20, with most classes containing about 10 students. All boys were required to speak both French and English and to study at least one other language, from a list of the 15 languages taught.

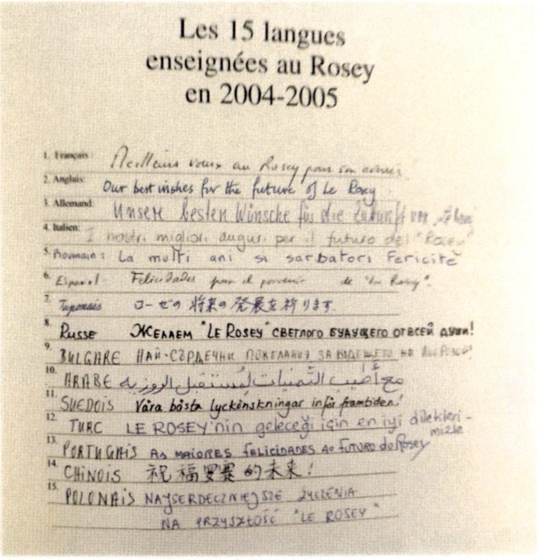

Our mandatory sports were of equal importance and were the main reason for our seasonal residence on two totally distinct, different campuses, both fully equipped for our academic classes as well as our sports. We resided at the main campus in Rolle, between Geneva and Lausanne, in the French speaking part of Switzerland during the fall and the spring terms. Our fall sports were European football (soccer), tennis and basketball. When we boys returned from Christmas holidays, we went to the winter campus in Gstaad, located in the German speaking canton (Swiss state) of Bern, in order to ski and to play ice hockey. After Easter, when we returned to the main campus, we ran track, swam and rowed.

We shared our dorm rooms with one to four other boys, depending on age. Dormitory buildings were segregated by the three categories: Junior, Moyen and Senior. In fall and spring, we lived in dormitory buildings adjacent to each other in Rolle. In winter, we slept in separate chalets clustered around a central hill in Gstaad.

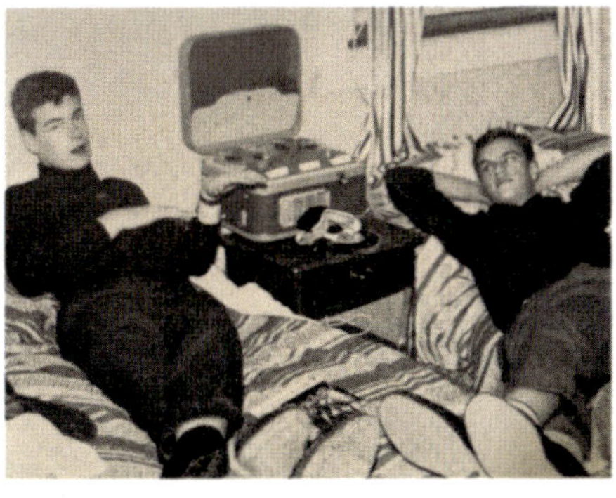

Typical Rosey dorm room

The small Alpine town of Gstaad was just beginning to establish itself as a ski resort for the rich and famous in the decades after the Second World War. Its low altitude of 1,000 meters had not previously made Gstaad a desirable ski destination like Zermatt, Saint Moritz or Davos. Instead, it was primarily a farming village. However, the parents of the "Rosey boys," and later the alumni themselves, built their own luxurious chalets near the school, forming a small, charming village, which was developed in an architecturally sensitive way to preserve the original Bernese look. The then-two principal hotels, The Palace and the Park, were renovated to accommodate the Rosey boys' visitors as well as tourists.

At La Clairière Leticia had been the only adult I related to. By contrast, at Le Rosey most students probably did not know the names of any of the numerous people who performed the comfortable services we enjoyed. I immediately appreciated and savored the relative luxury into which I had been transplanted. Unlike many of the other students, I enjoyed knowing the names of the various staff members and conversing with them while practicing my Spanish. Most of the service staff came from Spain and Portugal in search of the highly treasured Swiss francs to send home to their families.

The Rosey "hill" in the heart of Gstaad

We Rosey boys did not make our beds, wash our clothes, shine our shoes, or take any part in serving our meals. The staff, always politely addressed by the students, provided all these services almost without being noticed. Dirty shoes left outside our bedroom door appeared there, miraculously shined in the morning. Our beds were made up and the rooms were tidied daily. Our meals were served by uniformed staff. Rosey boys would greet and thank the staff appropriately. The meaning of *noblesse oblige* would be learned, as if by osmosis, in the overall environment Le Rosey embraced in the 1950s and 1960s.

Chapter 3: Time Off and John Lear

If not punished, the boys were allowed to leave school with a parent Saturday at noon and had to return Sunday evening for dinner. At midday on Saturday, parents would drive into the courtyard to collect their own children and any lucky friends who might be invited. Those of us who did not have parents living nearby watched this process with great envy, hoping for an invitation to accompany them. I noticed every detail of the cars and the clothes, as well as the relationships these parents had with their sons.

My best times during the first years at Rosey were when I went home with one of my classmates on Saturdays. There were five parents with sons my age who all took up residence along La Côte, the area between Geneva and Rolle. They were Betty Sicre, Marianne Alireza, "Pash Pash" Yehia, Jehanne Reynolds and Barbara "Bobo" Rockefeller.

I especially looked forward to going home with Emile Sicre (Sicre 2), another Junior with an older brother at Rosey. His mother, Betty, was an amazing woman who allowed her children to refer to her by her first name. An accomplished pilot, Betty had served as an air transport auxiliary attached to the RAF during the Second World War.

Since women pilots were not allowed to enter combat zones, they were given the extremely dangerous job of ferrying damaged planes to repair sites, and to deliver new aircrafts to their aerodrome destinations around Great Britain. Betty was fearless and had climbed Europe's highest mountain, Mont Blanc. She had also written a book about introducing hybrid corn to Morocco for larger crop yields, titled *Amid my Alien Corn.*

Betty Sicre, 1920-2018

I always enjoyed hearing the colorful stories of her adventures, which Betty told us in a very matter-of-fact way, and in so doing, taught us that we could do anything we aspired to. By the time I met her in 1959, she dedicated her life to overseeing the education of her children, while her husband lived in Madrid and aboard his yacht in Monte Carlo. Betty wore little make up, dressed in plain clothes and behaved like "one of the boys" with us. She attended all the sports events allowed for parents and gave us a lot of sound advice without preaching. At the Sicre's home, Betty would often cook hamburgers on a grill, and set us up in front of a television to watch sport competitions. I had never imagined that children could have such a loving, helpful and friendly home life. I looked up to Emile, who was one year older than I and was an accomplished young sportsman. He had a placid, tender way which differentiated him from others by making him unthreatening yet masculine.

The Sicre and Alireza families, while both friendly, were very different. The former was Hispanic-American, while the latter was a cultural mix of Muslim, Arab and American. These differences were apparent to us at our young ages but were also not viewed as exceptional or menacing. Any form of racial or cultural discrimination represented concepts that I had never encountered and certainly did not understand as a child.

Marianne Alireza, born 1921

Betty was very close to Marianne Alireza, who also lived near the school. She, too, had written a book: "*At the Drop of a Veil.*" It chronicled her marriage to one of the two leading, non-royal Saudi families; the other such family was the Bin Laden family. Marianne and her husband-to-be had met as young students in California. Eventually they went to live in Saudi Arabia. Like Betty, Marianne was a strong woman, a free thinker, the best possible example for independent women to emulate and for us to observe. I always felt welcome and cared about when I was with Marianne and Tarek, her second son who was my age. I envied the home lives enjoyed by Tarek and Emile, and I adored them both.

Another boy, John Lear, an older student who was six years my senior, was the son of William Lear Jr., the pilot who had developed the first successful, executive jet and the autopilot. By the late 1950's Bill Lear had become wealthy and founded the Lear Jet Company. Accompanied by his fourth wife, Moya Olsen, the daughter of the well-known stage comedian, Ole Olsen, the family moved to Geneva and split their time between Switzerland and Santa Monica, California.

John was a handsome rogue who shared his family's passion for planes, and he was frequently in trouble at school. At age sixteen, he had managed to get a pilot's license and he loved flying a red Bucker Jungmann bi-plane. A real daredevil, John buzzed the school in his plane one weekend while we all hung out of windows waving and shouting. His skill at flying amazed and entertained us. At one point he flew so close to our buildings that I could see every detail of his face.

A Bucker Jungmann bi-plane

As was customary, after dinner, M. Johannot would rise and make announcements to the entire student body. As soon as the boys saw Monsieur Johannot stand, we would all click a fork on our water glasses to silence those who had not noticed. The night Lear had buzzed the school, Johannot got up to talk about Lear's flying acrobatics over the school.

"I have an unpleasant announcement," Johannot started. "What happened today was not acceptable. As a result, Lear has been expelled. He will not be coming back to school." Then, as was his custom, he continued with "now let us move on to more pleasant subjects...."

The following Saturday, Betty and Marianne arrived in their respective station wagons for the ritual of collecting children for the weekend. I was talking with them, probably in the hope of soon getting another invitation, when I heard the distinctive, muffled sound of Lear's bi-plane. John had decided to make an impressive farewell statement.

The engine's sound increased to a roar as he maneuvered the plane in over the courtyard. By now, everyone was watching, some in shock, while some, like I, were dazzled. Again and again, he flew the plane in towards the group, scattering some. He would pull out of the dive just in time to avoid hitting a dorm. He even managed to touch the roof with his fixed landing gear sending decorative, red clay tiles rattling to the ground.

For his parting stunt, he planned to buzz his former dormitory room located behind one of the buildings bordering the courtyard. I watched him climb steeply, almost vertically, until he started his roaring descent toward the dormitory. In an interview many years later, John explained what happened.

"I had managed to start a three-turn spin, but I was too low, and I crashed. I shattered both of my heels and ankles and broke both legs in three places. I crushed my neck, broke both sides of my jaw and lost all of my front teeth."

All the boys who had been watching with a mixture of admiration and fascination followed Betty, who began to run from the courtyard, followed by a few other parents. When we reached the far side of the dorm, we could see John's plane smashed into the ground at a 45-degree angle, its tail elevated in the air.

"Stay back!" yelled Betty, as she ran directly toward the smoking plane. She passed a local farmer who stood frozen in shock with a cigarette dangling from his mouth. Betty paused momentarily to tear it from his lips.

"Stamp that out! Boys, stay back!" she repeated, as she ran up to the plane's open cockpit. John was alone, sitting in the aft seat of the two-seater bi-plane. The engine and the front seat were completely crushed together into one mass of crumpled red, rather like used Christmas wrapping paper. Betty reached into the cockpit fearlessly and unbuckled the handsome young pilot. She tried to pull him out, but John was too heavy.

"Get over here and help me!" she ordered the farmer, who obeyed. Together they managed to lift John out and lay him on the ground. I could see his shattered legs, limp in blood-soaked pants. Worse was his classic face: the top two thirds were intact, but from his nose down nothing was left, just indistinguishable skin, bone and dangling teeth. As Betty spoke to him, he spit out blood and gasped for air.

"I need three more big guys here right now!" she shouted at the group of boys waiting about 100 feet away. Obediently, three Seniors moved forward and carried John to a safe distance from the plane. I looked at the young man in shock as he spat out more blood, this time with teeth.

As Monsieur Johannot arrived with many of the teachers, he ordered us all back inside. We walked to the dining hall and ate lunch in silence as we heard sirens of an ambulance and fire trucks. I never saw John again, but Betty would answer my questions about his many operations and his struggle to walk.

Shortly after the crash, John developed gangrene in one of his ankles. Fortunately, amputation, which had been considered, was narrowly avoided and John was shipped to the Lovelace Clinic in Albuquerque, New Mexico for extended surgical repairs and rehabilitation.

Chapter 4: Last in My Class

I began to develop some feelings of calm and stability during my first year at Rosey, under the care and supervision of the Stickel's in their well-run Junior section. Even so, I often felt lonesome and cried myself to sleep many nights. Happily, I was gradually losing the constant fear of being beaten or molested. The main concern, however, was my inadequate grades. While I genuinely enjoyed Madame Stickel's fabulous history lessons, I was failing at all other subjects. The three years of virtually no classroom education at La Clairière was evident.

During classes I would frequently look around to see if the other kids understood the words the teachers were using. Although fluent in the languages of my instruction, the vocabulary was far more evolved and sophisticated than I had been exposed to before. This realization frightened me as much as if I were studying in a foreign language. I became frustrated and frightened and wondered if, perhaps, I was mentally challenged or just different from the other boys.

The first winter term in Gstaad, I lived in a five-bed room with a Swede, a Turk, my Saudi friend Tarek and an Austrian, Egon von Fürstenberg. Egon later gained fame through his wife, Diane, who developed a successful clothing line. The Turk, Kemal Dervish, went on to be an elected official in Turkey, the equivalent of a senator. He is frequently interviewed on major news networks regarding terrorism and Middle Eastern affairs.

Our room had one window with double panes of glass for added insulation. My bed was next to the window on the top floor of the main chalet. This building, known as the Rex, had been the headquarters of the Swiss army for the canton (state) of Bern during the war, while Monsieur Johannot was the young headmaster of the school and an up-and-coming army officer. The chalet faced the village, which was located below the "Rosey hill," and looked directly at the beautifully lit Palace hotel which dominated the village from the opposite hill.

The Palace Hotel opened in December of 1913. The main part, which is visible from everywhere in the village of Gstaad, is a large, beige, cube-like concrete structure with a tower at each corner flying festive flags. No other building in Gstaad is like it; all other construction is wood and designed to look like a classic chalet. Even some of the newer eight and ten thousand square foot chalets have authentic Alpine appearances. Several contain numerous subterranean levels for indoor pools, garages and party rooms.

We five roommates were coping, but we were still quite homesick, 11-year-old boys. Several of my roommates' mothers would come to visit their children and stay at the Palace hotel. By adjusting the window adjacent to my

Palace Hotel, Gstaad today

bed at exactly the correct angle, I could create a reflection of the illuminated hotel so that any given bed in the room could see it. As each subsequent mother came to Gstaad, after lights out, in the dark, her son would ask:

"Silvin, please give me the palace." Dutifully, until I got too cold, I'd "send" the reflection of where this particular homesick child's mother was staying, presumably waiting for Saturday when her boy could spend the night with her.

That winter I learned how to ski, and I loved it. My ski teacher, Cubby Bach, was a kind, gentle man who enjoyed teaching us children how to ski in single file down the easiest mountain in town, the Eggli. He was even patient when one of us would try to quickly break with the line to pass another student. Years later this technique served me well as we had night-time, torch carrying ski runs down the same mountain, accompanied by Mr. Bach and his friends who played accordions as we approached the glowing village below.

By the first spring trimester in Rolle my failing grades were clearly a trend and had begun to alarm Madame Stickel and other teachers. By the end of the school year, out of 33 Juniors, I was listed as 32nd. There was no pride in the fact that the child I beat was later diagnosed as "dull normal." When my father was advised that it was unlikely I could continue at Rosey, he came to Rolle for a meeting with Madame Stickel and Monsieur Johannot.

"He is like a little bird, Mr. Silvin," began Madame Stickel. "He is sweet enough, but I can teach him only so much. Do you realize that at his age he cannot perform the most basic mathematics and cannot even spell the word 'père'?" (father)

"Well, I have found out that the studies were not adequate at La Clairière" my father responded. Then turning to Monsieur Johannot; "After all, Louis, you recommended he be schooled there, but let's overlook that. I have a suggestion. I'll send him to a cram school this summer. He will return to Rosey before the other boys in the fall and repeat all his exams. If he does not pass each and every one, I'll have to find another solution for him. Is this acceptable, Louis?"

Johannot, a chain smoker, took a long drag on his cigarette. Clearly, this had not been his preference. However, the slightly veiled threat may have struck a guilty nerve.

"OK, but we agree, he passes all exams or he's out," conceded the colonel.

My head bobbed back and forth like at a tennis tournament as my fate was being decided.

"Yes, that's the agreement, Louis," my father confirmed.

Then with no word to me, he left. My thinking was not complex enough to feel much besides indifference at the thought I might soon embark on another schooling adventure. I was unconcerned about returning to Le Rosey and primarily focused on the immediate future, what the mysterious "cram school" would be. Consequently, all I felt about this "agreement" was a desire to please all parties, with no consideration as to the consequences for me. It was clear from the meeting that I was "a problem" and I had best figure out how to reverse that impression, or else face every adult's displeasure.

As I suspected, there was no cram school. A few days after the embarrassing meeting, I flew to New York with the other American based boys. As soon as I reached my mother's house in Bay Shore, she informed me I would spend each day with an elderly French couple. To my joy, I soon discovered two delightful, retired teachers. Madame Tschenne was severely handicapped with advanced osteoporosis, while her husband suffered from cardiac problems. They made me aware that I was their rebirth. As soon as I was delivered to their home each day, they lit up as if rejuvenated. From the very first hour, this "cram school" would be the best part of my instruction yet.

Vocabulary lessens were conducted while playing Monopoly in French. I discovered words such as "mortgage" and "construction costs," as well as their meanings. Even mathematics was fun as Monsieur Tschenne patiently taught me basic rules. This so-called punishment was much more fun than behaving like an adult at my mother's house. The summer became increasingly interesting as all my failed subjects were reviewed and explained in tender terms. The fact that I did nothing else all summer but sit with this octogenarian French couple became a constant thrill. Once dressed and having had breakfast in the kitchen with the cook, I eagerly sat by the back door until my mother or her driver would bring me the two miles to the Tschenne home.

In September my father met me at the airport in Lyon, France, the closest airport to his beloved hunting preserve, and he brought me to Rolle a few days before any other student returned. Driving with my father had never been a joyous occasion. I knew that, as an 11-year-old boy, I had to "behave" as a sophisticated adult. On one occasion I sneezed and was severely reprimanded for doing so in a "common fashion." When we stopped for meals, my father ordered his courses and, without consultation, side plates for me. It was patently clear that my presence was an uncomfortable, time-consuming obligation; not an opportunity for father and son to communicate. I did my best to behave as a sophisticated adult, and if I could not meet that standard, silence was the only alternative.

"I need not tell you that you have no options here. You ***will*** pass these tests. Think of the embarrassment you have been to me. My son the last in his class!

So, just stop causing all this trouble!" he exclaimed, as we drove along the lake road from Geneva and approached Rolle.

"Yes, father," I replied, not knowing how I could just will this success to happen.

Carlo Mastelli
1918 - 1974

On arrival at school, my worst fears were realized: Mr. Mastelli, the most dreaded teacher, would administer these two days of tests. I had not had any classes with this Italian gentleman, but my brother had failed his Latin course and had relayed stories about how severe he was with all the older boys he taught.

The first day of the exams, sitting alone in one of the larger classrooms, I desperately tried to solve the first mathematics questions while Mr. Mastelli stood behind me. Just his presence out of my sight was a threat to me. My hand shook, and I trembled as I started to solve a simple algebra equation. Frequently, he would gently say: "Now, Silvin, think that one through again." Or "Are you sure that you did not forget to multiply A by three?"

Gradually, it became apparent that this "tyrant" was trying to help and propel me forward. How could this be, I wondered? A voice erroneously grouped into a category of feared authority took on a tone of helpfulness. I became momentarily stunned that a possible batterer might actually have an interest in being part of his student's success and achievements. I gradually relaxed and read the questions in a more comfortable way, so as to better understand them.

During the dictation, he again stood behind me: "Silvin, listen carefully to how I pronounce the word. Do you not hear me emphasize the ending?" Or "do you remember the following rule… Let's write that word again."

Carlo Mastelli was actually doing his very best to *help* me. That an authoritarian figure could care about a protégé's success was a novel realization to me. In a sense he felt that my succeeding was his goal! There really were people like this in my new world.

Needless to say, I did very well on all the subjects. There had been no need for me to fear Mr. Mastelli. I had also learned that reputations were to be taken with a grain of salt until one could form one's own opinion. Mr. Mastelli taught at Rosey until his death 20 years later. He always took great pride in watching me progress through life, and asked questions about my career and personal life. In return for his concern and guidance, I always let him know how grateful I was for his secretive, yet pivotally important assistance and encouragement.

Chapter 5: The Woodwards

William Jr. and Ann Woodward

My parents had entered into a "Catholic divorce," a separation, during my time at La Clairière. This meant that my mother stayed in New York much of the year, while my father hunted in Europe. His companion was the infamous Ann Woodward who fatally shot her husband, Bill, at their Oyster Bay estate on October 30, 1955. This accident had occurred after a huge row the social couple had during a dinner given nearby for the Duke and Duchess of Windsor. A major media event in New York, Dominick Dunne chronicled it as the mystery unfolded and later wrote the *Two Mrs. Grenvilles*, which closely follows each detail of the story.

The Woodwards had two boys who were roughly the same age as my brother and I. Mrs. Elsie Woodward, the slain man's mother and one of New York's revered *Grande Dames*, insisted that her grandchildren, William and Jimmy, leave America and attend Le Rosey with us. Over the next years, the aging Elsie, who resided at the Waldorf Towers in Manhattan, was a source of kindness to me. My relationship with Ann was a different story. Oddly, my father always introduced her as "a wonderful shot." The irony of the statement obviously escaped him.

In my second year at Le Rosey, my Easter recess coincided with the world championship of live pigeon shooting held in Bologna, Italy. It was one of the few times I was asked to attend an event with both my father and Ann. I was quite happy about it because Ann's youngest son, Jimmy, was also invited, so we would be traveling together. I admired Jimmy very much. He was two years older, taller and appeared much more self-assured than I.

Carola Mandel aboard her yacht *Carola*

Women competed as a separate group in pigeon shoots. Ann's archrival and champion contender was another American: Carola Mandel. The Mandels lived in Chicago, Palm Beach and aboard their yacht: the Carola. Before it was so named, my father and Leon Mandel had participated in wild parties on board the vessel, when Mr. Mandel had sent it to Havana prior to the Cuban revolution. Leon Mandel was the owner of the Chicago based Mandel Brothers Department Stores before selling the chain.

The Mandels had met in Havana during Cuba's grand era before the 1953 Cuban Revolution. After their marriage, Mr. Mandel devoted his life to making his beautiful, young wife famous. He had succeeded in getting her onto the 10 best-dressed list. As a result, Carola was known as the "picture of Paris chic" and was generally recognized as a fashion leader. In the 1950's both Carola and Leon Mandel were eager to see the glamorous Carola become World Champion at pigeon shooting.

The Mandels sent their car driven by a uniformed chauffeur to pick us up at the station in Bologna. Leon had commissioned a specially designed Rolls Royce built on the Phantom limousine chassis and reconfigured as what the British call an estate wagon (station wagon). It was outfitted with two large armchairs, and a gun rack for Carola's prize guns. Their American chauffeur met us at the train station.

The 10-day long competition was nearing its end when we arrived in Italy. Some 20 women had already been eliminated. Ann and Carola were the two finalists for the championship. Even I, who hated these events, sensed the excitement. Again and again, both women successfully killed their birds as the competition continued and the tension mounted. Finally, Carola won. Her green eyes blazing with rage, Ann left the club hurriedly as Leon called reporters in Palm Beach and Chicago to announce his wife's championship, and to ensure that it would be picked up by the press.

When Ann competed in major shooting events, she always booked three adjacent rooms in hotels. She slept in the middle room and kept the two rooms next to hers vacant to ascertain that no noisy neighbor might disturb her rest. I'm not sure where my father slept during these tension-filled days.

Carola Mandel at a pigeon shoot

The celebration dinner for the end of the championship was a grand event in a large, lush garden lit by torches, held at a local nobleman's property outside Bologna. Servants dressed in Renaissance costumes served the food and drink. An angry Ann, Jimmy and I were seated together as my father socialized with other shooters. Suddenly she looked at me and said:

"You don't understand the challenge of pigeon shooting, do you?"

"I just hate to see these animals killed," I responded.

"You know, René, you will always be a problem to your father, and you will never be a real man like Jimmy." Her beautiful green eyes suddenly looked threatening and frightening to me, not just angry because she lost. This distant, austere and formal lady had become an adversary. Not understanding how I had challenged her, I was confused. Previously I knew, without judgment, that she was infamous and possibly scandalous. Had she been loving; she would have received my gratitude and protection in return. But this reaction forced me into an adversarial role with her.

I was crushed. I wondered what she could mean by "a real man." *Could I not become as tall and as strong as Jimmy? Could I not excel at a sport or a career?* That night and later on the train back to Switzerland, I decided to do my best to prove her wrong and become "a real man." The only problem was that I had to figure out what it meant!

Chapter 6: Famous Names Lead to a Lock Down

Le Rosey was a conservative, publicity adverse institution which strictly enforced its rules. By the time I was in my "Moyen years" a number of new boys from famous families were in attendance. Names like Rockefeller and Vanderbilt were not out of the ordinary, which understandably interested the press. Occasionally, one of these families would have liked an exception to one or another of Le Rosey's rules and policies. Johannot, always militarily strict, did not make exceptions, and he always protected his students' privacy with equal diligence.

Alexander Onassis and Philip Niarcos, sons of the two rival Greek shipping magnates, were also enrolled. Niarcos, a small and shy boy, kept to himself, so he was able to lead a normal school life without turmoil or apparent hardship. However, Alexander's "career" at Rosey was shorter.

Alexander's mother, the first Mrs. Onassis, had been told when the boys could receive visitors: Wednesday at noon and taken out with a parent at midday on Saturday. On Alexander's first day of school a large black Rolls Royce slowly pulled into the courtyard. As if expecting a problem, Johannot rapidly emerged from his office.

Athina Livanos Onassis and Alexander

"Mrs. Onassis," he greeted her, "how nice to see you. What can I do for you?"

"I want to see Alexander, Monsieur," she replied politely.

"Perhaps I had not been clear to Mr. Onassis over the phone and to you yesterday," he responded. "The rule is that parents can only see their son on

Wednesday at noon and again on Saturday. And this assumes that the child has not been punished."

"Oh yes, Monsieur," she replied with an anxious tone, "but I miss Alexander so much and I have a small gift for him. I just wanted to hug him and have a short talk with my son. I'm sure you will make an exception for me."

"Very well, Madame," Johannot conceded, "but I must tell you that this can *never* happen again, other than on the days, and at the specific times, we have discussed."

The following day, close to the same time, the large black Rolls Royce carefully maneuvered into the courtyard. Monsieur Johannot, marching like a battalion leader on parade, again met her by the car as her chauffeur opened the back door.

"Yes, Mrs. Onassis?" he inquired sternly.

"Monsieur Johannot, I need to see Alexander in the worst way. I won't take long, I assure you," she pleaded.

"Actually, Madame," Johannot responded, "you may take as long as you like. In fact, you *will* take him home with you permanently. It is obvious to us that you cannot comply with our rules."

Monsieur Johannot was always the quintessential Swiss army colonel. He also enjoyed the luxurious position of having a two-year wait list for students to attend his, the most expensive, boarding school in the world. He was adamantly opposed to any accelerated acceptances that would allow a student to bypass others who were awaiting acceptance at Rosey.

Simonne Bonnemain

Charlie Chaplin learned this when he phoned the school after he moved to the lake side town of Vevey, not far from Rolle. Monsieur Johannot's secretary took the call:

"Simonne Bonnemain," she answered in the Swiss custom of stating one's name instead of saying "hello."

"This is Charlie Chaplin." He spoke proudly. "I want to enroll my son at Le Rosey for the next academic year, starting in September."

"I'm terribly sorry, Mr. Chaplin," she replied, "but there is a formal acceptance procedure, *and* we have a two-year waiting period."

"I don't think you heard me correctly," the male voice continued, "*I am Charlie Chaplin…*"

In what became a famous, often repeated tale in Rosey history, Mademoiselle Bonnemain interrupted him, "It is you who does not understand, Monsieur. There is a two-year wait list, and *I am Simonne Bonnemain.*" She ended the conversation there. The Chaplin children attended other Swiss schools.

Barbara "Bobo" Sears Rockefeller, 1917-2008

Since Le Rosey changed locations from Rolle to Gstaad and back to Rolle again, each student had three different sets of roommates per year. My roommate at the time of this incident was Winthrop Rockefeller, the son of Arkansas' governor, and the nephew of Nelson Rockefeller. His mother Barbara, *aka* BoBo, lived at the recently completed Intercontinental Hotel in Geneva to be near her son. She often took me out on Saturday with "Winnie."

I enjoyed being with her very much. She was a no-nonsense, down to earth lady who was not impressed by any other Rosey parent and vocally *unimpressed* with the senior staff. Like me, she loved to cross the ocean by ship when she returned to her brownstone on East 67th Street. On one occasion I was able to join them and their 50 pieces of luggage on the Italian Line's Michelangelo when she and her son moved back to America. The bags required BoBo to hire a separate baggage car on the train from Switzerland to the South of France, and her own barge to ferry the cases from Cannes out to the Michelangelo which was waiting for passengers in the Bay of Cannes.

Winthrop "Winnie" Paul Rockefeller 1948 - 2006

A good lad, Winnie found the regimented life and strict studies at Le Rosey difficult to master. That night, after dinner, Monsieur Johannot stood to speak. Dutifully, we tapped a metal utensil on our glasses to create silence.

"Welcome back to school, boys," he began. "I have a very important announcement. I want you all to listen carefully. *Life Magazine* has requested to interview me and several of you. This request has been ca-te-gor-ic-ally refused." He broke down the syllables to emphasize his point. "I want to make one thing perfectly clear," he continued in his authoritarian voice. "No student is allowed to speak to any reporter. If anyone disobeys this order, he will be immediately expelled."

L to R: René, chauffeur, Prince Rainier, Prince Albert, Princess Grace and Louis Johannot

That night, while readying ourselves for bed, Mademoiselle Schaub came by each room with toast and jam. This was a bedtime tradition she carried out in one chalet or another each week.

"Good evening, Silvin. Hello, Rockefeller," she said. "Did you pay particular attention to what Monsieur Johannot said after dinner?" she asked, looking as squarely as possible at Winnie. Since she had a severely wandering eye, we were never quite sure of whom she was addressing.

"Yes, Mademoiselle," he answered.

"You must be sure to understand, because you are one of the boys interviewed," she said in her characteristically confusing sentence. Her nickname was "Vague" because she often made little or no sense.

"No, I got it, Mademoiselle," Winnie reaffirmed, as 'Vague' twirled around, bumped into the door and left the room.

In Gstaad, classrooms were spread out in different chalets. Each hour, when one class period was over, we boys crisscrossed all over the hill in the snow, to reach our classrooms. Within a few days of the ominous announcement, men with cameras began to appear on the paths between the chalets.

"Where is Winthrop Rockefeller," one asked.

"Show me which kid is Niarcos," shouted another.

Not being a target of these requests, I was amused at the sight of reporters and photographers until I saw young Niarcos running away from them. He clearly was frightened, perhaps more from Johannot's admonition than anything else. The diversion had become an annoyance.

Some boys just chuckled and continued walking through the snow as one photographer took pictures of as many students as possible, as we threw snowballs at each other. At lunch time, Monsieur Johannot did not wait for the end of the meal to make his announcement. Customarily, we students would be seated and have time to eat a bowl of soup before the headmasters, often accompanied by an invited parent, entered the room. As soon as we saw this procession, we all popped to our feet creating a cacophony of wooden chairs being pushed back on the wood floor. When the guests were seated, we were allowed to resume our seats.

That day, Monsieur Johannot was accompanied by Countess Consuelo Crespi. Her son Brando was at school, and he was a good friend of mine. His parents ran Vogue magazine Europe, while Countess Crespi's identical twin sister, Gloria Schiff, ran Vogue, USA. I had known that Brando's mother was coming to lunch and I was curious to see her. I had heard how beautiful and elegant she was. What I had heard, and the picture I had seen of her on Brando's night table, understated this tall, young, lithe beauty. She wore a one piece, leopard-skin ski outfit. As she strode regally into the hall, I was awe struck.

When Johannot reached his table and held out a chair for Brando's mother, he waved a hand indicating that we should be seated. Uncharacteristically, he did not sit.

"I must remind you of the announcement I made a few nights ago regarding *Life Magazine*. As you have no doubt noticed, there are photographers outside the chalets. While I cannot force them to leave the public streets, they are not allowed on the school paths. More importantly NO---BODY" (once again he emphasized the syllables) "is to speak to any of them, nor are you allowed to stop for pictures. I repeat my warning: any violation will be cause for dismissal from school." With that, he sat down, and lunch continued with the usual sounds of chatter and utensils rubbing plates in a crowded, poorly insulated room. I could not take my eyes off the magnificent Consuelo Crespi.

Countess Consuelo Crepsi

After lunch that day, while we were getting ready to go skiing, Brando brought his mother to the chalet we roomed in that winter and introduced her to several friends, including me.

"Brando has told me many nice things about you," she said, "and you simply must come and visit us in Rome." Although it was 20 years later, I took her up on the kind invitation!

The photographers did not leave the vicinity of the school. Instead, several of the students who were children of famous families, as well as their roommates, were confined to a specific chalet. We were not allowed to take our usual walks into the village that Wednesday and Saturday afternoons. Eventually, the reporters left. The magazine published a weak article with few facts and even fewer pictures. The brief exposure to what is now called 'the paparazzi' ended, along with the unpleasant confinement, and we were once again free to visit the village on weekends.

A week or so later, Countess Crespi left the Palace Hotel to return to her home in Rome. The hotel had (and still has) an antique, early 1950's Rolls Royce Phantom painted in blue and yellow, with the hotel's crest on the back doors. I happened to be in the village when the car we all saw so frequently drove through, with Brando's mother in the back seat next to the oversized window typical of that vintage limousine. Her skin was like a light pink satin. Her long, jet-black hair was immaculate, and she was wrapped in a Russian sable coat. I thought I had seen the most graceful lady in the world.

Over the subsequent two years, I would meet her equals.

Chapter 7: Hints of Cruelty

No one was ever randomly beaten at Rosey, as children were at La Clairière. The occasional smack, while not pleasant, was usually deserved and was consistent with the general customs practiced in European child-rearing in the middle of last century.

Joseph "Zuzu" Zürcher

There was one "teacher" who obviously took pleasure in hitting a particular group of us. Joseph Zurcher, (AKA Zuzu) was a sports teacher who taught gymnastics and skiing in Gstaad, and football (soccer), track and rowing in Rolle. Being a less senior member of the teaching staff, Zuzu also monitored the study hall where students did their homework in the evening. Zuzu's claim to fame was that, in decades past, he had been a former member of Switzerland's prize soccer team. The problem with Zuzu was that his frequent overreactions to a slight infraction of a rule would immediately cause him to lose control, which was the only obvious similarity to my earlier "schooling."

Overt and arguably hysterical homophobia was an obvious characteristic of Monsieur Johannot and some of his faculty members, especially this sports teacher. Their fear that a Rosey boy could possibly be "abnormal" or "deviant" in any way was palpable. Monsieur Johannot demanded that we all fit his idea of what a Rosey boy should be. As a result, and reminiscent of a detective investigating a crime, Zuzu took this cause to the extreme by searching for any signs that he could identify as "effeminate," regardless of the boy's age.

One of the classic punishments was called "la consigne," meaning consignment or detention. This meant that, instead of going into the village on Wednesday or Saturday afternoons, the punished boy was "consigned" to the study hall. Zuzu had delighted in inventing an optional, modified version of this punishment that he happily and proudly called "consignment by the hand." This meant, that Zuzu offered the option of either being consigned to the study hall while other boys had free time or coming up to Zuzu's desk in the study hall to take a good, strong slap across the face – like a man! La Clairière had taught me a high tolerance for pain, so I always opted for Zuzu's "consignment by the hand." The few times I experienced Zuzu's invention, I noticed a hint of pleasure on his face each time he slapped me or any other boy.

During soccer practice we wore a uniform of white shorts and blue T-shirts, the Rosey colors. Zuzu wore a blue sweat suit, a whistle hung from his neck which he used when a rule was broken. In soccer, like hockey, "off sides" is a common error. Zuzu moved around in the middle of the field as he coached the teams, blowing his whistle to identify an error.

Prince Egon and Diane von Fürstenberg

As mentioned previously, Egon von Fürstenberg, the son of an Austrian prince, attended Rosey during my first few years at the school. He was an attractive child and grew up to be a handsome man. He was tall, blonde, blue eyes: the perfect Aryan. Two decades after this story, he married Diane, who designed the well-known women's clothing line bearing her name. Along with me, Egon was one of the students Zuzu watched with a suspicious and hateful look, as if he had detected a mortal and contagious virus which could be eradicated at any cost by his piercing stare before it spread.

Egon von Fürstenberg

One day during soccer practice, I had noticed Zuzu was a bit more testy than usual. He was in no mood to explain a rule twice, much less to blow the whistle and stop the game. Egon and I were playing forward positions. I had the ball and was charging toward the goal. In the rush of the moment, Egon advanced ahead of me and beyond the opposition's two-man defense line, which was the classic "off sides" offense. Zuzu's whistle rang through the air as he ran toward Egon. He grabbed the boy's blonde hair, held his head erect and slapped him with all his might. I could see Egon's fair skin turn bright red where the large hand had struck. The poor boy stumbled and struggled to stay on his feet. My eyes shifted back to Zuzu, and I saw him pulling blonde hairs off his palm. Then, as if nothing were out of the ordinary, he started the game again. The entire team was clearly alarmed at how easily Zuzu could lose control and we shot concerned, stunned looks at each other.

That was Egon's last day at school. Unlike at La Clairière, we were all permitted to phone our families and Egon did so. The following day, his mother, Princess Clara Agnelli von Fürstenberg, flew to Geneva, came to the school in an airport taxi which waited until her son had packed his belongings, and subsequently drove them back to the airport.

Another frightening event took place that winter in Gstaad. Prince Rainier of Monaco's sister, Princess Antoinette, had sent her son, Christian de Massy, to Rosey. She visited Gstaad frequently with Christian's sisters. The three members of the de Massy family, mother and two children, looked exactly alike: black hair, blue eyes, olive skin and a large, aquiline nose. I had been to Princess Antoinette's home to see Christian in Eze-sur-Mer when I visited my father at his villa on nearby Cap Ferrat. The de Massy estate sat on a hill overlooking the Mediterranean, and was reached by climbing a steep, paved

Christine Alix, Princess Antoinette, Christian Louis and Elizabeth-Anne de Massy

incline driveway from the "Basse Corniche," the coast road near Monte Carlo. The de Massy family was as normal as possible, given their social status.

One snowy, winter Wednesday evening, Johannot rose after dinner to make his usual announcements.

"I have some most troubling news," he began. "De Massy was caught stealing from Cadonau today."

I had noticed that de Massy was not at his table. Cadonau was, and still is, a lovely gift shop, in the middle of the village, which at the time sold both school supplies and Swiss souvenirs. They designed the well-known "Gstaad my love" emblem, printed alongside a red heart, which decorates most of their merchandise.

"I have spoken with de Massy's mother, Princess Antoinette," Johannot continued, "and we have agreed on a proper punishment. De Massy will stay in the infirmary until tomorrow evening when, after dinner, he will be whipped here, in the dining room, in front of all of you."

I was dumb-struck. *A public flogging*? Astounded, I had never imagined such a humiliating event at Rosey. It seemed eerily like Zuzu's idea. I looked across the room at Zuzu, who smiled with pride as if his invention had been elevated to a new status.

Dinner the following evening was anything but a joyous occasion. All the boys were subdued, not knowing what to expect. The dining room in Gstaad had double, glass pained doors mounted on hinges. They made a noise rather like a wild west's saloon swinging doors. The table I was assigned to that winter was near the hall's entry and was headed by Mademoiselle Schaub. The older boys' and Monsieur Johannot's table were deeper in the room, and one had to walk past me to reach them. Mademoiselle Schaub was understandably somber that night; we spoke little. After the main course she rose and left the room, foregoing her custom of initiating the end of dinner by standing at the door and shaking hands with each boy who passed. She normally greeted everyone with "bon soir" uttered with the same lack of individual attention given by most flight attendants saying "goodbye" to passengers as they disembark.

During the dessert course, usually a piece of fruit, our muted chatter steadily decreased, then died out. Through the glass doors, I saw two figures walking down the hall toward the dining room. They stopped just before reaching the doors and waited. It was Mademoiselle Keller, the school nurse, and de Massy. The former wore her usual white, nursing uniform and de Massy was dressed in pale blue pajamas and a white bath robe.

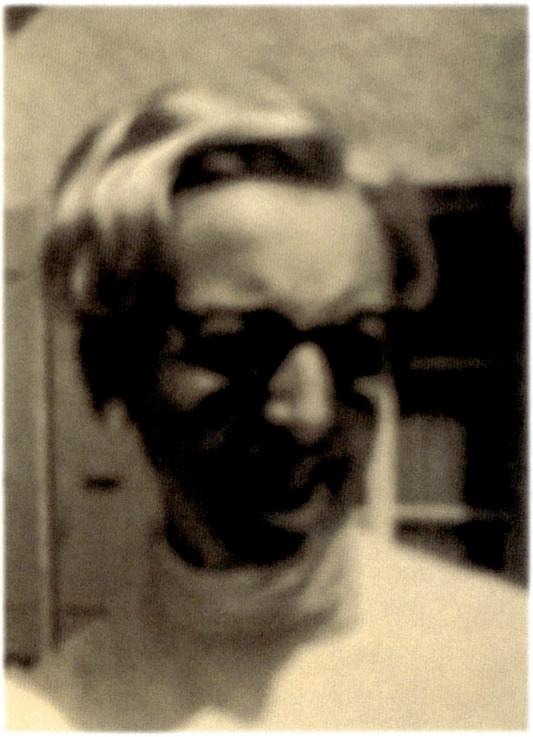

Mademoiselle Charlotte Keller

The two spinsters, Keller and Schaub, were close friends and shared a car. Like Schaub, Mademoiselle Keller had a facial abnormality. She squinted and fluttered her eyes which were mostly hidden behind thick, tinted, prescription glasses.

Monsieur Johannot rose. No one needed to tap their glasses to create silence. Johannot was a very accomplished horseman, and he was holding a riding crop in his right hand. As if on cue, the doors swung open and in walked de Massy and Mademoiselle Keller. The nurse's eyes were twitching more than usual, while de Massy, expressionless, stared straight ahead. They passed within inches of my chair to reach the middle of the room where Johannot waited. As if it were scripted, Mademoiselle Keller helped de Massy out of his bathrobe and draped it over her arms. Then Johannot spoke:

"Will all the ladies leave the room?" It was not a question.

Dutifully the few female teachers left as I lowered my head into my hands and turned my chair around, so that I was facing the door with my back to the imaginary stage.

Johannot spoke again: "Bend over and hold your knees!"

I heard a loud crack, and another and another. I counted them as I pushed my face deeper into my hands. Now the sound of the crop was mixed with sobbing. I had counted ten lashes when I heard the sounds of crying and slipper covered feet running through the dining room followed by the noise of the dining room's swinging doors being slammed apart. After several awkward seconds I heard a chair pushed back on the wooden floor, followed by many more. We all walked out in silence.

I never heard anyone refer to the events of that night again. I remained friendly with Christian de Massy and never mentioned it, nor do I believe any other student did. It was a dark day in Rosey's history, and we all knew it. Nobody cared to bring it up in conversation. While, for many boys it was a first exposure to excessive discipline, it was merely a brief flashback to my years in Villars.

Princess Antoinette did not visit Gstaad that winter. De Massy finished out the year but did not return to school the following September. I am not surprised that Prince Rainier never attended any Rosey meetings or alumni events.

Chapter 8: Reversal of Fortunes

Life had been progressing as well as I could have expected at Rosey. My grades were steadily improving as I moved up the list into the top 10 percent of "Moyens." I enjoyed skiing in the winter term, and I managed to steer away from Zuzu during soccer and swimming practice.

One continuing problem plagued me, however: Ron Agerev, two years my senior, who had also attended La Clairière. From my first through my third year at Rosey, Ron would pull me into a bathroom or out into a field to force me to perform sexual favors. I experienced the same feelings of panic and humiliation as I did in Villars when I was pursued by the filthy wood chopper. My greatest fear was being discovered and expelled, which played into Ron's hand. Perhaps my not having been able to come forward at La Clairière created the dynamic for my fearful, repressed silence. I assumed that no one would believe or help me. My only defense was to avoid places I knew Ron would be. So, I found detours while going from one class to another, or to take a circuitous route from a meal to a sport activity if I knew Ron would be there.

Finally, by the age of 13, I felt empowered enough at least to pretend that I could stand up to Ron. I was greatly assisted by Jimmy Woodward in whom I finally confided. Because Jimmy was older than I, we had little opportunity to be together and I was very pleased to see him one day in Lausanne.

Once a boy reached the "Moyen" group, he was granted the privilege of taking the train from Rolle to Lausanne or Geneva on Saturday afternoon, as long as he was back at school for dinner. My big treat was to save my allowance to pay for the round trip in second class and to have a pizza on the Rue de Bourg, a pedestrian street not too far from the station. I would walk up the hill from Lausanne's train station to the lovely old Place Saint-François, the center of town. I liked looking at the beautiful church and the small businesses, including the Pharmacy Golaz. I also enjoyed window shopping, admiring the beautiful watches, the latest fashions from Milan and Paris, and the expensive furs and beautiful jewelry.

Place Saint-François, Lausanne, Switzerland, 1960s

The southern Italian restaurant where we boys liked to congregate, still exists in the same location at the top of the steep, cobblestoned Rue de Bourg, on the second floor of an old building. Older students loved meeting girls from Lausanne's girls' boarding school, Brillamont. I felt very grown up indeed when I started going to the pizza restaurant. I happily squandered two weeks allowance whenever I went there.

One spring Saturday, as I climbed the stairs to the restaurant, I saw all the graffiti, many drawn by very talented kids. Passing by the kitchen, I enjoyed the smell of the pizzas cooking in a brick oven. I walked into the smoke-filled, crowded room feeling both very grown up and a bit intimidated. Jimmy was seated alone at a table by the window. He waved me over. My spirits heightened. The boy I idolized most in the world had asked me to join him *and* I had enough money to pay for my own pizza, even if it was a Margarita, the cheapest one on the menu!

Jimmy was in a talkative mood. He put me at ease by taking me into his confidence.

"Ya know, René, I hate Rosey and I don't see spending two more years here," he said. Jimmy always used my name René since he knew me from before I attended Swiss boarding schools.

"How can you leave? What will you do?" I asked bewildered.

"I can swing it. And, damn, I will, just as soon as I can get a driver's license"

"Wow, no kidding! What will you do?" I asked, my eyes widening.

"I'll buy an Alfa Romeo and drive around Europe."

My imagination went wild. This handsome rogue in a hot sports car driving along the Croisette in Cannes or the Champs Elysée in Paris! I envied him, and I imagined that many girls would want to jump into the car next to him.

"So, what's goin' on with you?" he inquired, inviting me to be his equal.

"Mmmm, ehhh, Jimmy, I'm in a jam," I said, hoping he might be interested.

"What's up?" he asked, encouraging me to expose my problem.

"It's Agerev," I said, exhilarated that I had uttered the dreaded name.

"He's just a jerk, everyone knows that. What's the deal?"

I had gone too far. How could I back out now? My heart raced. I could not speak, almost paralyzed by fear.

"What's the deal?" he repeated the question emphatically.

"Jimmy, I'm afraid of him." I said definitely entering the terrifying zone.

"Afraid of that little creep? Why?" he asked.

"He makes me do things…" I managed to say, my voice faltering.

"I'll beat the shit out of that fucking faggot," he said loudly.

I quickly looked around to make sure no one had overheard us. His words went straight to my heart. My immediate reaction was to be grateful that Jimmy was sympathetic and offering help. But then my confidence vanished, and my fear returned.

"Jimmy, please, PLEASE just leave it be," I begged.

"No way, Jose," he continued. "It will give me a big thrill to kick his ass. He's a damn weasel, anyway."

I'm not sure what Jimmy did or said to Ron, but Agerev never came near me again. However, he caused me much more harm. One day, shortly after our conversation at the pizza house, Jimmy came to me in the dining room.

"I need to speak to you after dinner. It's important," he said ominously.

What could be so important? Of course, I would meet Jimmy anywhere and at any time. We met by the fountain in the courtyard during the few minutes between the end of dinner and the beginning of the study hall period.

"There's stuff written all over the bathrooms and desks," he said.

"What kind of stuff?" I asked

"Shit like Silvin is a homo," he said.

The blood drained right out of my head. I felt faint for the first time in my life. Nothing could have been more frightening or more ruinous at the homophobic school. My panic was worse than when I'd been summoned to Beauverre's office for a beating. This pain would have far longer and worse implications. It would hurt more. A few minutes later, I entered the study hall and glanced at the long, wooden tables. Jimmy was right. The comments were everywhere: some in ink, some carved by a knife. Trying not to stare at the comments, I sat down in a trance, frozen by terror.

After the two-hour study period, instead of going straight to my dormitory floor, I ran to the main bathroom and opened all three stalls: *Silvin=homo, Silvin=homo, Silvin=homo.* I could not imagine any worse news. I felt friendless and alone. My enemies were everywhere. No war could be worse, no condition. I'd happily be starving or be a heroin addict than face the whole student body at a homophobic school calling me "a fairy." Nothing! The dreaded bowling ball feeling in my stomach reappeared for what I knew would be a very long stay.

That night I waited until I was sure everyone on the floor was asleep. I snuck out of the dorm equipped with a pen, my flashlight and a Swiss army knife. The consequences of being caught wandering around after 'lights out,' while very serious, were much easier to contemplate than this vicious labeling and likely teasing. I spent hours going to every desk and bathroom stall, trying to alter the words, desperately trying to make them unrecognizable.

It was futile. Day after day, more desks and bathroom walls displayed the dreaded words. They appeared like a rapidly spreading cancer, jumping out at me from everywhere. Within two days kids were giggling and making nasty comments as I passed near them. During these horrible days, the worst in my life so far, I carried another fear. I knew it would not be long before the military-minded Johannot would accuse me of the crime of homosexuality and would "interrogate" me.

Chapter 9: Humiliation

As I feared, my interrogation began just prior to the four-day long exam period that would be followed by our festive year-end ceremonies. One day, shortly before exam week, while in the dining room for lunch, Monsieur Johannot walked past my seat to reach his table. He lowered his mouth to my ear and, in a stern, commanding voice said, "My office, 14:30." The words were like a shout. His lunch guest that day was Audrey Hepburn who lived in a village near Rolle, where Monsieur Johannot and Mademoiselle Schaub were considering buying land in preparation to construct a building which would eventually house girls, so that Rosey would become coeducational. Sadly, I was in no mood to observe, much less appreciate, the elegant guest as I had Consuelo Crespi. I devoted all my will power and attention to remaining seated and not throwing up. Some of the longest minutes I had ever endured were creeping by. Eventually, the time came. I entered the office where both Johannot and Mademoiselle Schaub were seated.

Monsieur Johannot was smoking and was visibly angry. Mademoiselle Schaub dabbing at her face with a lace handkerchief, repeatedly mumbled, "Why did we ever take this boy?" I didn't know whom she meant, maybe me, until Johannot turned to her:

"Helen that's over, Agerev will not be back." Turning to me, he said: "Homosexuality is against the Rosey rules." The sentence sounded ridiculous. I stared at him unable to speak, even if my life depended on it.

"We have not decided what to do to you," he continued. "I will speak to your parents first. That's all I have to say right now, Silvin."

Was this man speaking a different language than I? What was he going to do *to* me? I could only imagine what including my father in the debate might yield. A chat with Princess Antoinette got de Massy a public flogging. Monsieur Johannot's pronunciation of the word "homosexuality" implied a far greater crime and more disdain, than theft. I left the room numb, my temples throbbing as Schaub dried tears from her face repeating "We should never have taken this boy."

Writing my exams, trying to think about my academic subjects, after enduring sleepless nights was nearly impossible. The only questions I wanted answers to were the ones that kept me awake: Would my mother still come to the graduation festivities, called the "Fête Sportive?" Worse, would Johannot speak to her then? And my refrain: *what were they going to do to me?*

Graduation day was a beautiful July morning. When my mother arrived, I approached her cautiously, like a dog who has soiled the house and is not sure if the master will hit him. After a few words I knew that my mother had not yet been included in the drama. I wondered what Monsieur Johannot might say to her: *That I was a homosexual, a trait that eliminated my qualifications to be a Rosey boy?* I wondered what her reaction might be.

"How did you do on your exams?" she inquired.

"Not as well as I had hoped, mother," I replied, missing the humor of the understatement. And then hoping to get away as quickly as possible: "I have to get changed for the swim meet. I'll see you at the pool."

Each year, several 100 parents and guests came to lunch at the Fête Sportive. Long tables were set up under the large, shady trees along the driveway and near the "Château," where the school began in 1880. The boys all wore a blue Rosey blazer, with the school's crest on the pocket, and Rosey's blue and white tie. Before and after lunch various sports events were organized to entertain the guests. There were swimming races and track events before lunch and a soccer tournament afterwards. That year I was to compete in the 50-meter freestyle swim race.

Betty Sicre and Ava Gardner

When I got to the pool, Mademoiselle Schaub was standing between my mother and Ava Gardner, who had come to see Betty Sicre's boys compete and her oldest son graduate. *What was Mademoiselle Schaub telling them?* I wondered. The race was a blur. I did not win or even place.

In mid-afternoon, Monsieur Johannot delivered a speech informing parents of important decisions and future changes. Then he conducted "la distribution des prix" (the handing out of awards) by explaining each one, and then calling up the proud student to collect a cup or a certificate, while the large group clapped. I had hoped to be called twice, once for winning the swimming race and again for being among the top Moyens academically. My mother expected to witness me win an academic award, which would erase the embarrassment of having failed all but one exam three years earlier.

The day lingered on while I so wished I could be somewhere, anywhere, else. When Monsieur Johannot started calling up the Moyens who achieved the best grades, I was shocked to be third. I had not even been listening for my name. As I reached the podium, he handed me a certificate, omitting the customary "congratulations." He propelled me off the platform with his handshake instead.

Chapter 10: The Punishment

The following day my mother and I flew to New York and drove to her home on the south shore of Long Island. My father was there that summer and would remain with us until hunting season began in Europe. Neither of my parents seemed to have spoken with Monsieur Johannot or anyone else from the school, so I kept struggling with my questions and fears. Within a week, my father announced that he and my mother were going to the Guggenheim Museum in New York City to meet Mademoiselle Schaub who was visiting the US. I became more fearful as I imagined the most horrible punishments. Upon their return that evening, the anger on my father's face clearly told me that the dreaded conversation had occurred. My mother's eyes were red and angry too.

"I am hot and do not want to talk to you yet," my father said, as they brushed past me. "You will eat in the kitchen, and I'll see you after dinner." After their meal, I was told to meet my father in a den off his bedroom. He was seated in a tall, Spanish wing tipped chair, looking like an angry, grand inquisitor. Fearfully, I stood before him.

"Are your sex organs normally developed?" he began. "Do you masturbate? How often? What do you think about when you do…?" The questions seemed endless. Not one focused on what happened or how I felt. Never did he ask for "my side" of the story. He simply believed that I had committed a serious crime, and he was searching for a physical defect which might explain the abnormality. I was prepared for him to order me to drop my pants for an examination, as if an "abnormally developed sex organ" was a scarlet letter identifying a homosexual. I guess he accepted my answers about my physical condition. Then, he issued his orders.

"You will not be allowed to use your boat, and you'll go to tutors and see a doctor all summer," he announced and dismissed me.

The summer before, I had been handed down a small boat with an outboard engine from my brother who was now at Georgetown University in Washington, DC. I had used it almost every day to collect mussels, clams, scallops and crabs. Then, I would cruise several canals where cooks and housewives would run out to buy my bounty. These were my happiest summer-time moments and are memories that I still treasure. I loved plowing through the huge wakes of ferry boats leaving the harbor to cross the Great South Bay to Fire Island. I gloated over my ability to flawlessly maneuver up to the fuel dock. In one summer, I had made enough money to upgrade the Johnson outboard engine. But this summer there would be no recreation and no extra pocket money for trips to Lausanne and Geneva next school year, assuming I was going back to Rosey, since no one had told me what might happen in the fall.

The "doctor" turned out to be a Catholic priest who was totally inept at dealing with children's problems. During our first session he announced:

"We will study the scriptures and pray very hard for your recovery."

Recovery, I wondered? What am I going to recover from?

"When I consider you to be healed," he went on to say, "I will allow you to help me with church chores and maybe to be an altar boy."

Although I understood none of this, the priest's terms were acceptable as they involved no beatings and, since I could not use my little boat, I might as well work in the church and the vestry.

I did not use the boat that summer with its pretty, new, red engine, which was moored in a slip next to the house. I had, however, convinced my father that the new motor needed to be run. So, between tutors and useless "therapy" at the rectory, I'd pull the hand starter, sit on the bow for as long as possible and cry. I hoped that the wonderful sound of the engine would drown out the noise, as well as the cause, of my sobs. Mercifully, the summer eventually ended. My father and I flew to Geneva and drove to Rosey for a meeting with Monsieur Johannot.

We did not talk as we drove along the coast road to Rolle in the rain. I only recall my father saying, "Little children, little problems. Big children, big problems..." followed by a deep sigh. On a rainy, late August evening, we pulled into the courtyard and entered the Château and Monsieur Johannot's living room. While smoking, he listened carefully, as my father detailed my summer activities. Eventually, he handed me a piece of paper with four names.

"Are these boys, homosexual?" he demanded.

"No, Monsieur," I answered totally unsure. I had never thought about it. *Was I suddenly an authority?*

Then he produced a second page with three names:

"These are your roommates this semester. Will you, errrr, well, stay away from them?"

"But of course, Monsieur," I responded as my father interrupted.

"Louis, the psychologist has assured me that he is not a fairy. Any tendencies that may have existed were eliminated during his work with a Monsignor."

"Mmmm…" continued Monsieur Johannot, puffing at a cigarette and never altering his gaze at me, as if he was watching a wild animal whose behavior was uncertain.

"We will watch you very closely," he finally said. "You will not be allowed to go to Lausanne or Geneva this fall, not even into Rolle. You will do extra sports instead."

I could deal with that, I thought. I had no pocket money anyway, so I wouldn't have been able to go into town. At least I wouldn't have to endure further idiotic conversations with a priest. The irony of this punishment caught my attention. I was identified as a "recovering fairy," but was confined to an all-male environment with other punished jocks.

I walked out to the car with my father, whose parting words have always resonated:

"I strongly recommend you never embarrass me again."

As I watched him drive away, I was conscious of many things. I could never count on any parental assistance, and I had to commit to a long-term effort to overcome the stigma of being a "fairy." The former challenge was more difficult to grasp than the latter.

But the issue of my budding sexuality was a concern to me. Clearly, I had homosexual desires and thoughts, but could these ever be translated into pleasant, voluntary acts? And, even if such a wonderful situation really existed, how could they be concealed? I assumed that the best I could hope for in my future sex life was for it to be secretive, embarrassing and humiliating.

I had heard of heroin addicts and wondered what was a worse, more dangerous and isolating curse: drug addiction or homosexuality? That bizarre and comparative question lingered in my mind for many years.

PART 3

VICTOR

Previous page: Rowing at Le Rosey

Chapter 1: Rowing

If I were to overcome the curse of having been branded "a homo," a goal I desperately wanted to reach, I deduced I would have to excel at some sport. Skilled young athletes against whom I had little or no chance of competing, headed up the more stylish Rosey sports of skiing and soccer. While I enjoyed both activities, I knew my limitations and had no illusions I could rise to the top of the Rosey teams in those events.

Suddenly, it became clear what path I could take that had the most chance of success. I knew I loved being on the water, and I had rowed dinghies my entire life. I was confident I had some basic rowing skills and I had great stamina and was strong and well-built for my age. I concluded the current sport stepchild, rowing, was to be my best chance for success.

Prince Karim Aga Khan

Rosey's rowing equipment had deteriorated since Karim Aga Khan, the school's last famous rower, had focused his athletic abilities on the sport. The position of Rosey's rowing teams relative to the other boy's schools along Lake Geneva had suffered a similar decline. Since Karim had graduated from Le Rosey, the year I started at La Clairière, rowing had gradually lost its glamour at the school.

Karim was the son of Prince Ali Khan and the grandson of Sir Sultan Mohamed Shah Aga Khan.

Weighing Sultan Mohamed Shah Aga Khan III in Dar-es-Salaam, 1946

To celebrate Karim's grandfather's diamond jubilee the prince was paid in precious gems. The precise amount of the diamonds had to weigh exactly the same as the prince. A public ceremony was held in 1946 in both Dar-es-Salaam, Tanzania, and Bombay, India, to determine the number of stones to be given.

The title "Aga Khan" has been handed down for 14 hundred years, since the death of the Prophet Mohammed, through his daughter Fatima. Muslims acknowledge that the Aga Khan is the direct descendant of Mohammed, and some 20 million Shia Imami Muslims believe that the prophet's divine right is passed down to the title's heir.

To store the rowing equipment, Rosey rented a barn-like structure in the small, charming port of Rolle, home primarily to a few dozen small boats. In the shed were five, four-man racing sea yawls. This category of racing boat is slightly wider than the better known "sculls" used, for example, on the Charles River in Boston, because our boats had to be seaworthy in the rougher European lake waters. Rosey's boats were kept three high on metal shelves and had all been repaired following accidents incurred while less careful teams had removed and replaced them during practice. Most sets of oars, painted with barely recognizable Rosey colors, were damaged. There was no training boat in which a coach could follow the teams to give instructions. Consequently, either the team's "stroke," which is the captain who sits in front of the coxswain, or "the cox" himself did his best to set a pace, steer the boat as straight as possible and do the coaching. The result was amateurish, poorly trained teams.

A WWI-era paddle steamer coming into Rolle

I found the walk down the mile-long hill to the port, the readying of the boats and especially the thrill of being on the water exhilarating. We rowed past the charming island park, the village of Rolle and many grand, lakeside villas. By late spring the classic paddle steamers, which are ferry boats that tour Lake Geneva, would pass by blowing whistles as they pulled up to the public dock to embark and disembark tourists. Their great round wheels would be thrust into reverse making a thumping sound as the huge WWI era boats gracefully pulled to a stop at the pier.

Not only was I in my element, but the "dos and don'ts" of the sport came naturally to me. That first year, I rapidly became stroke of the 14-year old's team. Like choosing a jockey, I selected the brightest, lightest coxswain available for my team: Bob Reynolds. Bob's older brother, David, was and is a close friend of mine. Their father was President of Reynolds Metals, International and their loving, Belgian mother lived near the school in the "Château de Vinzel," located in the town bearing the same name, where refreshing white wine is made and consumed in great quantities with cheese fondues.

Once a year, in late spring, we tied the best boat on top of an aging, blue Volkswagen bus and brought boat and oars to Ouchy, Lausanne's lakeside garden paradise, to compete in interschool races. I was overwhelmingly excited and eager to prove myself as stroke that first year. Many teachers and most parents who lived locally, including Betty Sicre and Marianne Alireza, came to enjoy the day and watch the races as they walked or sometimes ran to keep up with us, shouting their support for each of the age group categories.

Rosey inter-scholar races, Ouchy, Switzerland
Tom's mother Claire in foreground taking picture

My team won its race that day, beating out five other schools.
Following tradition, all teams and the schools' headmasters met in the restaurant of a nearby hotel for the awards. "My" Rosey team rose to receive their small pewter plates with the engraved date. As I returned to my seat, Monsieur Johannot stopped me, shook my hand and congratulated me. Unlike the artificial hand shake a year earlier, this one was as genuine as was his pleasure in our achievement for the school's honor and glory.

"You will ride back to Rolle in my car," he added.

I had left school only a few handfuls of times by car and had never been invited to ride in Monsieur Johannot's blue Chevrolet. That was a privilege reserved for teachers and, on rare occasions, a "committee member." The "committee" was a group of seven Seniors, almost always exclusively from the graduating class, more or less equivalent to an American student council. The committee members were elected by the students and approved by the headmaster. They sat at Monsieur Johannot's table in the dining room and had certain responsibilities such as monitoring the younger boys while in the study hall and checking tardiness at meals. They had the power to enter the headmaster's office to add a demerit to a student's name, which could lead to the loss of certain privileges and consignment. To the younger boys, these committee members were impressive, influential idols. Some were even feared.

We drove back to Rolle along the recently inaugurated "autoroute," the highway connecting Geneva to the other lakeside cities to the east. As we descended the on-ramp, we passed a new truck pulling a trailer loaded with several shiny, new sea yawls headed in the opposite direction. I twisted my head around and pushed myself up in the front seat to observe every possible detail.

"That's Geneva's rowing club's rig," Johannot informed me, aware of my attention. "Tomorrow the city clubs will use the same courses you just raced to qualify to be in the championships."

"What championships?" I asked.

"The Swiss National Championships," he replied. "The winner goes on to the European championships, while some go on to the Olympics."

"What's a city rowing club?" I inquired.

Johannot chuckled, drew on his cigarette and chose his words carefully.

"All major cities have a club. It takes a lot of money and professional training. The guys are real athletes," he said, terminating the discussion.

The words "real athletes" sounded eerily like Ann Woodward's admonishment that I would never be a "real man." I sat in silence, thinking, dreaming of equipment like I had just seen, and competing with Switzerland's city rowing clubs and becoming a real athlete.

I was truly enjoying many "firsts" in my life: being stroke, a team victory, a genuine sign of approval from a father figure, and a pleasant, fast trip back to Rolle. My thoughts returned to a more believable goal: One day, I *could* be a "committee member." Clearly, the vehicle to get me there was the exciting thought of more rowing victories.

Chapter 2: The Yehia Family

A wonderful, successful boy, one year older than I, had befriended me. It was unusual for friendships to develop between boys in different classes, but Ahmed Yehia was and is anything but usual. I had first become friendly with Ahmed while we shared a room in the school's infirmary. Neither of us cared to return to class when our flu had dissipated, so we put the thermometer on a lamp's light bulb located on a night table between our two cots. Needless to say, the ruse did not work. However, the bond it established between an 11 and a 12-year-old boy did work and has lasted for sixty years. In spite of the segregation of the classes by age, we did our best to see each other whenever possible.

Aly Pasha, Ahmed and Pash Pash Yehia 1949

I was equidistant in age between Ahmed and his younger brother, Aziz, and the three of us enjoyed each other's company. Aly Pasha Yehia, the boys' aging father, had been a popular western-oriented tycoon and philanthropist in Alexandria. He held the first pilot's license in Egypt and was the first Egyptian to attend Harvard University. His beautiful and elegant young wife, affectionately referred to as Pash-Pash, bore him these two boys late in his life. After their exit from Egypt in 1959, following the revolution, they lived in Geneva where they were pursued by numerous sycophants and phonies claiming to be able to retrieve parts of their vast, confiscated fortune from the Nasser government.

Aly Yehia, a kind and gentle man, had but one love during his Swiss exile: his older son Ahmed in general, and watching Ahmed perform at soccer meets, in particular. His Mercedes limousine would pull right up to the soccer field during interschool meets in inclement weather. Under an umbrella, Aly Pasha would watch the competition with kind eyes, eager to see Ahmed score a goal or use his "secret weapon" – a backwards kick coupled with a flip called "the bicycle." I could catch glimpses of Ahmed's beautiful mother in the back seat, hidden by tinted windows. On occasions she would ask me to join her inside the car and she would relate sweet stories filled with humor and love.

Ahmed came to be a star very naturally and with ease. During the first 10 years of his life, while still living in Alexandria, Ahmed's birthday on April 20th had been celebrated as a regional holiday, during which no one worked. The family lived in a "house" which contained 300 rooms, many of which Ahmed never saw. The palace was later used for official diplomatic events during the Sadat government era. One would think that such adulation and privilege bestowed on a young boy might adversely affect his mental well-being, but Ahmed was too self-assured and secure to adopt such a handicap.

Ahmed Yehia, 1965

Pash-Pash and Aziz were Hollywood aficionados. They would travel to Beverly Hills to be received by actors and producers who had, in turn, been royally entertained by the Yehias in Egypt and, later, in Geneva. Aziz became a walking encyclopedia about movies. He could recite any actor's academy award nominations by film and year or any given movies' director, producer and cast. On one occasion he enabled Le Rosey to win a general culture contest when questions on the history of films were introduced into the competition.

When Pash-Pash would enter the main lounge of the Palace Hotel in Gstaad, conversation would stop as everyone admired her looks, clothing and jewelry, mostly acquired from her close friend, Harry Winston. Many mothers were intimidated by her command of any gathering and, although for very different reasons, were as jealous of her as they were of Betty Sicre.

During the winter following President Kennedy's assassination, Jackie Kennedy and her children, John-John and Caroline, stayed with the family's close friend John Kenneth Galbraith at his chalet in Gstaad. One Sunday afternoon, during a children's party in the hotel's living room, all eyes were on the Kennedy family as Jackie played with the children on the floor by the hotel's huge, central fireplace. When Pash-Pash walked in and joined the games, Mrs. Kennedy and she shared the attention equally.

Jackie Kennedy, Ricardo Sicre and Princess Grace

Princess Grace of Monaco and her children were also in Gstaad that week. When she learned that Jackie had arrived, she asked her friend, Betty Sicre, if she could possibly arrange a meeting between the two First Ladies. Betty, always willing to oblige, was happy and perfectly qualified to make the introduction, since she knew both famous ladies well.

One spring break, Pash-Pash took her boys and me to Monte Carlo. We stayed at the Hotel de Paris, on the main square, where I had stayed with my parents

Monte Carlo with casino (center) and Hotel de Paris (right)

for the royal Monegasque wedding several years before. Ahmed's mother was an avid gambler, so we were offered many luxuries and benefits in the tradition that has become well-used in Las Vegas. Pash-Pash played in a private room which we, being under 18, could not visit. Although Ahmed's mother played for high stakes, it was nothing compared to another Rosey boy's mother, Helena, The Duchesse Serra de Cassano, who reportedly lost five million Swiss francs that weekend.

Ahmed, Aziz and I were not interested in the activities at the casino. Betty Sicre had brought her four boys to Monaco for a family reunion aboard their newly built Camper Nicholson yacht, the Rampager. We all knew each other because all four Sicre boys now attended Rosey. Betty's youngest son, Penn, was an adorable, enthusiastic and bright boy whose "Rosey name" was Sicre IV because he had three older brothers at school. Early on, during his Junior years, a newly assigned roommate had seen the laundry label "Sicre IV" sewn into Penn's clothes. Not having yet understood the school's nomenclature, the new arrival asked Penn: "Of what country are you king?"

Yacht Rampager in Monte Carlo

Since the Hotel de Paris is a short walk from the harbor, we all made the trip back and forth, from hotel to boat, several times a day. The Rampager was unique in that, unlike other new steel yachts, she was designed with children in mind. What is now called Sun Deck on large, new yachts was a children's play and dormitory area, and the vessel was loaded with the latest water sports equipment. It was a wonderful, joyous holiday and distraction from our studies. I envied the Sicre boys' family life, as always. I very much appreciated being included, especially since this was a "family reunion" for them.

While splashing around in the sea near Monte Carlo's harbor, we all discussed the sports we excelled in at school: Ahmed at soccer, Emile Sicre at swimming and track, and me as a promising rower. That night, lying on beds on the Rampager's sun deck, looking at stars, we talked about the relatively new swimming pool back at school. It had a five lane, 25-meter racing section and a deeper diving area. The unusual design included a bridge that crossed the transition area between the two sections.

Le Rosey Rolle campus swimming pool

Then Ahmed said something that would stick very firmly in my mind:

"Some anonymous parent who wanted kids to excel at swimming gave the money to build the pool."

The previous spring one of Rosey's more famous alumni had visited the school. Mohammed Reza, Shah Pahlavi of Iran, had remained loyal to, and involved with, Le Rosey since he had graduated two decades earlier and before ascending to the Peacock throne of Iran. Amazingly, he always included his attendance at Rosey on his biography. As a result, and as one might imagine, there were many children of wealthy and well-positioned Iranians at Rosey, and the Shah was always hospitable and helpful to Rosey alumni while living in or visiting Teheran.

The Shah had recently divorced his wife, Princess Soraya, most probably because she had not borne him an heir. His new wife, the 21-year-old, regal,

Farah Diba, became Farah Pahlavi, Empress of Iran. Shortly after visiting President Kennedy in Washington, DC, the newlyweds came to Le Rosey for the first time. They arrived for the private visit, relatively unceremoniously, in three black cars: a Cadillac Fleetwood and two Mercedes full of bodyguards. The Royal couple emerged from the back of the Cadillac. The Shah was conservatively dressed in a dark business suit, while his bride wore a blue chiffon dress which showed her tall, slender figure to advantage. Until that point, I had believed there could be no woman more striking than Consuelo Crespi, but I had now seen her equal.

After a brief meeting with Monsieur Johannot, the Shah and Farah walked together down the driveway and around several of the school's buildings. A few bodyguards followed some distance behind them as the Shah presumably related various childhood experiences to his new empress. They ended their tour by admiring the new swimming pool. I had watched them return to their cars. "Shah," as Iranians respectfully referred to him, waved the chauffeur into one of the other cars. He then chivalrously helped Farah into the front passenger seat and took the wheel himself.

I wondered if the Shah might have been the generous donor of our wonderful new pool. I also wondered how an alumnus or parent might be persuaded to make such a generous donation. I knew what kind of equipment we needed to compete with the best rowing teams. I also knew how to train the rowing teams we would need. Now I had an idea about how to acquire the equipment the rowing team needed in order to reach higher levels of performance. Now I had to figure out how to turn the idea into a plan.

President Kennedy, Shah of Iran and Empress Farah

Chapter 3: New Equipment

My plan germinated that winter in Gstaad. Given our first victory at the rowing races, I decided to conduct an informal poll to see which students might like to sign up for the sport. To my surprise, several boys who had not previously expressed any interest in rowing enthusiastically agreed to try out their abilities after Easter when the school reconvened in Rolle. Armed with my list, I asked if I might have a few minutes with the headmaster. I had never requested to meet with Monsieur Johannot, and to my knowledge, nobody had. That just wasn't done.

"Monsieur Johannot," I began, "it seems that many boys would like to sign up for rowing next spring. In fact, I have asked around and here are some names."

Johannot looked at the list. His expression indicated indifference, I thought, because the names were not any of the school's jocks. All the "real athletes" were otherwise committed to track, soccer and swimming. Before he could terminate the unprecedented "meeting" with a student, I added:

"Monsieur, I was thinking that, if more boys want to row, we might be able to update the equipment." He looked at me curiously. I thought he was about to accuse me of impertinence as I continued speaking.

"In fact, I was hoping you would allow me to write the parents of all the boys who sign up and ask them if they would contribute money for that purpose."

Johannot, puffing thoughtfully on his cigarette, replied: "Very interesting. Draft a letter and let me look it over." He turned his chair back around towards his desk indicating that I should leave.

"But I already have, Monsieur," I said, reaching into my pocket for another hand-written note. Johannot looked somewhat taken aback.

"Here's a letter," I added.

Johannot took the paper, read it and replied:

"No, you cannot say anything like 'our equipment is damaged' and 'we respectfully request that you make a contribution, so we could acquire new boats.' Rewrite your letter saying that a small contribution to make minor additions would be appreciated. In fact, say that there is a five hundred Swiss franc maximum donation. You cannot leave the request open to people like..." he looked at the list again, "Mr. Niarcos or Elizabeth Taylor."

A second draft letter was approved and sent to each prospective rowers' parents. After what I thought was an eternity, some two weeks later, my mailbox contained more letters in two days than I had received in two years. Almost every envelope contained a check for "SFR 500" accompanied by notes from the donors wishing us well. Since I never expected one, I was not surprised that there was no letter or check from my father. Bursting with pride, I brought the entire pile to Monsieur Johannot upon his return from one of his frequent absences due to military duty.

"Very good, Silvin. Since this was your idea, we will progress as follows. You go to the Cantonal Bank in town, open a checking account in this name," he scribbled a few words on a piece of paper. "Deposit all the checks, keep good records, give me a list of what you think you need, and we'll go from there." The words "you need" hit me. This was *my* project, and I was determined to make it a success.

My list did not take long to create. It was detailed and specific. I set priorities: new oars, a custom-built vehicle to tow boats to competitions, a speed boat for a coach to monitor the teams, major repairs to the existing sea yawls and the shed in Rolle's little port. Johannot priced out the list and told me that we had enough money to order every item. I was ecstatic.

I would have to wait for the spring term before seeing any of the new equipment. Little did I know that the delay would open my eyes to new and exciting worlds, because I had been invited to spend the Easter vacation in Paris with my new roommate, Nicolas Politis.

Chapter 4: The Dietrich Weekend

Although rowing consumed all my available free time while the school was in Rolle, I had ample extra energy in Gstaad to be involved in school activities other than the enjoyable, yet obligatory, two hours of skiing every afternoon. By the mid-1960s, Gstaad had become referred to as "Hollywood East" because numerous well-known actors had children at Rosey and had subsequently built chalets, mostly on the "Palace hill" behind the main hotel.

American citizens working abroad at this time were not required to pay U.S. income taxes if they had a legal foreign residence. As a result, Liz Taylor, David Niven, William Holden, Julie Andrews, and other Hollywood celebrities as well as business tycoons chose Gstaad as their European address. Thus, they enjoyed the dual advantage of being near their sons during the three winter months and protecting their income from the IRS.

I had befriended Michael and Peter Riva, Marlene Dietrich's two grandsons. Michael was a delightful, blonde boy who was amazingly "all American," given his family history. His mother, Maria Riva, was Dietrich's only child, whose sons were adored by their grandmother.

I thought it would be a good idea to start a "ciné club" and to ask certain parents to present a film of their choice to the students. Several actor/parents accepted the invitation but none more dramatically than Dietrich who chose to present *The Blue Angel.*

Dietrich was responsible for the boys' tuition at Rosey but had been falling behind in payments. Coincidentally, the Palace Hotel had been pleading with her for years to perform in their cabaret restaurant Maxim's, adjacent to the main lobby. Maxim's was named for and designed after the well-known Paris restaurant in the Rue Royale. The brilliant, no-nonsense legend concluded that she could kill several birds with one stone during a blitz-like, 48-hour visit to Gstaad at the height of the winter season. Her schedule was an afternoon presentation of *The Blue Angel* to the Rosey ciné club at the charming, small movie theater in the village, followed by her performance at a gala dinner in Maxim's. She had allowed Michael to invite me to sit at her table in Maxim's for dinner and the concert afterwards. This was without a doubt the most exciting event of my life to that point.

Maxim's night club in the Gstaad Palace

I used my entire month's allowance to send flowers to Dietrich's room prior to her arrival. I met her at the movie house on Saturday afternoon. Unlike other parents who presented their films, she had given me specific instructions as to how the event was to unfold. As soon as everyone was seated, the lights would be dimmed. Without an introduction, Miss Dietrich would enter through a back door and proceed down the aisle to the stage. Imagining a dignified walk down the aisle, I was completely surprised by her grand entrance. Wearing a tight, white ski outfit and white boots, she ran down the aisle, taking huge, confident strides. In her mid-60s, she looked 20 years younger and exhibited the energy of a young woman.

Her introduction to *The Blue Angel* was riveting. She relayed how she got this first big role in great detail and included many charming anecdotes. After her 10-minute monologue, during which there was not a sound in the room, she proudly marched back up the aisle, into the Palace's waiting car to prepare for that night's performance.

A second dramatic, and much less happy event was taking place that same weekend. Ahmed's father, Aly Pasha Yehia, was dying. His last wish was to spend time with Ahmed, his first born. Pash-Pash called Monsieur Johannot:

"My husband's health has deteriorated," she explained, "and we need Ahmed in Geneva for the weekend."

"But Ahmed is punished," responded Johannot, "and he cannot leave school."

"The impertinence!" exploded Pash-Pash. "Are you totally shameless?" After an uncomfortable silence, she continued:

"I'll make one concession and I recommend that you consider your reply very carefully, Monsieur. My husband and I will travel to Gstaad in an ambulance. I will take Aziz to the Marlene Dietrich gala, while Ahmed will stay by his father's bedside in the hotel. And for as long as is necessary. Have I made myself perfectly clear?"

The colonel, like anyone who was close to receiving Pash-Pash's *real* wrath, realized that this was an order not to be countered.

Ahmed lent me his dinner jacket to attend the gala. As I put on my first "black tie" and Ahmed's Scottish tartan plaid jacket, before they were popular, I felt very dandy. Seeing a parked ambulance near the front door of the hotel was like having a bucket of ice water thrown on my face. I thought of Ahmed's gentle father upstairs and wondered what it must be like to prepare oneself to leave the world, what exactly a loving father might say to a son in this situation, and how my friend Ahmed might feel as he listened.

Maxim's at the Gstaad Palace looks very similar to the original in Paris with red velvet décor and banquettes built along the walls. One difference is that it has a stage at one end of the room for performances, and an elevated platform at the other. Our table of four was in the front and center of the raised area. The Riva brothers and I shared it with Mimi Johannot, the headmaster's wife.

Mimi was a dear lady who raised four wonderful children, and always seemed to be so mismatched with her stern, militaristic husband. She often consoled the younger boys, while her eyes said: "I know you are homesick and the rules are tough, but you will be just fine. I know you will make it." She was more human and genuine than 'Vague' and more sensitive and perceptive than any other faculty member.

I do not recall a single morsel of the food served, because my focus was entirely centered on the anticipation of the show. I did not even notice any other guests except for one banquette with its two occupants. Aziz, in a black tuxedo, the only other Rosey student in the room, was seated alone with his mother who wore a plain black, formal dress and a magnificent diamond tiara. I later learned that Queen Elizabeth has the twin tiara. Even Her Majesty could not possibly wear it any more comfortably or elegantly than did Pash-Pash.

Marlene Dietrich (1901-1992) as she appeared at the Gstaad Palace

While her heart was breaking because of her husband's deteriorating condition, she held her head erect, her posture perfect, her green-blue eyes sparkling along with her jewelry. Her composure seemed perfectly calm as she nodded ever so gently to everyone who wanted to be noticed by her. Her demeanor then, as always, reflected her frequently used expression: "Noblesse Oblige."

When the BIG moment came, the lights were dimmed, the curtain was raised and there she stood, Marlene Dietrich in all her glory. She wore a floor length, white Swans down coat with a long train, perfectly arranged in a circular pattern around her feet. The open 'coat' was more like a cape with a tall white feather-like collar and puffy fur sleeves. The tight, floor length dress was made of sequins and beads which cleverly disappeared at the top of her breasts, melting into a skin-colored bodice. The lower part of the dress was sufficiently tight to allow her to move her legs sensually to maximize our awareness of her beautiful figure and the drama of the moment.

As Marlene walked around the stage, telling more wonderful stories in between songs, she created a magical fantasy. The well-choreographed performance included a description of her career, punctuated by her well-known, signature songs. When she sang "*Falling in Love Again*," I'm sure every person's individual love story was reignited in their minds as they listened to her deep, sexy, accented voice:

Neffer Vanted toooo
Vatt am I to dooo?
I kaant help it!

I looked over at Aziz's booth and saw even the regal Pash-Pash touch her eyes.

After the performance and many curtain calls, to which she generously obliged her appreciative audience when they begged for more, we met in the "bowling alley" situated on the hotel's lower level. It was very rustic, typically Swiss room, paneled with white pine and had a low ceiling. Most nights, a barman served the few tables drinks, while some folks bowled on a pair of two-thirds scale lanes. Tonight, however, the room was closed off for Marlene and her family. The only exceptions were Mimi and me.

Dietrich had changed into a pale pink classic Chanel suit, her blonde hair loose and flowing. She was no longer the quintessential performer, but simply a happy grandmother enjoying her family and relaxing after an exhausting day.

As we were about to end the evening, Mimi asked:

"You will come to school for lunch Monday?"

"No, thank you," Dietrich replied. "But I will come by your husband's office just before noon Monday, as I leave Gstaad."

I caught a different look in her eye and there was something in the way she delivered that last sentence which told me:

"If you liked tonight's performance, don't miss Monday's...."

We all parted. There was no kissing of hands, just strong hugs and real kisses.

Chapter 5: Monday's Dual Dramas

I spent the following day, in a strange daze. The events of the preceding 24 hours, both entertaining and tragic, had overwhelmed me.

At the foot of the "Rosey hill" in Gstaad was von Siebenthal, a food and gift store where the well-known, hand painted, Bernese Oberland china is sold. Herr von Seibenthal was a large, jovial man who made hot dogs in the food store's window on days when Rosey boys would come by. I bought two and ate them while sitting on the concrete wall adjacent to his store. I looked up at the imposing Palace Hotel and thought about Marlene Dietrich and Aly Pasha. I knew that both events had affected my life in a significant way. I hoped that, perhaps, Ahmed's father had had a spontaneous recovery. My life was progressing so well that I had fooled myself into believing that there was justice and perfection in the world.

I had put Ahmed's tuxedo pants under my mattress in a vain attempt to press them. Toward the end of the afternoon, I packed up the dinner jacket and brought it to his room hoping to find him and listen to any small piece of information he cared to reveal about his experience the previous night. Imagining such a conversation put the gala event into a balanced perspective. In fact, the gala suddenly became a diversion in the real story of the moment. But Ahmed's room was empty, and the other boys on his floor in the Chalet Ried had not seen him all weekend.

After morning classes on Monday, I deliberately hung around the front door of the main chalet, the Rex, hoping to get a final glimpse and, ideally, a word with Dietrich. A few minutes before lunch time, the Palace Hotel's Rolls pulled up beside the front door and Dietrich walked into the building.

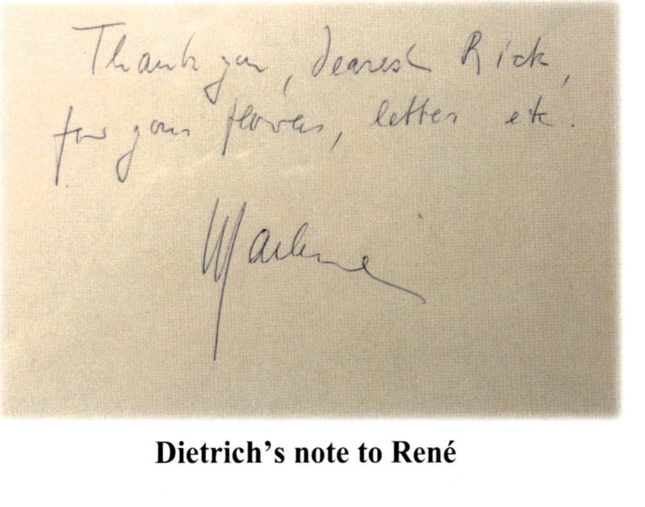

Dietrich's note to René

“Please bring me to Monsieur Johannot’s office,” she said, after handing me a note. “I’ll only be a minute and then I’ll say good-bye, because I am returning to Paris now.”

We walked up the narrow stairs, while several boys identified her and pointed. Monsieur Johannot’s office door was open. He was alone. I stood outside as Dietrich walked in. Over her shoulder she had slung a fur purse, which she unzipped as she removed four envelopes. There were no polite greetings. She immediately got to the point:

“This is for Peter last year.” She slapped an envelope on his desk.

“This is for Michael last year.” Out came a second packet.

“This is for Peter this year.” A third bundle hit the desk.

“Lastly, this is for Michael this year.”

A final ‘plop.’ Dietrich’s overdue bills had been paid with her one-night performance. What a brilliant star, I thought.

Johannot had not even had the time to stand. He sat still and was very silent. Marlene turned around to leave, took one look back and added in a particularly deep voice:

“So, I guess I ‘von’t’ hear from you for another two years.”

She walked out, taking my arm as we descended the stairs. She left the building and Gstaad.

At lunch I asked Mademoiselle Schaub where Ahmed was. She informed me that he and his brother had gone to Geneva because their father had slipped into a coma.

Aly Pasha died the following day. I longed to see the boys and to touch their shoulders, but that would have to wait until after the funeral.

Ahmed returned to school at the end of that week. On Saturday we met at Pernet’s, the tea house in the middle of the village. He revealed some of what his father had said, including his advice and guidance. Amongst other things he told his son was that Ahmed *would* go to Harvard.

That summer Pash-Pash took Ahmed to Boston for an admission interview at Harvard, the only meeting she had scheduled for him. Why should she waste her time going to colleges her son would not attend? Ahmed later told me that during the meeting, the assistant dean of admissions said:

"I see that you are an Egyptian refugee living in Switzerland and you attend Le Rosey. How can you possibly afford such a life?"

"Well, sir," Ahmed replied, "I was 10 years old when we left Egypt, but my mother is waiting outside. Perhaps you might ask her that question," which the poor, misguided fellow did.

Ahmed told me what ensued: His mother rose out of her seat, looked the man straight in the eyes and began:

"How dare you? How DARE you ask me how or under what circumstances my late husband and I escaped Egypt? And what, may I ask, has that to do with Ahmed's capabilities and his credentials to attend Harvard? All you need to know is that his tuition will be paid *when*, not if, he is accepted."

Ahmed went to Harvard College and was the star on their soccer team. He went on to Harvard Business School before he and I embarked on an entrepreneurial business venture that lasted 25 years.

Chapter 6: Paris

I was friendly with a somewhat misunderstood Greek boy my age named Nicolas Politis. "Nico" was shy, tall and handsome. I thought of him as a "Greek god." His sophistication and intellectual prowess were difficult for some of our peers to recognize and understand. Today, he might be called a handsome "nerd."

All students were allowed to receive calls from parents only during the dinner hour and I noticed, with some jealousy that, during his first term at school, Nico received more calls from his parents than anyone else.

Francoise Michel

Mademoiselle Francoise Michel, the floor master of the "Moyens," was a buxom, slightly overweight and vulgar woman who was also Zuzu's girlfriend. One of her duties was to answer the incoming parental calls and get the appropriate boy to the phone. I would watch her stomp into the dining hall, bosoms bouncing, while she made a very noticeable racket as her excessive weight slammed her high heels into the wooden parquet floor. When she was within ear shot of her target, some 20 or more feet away, she would shout out a loud, "POLITIS TELEPHONE!" for example. It seemed to me that the boys who were summoned frequently by Mademoiselle Michel were also the most secure. If I received one call per three-month term, I was lucky. Mademoiselle Michel would invariably laugh as she brought me to the phone because my father used an obsolete, 'old French' word for "talk."

"Your father never needs to say who he is calling for," she would say. "As soon as he says 'causer' instead of 'parler' I say: Hello Monsieur Silvin, I'll get your son." And she would giggle as she stomped away.

Nico and I sat at the same dining room table, so we could speak together at every meal. I always asked him what he discussed with his parents who, on occasion, also asked about my news. Prior to that Easter vacation, Nico returned from a call, saying:

"My mother wondered if you want to come with me to Paris for Easter."

"God, Nico, I'd be thrilled, thanks! I'll write my father and ask him." I was elated.

Once a week, each boy would bring a sealed letter addressed to a parent into the headmaster's office in exchange for their allowance. I wrote asking permission to go to Paris. My father was receptive to the idea, possibly because he endorsed most things that furthered my knowledge of France and French culture.

Nicolas Politis

Several boys, including Nico and I were driven to Geneva's airport in the school van by Eric Fischer, a teacher whom I admired. One of the other students, on his way home for the break, was the son of the President of the Democratic Republic of Congo, Joseph Kasavubu, that country's first President following its independence from Belgium in 1960. Another student was an Irish boy, Roderick Mullion. When we reached the check-in counter a porter and a representative from the Congo's embassy in Bern, approached young "Kasa" with a heavily laden trolley full of suitcases and boxes. Eric Fischer's eyes widened as the bounty was placed on the scale.

"That will be well over one thousand Swiss francs in overweight charges," said the surprised counter attendant.

"How much exactly?" asked Kasa.

"One thousand seven hundred," she said a few seconds later.

"I'll take the boxes over to air freight," interrupted Mr. Fischer.

"No!" interjected Kasa, as he pulled out four 500-franc notes from his pocket: more cash than I could remember ever having seen, and as much money as the teacher earned in a month.

As Nico, Mullion and I proceeded through passport control, we heard the loudspeaker announce, "Mr. Mullion, your plane is ready at gate 15, the far end of the boarding area."

Amazed, I watched young Mullion walk off and board his father's four-engine plane. I had not even heard of long distance, private aircraft before, much less known anyone who had one.

Nico's father sent a driver to pick us up at Orly airport in a handsome two-tone beige Bentley. His Greek parents lived in Paris and Gstaad, his father was a leading Parisian, real estate developer and his mother was a delightful, elegant woman. They had recently built an apartment building on the fashionable Avenue Foch in Paris and had retained the entire top floor for their home, some eight thousand square feet of beautifully decorated rooms designed in an eclectic mix of contemporary furnishings and traditional antiques. All the other floors in the building had two or three units.

When we got to their building, a private elevator brought us directly into the foyer of their apartment. I was dumbstruck with the beauty and grandeur. The oval foyer had refined, painted murals of classical Greek scenes and rounded doors that led into the various rooms. Nico's mother greeted us affectionately. She described some of our plans for that week: we were going to the theater on three different nights. Imagine the elation I felt because I had never been to the theater. I savored each detail of the buildings and the performances, while I admired the friendly, easy-going relationship Nico had with both parents. We actually laughed and told jokes which, even when silly, Nico's parents seemed to enjoy. Clearly, this was their intelligent, wise way to better understand what was happening in their son's life.

I had noticed the names of the other residents on a panel inside the building's lobby: "C. Ponti," "A. Onassis." Nico had told me that Sophia Loren and her husband, Carlo Ponti, had been one of the original investors in the building. I hoped I would be able to catch a glimpse of them.

The following night we went to see the popular Johnny Hallyday perform at the Olympia Theater. When we reached the garage, there was a Rolls Royce waiting near the bank of elevators, a uniformed chauffeur standing at attention next to the limousine's passenger door. We had walked past him towards Nico's parents' car when an elevator door opened, and the Pontis emerged heading for the Rolls and their driver. Nico's parents turned us both around and guided us back to be introduced to their neighbors.

Carlo Ponti and Sophia Loren

I really did not know much about Sophia Loren then, but even a teenage boy could not ignore her grace and beauty. It occurred to me that "buxom" could be vulgar *'a la'* Mademoiselle Michel, or elegant and alluring like this goddess who stood in front of me. Her classic features lit up as she spoke not only to the adults, but also to Nico and me. I kissed her hand, as I did each night to Mademoiselle Schaub upon exiting the dining room, again thinking that manners are one thing, but bestowing their application to a worthy recipient is quite another. I added this goddess in the floor length black satin coat to the list of women who had almost made my knees buckle beneath me: Countess Crespi, Audrey Hepburn, Empress Farah and now, Sophia Loren.

The Politis made sure that Nico and I did as many activities and saw as many cultural events in Paris as possible that week. They carefully balanced our experiences, so that we also engaged in pastimes that all teenagers enjoyed. Nico and I were able to lunch at "Le Drugstore" on The Champs Elysée where adolescents hung out. We ate expensive, trendy hamburgers and listened to the latest music. To this day, I often think about Nico, his late father and delightful mother.

On the Swissair flight back to Geneva, I dreamed of what our new rowing equipment would be like and how we could best put it to maximum use. I knew that I all my energies had to be focused there in order to excel. I was also aware that an odd, detached sensation was emerging in me. I was becoming an observer of life rather than an active participant. I had to pretend not to be sexually attracted to other boys. If I could learn how to conduct myself in a refined way and learn how to become a jock, could I not learn how to be attracted to girls? I was becoming an "actor" on my world's stage. I understood that the focus on survival at La Clairière had left a lasting impact on my ability to succeed through sheer endurance.

Chapter 7: The Silvin

The first day back at school, my plans were temporarily postponed due to a very unusual event. We learned the two Alireza boys were to abruptly leave the school the following day. The buzz went around that the children's Saudi Arabian father had divorced his wife and requested that his sons be immediately repatriated to Saudi Arabia to continue their education in a traditional Arab environment. Under Saudi law, a husband had merely to say "I divorce you" three times in succession to make the act binding and final. The boys were told to pack their belongings in preparation for the arrival of a car from the Saudi embassy in Bern with an official who would escort them back to Jeddah.

The clever, kind and dedicated Marianne learned about her and her children's fate through a phone call from Mademoiselle Schaub. Marianne immediately confided her distress to her close friend, Betty Sicre, who was not about to allow such an injustice to occur without a fight. Betty raced to the school, grabbed both boys, brought them to a waiting boat and crossed Lake Geneva to Evian, France. There, Betty had a private, chartered plane standing by which took the entire group to Madrid, Spain. By the time the embassy car reached Rolle that following day, Marianne and her children were aboard a TWA flight to Los Angles. The story is well chronicled in her book "*At the Drop of a Veil*" which Johnny Carson enjoyed so much that he invited Marianne to appear on *The Tonight Show* to discuss the amazing story.

After the dust settled, I asked to see Monsieur Johannot about the new equipment. The suspense was killing me.

"Well, Silvin, most of the money raised has been spent. The boats and the storage racks have been repaired, especially the Cyril."

The Cyril was our best racing boat. It was named after Cyril Hughes the "Mr. Chips-like" figure and former headmaster of the "English side" of the school.

Something about its design, the angle of the bow and the placement of the seats allowed me to go faster with the Cyril than with the other boats: Rosey I, II, III and IV.

"New oars will be delivered next week," he continued. "The speed boat you felt necessary for training the other teams can be picked up in Geneva any time. There will be a delay in the arrival of the trailer."

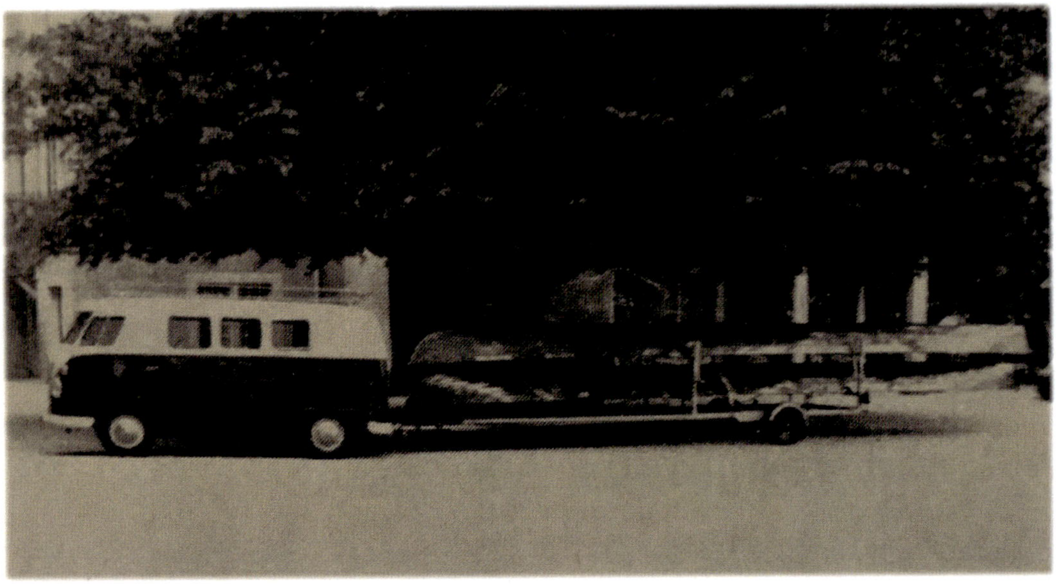

Le Rosey VW bus with custom trailer carrying racing boats

The "trailer" was a custom designed set of two shelves which attached to the back of the school's aging Volkswagen bus, so that the boats and the oars could be stacked, secured and safely transported to regattas.

"That is great, Monsieur," I replied. "We really do not need the trailer until the interschool races, but the speed boat will make all the difference in the world for the younger teams' training. Monsieur Johannot, I was hoping we could name the new boat 'Mimi' after Madame Johannot."

The "Silvin"

"That's very nice, but I have a different idea. The boat will be called 'the Silvin.' After all, we would not have her if it were not for you."

When I regained my composure, I continued with my requests.

"Monsieur, I would like to ask your permission to coach all the younger teams from the speed boat with a loudspeaker. Is that possible?"

He took a puff from his ever-present cigarette and thought about my question for what seemed like an interminable period.

"OK," he began, "there are a few logistic issues. You will need a license to operate the boat here in Switzerland. Since you are 16 you are eligible to take the test in Geneva, but you will need to practice first. I'll have to give some thought to what regular school activities you can omit so as to have the extra time to coach as well as row on your team."

Several thoughts raced around in my mind: A boat named after a student, me, was unprecedented in Rosey history; learning how to coach would be a challenge and would certainly further infuriate Zuzu who had 'played at' being a rowing coach; finally, getting out of a few boring activities so I could spend more time on the water was a definite plus.

"One final thing, Monsieur, I do not need to practice to be able to take the test for a license. I am used to outboard engine boats. Please believe me. Can I not take the test when we pick the boat up?" I implored.

"You seem very confident. It is a difficult test, and you can only take it once a year."

"It will be fine, Monsieur, I promise," and the meeting was over.

A few days later, Monsieur Johannot and I went to the docks in Geneva where the Geneva rowing teams' equipment was kept. A new Boston Whaler with a powerful engine was ready, as was an officer sent from the port of Geneva to give me both a written and sea trial test. I looked over all the boats belonging to the city of Geneva. Only our repaired Cyril was their equal. There were many more boats, sets of oars and facilities. But all I needed was one good boat and dedicated teams. We had the former, and I'd try to create the latter.

At the rowing club, I was introduced to a formal looking man in a suit. He brought me into a meeting room used by the Geneva team and handed me a written test. I had learned the terminology, and all the navigation rules were more or less the same as I had practiced on the Great South Bay off Long Island. Then we proceeded to the Whaler. In the middle of both sides the word "Silvin" was written in blue script. The instructor watched as I pumped gas into the carburetor, found the choke, and gave the engine one hard pull. She lit right up and purred, and I noticed the smell of the exhaust rising with some fumes.

Rowing Club Geneva, Switzerland

"Whoever mixed the fuel has put too much oil in with the petrol," I said. "The fumes should not be this white," I added.

Johannot and the instructor looked at each other.

"Now what would you like me to do next?"

The instructor got into the boat and ordered me to maneuver around the small harbor, to pull up to a fuel dock, to use the reverse gear and to pass other boats outside the port. After ten minutes he told me to return to the dock. I jumped out and secured two lines as he looked at Johannot and said:

"This kid knows what he is doing. I'll mail the license next week. But he can drive the boat back to Rolle right now, no problem."

It was a warm, sunny, spring day without a ripple of a wave on Lake Geneva. The 33-kilometer trip back to Rolle was invigorating and over too quickly. I loved the smell of the water and even the oil rich fuel mixture.

Chapter 8: All Bullies Are Cowards

After an initial observation period, Zuzu gradually retreated from interfering with how I was learning to run the sport. I enjoyed explaining the very basic concepts of caring for and using the equipment to the boys. At the beginning of the spring term, I wanted to teach the prospective team members how to remove the boats from the shed without damaging them, how to enter and exit these paper-thin vessels and, most importantly, how to row in perfect harmony with the team captain, the stroke. The important position of coxswain, or "cox" had never been properly exploited, because no one had bothered to teach smaller, less athletic boys who wanted to row, how to maneuver a 40-foot, powerless boat. Since the slightest error could result in a costly accident and the loss of use of the boat, that position had been relegated to teachers who were too heavy and generally poor mariners.

Zuzu and I came close to a conflict on several occasions. Excessive yelling, abusive discipline and threats were his way of dealing with the student rowers. Our final confrontation took place one early spring afternoon. Each day he unlocked the shed and asked one boy to take the bow of a designated boat while he took the stern. Together they lifted it a few inches so as to not touch the rack above, and ever so carefully removed it from the shelf and the shed, and then placed it on two tresses by the dock. The boat would then be flipped from the upside down to the upright position. On this particular day, the young boy Zuzu ordered to lift the boat was not strong enough. He wasn't able to properly remove it from the storage position. This resulted in a crack in the boat's side, followed by a screaming Zuzu hitting the frightened boy twice in the face: Zuzu's favorite, "a pair of slaps."

"Don't hit him!" I screamed, shocking both myself and Zuzu. When I saw his stunned look at being admonished, I continued:

"There is no reason to terrify these boys. There will only be more accidents and you'll never get them to learn the sport or to give it their all during a race. Surely, we can make this fun."

"Sports at Rosey are not supposed to be fun, Mademoiselle Silvin," Zuzu replied, using the insulting female title of Miss. "If you are so clever, show me how to make these kids from so-called high society families prepare the boats."

"Great!" I said. "But no rowing today. We teach every boy here only how to remove, replace and wash the boats and oars. And once we have mastered that, we spend one entire day learning how to enter and exit a boat, and only Rosey III. No rowing until everyone is comfortable doing that." Rosey III was in such bad shape that I did not mind using her for risky training.

"Well, Miss Silvin, do you think we will ever get the boys on the lake?" he asked in his most sarcastic tone.

"Oh, yeah, we'll get them on the lake, but only when they are ready. And we'll keep the boats safe, and we will win every interschool race in June, and we will never hit ANY kid".

"OK, if you are so brilliant, show me how to have Reynolds lift a boat." He said, pointing at Bob Reynolds who was the smallest boy there.

"Reynolds will not lift a boat" I answered. "He can flip one and I'll bet he will cox the under 18 team in June." I had seen Bob maneuver his father's power boat in the South of France. He was a natural.

"Ridiculous!" Zuzu chuckled. "OK: flip a boat with him."

I took the young boy, whose eyes were about to pop out of his head, over to a boat resting on two tresses.

"I've never done this," he said, obviously worried.

"Bob, it's easy. It's not about strength, just coordinate with me." I tried to assure him.

"The accidents during flipping happen because we never know which way Zuzu wants us to turn them," said young Bob Reynolds. "He says 'right' or 'left' and we never know if it's his right or ours," he said quickly, as he choked up.

I positioned the clever young boy at the boat's bow and I walked to the stern. I looked around. Even though one could not see it, Geneva was to my right,

Bob's left, and Lausanne to my left, Bob's right. Everyone knew where the two cities were relative to Rolle. We each took one end of the boat which weighed several times Bob's weight.

"OK, Bob. Just look at me. Do NOT look at Zuzu. Gently sway her three times on my count. Then we will flip her toward… Geneva. Clear?" He nodded still wobbly. "So, toward Geneva: one… two… three: GENEVA…" The boat flipped over perfectly.

From that day on, we never damaged a boat in regular preparation periods again, and we always used the simple "Geneva" or "Lausanne" rule to indicate which way to flip or lift the equipment. More importantly, Zuzu started coming to practice less and less, especially once Monsieur Johannot had given me the huge old-fashioned steel key to the shed. Most importantly, no boy was ever hit at rowing practice again. I had learned the best lesson of my life to that point: All bullies are cowards. It did not matter if my strong, immediate response to abuse had been an act on my part or not. It had been a spontaneous response which achieved the goal. I supposed most confrontational interventions were, in some way, meant to trick the aggressor into believing his opponent was very strong.

René (Left) coaching younger students

That spring was the first time in my life that I felt unthreatened and happy. I spent four hours each day either rowing or coaching the three other teams selected by age groups. We rehabilitated an abandoned yet solid, old training boat which I used to acquaint new rowers with the art of the sport before they entered the delicate racing boats. When teams were selected, I'd follow their boats with the Boston Whaler to give instructions to both the cox and the stroke while they practiced. As the interschool races neared, I had convinced Johannot to allow me to spend more time on the lake and to reschedule some teams' hours so that I could both practice with my team and coach the others.

One day in early June, the made-to-order trailer was delivered. I looked it over with more pride than if it were my own first car. I knew that we could now safely transport enough equipment to the races without incurring damage. Furthermore, we would no longer tire ourselves with all-night trips back and forth to Lausanne, with a boat precariously tied onto the roof of the school's VW van.

That year, Rosey won every single race at the interschool competitions for the first time in its history. During the awards presentation, I was ecstatically satisfied, yet almost embarrassed to sweep the event. Our schools' teams answered the call, one after another, to collect every first prize. Like the year before, Johannot asked me to drive back to Rolle in his car.

"I'd be happy to, but I have to bring the Whaler back."

"Zuzu can do that," he said, dismissing my concern.

Racing west along the 'autoroute' toward Rolle, Johannot began:

"I never thought we could have a clean sweep of all first prizes. I am very proud of you. Make sure we do this again next year."

"Actually, Monsieur, I think we can do better than that. Beating the schools will not be a problem," I began somewhat sheepishly. "BUT I have seen the times that the Zürich team did in both the two and five-kilometer races. We're very close to their time. If Zürich is the best team in Switzerland, I know we can at least place in the Swiss Nationals, if we really work at it."

"I've told you before, Silvin, only city rowing clubs can enter the Nationals. We are a school not a city club."

"But I don't understand," I insisted. "If our racing times are competitive with Zürich's, what reason would anyone have to stop a new club from qualifying, even if it is called 'Rosey' and not 'Zürich'?"

He remained silent for a long time, taking advantage of the no-speed-limit to approach 100 miles an hour. The driving rule in Switzerland was to keep the left turn signal on as long as the car remained in the passing lane. I watched in front of us and listened, but I never heard the turn signal stop clicking until we exited at Rolle. What was he rushing for, I wondered?

That night, after dinner, Johannot rose to speak. As usual glasses were tapped, and the room became silent.

"As you may have heard, Rosey took every gold medal at the interschool races today. A first for us!" Then, as was the custom, he shouted, "hip hip hip" and we all hollered back "hurrah!"

He continued: "Our oldest team's time is good enough to compete with Switzerland's city clubs. I have just spoken to the rowing authorities in Bern, and they have agreed to test us to determine if we can register as a city club."

Again another: "hip hip hip ---- hurrah"

"No" he continued, "that's weak. Really DO it! "HIP HIP HIP" and we hollered at the top of our voices:

"HURRAH!"

I held my hands to my head and choked back tears of joy. We were becoming *real athletes.* This was not imagined, it was real, and I had to live up to the challenge regardless of how I had to conceal my inner self and my emerging sexuality.

Chapter 9: A Committee Member

As mentioned earlier, Le Rosey had a seven-member student council called "the committee." At the end of each school year, the students voted to elect the committee which was to serve the following year. Only boys from the three-year "Senior" group of students were eligible. Rarely was any committee member elected from a class that wasn't graduating the following spring. The committee members had certain duties and powers. One sat at a table by the dining room entrance at all meals, taking note of who arrived late. They also "kept study hall," meaning they sat at the teacher's desk during study hours for, made sure silence was observed and granted permission to go to the bathroom. Finally, a committee member acting as chaperone accompanied younger boys on some school outings.

René at Le Rosey, 1965

Corresponding favors were bestowed on these students: they could enter the headmaster's office and access a student list to add demerits beside the name of the offending boy. Different types of symbols were translated into fines which were debited from the offender's weekly allowance, or into punishments, "consigning" the child to study hall when others were allowed to go into the village supervised by another committee member. These boys were looked up to by the younger kids. Sometimes they were consulted regarding discipline or scholastic problems, and generally enjoyed a privileged and admired position at school. They sat at Monsieur Johannot's table for all meals and, by no coincidence, were usually the best sportsmen at the school.

As the first student to be "coach" of any sport, I had been catapulted into a different category. Importantly, rowing had become a respected and desirable sport for many reasons. First of all, we had a lot of fun. Secondly, in an environment when boys rarely left campus, we practiced on the lake every day and entered into competitions away from Rolle. Finally, there was never any need or reason to discipline any boy who signed up for rowing. The worst "punishment" they could receive would be to not qualify for the appropriate team or event. This classic win-win situation was based entirely on positive reinforcement.

I was elected to serve on the committee two years before I was to graduate, starting in the fall term of 1964. To my knowledge only two other boys had held this distinction: Betty Sicre's oldest son Ricardo, and Ahmed Yehia, who was at this time completing his second year on the committee. Ricardo Sicre had gone on to win *the* prize award on graduation of "Meilleur Roséen" (Best Rosey Boy) and I would be 'campaigning' for Ahmed to win it.

Initially, being a committee member created quite a conflict for me. While I was enormously flattered at being a rare "non-graduate" on the committee, I could not imagine myself as a disciplinarian. Running away *from* discipline rather than enforcing it, had been the focus of my survival. I soon understood that one could have authority without having to *use* it.

President Joseph Kasavubu, 1915-1969

Eating with the omnipotent headmaster had many advantages. We knew which guests were scheduled to dine with us on subsequent days, and we knew ahead of the rest of the school about important upcoming announcements and events. One night that fall term, Monsieur Johannot laughingly announced to the table that Kasa's father had been overthrown that same day by a rebel leader, Mobutu Sese Seko, in Zaire. At this early hour it was not known if the senior Kasavubu, who had earlier studied to become a Catholic priest, was alive or dead. Shortly, the buxom Mademoiselle Michel pounded her way into the room shouting "Kasavubu, telephone!" I watched my friend run out of the room, as Johannot said "Well, boys, in a few minutes we will learn if his dad is cooking in a pot in Kinshasa or living it up on the Riviera."

The comment struck me as insensitive and cruel. Fortunately, the outcome was more like Johannot's prediction of a luxurious exile. Maybe Johannot was in a bad mood because, only the day before, a younger student had accidentally shot him in the ass at the school's new shooting range. Needless to say, shooting was not one of the activities that interested me.

Another evening, Johannot arrived at dinner to say:

"Silvin, either your father or Mullion's is a liar."

"Excuse me, Monsieur?" I asked, confused.

"I received two calls today. One was from your father and the other from Mullion's father. Both announced that they had won the Grand Prix of Paris, and both told me to take some teachers out to celebrate. I did not know that your father owned racehorses."

I smiled as I realized why he had misunderstood the two phone calls, and that both fathers had told the truth. Although Ann Woodward had owned two double crown winners (Apache and Nashua) before 'the accident,' my father was not a devotee of horse racing.

Pigeon shoot club Bois de Boulogne
Paris, France

"I think you misunderstood, Monsieur," I explained. "There is a week-long sports event in Paris now. Mullion's father must have had a horse in *that* Grand Prix. I assume my father won the Grand Prix of live pigeon shooting."

"Good, we'll enjoy two meals in Geneva," he said laughing.

While I respected Monsieur Johannot, I was always keenly aware that he had never "forgiven me" for having been labeled a homosexual. As such, I was not quite acceptable as a perfect example of his school. That spring I was struck by a quote from Johannot in *Life Magazine,* which perplexed me. Johannot had said: "The only reason I always try to meet and know the parents better is because it helps me to forgive their children."

After pondering why a headmaster would say such a thing to the very press he distanced us from, I wondered if his rather intimate knowledge of my father had helped or hindered him in "forgiving" me.

Typically, I learned news about my parents through the headmaster rather than directly from my parents. On a previous occasion, Johannot told me that I was not leaving for Nice the following day for the Christmas holiday as planned. I was staying at school instead. My father had been in a serious car accident while returning from hunting in Italy. I remained at school, worried and with no further news for a week, until my father phoned me to say he was sorry that I had spent Christmas at school.

Ahmed and Lady Charlotte Anne Curzon Palace Hotel, Gstaad

Now that I had become a "Rosey jock," a coach and a committee member, the opposite sex began to show a definite interest in me. The two all-girls boarding schools that Rosey boys interacted with during the fall and spring terms were Montesano in Gstaad, and Brillanmont in Lausanne. That first winter, Seniors were allowed to go to the "Hi-Fi," a discothèque in the basement of the Palace Hotel on Saturday and Sunday afternoons to meet the Montesano girls. We bought Coca Colas and listened to the new big musical fad: The Beatles.

I used to watch Ahmed dance with a tall, blonde beauty: Lady Charlotte Anne Curzon, the Earl of Howe's daughter. A decade later her noble British parents attempted in vain to marry her to Prince Charles. At this stage, however, she was innocent, extremely beautiful and sensual. More importantly, she was deeply in love with Ahmed. The best part of my late afternoons at the Hi-Fi club was racing down the Palace hill and back up the Rosey hill to monitor dinner's attendance.

A more secure and mature boy during a different period in history might have had the wisdom to understand that I was looking more at the boys than at the girls. But, I dearly wanted recognition, which meant safety. And recognition at an all-male, athletically oriented, military academy-style school meant having a 'girlfriend.' The first year I was on the committee I dated the daughter of a British knight who attended Montesano. She was also blonde and a friend of Charlotte's. If emulation is the best form of flattery, I was clearly flattering Ahmed. In a sense he became my instructor.

When we returned to Rolle, I met an enchanting young Brillamont girl. Elizabeth Marie Therese Walker, named after one of Louis XVI's children, was the daughter of a former dancer, now an aging beauty living in Cologny, the exclusive suburb of Geneva. Germaine, Liz's mother, had had a long-standing affair with John Ringling North of the Ringling Brothers Barnum and Bailey circuses.

I had not learned the self-confidence to appreciate women without a sexual overtone being implied. I so very much wanted to have "my girl" present at a rowing regatta or the annual school ball in the spring term in Rolle. Once a year, the main dining hall was decorated for the event. Each time a different theme was created. For example, a Roman garden or a French Château. Monsieur Stump, the brilliant and sensitive art teacher, led the month-long preparation of the fantasy space. We erected scaffolding to protect the room's oak paneling so that we could affix hand painted scenes that depicted the soirée's theme. Frankly, I enjoyed the artwork and the preparation more than being 'trapped' in a corner by the sexy and beautiful Liz during the ball. Acting out that scene was uncomfortable and actually made me nauseous.

Having a girlfriend was an embarrassing ruse. I believed and felt in my depths that as a sports team leader and committee member who had previously been ridiculed as a "fairy," I needed protection. Sadly, for both of us, Liz was my protection. She attended all the regattas, always beautifully dressed thanks to her elegant mother's purchases. She telephoned regularly at the specifically allowed times which gave me more pleasure than any sex act, and she was genuinely interested in my life.

Our relationship deepened when she had an old fashioned "coming out party" at her uncle's Oyster Bay, Long Island estate the following summer. Her uncle knew my mother as they were part-time neighbors in South Carolina, where they both owned islands off the coast of Beaufort. The Walker's island was named Spring and my mother's Saint Philips, which many years later, was sold to Ted Turner and became one of his homes.

I met Liz and her mother at the USS United States when they docked in New York for the event. The black-tie evening, which was well-written up in the

New York society papers, was one of *the* coming out parties of the season. The other had been held in Southampton, New York the previous week where a young, intoxicated guest had been injured while swinging from a chandelier in the ocean front mansion during the party. Several reporters were waiting at the gates to Liz's event, hoping to cover a similar scandal. But, this Rosey boy did not swing from his host's lighting fixtures! I could behave as I had been trained to and, as long as I was not cornered into having to perform sexually, I was safe and confident about my presentation.

The long driveway, lit by torches, led to the large white tents set up on the huge property. A band played all the latest 60s music so that beautifully dressed young ladies could dance with their prospective beaux. It was all an unreal fairy tale.

All I could think about that night, and at all the other events surrounding the major coming out party, was getting back to Switzerland and, specifically, to rowing. I was also determined to continue something I was privately very proud of: I had served a full year on the committee without ever adding a single demerit to a fellow student's name. I reveled in the satisfaction of knowing that the oppressed need not necessarily become the oppressors. Having been reelected to serve a second year on the committee was proof of that. This was a *real* reward for having behaved according to my principles.

But first, I thought, my team will compete in the Swiss National Rowing Championships! I could focus all energies on that goal, while repressing my sexual feelings.

Chapter 10: My Team

I was particularly proud of our coxswain, Bob Reynolds. His older brother, David, my contemporary and still a close friend, had coxed older boys and Bob's progress was a source of pride. As "cox" Bob was seated in the stern, and the only team-member to face forward and see the course. As such he was responsible for steering the boat throughout a race. The rest of the team faces the cox and could not see where we were headed. As stroke, my position, directly in front of Bob's, sets the pace and length of each stroke.

The other members of the team were, in their seated order behind me: Hans-Björn (Teddy) Püttgen, Kelvin Vanderlip and Tom Pierpoint. Oddly enough, given the international makeup of Rosey's student body, four of the five team members were American. Teddy, the only European, was a Swede.

We were all misfits in one way or another. Perhaps that is the reason we had initially signed up for the sport. In spite of our very different psychological make-ups, we had a few essential characteristics in common: we were competitive, stubborn and would go to great lengths to achieve recognition. Whatever our differences and oddities, we were prepared to combine our strengths to realize our common goal: win.

Our team contained all the elements of the classical "fight to the death" group. As stroke, the responsibility of coordinating the team was mine. I had to channel all of our serious differences into a new persona with an iron-clad will, so that each of us could rely upon all the others' strengths. We were not destined to be the sort of childhood pals who find a lifelong bond, as I did with Ahmed Yehia or David Reynolds. Somehow being best pals outside our sea yawl did not matter. What did matter was that our combined energies had mystically come together as a unified rowing team.

Teddy Püttgen

Teddy sat directly behind me. His charming parents lived above Lake Geneva near Vevey, a 30-minute drive from Rolle. His father seemed to have the same adoration of Teddy's accomplishments that Aly Pasha had for Ahmed's, and his silver-grey sports sedan could always be seen in the school's central courtyard at the exact allocated times for the parental visits.

Elin Vanderlip at Villa Narcissa

Kelvin Vanderlip was seated behind Teddy. "Kel" was a delightful and good-natured teenager. Like with me and Tom, I suspect there were secret goblins buried deep in his head. Elin Vanderlip, Kel's Norwegian born mother, was the daughter-in-law of one of the Bank of America's two founders. She was both a generous and frightening local parent, whom we frequently saw while the school was in Gstaad, where she rented a typical, charming Swiss chalet not far from the Palace Hotel. While she invited Kel's friends to her chalet, I did not sense any of the warmth that we experienced at Betty Sicre's chalet. Once Elin's children had left Rosey, she returned to live at her historic house, Villa Narcissa, in Palos Verde, California, where she became known as the "Chatelaine of Rancho Palos Verdes."

Tom Pierpont throwing a shot put ball at a field & track event
Second from right: Fritz Gunter Sachs, who at the time was married to Brigitte Bardot

Tom Pierpoint was built like a concrete cube with unusual strength for a youth of his age. He was a very accomplished sportsman who was on several Rosey teams. His attractive and youthful single mother, Claire, led a somewhat secluded life in Geneva. On one occasion, Tom kindly took me to their home. We all enjoyed ourselves, especially an evening ride back to school in Tom's mother's Mercedes sports car. Tom's strength and abilities as a rower definitely made him an important and contributing team-member.

Shortly after our return to Rolle at the beginning of the fall term, a member of the National Rowing Committee arrived to assess our abilities to see if we would be permitted to race in the qualifying meet for the Swiss National Championships in June. He surveyed the waterfront around Rolle and used the school's Boston Whaler to drop rock-laden plastic buoys at one and two-kilometer distances, each one a racecourse. Then, conserving all strength, we slowly brought the Cyril out to the makeshift starting line for our first race. We waited for the sound of his blank gun.

As stroke, in the first seat of the yawl, I sat closest to young Bob Reynolds, our cox. My hands, as well as those of the other three team-members, were bloody from having over-practiced the previous ten days. Unfortunately, this day we did not enjoy ideal conditions: the lake was rough, and the wind was coming from the opposite direction. As we approached the starting line, I turned around to face my teammates and said:

"OK guys. We all know it's rough today. All that matters is not to catch 'a crab.' And don't hit 'front stops.' If we can run the courses that way, we will do it in good time." These two seemingly minor infractions can reduce the boat's speed enough to lose an otherwise well-executed race.

A crab is when an oar hits the water after a stroke while the rower is moving his seat forward to take the subsequent stroke. If an oar touches the surface, the boat slows. Always a challenge, this feat would be made more difficult by the rough waters. Front stops are the front ends of the rails the seats slide along. As a rower prepares for each stroke, sliding forward, he must come as close to the end of the rails as possible without touching the stops, thus maximizing the distance the oar will be in the water. Touching the rail's end causes the boat's bow to dip ever so slightly which, in turn, slows the craft down. An accomplished rower, watching a race from the shoreline, can tell if any team-member hits front stops because the bow dips deeper into the water.

We observed these two simple rules used in rough water races for both distances. I did not set a pace that increased the risk of incurring either infraction. When both courses had been completed, we returned to the dock.

Bob, our cox, needed to guide us flawlessly in our approach to the pier. This must be accomplished in a seemingly effortless maneuver. The cox turns the boat toward the dock, ideally into the wind, and orders the necessary number of strokes which the team captain controls. Since the boat has to come alongside the pier and the oars are ten feet in length, several commands have to be meticulously followed as not to damage the paper-thin boats or the fragile ores. After the last stroke, and as the vessel approaches the dock, the command is "easy!" This means all oars are out of the water in perfect synchronicity and held inches above the surface.

The cox then steers the gliding boat toward the dock. Once the craft is nearly at its destination, the second command is given, "easy oars!" At this command, the rowers place their oars onto the water's surface, parallel to the water. The boat glides along and gently slows down.

Finally, at the very second before reaching the pier, the last command is "stop the boat!" The oars are immediately turned to right angles in the water, which if done properly, acts like a set of disc brakes in an automobile. The rowers who have their oars on the side next to the dock must immediately and simultaneously pull in their oars at just the right moment to allow the boat to come to a stop within a few inches of its destination. Nothing is more beautiful than a racing boat's perfectly executed 'landing.' We carried out one such docking that day.

The official looked at me and said: "The times are fair given the conditions. You'll be allowed to compete in the qualifying races for the under 19-year-old category in Lucerne next April."

"Do you not mean under 18?" I asked, surprised and worried.

"No," he replied. "We are changing the age group you are eligible for from under 18 to under 19."

This was seriously bad news. The teams we would face were to be a full year older than we; therefore, they would be bigger and stronger and more experienced. In my confusion and consternation, I heard him ask:

"And, by the way, the docking was impressive. How old is this boat?"

"Six years old, sir," I answered.

"I guess you don't use it often?" he inquired.

"On the contrary, she is used several times a day, monsieur. Our cox has been docking boats all his life." I winked at a very happy Bob Reynolds.

"Amazing that it has no scrapes," he muttered, and wrote notes on his clipboard.

As we walked, almost danced, back up the hill to school, we could hardly control our excitement. Clearly, we had met the criteria for participating in the qualification races. We snatched apples off trees along the path, took a few bites and threw them at each other giggling.

Underlying the elation, was the very real concern of what it would be like when we actually met the highly respected city clubs, especially Zürich? How could I be sure each team-member would conform to the overall team's needs? Would Vanderlip and I be strong enough to endure the rigorous training we faced? Clearly Tom and Teddy were more powerful than we.

Kelvin Vanderlip

The National Championships were eight months away, but we would only be able to row for a total of four and half months, due to our being in Gstaad all winter and regularly scheduled school vacations. That was not a lot of time. Worse, I thought, was how we would do in Lucerne facing older athletes. The city teams would be able to practice all winter and into the early spring. We, on the other hand, would be returning from Easter break just two weeks before the qualifiers. There was no time to lose.

Another issue required immediate attention: rowing had not been previously practiced far into the fall term, once the weather changed in October. At dinner that night, Johannot asked me for details about what had occurred. After he expressed his satisfaction with the day's results, I said:

"Monsieur, we will be at a considerable disadvantage by spring term. We cannot row all winter like the city clubs, and the new rules will have us compete with under 19-year-olds."

"That is exactly the kind of problem I warned you about, Silvin," he responded. "I have no control over National rules like I do with interschool events."

"What would you think about allowing us to row this fall?" I asked, knowing that changes to the curriculum were not easy to convince this army colonel to implement.

"Mmmm," he thought, "you would be totally unsupervised, because Zuzu will be coaching soccer. But, I guess that does not matter." He paused a while before concluding, "OK. I'll release your teammates from other sports. Since you are the only committee member you will be held responsible. Is that clear?"

"Yes, monsieur," I said, trying to conceal my joy, but worrying about what that warning might entail. Having my request granted was a thrill but being responsible for our team's behavior was a daunting thought. My earlier childhood experiences had created an instinctual adversity to "supervise" my peers.

The weather during the fall months of 1965 was some of the worst anyone could recall. It rained almost every day and it was unseasonably cold. Monsieur Johannot had even broken his rule and turned on the dorms' heating systems prior to October 15. The swimming pool was also shut down early, but we practiced on the lake every afternoon, rain or shine.

On rainy days we did distance training to increase stamina. I had placed cut-open plastic bottles next to Bob and Tom to bail water from both of the boat's extremities when we would break for rests on torrential rainy days. After practice, we would race back up the hill to run into hot showers after having been in the cold rain for two hours. Most of that fall, the physical pain was nearly unbearable: arms, backs and shoulders were always sore. The worst was our hands: huge blisters led to bloody sores. But no one complained.

On one stormy day a teacher came to the dock to drive us back to school in Rosey's aging VW bus. The seats behind the driver had been removed to create more space and the rain-soaked team was all seated on the metal floor. The double side doors had clearly not been adequately bolted into position. As we raced around a curve in the road, the doors flew open and Teddy, hovering next to the doors, rolled out onto the pavement. The teacher screeched to a stop as we all ran back to find a stoic Teddy with only scrapes and a few cuts. We climbed back into the bus, secured the doors and continued up the hill as if nothing had happened. Such was our resigned determination to "carry on" and was typical of our cohesive behavior as a brave and robust team.

By December, we had gained considerable strength and stamina. We decided to do as many useful exercises as possible during the winter term to maintain our physical progress. Rosey had no gymnasium at either location, so we improvised using any horizontal bar we could find for pull-ups. We did push-ups and other exercises that required no special equipment. Skiing would help us maintain our endurance. The usually enjoyable winter term seemed agonizingly long, but it eventually ended with the Easter break.

My team reunited in Rolle for the final countdown.

Chapter 11: Foolishness in Lucerne

Altstadt (old town), Lucerne, Switzerland

We took full advantage of nearly perfect weather during the fortnight that preceded the Lucerne event. We rowed twice a day, rising at dawn to row before breakfast. Racing boats on the lake in early mornings was a novelty for the residents of the waterfront properties, who appeared to enjoy the excitement. Many waved as we moved along, but we were unable to acknowledge their greetings. The local paper had published an article about Rosey's designation as an official club. Several shopkeepers asked questions as the excitement spread from the Rosey kids to much of the town. In this context "Rosey" became synonymous with "Rolle." The locals would never have dreamed their tiny village would compete for any sport on a national scale. The barriers between the well-to-do Rosey students and our working-class neighbors were coming down. We now had a common goal and our differences were being forgotten.

The day before the scheduled event we loaded two boats and two sets of oars onto our fancy trailer, just in case we needed an extra boat. A young British teacher, Colin Waller, drove the bus, with his wife beside him. We huddled in the back. None of us had ever been away from school during weekdays, which added to the excitement. We left Rolle early so that we could reach Lucerne in time for a practice race and to survey the course. After practice, we ate a hearty dinner in the small, inexpensive hotel and were told by Mr. Waller that lights would be out in our two rooms at nine o'clock.

I was rooming with Vanderlip, while Püttgen and Pierpoint shared the next room. Shortly after nine, we decided to sneak out of the hotel. Within seconds we were dressed and had tiptoed down the hall and out onto the street. Our teen-age desire for adventure had trumped our sense of responsibility as we explored the entire area.

A four-lane highway, spanning the river approximately 100 meters below, was being built through that part of town. When completed, there would be two separate parallel bridges; one for traffic in each direction. At this stage of the project, one bridge was finished and temporarily served traffic heading in both directions. The second bridge was under construction and that is where our motley crew found its adventure.

The two bridges emerged from parallel tunnels and sloped downwards. We noticed that the unused tunnel contained construction material, including an 'A-frame' scaffolding unit which rolled along tracks, presumably for work on the tunnel's ceilings and to transport heavy materials. The unfinished bridge we were on ended abruptly over the river.

We were totally out of control, like a pack of animals that had escaped from a fenced in back yard. Actually, we were not much smarter. We explored the tunnel and climbed aboard the A-frame rail car. It had an iron, circular brake control which one of us quickly loosened. It started to roll down the slanting bridge.

Clickety-clack, clickety clack; faster and faster we went. Kel grabbed the brake wheel and tightened it as the vehicle screeched to a halt.

"C'mon, let's push her back up the hill," urged Pierpoint, "and get it going faster!"

Highway bridge, Lucerne

On the second run, we became blinded and mesmerized by the increasing sound of the wheels on the tracks. Through the darkness, surprised and frightened faces stared at us from cars using the other bridge only a few meters away. Our speed increased as did the repeating 'clickety-clack.' Shortly, we could see the rails end directly in front of us. The steel brakes locked onto the metal wheels, but the over-weighted cart kept skidding along the rails throwing a fantail of sparks behind us.

The rail car came to rest a few feet from the cliff. Our irresponsible adventure had nearly turned to tragedy. British folk wisdom claims "the universe takes care of drunkards and fools." We had not been drinking, but we certainly had been fools.

We climbed down the bridge's scaffolding and walked back to our hotel. It was 2 AM. We had to attend a daybreak registration procedure. The Wallers never knew what had happened but noticed our weary faces and sluggish movements.

"Good morning gentlemen," Waller said, as we entered the hotel's restaurant for breakfast at the agreed upon time. "We certainly are not bright eyed and bushy tailed today. Didn't sleep well, eh?"

A muffled mumble was our response.

Our performance on the lake was as embarrassing as was the recollection of the previous night's reckless events. We splashed our oars into the water, rather than cutting through it. Vanderlip 'caught a crab', and we all 'hit front stops' several times. I thought we were a sloppy bunch of hoodlums and miserably felt like one myself.

Eight boats raced: seven cities and Rosey. Amazingly, we came in fifth behind Zürich, Geneva, Lugano and Bern. The five best teams would be qualified to compete in the National Championships. The big day was ten weeks away and would be held at the hometown of the reigning champions, Bern. Until that time, Zürich had been undefeated, and the championships had always been held in Zürich.

We had received a reprieve. I was not about to tempt fate so foolishly again. Sitting on the floor of the noisy bus heading back to Rolle, I talked with my team.

"We screwed up big time."

"We were assholes," agreed Tom. "It's a miracle we were not eliminated or even killed."

The rest of the team was in full agreement. We would have to behave more maturely if we were serious about winning.

Chapter 12: Final Training

In the weeks that followed Lucerne, I thought of little else besides rowing practice. Even the usual agonizing wait for college acceptances was eclipsed by my concentration on rowing. Most boys in the graduating class applied to many universities. My father had instructed me not to.

"There is no use spending money on each individual application," he explained. "Your brother went to, and graduated from, Georgetown and that is what you will do. After four years, you will go to graduate school. Then, and only then, will I allow you to pick a University under the nonnegotiable condition that you study either business or law."

I wanted to study history, but a 'discussion' with my father about something four years away was senseless.

Like all high school graduates who are headed to college, I was relieved to have an acceptance letter in my hand. But that letter, placed in the same mailbox as my 500 Swiss franc contributions to update the rowing equipment 18 months previously, was of far less importance. My attending Georgetown University later that year could have been a century away. My focus was on doing well at the National Championships and another very improbable dream: becoming "Meilleur Roseen," which title both of my heroes, Ricardo Sicre and Ahmed Yehia, had won the two previous years respectively.

Ricardo "Rick" Sicre

I wished I had paid more attention to the teams which beat us in Lucerne. Obviously, there were no videos of the race in those days. Vanderlip and I tried to recreate the race in our minds to better familiarize ourselves with whom we would meet in Bern later that fall.

"The guys from Zürich were huge!" Vanderlip said, reminding me of an important detail.

"Their stroke looked like he was laughing at us, did you notice that?" I asked.

"I think everybody was, especially when I caught the crab!" said Kel.

We continued our twice a day practices, rain or shine. An ever-increasing number of "Rollois" took an interest in the upcoming national competition, as well as in our early morning sorties. Another article appeared in Lucerne's paper after the race. It related details of the event and spoke of the first three finalists. The last paragraph read:

"A new team has qualified to compete on the Aare River. Le Rosey, the exclusive, international boarding school in Rolle." We certainly could not have appeared to be a threat, based on our sloppy performance, so did not merit further consideration.

Aare river in Bern

The Aare River meanders through the charming Swiss capital forming a peninsula of the old part of the city with its immaculately preserved medieval streets. We had never rowed on a river before. Our practice had strictly been on lakes: Geneva and Lucerne's Rotsee. I wondered how different this would be.

One night at dinner I asked Johannot: "Monsieur, how fast is the Aare in Bern?"

"It flows pretty well. All depends on which part and on rainfall," he answered.

"Might I call the rowing club in Bern from your office tomorrow and ask for details about where the course will be set up?" I inquired.

The following day, I went to the headmaster's office with a piece of paper I had received in Lucerne from the rowing committee. It had their address and phone number on the top. The secretary I spoke with explained that the two-kilometer course would be set up to run through the city's center where the river narrows. I tried to imagine how races begin on a river with a current.

"How do you create a starting line on a river?" I asked.

"There is a pedestrian bridge which we close off. Officials catch and hold the boat's sterns. When the gun is fired, the boats are let loose," she explained.

I tried to imagine the difference in the starting techniques from the still waters of Lake Geneva. However, I had a greater concern.

"But, Madame, it's a straight course, right?" I asked.

She chuckled. "There are no two kilometer straight-aways on the Aare."

I thought of Bob Reynolds. He was a great pilot, but this would be a totally new experience. Bob never let us wander over into competing boats' imaginary lanes, a cause for disqualification. Even more to his credit, he was able to steer a straight course in conditions where other boats would have drifted out of their lanes. But, a curving, fast flowing river would be totally different from what we were used to and, presumably, required a great deal of courage and skill.

During training over the next weeks, I told Bob to steer us through an imagined, circuitous course. We progressed by rowing around the small island near the village's dock at our top speed trying to keep an equidistant position from the island's shore. We repeated the exercise in both directions to simulate turns to both port and starboard. As I feared, positions one (mine) and three caught many crabs when the boat turned to port and, conversely, seats two and four were similarly cursed when we veered to starboard. We

The island, Rolle, Switzerland

repeated the exercise over and over again while I changed the frequency and length of strokes when the boat listed during a turn. Eventually, we mastered a harmony between speed and flawless strokes.

Another alarming problem was that, in their zeal, some team members 'rushed' me. 'Rushing' is the term used for trying to increase the pace that the stroke establishes. An analogy would be if a musician tried to speed up the tempo of a piece by his own playing, instead of following the conductor. Its effect is to disharmonize the team and lose a race. Eventually, we were able to overcome this common problem and began rowing in total, synchronized harmony.

Back around the island we raced, twice in each direction to approximate two kilometers. By the end of that day's training, our performance was as near perfect as possible.

A few weeks before the big day, Johannot brought a copy of Switzerland's widely circulated Zürich paper, Neue Zurcher Zeitung (NZZ) to dinner. He opened the paper and put it in front of me. In German, the headline read:

"Will Zürich take back the National Rowing Cup?"

Again, only one line at the end of the article introduced the new underdogs.

We were as prepared as we would ever be. The four of us had become accustomed to the constant pain involved in rigorous training. Erroneously, I imagined and hoped that there would be no more surprises before we went to Bern one week later.

Chapter 13: The Swiss National Rowing

Tournament Bern 1966

The same gentleman who had clocked our times to qualify us for the Lucerne race returned to the school a week before the Swiss Championships. We were told to meet him in the schools' infirmary, which I thought was very odd. There, the squinting nurse, Mademoiselle Keller, handed us small plastic cups and told us to urinate. Turning our backs to her, we all complied. The following day, I was called out of class by Johannot's secretary.

"There seems to be a medical problem, Silvin," Johannot began, when I entered his office.

"I don't understand."

"Unusually high doses of albumin were found in the team's urine," he explained.

"What does that mean?" I asked, never having heard of 'albumin' or imagining any health issues could interfere with our plans. We had never been near, or even heard of, 'performance enhancing drugs.' Although we were in constant pain, no team member had ever been ill.

"As it was explained to me," Johannot said, "traces of this protein in urine means that muscles are being excessively overworked and broken down."

Not familiar with those terms and puzzled, I repeated my question. "What does that mean, Monsieur"?

"You may have overworked the team and risk being disqualified."

"DISQUALIFIED?" I said in a louder voice than ever before in his presence.

"They will test you all again two days before the race, in three days from now" he said, raising his shoulders as if to say, "There is nothing further I can do about this."

That night, Mimi Johannot, came to my room. We were alone because my roommate, another committee member, was tutoring a younger student.

Anne-Marie "Mimi" Johannot

"Silvin," she began, "Monsieur Johannot has told me about the albumin issue. As you know I am a chemist, a dietician and an amateur hematologist, you know: a blood specialist. Albumin in the urine *may* mean overworking the muscles or kidney failure. There is another reason this may have occurred in a young man. My guess is that you can solve this problem easily." She paused, and I stared at her. I knew she was doing her best to help me, but I was totally in the dark about her point.

"Silvin, if the urine sample was taken shortly after ejaculation, unusually high doses of albumin would be present. Do you understand what I am saying?" She asked after spitting out the sentences.

"Well, yes, Madame, that's pretty clear," I said.

Mimi winked and left.

The next morning at practice I spoke to the team about this touchy but also somewhat humorous problem.

"Guys, please don't ask me why, because I really don't understand any of this, but do me a favor, OK? Just don't jack off before you piss in that cup again in two days. It seems that might be the issue with this albumin stuff."

We all roared with laughter, made a few risqué comments and began our practice.

I will never know whether it was Madame Johannot's brilliant and compassionate assistance, or the fact that we took a day off from practicing before the subsequent urine test. Nevertheless, the urinalysis results were within acceptable norms, and we were now definitely going to Bern.

As we did for Lucerne, we loaded the same boats and oars onto our trailer and, accompanied by several curious teachers, we went to Bern the evening before the race. Nobody had to tell us that "nine o'clock lights out" was not a recommendation. We all knew it was an order to be obeyed.

The river Aare, Bern

The following day we drove through the charming streets of Bern, which had recently been voted the "most flowered European City," to a boat landing where all the teams were getting ready. The crystal-clear day made the distant Alps visible and enhanced the beauty of the steep, green river banks.

I held a final strategy discussion with the anxious team. "Bob," I said to young Reynolds, "just remember everything you learned racing around the island. Use the closest bank as an orientation point through the course. If another boat drifts over, check your position based on the distance from the shore. I'll be watching also. Let me know when we are approaching turns in the river."

Facing the others, I said, "We'll start off with long, hard strokes to try to pull ahead early. The current may work in our favor that way. We have been issued slot number three, so our best bet is to lose at least one neighbor quickly."

Our position on the starting line was regrettable. We all knew it. Being adjacent to a shore would have meant watching only one immediate neighbor.

In the third position, Bob would have to guide us into an imaginary lane squeezed between the boats numbered two and four, Bern and Zürich, respectively.

"I'll bring the pace up to our maximum early on," I continued. "But I won't be rushed. And remember when she lists, you have to make damn sure to keep the oars high when moving forward to avoid crabs. I'd rather shorter strokes to hitting the front stops." Now that training was over, the boat's seats had been properly put back together.

"No one looks around. Leave that to Bob. Just kick ass." I had finished my not-so-well delivered pep-talk. Something was missing. I believed we were overly anxious. *That*, in turn, made me nervous.

We rowed upstream and passed the starting line bridge. There were five men on a lower platform with large signs numbered one through five. Coincidentally, we maneuvered the Cyril to turn around at exactly the same moment as the Zürich team executed their U turn. Even though I had not been paying full attention in Lucerne, I'd have recognized Zürich's stroke in a crowded airport: a large, blonde with a sarcastic grin.

"Ich wuerde Dich ausquestschen wie die Zahnpaste von der Zahnpastentube." ("We'll squeeze you out like toothpaste from a tube") He yelled over to us.

Fortunately, my teammates did not understand enough German. I nodded and said nothing. We drifted downstream passing under the bridge. Bob gave the "stop the boat" command, and the official grabbed onto our stern. Bern's boat was already positioned on my left and Zürich's boat eased into place on my right, facing the direction the stroke looks as he rows. Now my opponent was very close and stationary. I would be able to watch him throughout the race.

"Reicher Fagot!" he yelled at us. We all understood that part: 'Rich fag.'

The magic word had been uttered. A common cause had been handed to us on a platter as unknown power surged from within each of us. The race had now become something very personal, at least for me. We had to win to prove that he was wrong about us, and for all the underdogs and all victims of prejudice. Winning was the only weapon against being ridiculed. I turned around, looked at the team, and said,

"You got that, guys, right?"

Pierpoint's eyes were furious, Püttgen and Vanderlip nodded; their lips pressed firmly together. Then,

"On your marks, get set……" A long pause followed as we stretched our arms as far forward as possible advancing the seats to a millimeter from front stops, waiting….

"BANG!" The boats were released into the current.

We took huge, long strokes with all our might. Within seconds, only the three middle boats were still in the race. I could see the Zürich boat clearly; that was the direction of my oar. Turning to look at Bern would be a costly mistake, but I knew she was right there. I could hear, even feel their teammates struggling to keep up with us. Faster and faster we rowed, as we approached a first turn in the river, which only Bob could see. There had been little splash to our strokes indicating perfect execution. Each move forward for the next stroke advanced me to within a foot of Bob's face.

"Turning to port in about two strokes," he whispered.

I shortened the length of the strokes somewhat, but we kept giving every ounce of strength we had. The boats all listed and righted themselves. Neither Zürich nor we incurred any crabs on the curve. Onwards we raced. I could now see Bern's stern through the corner of my left eye, which meant they had not managed the curve as well as we had. I saw the one-kilometer mark on the shore. The race was clearly between two teams: Zürich and Rosey! The two boats' strokes were not synchronized, so that as Zürich executed a stroke they inched ahead while we positioned ourselves forward for the next stroke. Similarly, we moved ahead when we rowed. But, Zürich was gradually increasing its lead.

Then Bob spoke again, "Turning to starboard in two strokes."

That was great news. Zürich would be on the outside and Bern was sufficiently behind that we need not be concerned about ramming her oars. After the second turn we were again neck and neck with Zürich. Neither team had made the slightest error. I could hear my teammates' breathing and even our opponent's, along with grunts of power. There was now another noise which grew louder each second. People were shouting at us from the river banks as they ran along trying to keep up. I saw Monsieur Mastelli, the previously feared Latin teacher who had helped me pass the repeat exams my first year at Rosey. He was screaming.

"Rosey, Rosey!"

Then he ran by my heroine, Betty Sicre. She, too, was screaming at us.
"GO GO GO!"

I brought the pace up to our maximum, knowing that we were only a few hundred meters from reaching the finish-line. Another good piece of luck was thrown our way: Zürich's stroke turned to his left to check our location. Again, we inched forward. But, it was still close enough that the boat which crossed the line with their oars in the water would probably win by a hair.

We pulled harder and harder as we crossed over the line and coasted, panting, trying to sit erect. At this moment, I still was not sure who had won. Clearly, Bern was third, but what about us? I looked around at the exhausted team. A loudspeaker broke in:

"First place: Le Rosey, Rolle. Second, Zürich; third, Bern…" The announcement passed into oblivion as a feeling of elation overcame our fatigue.

A nearby pier was full of spectators lined up behind a fenced-off area. On the water's edge stood rowing officials. One waved us over. Once again, Bob brilliantly maneuvered the Cyril up to the dock with commands in English:

"Easy, easy oars, stop the boat."

The gentleman who had checked us out eight months earlier reached over, and put large plaques suspended from blue ribbons around all our sweaty necks. I looked down at mine. It read:

"Swiss National Championship, 19-year-old class, 1966, first prize"

That night, back at school, the entire dining room was buzzing with the story. Teachers at many tables had been in Bern and they related specific details. After dinner, Johannot rose to speak.

"Your school is the Swiss National Champion at rowing!" Let's hear it for the team:

"Hip, hip, hip"

I watched as everyone shouted back: "Hurrah!"

"No, too weak," Johannot repeated twice before he was satisfied with the noise level.

"Everyone stand up and really do it!"

"HIP HIP HIP"

Everyone responded with a 'Hurrah' that nearly shattered the windows. I looked at the team seated at a table behind mine. Jubilation showed on their faces.

Johannot had more to say. "I think it is time that you throw the team into the pool fully dressed. And there will be no study hall tonight. To the trees!"

Throwing a committee member in the pool on his birthday was a frowned upon custom. Now, Monsieur Johannot was recommending it. "To the trees" meant we could raid the cherry trees, a once-a-year treat, usually offered after final exams.

Final exams were ahead of us, as was the vote for "Meilleur Roséen." We also had one more rowing regatta: The European Championships. We would represent Switzerland at that race to be held in Zürich three days before our final exams.

Chapter 14: The Real Victory

Zürich, Switzerland

The European Rowing Championship competition was held in Zürich, shortly before the beginning of our final exams. Le Rosey represented Switzerland and competed against Germany, Italy, France, Spain, the Netherlands and Belgium. Had the venue been in a foreign country, I doubt that we would have been able to compete. Missing one day of school for a regatta reached by using our old bus was one thing. A lengthier trip would have been entirely different.

Monsieur Johannot had informed all the team's parents of our victory in Bern and the upcoming meet in Zürich. My father called a few days before the competition. Mademoiselle Michel barked out her usual "Silvin, telephone" announcement in the dining room.

"Your brother and I will watch you race in Zürich," he announced. "I have reserved a suite at the Baur au Lac Hotel so that, if you place in the top three, we will invite your team, and any teachers who accompany you, to celebrate afterwards."

My father and my brother met us at the docks in Zürich as we prepared for the race. The course was set at the up-scale residential area of Zollikon, slightly to the east of down-town Zürich. As in Bern, the weather was beautifully clear. The city and lake, bearing its name, looked like Walt Disney had used the scenery to inspire the creation of his Magic Kingdom.

Rowing Club docks, Zürich

Unfortunately, unlike at Bern, no opposing team shouted insults to ignite an extra human motivation deep within us. Although, we executed a flawless race, we were outclassed from the start as Germany took, and kept, the lead. We finished fourth, behind Germany, Italy and the Netherlands.

After the race, there was no pulling up to a victory pier. We simply rowed to the main dock, took the Cyril out of the water and prepared to mount her on our trailer. My father walked over and said:

"It looked like, if you could have given your blood to row faster, you would have. However, since you were fourth, we'll say goodbye and let you go back to school. I'll see you at graduation."

The Cyril, Zürich, Switzerland

I was neither surprised nor disappointed by the fact that there would be no party at the hotel. My father had clearly emphasized 'if you place' when he issued the invitation, and I knew he was not about to amend his offer. I felt much more at ease driving back across Switzerland to Rolle with my teammates than worrying about what might have occurred at a "celebration."

Final exams had none of the usual stress of previous years. I was going to college in Washington, DC and although I wanted to do my best, my thoughts and concerns were on my hope of being elected "Meilleur Roseén."

The unfortunate title translates as "Best Rosey Boy." Just prior to graduation each year, all students, teachers and employees would meet in the main study hall to cast their written votes. Monsieur Johannot would introduce the ballot with these words:

"This is the most important decision of the year." Actually, it was the only vote all three groups from the school participated in. "I want you all to think of it like this: if I received an invitation from the White House in Washington, to send a boy to represent Le Rosey, who would you want to go?"

The award, a pair of gold cufflinks engraved with the school's crest, was given at the graduation ceremony. It was the last, and most anticipated, prize of the day, presented after all other sports, academic and special honors.

On graduation day, like most of the senior class, I was wearing a white Rosey blazer, with the school's gold buttons and crest, along with a Rosey tie. For unexplained reasons, my father had decided not to attend. Instead, my mother would represent him.

Of course, I had invited my "girlfriend," Liz Walker. Her mother had sent her gold Mercedes to bring her, my mother and brother from Geneva to Rolle. I did not need to hide as I did five years previously, when I fretted that Johannot would tell my mother that I was "a fairy."

That morning, before the guests arrived, the boys customarily asked their pals and some teachers to sign year books. Monsieur Johannot inscribed mine as follows:

"I have often claimed that modesty was a serious flaw because, when one knows their worth, there is no reason to hide it. For you, however, pride could be the real danger today. When I think about the number of awards you will win, at the place you have taken at Rosey these last years and in our hearts for seven years, you can well be proud. We know that you will always be a very good Roséen and that our separation does not really mean you are leaving Le Rosey. We will stay friends who know they can count on one another for life. Good luck and thank you for everything you have given to your school, which is also proud to have contributed to your being a man. Your friend, L. Johannot, Rolle, July 5, 1966."

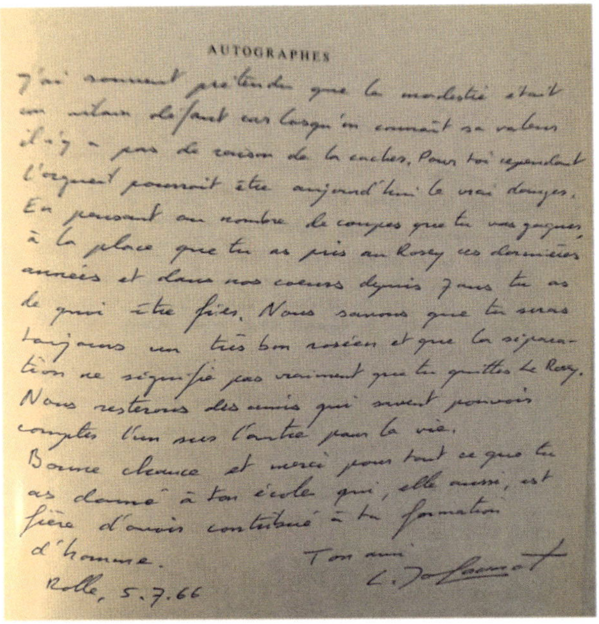

AUTOGRAPHES

J'ai souvent prétendu que la modestie était un vilain défaut car lorsqu'on connaît sa valeur il n'y a pas de raison de la cacher. Pour toi cependant l'argument pourrait être aujourd'hui le vrai danger. En pensant au nombre de coupes que tu as gagnées, à la place que tu as pris au Rosey ces dernières années et dans nos coeurs depuis 7 ans tu as de quoi être fier. Nous savons que tu seras toujours un très bon roséen et que la séparation ne signifie pas vraiment que tu quittes le Rosey. Nous resterons des amis qui savent pouvoir compter l'un sur l'autre pour la vie.
Bonne chance et merci pour tout ce que tu as donné à ton école qui, elle aussi, est fière d'avoir contribué à ta formation d'homme.

Ton ami
L. Johannot

Rolle, 5.7.66

Louis Johannot's inscription in René's year book, 1966

I read the atypical, somewhat emotional and detailed inscription several times, pondering what Johannot meant by we "are proud to have contributed to your being a man" and "we know you will always be a good Roséen," when one of my favorite teaches approached me.

Max Radoszycki was a young Frenchman who taught French language and literature as well as English to French speaking students. He was a very principled man who demanded respect but was always fair and ready to help any student who legitimately needed assistance in furthering themselves and their studies. Conversely, he had little patience with Rosey boys who did not carry through on homework assignments or who, he sensed, were disinterested in education.

Max Radoszycki, 1934-2015

"Rado" as he was affectionately referred to, pronounced a bizarre and, I thought, ominous statement.

"After the awards, I *must* speak with you. Whatever happens, whatever you feel, promise that you will not leave school without finding me first. Promise?"

"Yes, Monsieur." I wondered what he could not say right then and there.

The lunch tables had been set up along the pathway between the main school buildings and the swimming pool. Like other years, a soccer match as well as swimming and track competitions were held before and after lunch. At around 3 PM, the group assembled on the lawn adjacent to the "Château." In anticipation of his attending the event, my father had sent a sufficient number of cases of wine to serve all the adult guests.

Elizabeth Taylor with sons Michael Jr. and Christopher Wilding

Elizabeth Taylor and Richard Burton arrived, because Liz's two sons Michael Jr. and Christopher Wilding were at school. The two lovely boys were the offspring of Liz Taylor's marriage with Michael Wilding, which had lasted from 1952 to 1957. Michael Jr. had been overly disciplined for minor behavioral problems. Not only because he had his mother's magnificent blue eyes, had I genuinely liked young Wilding. As a committee member, I had argued strongly in his favor at a meeting with teachers about the boy's future at school. His mother sought me out.

"I'd like to thank you," she said, "for what you did for Michael."

"He is a good boy, Miss Taylor," I answered. "It was my pleasure to assist him. Rosey is not easy on the younger kids. The rules are rigid, and he needed a little leeway."

She put her hand on my arm and said, "Still, thank you. And congratulations for becoming Swiss Champions."

The Burtons then entered the Château where guests were gathering. This was the same building where on a damp night, four and a half years earlier, my father had told Johannot, "Louis, I assure you he is not a fairy."

William Holden was right behind Taylor. My mother and I had lunched the previous winter with him and his wife, actress Brenda Marshall, at their rented chalet, "Les Aroles," in Gstaad. Having overheard the conversation with Liz Taylor, he asked me, "What's this about Swiss Championships?"

William Holden, 1918-1981

"Well, sir," I replied, "our team won the Swiss National rowing championships last month."

"Good God!" he said in a loud voice. "That donation you asked for two years ago? I thought that was – well – a lot of crap. Bravo!"

"Actually, sir," I said "without all of your contributions we could never have done it. Thank you again."

My two favorite mothers were also there: Betty Sicre and Pash-Pash Yehia. Although their older sons, my friends, Emile and Ahmed, had graduated, these two very different idols still had younger boys at school. Interestingly, both their first-born sons had won "Best Rosey Boy." The differences in the exceptional ladies' characters were clearly defined with what they had to say.

"Silvin," Betty began, "you've done better than I could have expected. I want you to know that I appealed to the powers that be a few years ago when they wanted to throw you out when the homosexual issue was raised. I did my best to clarify what happened and to bring them into the 20th century."

She had just uttered some very frightening and disturbing words, terms that made me break out in a cold sweat. I wish I could have responded more eloquently and forcefully to this exceptional, advanced lady. All I could manage to say was:

"Thank you, Betty. Some of my best memories include you." I kissed her on both cheeks.

Pash-Pash was more regal: "Whatever happens to you, never forget you have inner strength and good breeding. Nothing can substitute. Because I value that, I have introduced an award that will be given for the first time this year: Ahmed and I have called it 'le Prix de Solidarité.' Pay special attention. To us, it means 'the most likely to *overcome*.' Aly Pasha would have wholeheartedly endorsed this award."

While delivered majestically, her comments were clear. I had respected her late husband so much that my dream of possibly becoming "Best Rosey Boy" was eclipsed by the thought of being "most likely to overcome adversity." I kissed her hand. She grabbed and hugged me. As with a ruling monarch, I knew one responded to such unusual and overt actions respectfully. One never initiated exceptional gestures like this. If such an honor was offered, you acknowledged it humbly. I held her as strongly as I dared.

"Thank you, Pash-Pash," I said. "I only hope we will remain close as our paths separate."

"Geography is meaningless in our age," she concluded, "we will be together forever. And never forget Aziz, he needs your strength."

"I promise, Madame," I said bowing.

I was in a daze as the day progressed. During the awards ceremony, I sat at a table for four with my mother, brother and Liz in a shaded area in the middle of the gathered guests. Johannot stood on a platform and made many announcements, including the fact that, as of the following academic year, Le Rosey would become co-educational. Buildings had been acquired near both of the school's locations to house some 80 girls, ages 12 through 18.

He then read a list of college bound graduates and proceeded to the academic awards. Again, I was third among the Seniors academically. I rose and walked past other tables to receive a certificate. Johannot's behavior toward me was welcoming and pleasant. Much different from five years before, when he rushed me off the platform as I received the same honor.

The sports awards were preceded by a description of the rowing race in Bern. Again, I was called up to receive a medal. Before the end of this part of the event, I was asked to rise again for an "overall best athlete's" prize. Then Johannot distributed a few more unusual trophies. He explained the last one.

"The Yehia family has introduced a new prize this year. It is called "Le Prix de Solidarité." Madame Yehia suggested the recipient and we, in the director's office, approved the nominee. It will be given each year to the graduate who is the most likely to succeed and overcome adversities. The gift is a gold clock engraved with the distinction. It is presented to: ....Silvin!"

Again, I passed the gathered crowd to be presented with a box that contained the 60s looking modern clock. I cherish it to this day as it ticks away near my bed.

The ceremony was drawing to a close. It was time to announce the winner of *the* last award. Again, Johannot described "le Meilleur Roséen" in the same way as he introduced the voting procedure:

"If President Johnson asked us to send a representative of our school......"

He explained that equal weight was given to the three voting groups: teachers, students and employees. He concluded by saying:

Hector Verykios

"Something totally unprecedented has happened this year. The votes of all three groups were divided equally between two students. We have no choice but do something we never have done, which is to present the title to two boys this year. I call Hector Verykios and....Richard Silvin"

Hector was a friend with whom I had roomed during two terms. He was a solid and kind Greek boy, the son of his country's ambassador to Switzerland and later other European countries, including Great Britain. We both rose to collect the sets of cherished cufflinks.

The improbability of what Johannot had claimed did not register. I was delighted at the outcome and, by now, I was somewhat self-conscious and ready to leave school for the very last time as a student. People began to say their good-byes to friends, parents and teachers. Cars rolled up to collect various families. Countess Crespi kissed me, saying kind words as she and her family entered a Cadillac limousine.

I then noticed Mr. Radoszycki standing alone in a clearing nearby, looking in my direction, beckoning me with his facial expression.

"You know that I am completely committed to education at Le Rosey, do you not?" he began. Before I could reply he continued, "It is my intent to work here until I retire. I will always be loyal to the institution and the people who run it. Otherwise, I could not commit myself to the school. In spite of this, I am willing to tell you something which is so important that it could jeopardize my career."

This was all so strange, I thought. Where was this explanation, delivered by this heretofore straightforward and forthright teacher, going?

"Yes, I understand, Monsieur Radoszycki," I said, using the tone of my voice to implore a conclusion.

"Something has happened with the Meilleur Roséen award that I feel compelled to tell you," he proceeded. "There was no equal counting of three different sets of ballots. Think about that. It's impossible. Monsieur Johannot asked the teachers to vote twice urging us to alter our original choice. He felt that the school needed a representative other than you to leave here with the title. I would never live with myself if I did not tell you. I ask you to never repeat it as long as I am alive. Please honor me by calling me Max."

I walked away deep in thought, avoiding my family for a few minutes. It was clear: everything that happened at La Clairière and the horror of being "outted" as homosexual at Le Rosey was old, past history. The rowing victory was merely a symbol of recognition in a lifelong effort to surmount childhood goblins. In fact, even shared, the gold cufflinks were that as well. What I had just been told meant nothing to me, other than the reaffirmation that totally honest people like Max Radoszycki did exist.

I knew that prejudice reigns in the minds and actions of bigots but need not be taken personally. To do so would allow racists and extremists to win. This epiphany was:

the real victory

I never rowed in competitions again, I never once wore the Rosey cufflinks. I gave them to my brother who left them to me when he died. I never took the headmaster or his institution seriously and distanced myself from most alumni activities. I had won.

I was free to proceed with my life.

AFTERMATH

"You may weather the storm, but will you weather the aftermath?"

Anthony T. Hincks

I thank you gentle readers for sticking with my story until the end and apologize for having dragged you through this book's particularly dark Part One. Hopefully, you will agree that Part Three is an uplifting story. In the words of one of my more sympathetic readers:

"I was concerned, given the beginning of the book, that the remainder might be about someone wallowing in self-pity. However, the author clearly did NOT take that path; rather, he decided to take charge of his life and free himself."

After the original *I Survived Swiss Boarding Schools* was published in 2006, I received many letters, mostly from former Rosey boys and, luckily, from a few men who had attended La Clairière as children. One person who wanted to remain anonymous posted this heart-felt comment on Amazon:

"This book gave me insight into what my father might have experienced when he was a student at La Clairière back in the 1950's. He had told me on several occasions that he felt the school had ruined his life forever, but I never quite knew what he meant. After reading this book, I had a clearer picture of what he might have experienced there."

The few letters I received from former children at La Clairière were all eerily similar. Many, like I, had never spoken about that school's worst stories; neither to their parents or siblings when they were children, nor to their spouses once they were adults. One letter, from a well-known American personage, stands out and deserves paraphrasing to protect his identity:

"I didn't think La Clairière was as bad as you described," this former sensitive and kind child wrote me 60 years after leaving the school. "The worst thing that happened to me was when Monsieur Beauverre discovered my pet rabbit, snapped its neck, cooked it and made me eat it."

Trust me, my imagination is not vivid enough to invent this anecdote.

While I was writing the first version of this book in 2006, John Kerry had recently been the democratic nominee for president and, as was widely reported, the senior Massachusetts Senator was considering a second run for the nation's highest office. I happened to notice that, on his official website, he mentioned he had attended La Clairière for one year, during the same period as I. Given his high public profile, I felt it appropriate to notify his office that I was writing about the school, and that I planned on revealing some upsetting details. I never heard back from Senator Kerry, but the reference of having attended La Clairière was removed from his public chronology the day after I sent my email.

Le Rosey, with its then-120 students was considerably larger than La Clairière with its 30 children. Therefore, it is understandable that I received many more letters about Le Rosey than I did about La Clairière. I was heartened that nine out of ten letters received from Rosey alumni were extremely positive. Most former Roséens, as we refer to ourselves, were overwhelmingly supportive. A small minority chose to interpret the work as a direct assault on the school, which they consider their substitute family. Sadly, my brother fell into this group. His adversarial reaction started when I handed him the book in manuscript form. Before he had read any of it, his reaction was from the playbook of his Swiss banker "doctrine": Never reveal family secrets, especially scandals, which would be best left untold forever.

As a result of my only sibling's strong, negative reaction, I agreed not to promote the book and to just let it die out. In spite of this neglect, which was difficult for this new author whom, like all new authors, believed he had written a masterpiece, more copies were sold than I expected. Today, used copies of the original $14.95 book are frequently for re-sale on Amazon for several hundred dollars. This validated my belief there was a market for a re-written book, which was the genesis of this current effort.

I have observed that boys who spend many years in boarding schools fall into two distinct groups after graduation. Some, like I, decide to close and discard the figurative "book" and move on with their lives. Others, who have adopted the school as a family substitute, remain very attached to the institution. They serve on the alumni association, go on holidays together and develop an idealized set of memories from their childhood. This is cemented together due to the fact that Rosey boys are, by definition, a minority of their own, given the wealth they were exposed to and the unique education they received.

Since I love Gstaad, I did vacation there every year once I entered the business world. As a result, I would meet many Rosey teachers and some former students on the ski slopes, or in restaurants and cafés.

Palace Hotel seen from the village of Gstaad today

Furthermore, in the early 1980's when AMI, the company I worked for my entire career, decided to create a network of private hospitals in Switzerland, I moved back to the country of my roots. The corporate offices and my home were located in Lausanne, close to Rolle. If I were not travelling at the time of the annual, year-end *Fête Sportive*, I would attend the school's graduation event.

So it was that, in a pre-social media era, during mostly accidental meetings I was able to learn news about many of the people mentioned in this book. Please allow me to share their stories with you.

Antoinette Stickel died at the young age of 55 in 1978 of cardiac arrest. Shortly thereafter her widower husband, Charlie, whom I revered above all other Rosey teachers, remarried a Belgian lady and moved to Brussels. He died in 2010 at 88 years old.

Of all the teachers mentioned in this story, the Stickels remain among the few whom I carry in my heart to this day and feel lucky to have had in my early life. Of course, Carlo Mastelli and Max Radoszycki are the two others.

Carlo Mastelli died at 74 years old in 1992 and, like many of the teachers in my era, remained associated with the school until his death.

Similarly, Max Radoszycki taught at Rosey from 1961 until his retirement in 1999. He taught me many things, including giving me an early glimpse into what has only recently become commonly referred to as "election fraud." This compels me to have a special reverence for him. Max died at 80 years old in 2015 after a valiant struggle with cancer. Those fortunate students who, like I, revered him have described him as a mentor, savior and friend. Nicolas Ullmann one of Max's other ardent admirers said: "This was a man who never accepted mediocrity."

Obviously, both the lakeside town of Rolle and the ski resort of Gstaad have grown, albeit in a very controlled "Swiss way" of managing growth, while respecting their history and architecture. Gstaad's marvelous Palace Hotel has been modernized and expanded. A new five-star hotel, the Alpina, now stands on the site where a small, alpine-like hotel bearing the same name, existed during the time this story occurred.

Alpina Hotel, Gstaad

John Lear's story following his plane crash is best described in his own words:

"When I could walk again, I worked selling pots and pans door-to-door in Santa Monica," California, where his family lived. Now in his late 70s, he owns the only permitted gold mine operation in Clarke County, Nevada where he lives with Marlee, his wife of over 40 years.

I remained close to several of the mothers mentioned in the book. Marianne Alireza is still alive and lives in Jeddah, Saudi Arabia. She has recently celebrated her 96th birthday and is often surrounded by her four loving children. David and Bob Reynolds' lovely mother Jehanne marked her 98th birthday at her home in Gland, Switzerland in May of 2018. I remain in touch with both Mrs. Reynolds and her son, David, who is the executor of my estate.

Jehanne Reynolds, May 2018

David Reynolds 2018

The elegant, Pash-Pash Yehia lived on as a grand lady at her home in Istanbul, Turkey until her death in 2009, at the age of 80. Ahmed was by her side. She struggled with bi-polar depression for 30 years and managed to survive in spite of having lost her younger son, Aziz, to suicide in 1984. The sensitive and sweet Aziz left behind a very personal and detailed letter. Ahmed and I have remained close friends to this day.

Pash Pash Yehia, 1929-2009

Ahmed Yehia and René Silvin 2017

We worked together at AMI for 20 years, the New York Stock Exchange company which owned the world's largest and well-respected international chain of acute care hospitals.

Prince Shah Karim Al Hussaini, Aga Khan IV Born 1936

Prince Shah Karim Al Hussaini, Aga Khan IV, is the 49th and current Iman of Nizari Ismalism. Now 81, Forbes lists the Aga Khan as one of the world's 10 richest royals. As one of his many achievements, he has been a central figure in the independence of both African and Central Asian countries.

Princess Zahra Aga Khan Born 1970

His daughter, Princess Zahra Aga Khan, a former "Rosey girl" is now 47 years old and is the director of the Social Welfare Department of the family's "Secretariat" (foundation). She is also active on the Rosey Foundation board.

Mohammad Reza Pahlavi, the late and last Shah of Iran, ruled his country from 1941 until 1979 when he was overthrown during the Iranian Revolution. Within a few months, he was diagnosed with Waldenstrom's macroglobulinemia, a rare type of blood cancer. He was refused treatment in New York and instead was cared for in Egypt. Since the Shah's death, his widow, the exiled Empress Farah, has received many honors and awards for her work at numerous charities, notably the IFRAD (International Fund Raising for Alzheimer Disease). She lives in Washington, DC and Paris, France.

Shah of Iran 1919-1980

Empress Farah born 1938

The Woodward family all had tragic and dramatic ends. Ann (which is spelled Anne on her tombstone) and my father spent much of the 20 years following Bill Woodward's death together. Their main activities were hunting and pigeon shooting. Twenty years after killing her husband, Ann committed suicide by swallowing a cyanide pill. It is widely speculated that Truman Capote's book *Answered Prayers* was the catalyst for her final act of depression. The day of her death, she went to the hairdresser, retrieved some pieces of jewelry from a safe, and dressed in a designer evening gown before going to bed and consuming the poison. On her bedside table was a note simply saying, "Remember Ann Woodward."

In addition to the NBC miniseries *The Two Mrs. Grenvilles,* the 1966 all-star cast classic film *Madam X*, starring Lana Turner as Ann and Constance Bennett as Elsie, loosely parallels the Woodward drama.

John Léon Silvin, 1903-1990

When Elsie Woodward was told of Ann's suicide, she said: "She killed my only son and now she is dead. I guess that's the end of that."

Elsie died in her Waldorf Towers apartment in 1981 at the age of 98. She outlived her grandson Jimmy, but mercifully was spared knowing about the death of Woody.

Three people attended Ann Woodward's funeral in New York. This included my late mother. After Ann Woodward's death, my father stopped hunting and returned to live with my mother. They wintered in Boca Raton, Florida, and spent the summers in Vichy, France, near his former hunting preserve. He died in 1990 of lung cancer.

Nancy Silvin shortly before her death 1908-1993

As is somewhat customary with older, well-to-do South Florida widows, my mother abused sleeping pills and tranquilizers. Each summer, I would fire her doctor and take her to a clinic in Switzerland to rid her of the horrible addiction. Within a month of her return to America, her medicine cabinet was, once again, full of large bottles of tranquilizers and sleeping pills. She died of a stroke in 1993.

In her defense of taking my father back after his 20-year absence, one must consider her upbringing in an early 1900s, middle class, Italian-American household, where girls were taught to *obey* their husbands regardless of any abuse. However, several of her friends have repeatedly told me that having to obey her husband's command to put me in a boarding school at age seven was the heartbreak of her life.

Jimmy Woodward, 1946-1976

My two defacto-stepbrothers Jimmy and William (Woody) Woodward III, both also died prematurely by suicide. Jimmy served in Vietnam, where he became addicted to heroin. He told me that, in Vietnam, he practiced live-fire Russian roulette and was captured and tortured toward the end of the war. He barely survived his first suicide attempt when he jumped from the fourth floor of a New York City hotel in early 1976. After he was released from the hospital, he repeated the effort a few months later, this time succeeding by jumping from a higher floor's window. This story is recounted in Xaviera Hollander's book, *Xaviera,* in the chapter amusingly, but tragically titled: *Jimmy Don't Jump Again.*

William "Woody" Woodward III
1944-1999

William (Woody) Woodward suffered from manic-depression. When his illness allowed, he worked as a journalist and served as New York State's Deputy Superintendent of Banks. He married but was estranged from his wife and children when he jumped from the kitchen window of his 14th floor Manhattan apartment in 1999 at the age of 54.

Marlene Dietrich with grandsons Peter and Michael, 1957

Marlene Dietrich's long and brilliant career came to an end on September 29, 1975, when, during a performance in Sydney, Australia she fell off the stage and broke her hip. She spent much of the next 17 years secluded in her Paris apartment. She is buried in Berlin, Germany. Dignitaries, royalty and 1,500 friends and admirers attended her funeral. Her grandson, Michael Riva became a successful art director and production designer. He died from complications following a stroke while working on the film *Django Unchained*, in New Orleans in 2012 at the age of 63. His brother, Peter, who is also a Rosey boy, is a recognized literary agent and producer.

Alexander Onassis did not receive any formal education after his very brief stint at Rosey. Instead, a long line of instructors tutored him. He went on to become an accomplished pilot and ran the Olympic Aviation Company, which operated small planes flying between Athens and the Greek Islands. During this period, Alexander conducted numerous heroic-piloting acts while shuttling sick tourists back to Athens for treatment, usually in inclement weather. In January 1973, Alexander died following head injuries sustained during a plane crash while training new pilots. The plane being used was an amphibian aircraft his father, Aristotle Onassis, kept aboard his yacht, the Christina. Alexander was only 24 years old.

Athina Onassis Niarchos 1929-1974

Alexander Onassis 1949-1973

His mother, Athina "Tina" Livanos Onassis Niarchos died in 1974 under suspicious circumstances at her home in Paris at the age of 45. The official cause of death is a lung edema but is also believed to be from a drug overdose.

After divorcing Onassis and the Marquis of Blanford, she married Onassis' life-long archrival, who was also her brother-in-law, Stavros Niarchos.

Le Rosey continues to be referred to alternately as "the school for princes and kings" and the "most expensive school in the world." Both characterizations give an outsider a distorted and prejudicial opinion of the venerable institution. The school has always excelled in its international approach to education and its dedication to physical fitness. In recent years it has successfully added a cultural element to the overall curriculum.

Anne and Philippe Gudin

In the school's 138-year history it has only had four headmasters and three owners. The current owners, Anne and Philippe Gudin bought the school from Louis Johannot and several smaller shareholders in 1980. Philippe Gudin ran the school until five years ago when he passed the reins to his capable son, Christophe.

Christophe Gudin

The main campus in French-speaking Switzerland is still clustered around the 14th Century "Château du Rosey" in Rolle and has expanded to handle 420 students. The most impressive of the many new buildings is the Carnal Concert Hall designed by Bernard Tschumi, which opened in 2014. The school became coeducational in 1967 but the girls are housed at separate campuses.

The educational philosophy is based upon the principle of "multiple intelligences," meaning a combination of academic, sporting and cultural programs. The student body has undergone various changes in nationality over the decades. During the 1950's and 1960's a significant majority of the boys were American. By the 1970's Arab and Iranian students made up the largest groups. In the 1980's Japanese and Koreans were dominant, while

Russians briefly took that spot in the 1990's. This latter situation led to some challenges, which caused the school to adopt a "10% quota system" whereby no single nationality can comprise more than 10% of the student body.

Le Rosey Rolle today with concert hall upper left and the château upper right

The Gudin family had plans to sell the Gstaad campus and transfer the school's winter campus to the nearby Bernese town of Schönried, where the girls have been located for 40 years. Due to zoning complications and a successful campaign led by neighbors in Schönried, the plan is currently in abeyance.

After they sold the school to the Gudins, Louis and Mimi Johannot remained active in Rosey life. Louis and Mimi divorced in the early 1970's and both continued to live in Rolle, near the school. Monsieur Johannot died in 2009 at age 90 and Mimi passed away five years later in her mid-90s. Over the decades after graduation, I developed an understandably complex but, fortunately, positive relationship with both Johannots. I came to admire and understand Colonel Johannot's strict adherence to discipline. Although today we would view him as irrationally homophobic, such behavior was not uncommon in educators in the 1950s and 60s. If possible, Mimi became even more compassionate and loving as the years passed. I always delighted in being in her presence.

After the couple divorced, Mimi began working in Switzerland's health care sector, which offered me the opportunity to invite her to conferences in Geneva and Paris. We also visited Princess Marcella Borghese together on several occasions. At each soirée, the Princess' table would include famous names like designer Emilio Pucci, Revlon founder Charles Revson, and Brazilian plastic surgeon Ivo Pitanguy.

Baron Christian Louis de Massy has had 4 wives, bearing 3 children. He wrote *Palace: My Life in the Royal Family of Monaco.* He founded his company Monte Carlo Lifestyle in 2001, and lives in Miami, Washington, DC and Monte Carlo. Neither he nor his uncle, the late Prince Rainier ever returned to their *alma mater*, Le Rosey, after the baron left the school.

Shortly before I left Rosey, Joseph Zurcher married a delightful lady. She is credited with softening his hysteric homophobia and they had two children who are modern, productive members of Swiss society. Zuzu died in February 2016 at the age of 91, and his ashes are scattered in Gstaad.

Professor
Hans Björn Püttgen

Teddy Püttgen has gone on to have a brilliant career as one of Europe's most respected experts on energy. Today Professor Püttgen leads the prestigious Swiss Federal Institute of Technology in Lausanne, Switzerland.

Kelvin Vanderlip

Kelvin Vanderlip lives in the family's ancestral home, Villa Narcissa, referred to as the "only hidden gem in the South Bay." He loves being in Aspen, and enjoys flying and antique cars, and is what I consider a modern-day renaissance man.

Tom Pierpoint

After Tom Pierpoint graduated from Carnegie-Mellon and NYU, he had an illustrious career as an aerospace computer scientist. One of his early accomplishments was as a key member in the team that developed what has become today's GPS. Before retiring in 2013 he worked with the Swiss air force, developing their F-18 fighter jet missions. He lives in Southern California with his long-term partner, Dana. Together they raised 2 sons, and currently have 3 grandsons and 4 great-grandchildren. He visits Switzerland regularly and, arguably, more than any other member of the team, has remained loyal and connected to Le Rosey.

Ron Agerev co-founded a wealth management company and has been very active in various boys' clubs.

BOOK TWO

Walking the Rainbow

All That Glitters Is Not Gold

To the loving memory of my angel, Robert D.

Mann Ph.D.

...and to all the other innocent victims whose full lives and brilliant careers were prematurely and cruelly aborted.

Part 1

INNOCENCE

1976 – 1981

Aboard the SS France, 1974

Chapter One

September 3, 1976

Beverly Hills, California

I stood outside one of the few tall office buildings in Beverly Hills with an energized sense of both anticipation and elation. At age 28 I had successfully negotiated the sale of my father-in-law's bankrupt hospital design company to American Medical International, Inc. (AMI). AMI was the first company in a relatively new industrial group called "investor-owned hospital corporations" and was one of three hospital companies listed on the New York Stock Exchange. The others were Humana — before it transformed itself into an insurance company — and Hospital

René working with a government architect in Germany

Corporation of America (HCA) founded by Tommy Frist, the father of Bill Frist, who went on to become Senate Majority Leader.

Over the previous five weeks, AMI's Chief Executive Officer Royce Diener and I had negotiated the sale to AMI of my father-in-law's small but well-respected firm. I had tried to "peddle" the firm to several other companies that seemed to represent a good fit, including consortium members with whom we had successfully collaborated on large projects. Our declining sales and deteriorating balance sheet turned out to be a consistent roadblock in our exploratory conversations with architectural and construction companies, with whom we had teamed up, building hospitals in the United States, France, England and Germany.

In a "last creative gasp," I went to the Library of Congress in Washington, D.C., not far from our corporate office, and asked to see the annual reports of the three publicly traded hospital companies. Five years of reports were available for each company, and I promptly spread all 15 reports out on a large desk and read them carefully. It was clear that one company, AMI, had initiated a strategy to expand internationally, beginning with the UK, and was interested in telling its shareholders how many communities it served. That figure had progressed from 20 to 35 communities and finally, in 1976, to 50.

Our little company served 200 communities in three countries. While we did not own facilities, we consulted at many prestigious hospitals on both design and management challenges. The company's founder, my father- in-law, was in deep denial about our precarious financial condition. He was equally oblivious to the fact that, in the U.S., the funds allocated to hospital construction projects under an act of congress called "Hill-Burton" had dried up, seriously impeding our major source of revenue. Our 60 consultants and architects had dwindled to an overworked 40 and we were on Cash On Delivery (COD) terms with all our suppliers. On numerous occasions I would fly to clients literally begging for payments to be made because my payroll was due the following day.

Our lines of credit were extended because I had managed to obtain a design-and-management contract to run The American Hospital of Paris. In prior years the hospital had been considered one of the world's most respected and well-known hospitals, and our mission was to prepare a plan for a phased expansion of the antiquated facility. Living in Paris and working at The American Hospital, I traveled to Cologne, Germany, every week to participate in team meetings relating to the construction of a 1,000 bed, ultra-modern new University hospital. Unfortunately, these two lucrative projects were not sufficient to cover the large losses incurred by the American side of the company, so we faced bankruptcy and foreclosure.

After reading the 15 annual reports of the investor-owned hospital companies, I summoned up all my youthful courage and called AMI's CEO.

My heart pounded as the phone rang. "AMI. How may I direct your call?"

"Ah, I'd like to speak to Mr. Diener, please," I said sheepishly.

"One moment please."

Another anxious moment while I heard a phone ring.

"Mr. Diener's office," said a soft yet professional voice.

"May I speak with Mr. Diener?" I inquired.

I looked across my desk at my partner, Ahmed Yehia, a childhood friend who had recently returned from a three-year stint at Proctor and Gamble where he had been a young product manager in the foods division. Amazingly, he personally committed to try to salvage me, the company and my in-laws from bankruptcy and possible legal reprisals due to what our bankruptcy attorney had called "irresponsible misuse of creditor's funds."

The phone rang again.

Royce Diener, 1976

I heard a deep, highly confident voice.

"This is Royce Diener."

I stared at Ahmed in astonishment, fully expecting to have been stopped well before actually speaking with a man of such relative importance.

"Mr. Diener, my name is Rick Silvin and I am the President of Friesen International in Washington, D.C. Thank you in advance for taking my call," I said, hoping that the trembling in my voice was not overly apparent.

"I know of your company. You fellows beat us on the American Hospital of Paris contract. What can I do for you?" he replied pleasantly. Again, I looked at Ahmed and shrugged my shoulders as if to say, 'he actually wants to talk to us!'

"Mr. Diener, I see that you are leading AMI into becoming an international health care services company, penetrating as many communities as possible," I said, still gazing at Ahmed in shock.

"Yes. How do you know that?" he asked.

"I took the time to dig into and interpret your last three annual reports," I said, gaining a tiny bit of confidence.

"Mmm, interesting. So, again, how can I help you?" he repeated.

The biggest moment for Ahmed and I, since we had obtained MBAs from Harvard and Cornell University respectively five years earlier, had arrived.

"We are working on several hospital projects in Europe, sir. Our corporate brochure highlights the fact that *we* serve 200 communities." There was a prolonged silence.

I continued, "We are looking for a strategic alliance with a bigger, reputable company so that we may pursue larger, lucrative contracts in the Middle East," I said, my voice still shaky. "I'd like to come to Beverly Hills and explain myself in more detail. But, sir, I must put up-front the fact that we have gotten ahead of ourselves and are experiencing a severe cash flow problem."

That was code for "we're broke."

During the ensuing month, I shuttled back and forth to Los Angeles as a deal to acquire our floundering company was formulated. At one meeting, I handed my new hero a list of seven criteria to acquire the company. Six of these would handle the honoring of aging payables, irresponsible pledges to Universities and charities and delinquent accounts, plus enough money for my father-in-law to retire comfortably. The seventh item on the page read:

"R. R. Silvin will stay for six months to train any manager AMI puts in charge of the company."

Diener had the paper in his hands and reviewed it in his careful manner. His handsome sun-tanned face showed no emotion. His pure white hair on a relatively youthful visage gave him a distinguished look of self-assurance.

"I'll not further negotiate the terms," he began. I could hardly believe my ears. Then he added, "Six items are accepted in their entirety, but item number seven is rejected."

I was dumbstruck. All I wanted was to extricate myself from a miserable and humiliating business and family experience. There was also a different hope — to achieve another kind of freedom. I knew I was gay, and I wanted to "come out." I believed that establishing financial independence for my in-laws would also be the time to explain my sexuality. I assumed that I would have to vanish and start life over again in a different business sector, and probably a different country.

"You'll work for AMI for five years and report to me, or there is no deal, Rick," he said. "It will take at least that long to see the emergence of a substantial international department."

"That's impossible, sir. I simply can't." "Why?" he

demanded.

"I cannot deal with one more creditor," I said firmly. "Do you realize that I get threatening calls at home in the middle of the night demanding payment for one financial obligation or another?"

Diener laughed aloud and picked up a phone.

"Get me accounts payable," he ordered. "Yes, this is Royce Diener. Cut a check to Friesen International for $225,000 and book it as an advance on the acquisition. Bring it to my office right away."

He turned to me adding,

"That will carry you over until the deal is finalized. After which, there will be a new accounting department which will handle all your payables, including the payroll. You will never *ever* speak to a single creditor again. I promise," he affirmed.

"There is another . . . errr . . .problem, Royce," I added. We had advanced to a first-name basis during the negotiations.

"I am gay and will be coming out of the closet…"

After thinking a while Royce began,

"I'm a Californian conservative." I imagined our deal flying out the window. "That means I am fiscally conservative and socially liberal. You are discrete and will be a fine representative for our new international division. You have not told me anything more significant than if you had said you were a vegetarian."

I so wanted to jump up and kiss him, but I restrained myself.

I was raised in homophobic Swiss boarding schools, and at 28 was tired of perpetrating the hoax of pretending I was straight. I had married while living a serious lie. It never occurred to me that any business executive I knew might comprehend all these parameters, be prepared to put them into perspective, *and* ask me to represent him professionally in a conservative industry. I wondered if I was dreaming. This new reality was simply beyond my wildest hopes and expectations. Ahmed and I, two young bucks, had successfully saved a family from bankruptcy and a company from disgrace while honoring all its debts.

....

I looked up at the modern ten-story black AMI building as the previous five weeks flashed through my mind. Today was *the big day* — the day of the signing of my first Securities-and-Exchange-controlled transaction, a deal that would end several years of horrendous financial and emotional hardship. I rode the elevator to the top floor and entered the wood-paneled lobby. I was friendly with the secretarial staff and knew all the senior executives — some of whom viewed me as a curious threat. I would be reporting directly to the Chief Executive, even though initially I would "only" carry the title of Vice President. This represented an unusual break with traditional reporting lines, because I would bypass the higher layers of Executive and Senior Vice Presidents.

I walked into the large board room. A huge custom-made wood table occupied the entire space. A door at the far end of the room led to a kitchen where a uniformed French chef attended to the needs of participants of meetings and served meals enjoyed by a select few elite guests. Some 20 piles of paper were neatly stacked along the periphery of the table, each requiring both my and Diener's signatures. Royce emerged from his office in a fashionable white suit. He smiled and put out his hand to congratulate me.

"Well, let's get this thing done. We should rejoice! After all, the lawyers nearly killed it several times in just a month," he said, laughing.

I had bought a flashy pen that I removed from my pocket along with a pack of Rothman cigarettes. I lit one with a DuPont lighter my aunt had given me ten years earlier. We each greeted several attorneys who had prepared the numerous documents. These included a stock-purchase agreement, a generous retirement package for my father-in-law, an employment contract, and settlement agreements to George Washington University (where Freisen had pledged $250,000 for a chair in Hospital Administration), another settlement agreement to The Kennedy Center in Washington, D.C. (for its building fund), plus several SEC required documents.

I followed Royce as we signed each pile of papers, feeling so relieved and excited about the future. I wondered what "gift" I might buy myself to celebrate. I did not need a car, as Royce had already bought me a new green 12-cylinder Jaguar XJS. I certainly could not envision a trip because I would be traveling constantly as of the following Monday.

Suddenly, unpremeditated, I settled on two "gifts." One was healthy and the other definitely was not.

At the far end of the table, I crushed my cigarette into a Venetian glass ash tray and threw the nearly full pack of cigarettes into a trash bin.

"What's that about, Rick?" asked Royce.

"That's my gift to myself for completing the transaction," I replied proudly.

We both laughed.

"Great idea," he added.

I did not tell him what I chose as my second "gift." That night, after a celebration dinner, I would go to Los Angeles' largest bath house for the first time. The moment had finally come for me to begin to get a life.

Chapter Two

1977

Pines Harbor, Fire Island, NY

Slip #1 at the Pines Harbor
Fire Island, NY

During my first year at AMI, I traveled constantly between Washington, D.C., Beverly Hills, and Europe and, for fun, The Fire Island Pines. My boat was moored there in slip # 1, one of only four deep-water docks.

I scheduled my business trips so that I could spend a few nights every month on the slick new twin-engine Sea Ray, "Les Beaux." The name was a takeoff on the delightful French village in Provence of *Les Baux*. It translates as "The good-looking ones." I *was* good looking, young and had more disposable income than I had ever imagined. Importantly, I had not previously experienced any sexual act I enjoyed and, in the late 1970's, The Pines was a gay man's sexual Mecca. I dove in!

If I were transiting through New York, I'd fly into The Pines on the sea plane from Manhattan. If I could steal a night or two from Washington, a newly inaugurated non-stop flight from Washington National into McArthur Field in Islip was miraculously available. I worked hard and played just as hard. The contrast invigorated me and fed into the desire to do each distinct activity to the fullest and to the best of my abilities.

I had befriended a handsome young hustler in Washington who

"serviced" several members of Congress, and who was at the center of a secretive web of young men who earned their living similarly and which, later, became known as the "Capitol Hill Page Scandal." David was breathtakingly sexy and would meet me at one or the other jumping points to go over to Fire Island. If we arrived during daylight, he would lay on the bow of the boat as people gawked in awe of his muscular body and handsome face. Sitting at The Boatel's bar, every man there was willing — and delighted — to have several drinks with us.

Late night substance-enhanced parties took place on the boat daily. Whenever we "surfaced for air," we would enchant guests with stories of our previous week's adventures. David talked of his outrageous sexual experiences with Washington celebrities who were allegedly straight, and I revealed stories of my international travels. We were part of "the A group" and we enjoyed every second.

I knew most of the owners of the boats on the "gay side" of The Pines harbor. We all ate and partied together. On several occasions we were irresponsible, and we miraculously escaped severe injuries or fatalities. It was not unusual for a party boy to fall off a boat while skipping from one cocktail party to another. One night, after a drunken dinner on a neighbor's boat I was dared to "plane" my vessel and cross the sandbar between Sayville and The Pines. When a boat accelerates, the bow raises. At higher speeds it may plane, thus flattening out and drawing (requiring) less depth. At the very most, only a few inches of water would be the difference between a foolish adventure and brutal injuries. Giggling in the wee hours of the morning, I maneuvered out of the harbor and pushed both throttles to their maximum. Many barely clad men stood on the bow in an attempt to make the boat plane which, inexplicably, it did, while no innocent clam boat stood in our path.

But there was another phenomenon gradually occurring: a few of the most energetic all-night dancers were complaining of uncharacteristic fatigue and were returning to their boats or hotel rooms early. They all had one oddity in common — swollen lymph nodes in their necks, groins or under their arms.

Washington, D.C.

Back in my Georgetown office in Washington, D.C., Ahmed and I were hard at work trying to revive the company with the new capital at our disposal. We learned that, if well justified, Royce Diener approved all our business development plans, as well as appropriate additions to the professional staff.

Several oil-rich Middle Eastern countries, notably Kuwait and Saudi Arabia, were in a race to develop their national infrastructure. That always included the construction of hospitals and, in some cases, complete hospital networks. We carefully monitored international "requests for proposals" (RFP) for every aspect of hospital development in the region and noticed that American firms were being left behind by the large European consortiums.

We concluded there were two reasons for that: a lack of a proven track record, and a new law enacted by President Jimmy Carter. The "Foreign Business Corruption Act" of 1977 was intended to "add morality" to business conducted by American companies overseas. Now that we were a division of a New York Stock Exchange company, it was of primary importance for us to strictly comply with this new, restrictive law.

We knew, however, that the European consortiums had no such limitations and, worse, several Western European governments actually underwrote the substantial development costs which we all had to incur directly during the many months of studying for and, ultimately, bidding on these projects.

One of the most lucrative and, therefore, hotly pursued contracts, was for the development of a health care plan for the country of Kuwait. Ahmed and I studied the RFP and prepared a proposal for Royce Diener's approval, which would allow us to compete with the usual front-runners. I brought the completed document to Beverly Hills and presented it to him.

"This is a significant amount of money, Rick," he said after careful review of the plan, which included several months of a development team's time and overseas expenses, the preparation of elaborate demographic studies, maps and hospital models. "There are no guarantees you will be successful. In fact, American companies typically have not been awarded these contracts."

"That's true, Royce," I replied, "but, a job like this will not only double our division's annual revenues and catapult us into profitability. But more importantly, it will position AMI to get the much larger hospital management contracts in the area which will be awarded over the next few years. And besides, Royce, we have a secret weapon."

“Oh, really, and what exactly is that?” he inquired.

“His name is Ahmed Yehia,” I replied as Royce smiled. “As you know, prior to the Egyptian revolution, Ahmed’s father was an enormously influential businessman in the region and is still known to many of the leaders and decision makers for his world view and integrity. We believe that, while this is insufficient to *get* the contract, it creates context and affinity that will be sufficient to get us in the door, to be heard and be judged on our merit. With the funds described in this proposal, we will produce a crackerjack plan to present to the Kuwaiti Minister of Health.”

Jaber Al Ahmad Al Sabah, Hospital Kuwait, part of AMIs master plan

“You are, of course, aware that three seats of my five- member Executive Committee are held by Jews?” he said, staring at me with a stoic and wise look.

“For now, they will be dealing with Ahmed and me. We’ll have this discussion again if we are lucky enough to reach the stage of bidding for the management contracts once the hospitals are built.”

“You know that if you are not successful, these expenses will create a serious loss for the year. You will not reach your projections and your credibility may well be irreparably painted.”

“Yes, I do, sir,” I said, understanding what was implied.

“Good luck and keep me closely informed,” he said, standing and ending our meeting.

During much of the rest of 1977, Ahmed stayed in Kuwait with his revolving team of expert demographers, consultants, architects and model builders. I visited periodically until, in late November, to the surprise of the huge international construction consortiums, we were awarded the contract to set up the country's master health care plan, which would include the development and construction of six major, modern hospitals.

In early December I received a call from Royce.

"Rick, I want you and Ahmed to move to AMI headquarters in Beverly Hills. The consulting division can now stand on its own. Ahmed will oversee the Kuwait project from here. But I need you in Beverly Hills to begin the development of an international network of hospitals. Bring whoever is essential for Ahmed. We'll gather a team for international development here."

"When do you actually want me to move?" I asked, looking at a pile of drawings, papers and contracts on my desk.

"As far as I know, there are many seats available on several flights tomorrow." The phone went dead.

I stared out at the Potomac River and the newly finished Kennedy Center. I recalled how we had struggled to survive on shoe-string budgets while our now-retired founder had vowed to contribute $50,000 for the Kennedy Center's construction. Given our precarious financial position, it was an embarrassing pledge that AMI had honored. By doing so, Royce had earned my respect and appreciation for life, as I had the added perk of using a private waiting room reserved for large contributors during intermissions at Kennedy Center performances.

I knew that my days as a hospital design and management consultant were over, and I wondered what life in a rapidly growing large corporate structure would be like. Importantly, I would be involved in the acquisition and construction of hospitals our company *owned* — a huge difference from consulting for municipalities and governments with no long-term accountability. While I had managed one U.S. government-supported hospital in Paris, would I be able to run a new hospital network of "for profit" hospitals? Where would they be and how would we be viewed by our host governments? These challenges swirled around in my head.

There would also be an exciting and pleasurable additional change to savor . . . living in one of the centers of the gay world during its "sexual revolution."

Later that night, Royce called again.

"Rick, remember those available seats on the plane I spoke of earlier?"

"Of course," I replied. "I'll be in Beverly Hills Monday morning. My secretary will take care of packing up my apartment and sending my gear out later."

"You'll need to change those plans. I want you in London Monday to meet Stanley, AMI's General Manager in London, and travel to Switzerland together with him. We'll rent your condominium in Washington from you to serve as a corporate residence. Naturally, I will disclose this in the 10K, and it will have to be at market rates," concluded the ever ethically mindful Chief Executive, who would never have knowingly violated his fiduciary responsibility to AMI's shareholders.

Chapter Three

1978

London, England & Lausanne, Switzerland

AMI had recently made a significant investment in London, England, when it acquired the famous Harley Street Clinic from Doctor Stanley Balfour-Lynn. His new role was managing director of International Operations, and he also reported to Mr. Diener. Royce put Stanley and me in touch to investigate a possible expansion of private hospitals onto the European continent. Initially, I had some reservations about meeting the debonair, allegedly severe and demanding physician turned hospital entrepreneur.

After a wild weekend on Les Beaux at The Pines, I boarded a British Airlines Concorde and flew to London. Stanley sent his uniformed chauffeur with his Rolls Royce to the airport to bring me to what would become one of my "homes away from home," Claridge's Hotel on Brooke Street. The following morning, the same dignified driver was waiting in front of the hotel to bring me to meet the mysterious Doctor Balfour-Lynn.

Upon arrival at AMI's luxurious offices on Wimpole Street, a block away from The Harley Street Clinic, I was escorted into his grand office. It was magnificently decorated with British antiques. A large, carved wood fireplace mantle dominated the room, and tall floor-to-ceiling windows made the space bright and cheery. Stanley's huge desk in a far corner was bare of the typical stacks of paper and boasted a very visible sign that read, "IT CAN BE DONE."

Doctor Stanley Balfour-Lynn

Stanley was reviewing his correspondence with his male secretary, Jeffery. The amusing procedure consisted of Jeffery opening each letter with a silver letter opener, showing it to his almighty boss, who would then, most often, order the document to be placed in a shredder located next to Jeffery. From time to time, Stanley would dictate a response and proceed with the show.

After a few seconds of my witnessing this ritual, Stanley rose to greet me. He was immaculately groomed in a well-tailored blue suit, a monocle hanging from his neck. Although balding in his late 50s, his skin was youthful, as were his movements.

"Lovely to meet you. Mind if I have a manicure while we chat," he said rather than asked. A manicurist was already seated and waiting with her utensils at a table in the opposite end of the office.

I instantly liked the extravagant gentleman and knew that we would become great friends. His theatrics were both obviously superficial and very amusing. Equally apparent was his brilliance and gusto for excitement. While I intuitively knew we would do our best for AMI's European endeavors, I had no idea of how much fun we would have and how profitable our efforts would ultimately become.

While I sat across the table from Stanley and his beautician, we discussed the reason for my visit. We were going to Lausanne, Switzerland to see a historic, closed, previously grand hotel in the middle of the city.

Between the ages of seven and 18, I had attended Swiss Boarding Schools near Lausanne. In a way, I was going back to my roots and people I understood. We checked into what would become another of my new "homes" — the Lausanne Palace Hotel, a few blocks away from the boarded-up Hotel Cecil. During my childhood, the grand old building was an operative but dilapidated hotel. It was now an embarrassment to the city. While it dominated a beautiful hill overlooking Lake Geneva and Evian, France, off in the distance, it had not been maintained in a fashion which attracted wealthy tourists who preferred two other local hotels: the Lausanne Palace and The Beau Rivage at Lausanne's lake-side section of Ouchy.

AMI had previously entered into an agreement to acquire the property, subject to certain conditions we were examining. After two days of inspections with Lausanne's preeminent architect, Pierre Jacqerot, and meetings with an attorney who had worked on obtaining approval for the foreign investment, we decided to proceed with the acquisition. Believing that a change of venue would create some mental clarity, we left Lausanne to overnight at the new President Hotel in Geneva before boarding separate flights the following morning.

After dinner, we went to the hotel's bar for a night-cap where we met two men. One would become my friend and partner to this day, and the other would interject a practically unnoticed detail that would alter the future of health care over the following decades. While ordering drinks, a short unusual-looking, bearded, well-dressed hotel executive entered the bar and introduced himself.

"Good evening, gentlemen, my name is Jean-Claude Salamin, and I am the hotel's night manager. How do you like your accommodations?"

"The new hotel is adequate," said Stanley in his fashion of distancing himself from "employees."

"Without being indiscrete," continued Jean-Claude, undeterred, "may I ask what the nature of your business is here in Switzerland?"

"We represent a company that owns and operates hospitals," I answered, observing Stanley's discomfort at being questioned. "In fact, we are considering buying an old hotel with the intention of turning it into an acute-care hospital."

"May I ask which hotel?"

"The Hotel Cecil in Lausanne," I said.

"That's rather amusing. I live in Lausanne and am very familiar with the magnificent building and its unusual story. It is rather tragic that such a piece of Switzerland's history has fallen into disrepair and disgrace. I can imagine that monument restored to its former magnificence. But you said a 'hospital.' I do not understand."

"I owned an old hospital lodged in the center of London," interjected Stanley. "Our company restored and transformed it into an up-to-date hospital. We believe that the same efforts can make that old hotel into a first-class hospital."

"We have a few obvious problems," I said.

"Again, might I query what those are?" asked Jean- Claude in his nearly perfect, yet heavily French-accented English. His charming blue eyes twinkled in the dimly lit bar.

"Well, the first is management," I said. "There are no graduate schools of hospital administration in Switzerland, and we plan to operate our hospitals based on sound, yet locally adapted, American hospital management techniques."

"The second?" inquired Jean-Claude.

"We are not sure the Swiss system of private healthcare is ready for a well-equipped, acute, highly technical hospital," I said.

"Well, I'll take the second concern first," answered a super-confident Jean-Claude. "If you create the finest private hospital in the Canton of Vaud, it cannot miss. But it has to be the *very best* run, equipped and promoted. We are an overly insured population and supplementary, private hospitalization policies are common here. No one has adequately filled that need. As for the second concern of finding an appropriate manager, I am your man! You can teach me these 'American hospital management techniques' — no problem."

Stanley and I looked at each other wondering if we had met a complete nut or encountered one of the very best coincidences of our lives. The latter turned out to be the case.

"Excuse me, Messieurs," interjected a Frenchman sitting close by. "I am a physician from Paris. Perhaps we have something in common."

"What is your specialty?" asked Stanley.

"I am a pulmonologist," he replied. "I am here in Geneva to inform certain authorities of a bizarre circumstance we have observed in Paris. Two women of the night have died of a rare and heretofore curable form of pneumonia. Speaking vulgarly, they were drowned by protozoa we all have in our lungs, but which healthy immune systems can control. So bizarre!"

I wanted to inquire how exactly a "healthy immune system" was defined and how it was measured. But, understandably, the Frenchman's prophesy was of far less interest to us than our

Harvey Milk and George Mosconi

immediate business concerns that night in 1978.

Flying back to Washington, I read about the murders of Harvey Milk and George Mosconi in San Francisco. Harvey Milk was the first openly gay elected city official. He had run for a seat on San Francisco's city council on several occasions, each time gaining more votes and support. His rational "no nonsense" approach to campaigning had gradually positioned him as a champion not only gay rights, but for all human rights. He was serving his first term with another human rights advocate, Diane Feinstein. The city's Mayor, George Mosconi, was working closely with them to address what they saw as an alarming trend. The previous years any progress towards gay equality in America had been halted due to the political climate.

A disturbed anti-gay conservative member of the San Francisco city council, Dan White, had abruptly resigned his seat. When he asked to be reinstituted, Mayor Mosconi had refused to make an exception to the law and allow it. The enraged White had entered City Hall, shot and killed both the Mayor and Harvey Milk. The gay community was in deep grief. Many feared that we had lost our hope to identify a "Martin Luther King type" of leader, who could galvanize the community and create a national awareness of the discrimination gay men and women had endured for decades.

The gay community had made some inroads in achieving some acceptance after the Stonewall Inn riot in Greenwich Village in 1969. That event marked a change from silently enduring prejudice and discrimination, to demanding the rights offered all Americans under the Constitution. The violent late-night demonstrations occurred at one of those odd crossroads of history when many elements had come together to explode into a major event. Unfortunately, in the ensuing decade much of the progress which was evident after Stonewall had deteriorated. Milk and his colleagues were working on reversing the conservative trend. His main crusade was to protect gay San Franciscans from being fired or denied lodging based on their sexual orientation.

The article I was reading enumerated several of Milk's requests, notably a demand that all gay Americans "come out." His position was that, as long as we hid our true selves and sexuality, we encouraged repression and discrimination. That idea became a requirement in my mind, and I decided to follow the slain civil rights advocate's appeal. I decide to come out to my parents.

The Stonewall riots, June 27, 1969

Chapter Four

1979

Los Angeles, California

My first year working in Los Angeles was a great learning experience both personally and professionally. At work, I had to quickly become skilled at surviving in an expanding, publicly traded company surrounded by many ambitious and some ruthless executives. I called the corporate office "the shark tank." Similarly, my personal life was completely different from my previous days. In Washington, D.C. I was an obsessed workaholic, wedged in a challenging space between despair and hope, and whose sole focus was to keep a small, fledgling company from tipping into a black hole. I had not learned anything at graduate school that could guide me during such adversity. Ahmed and I ran the business by "the seat of our pants," creating a *modus operandi* week by week, to find ways to meet our payroll.

As Royce had predicted, those days were completely over. While I worked and traveled more hours a week than anyone I knew, I was exhilarated. More importantly, perhaps, there were obvious fruits to our efforts. We were able to define strategies and set actions into motion to accomplish them. It took me a few years to confidently believe the long-term projects we began would actually become realities. I had become too accustomed to setbacks due to lack of funds and fighting windmills that never stopped turning for long.

AMI's Chief Operating Officer, Wally Weisman, was an understandable and ominous obstacle from the start. It was unprecedented for a Vice President with profit and loss responsibility to report "around" a senior officer to the Chief Executive. Royce was the quintessential internationalist and Renaissance man. He knew that the flexibility needed to create a network of hospitals in disparate countries presented challenges that the black-and-white thinking and unworldly Wally could not comprehend. While I tried to keep Weisman informed about my activities, a feeling of tension and visceral mistrust gradually emerged. It was clear to me from the beginning that my life at AMI was limited to Royce's tenure as its Chief Executive.

My large corner office at the AMI building in Beverly Hills was only a mile from West Hollywood with its trendy gay bars. Most evenings after work, I would drop by one of these gathering spots, usually Rage or The Revolver, for drinks while I watched the handsome, young men I nicknamed MDA's. This was a "*jeux de mots*" (play on words) of "model, dancer, actors" and also the name of the new sex-enhancing drug that many of these beauties used.

On Saturday nights I would dance at Studio One, the largest gay bar I had ever seen or imagined. Located a few blocks from Rage, it occupied two floors in a large warehouse-type structure. The dance floor was about 6,000 square feet, and by midnight it was jammed with men. The best disc jockeys played the latest disco music while we danced, usually shirtless. I felt a compelling desire for emotional connection with a view toward creating a special lifestyle of my own choosing. Several "regulars" looked more like world-class athletes and moved more like Olympic gymnasts than dancers in other bars. The music was so loud that one could literally feel it pounding through one's entire body. As the night wore on, the sexual tension rose exponentially.

I rarely asked anyone to dance. Instead, I would either simply take the arm of a young man standing nearby and guide him onto the pulsating floor, squeezing through sweaty young men, or I would begin dancing alone. Before long one or more guys would join me, usually to dance for several hours. Both techniques worked more often than not.

Tracy

One Saturday night, while standing on the narrow side pathways along the dance floor looking for a partner, I saw Tracy. His large green-blue eyes sparkled from a handsome black face with shortly cropped hair. His smile was youthful and radiated a happy innocence that was hypnotic. His football player-like smooth, shiny torso did, in fact, hypnotize me. We danced that Saturday night until closing, after which we went to my penthouse condominium on Ocean Avenue in Santa Monica, which had been professionally decorated and furnished while I was in Switzerland.

We quickly developed a curious and happy sexual relationship. Tracy was a graduate student at USC (the University of Southern California) and had a part-time job. Busy and secure as we both were, neither one called or saw the other during the week. We met at Studio One every Saturday and spent the night in Santa Monica. Then Sunday mornings we would part ways after brunch at a fashionable breakfast place somewhere on the West Side of town.

Most Sunday afternoons, after Tracy returned to his dormitory, I would walk the short distance from my apartment to Royce's impressive beachfront home. We sat by the pool or played paddle tennis. As day turned to evening, we ate cheese and fruit and sipped quality wines from Royce's well-stocked wine cellar. He never questioned me about my life away from work, nor did he interrogate me about office politics. My admiration, respect and love for him grew weekly.

Eastern Long Island, New York

Against Ahmed's advice, I decided to follow Harvey Milk's request and explain my sexuality to both my parents and a dear lady, Nonnie, who had been a huge influence in my very early years.

I began with her, in part, because I was most concerned about her ability to grasp the concept of homosexuality and, conveniently, she lived in Islip, Long Island, near the ferry docks to Fire Island.

I drove to her modest home near the village's Town Hall. Each visit I recalled with joy the happy times I spent in this small dwelling during most of my first six years while my parents lived in Europe. Nonnie and her husband "Mr. Lee" were poor but very loving. When I was a child, Nonnie tenderly bathed me in only a few inches of warm water to conserve energy. Any sense of security I have, emerged during those years and from their simple, but flawless logic.

Upon my arrival, Nonnie would always serve me tea in one of the cups I routinely sent her from a foreign country to add to her cherished China collection. Each cup sat atop a piece of the packaging in which it had arrived, with the stamps, so that she could easily recall

René at 3 years old with Nonnie

its country of origin. I walked up the three red brick front steps where I had sat for many hours as an infant and knocked on the door. Obviously, Nonnie was ready for my arrival and had our little party all set up. Nothing was different that day, but I feared the discussion certainly would be. Instead of entertaining her with my usual tales of international travel and business, I would have to "come out of the closet."

After gently easing herself into her well-worn rocking chair I began.

"Nonnie, you *do* know how much I love you, right?"

"Ayun," she affirmed, in her usual way of saying yes.

"Well, I fear that I have been hypocritical with you."

"There is not a lying cell in your body, René," she began, using my middle name, which everyone had called me during my childhood. "You were as good as gold when you lived here, and I'll not be believing anything else." She chuckled and rocked back and forth in her chair.

"Nonnie, I am homosexual." I spat out the words before my courage disappeared. "Do you know what that means?"

"Oh, sure, René, I know all about gay men," she replied to my complete astonishment. "I watch Phil Donahue right there on that television every day."

I laughed aloud as I noticed a frown appear on her face and watched her formulate her next sentences carefully.

"I am concerned about one thing, René. I never taught you a single thing about cooking and keeping house. I guess I should 'of.' I wonder about who will be taking care of you and prepare your food?"

My laughter turned into tears of joy as I jumped up and hugged her fragile body as tightly as I dared without hurting her.

The rest of the visit proceeded exactly as was the custom. When it was time to leave, she walked me the few feet to the front door, kissed me and said: "Good as gold, René. You just always remember that. Good as gold," and she wiggled the "life-line" buzzer hanging from her neck. It allowed her to continue living alone with confidence since her recent stroke and was the best gift I ever gave anyone.

As I rode the ferry over to The Pines, I felt so relieved and thankful. I had the unrealistic expectation that a similar discussion with my supposedly sophisticated parents would also be unproblematic. I planned to stop by their home in ten days when I returned from Europe.

Boca Raton, Florida

Then in their mid-70s, my parents had recently moved from a house to a condominium in a new high-rise on A1A, across from the well-known pink Boca Raton Hotel and Club. They owned both places for two years while my father prepared the apartment and ascertained that *his* decision to downsize was correct.

My relationship with them was formal in the extreme. I barely knew them. I'd lived mostly with Nonnie during my first happy six years. After that, I spent ten years in strict and homophobic Swiss boarding schools. From there I went to Georgetown University and, later, graduate school, in addition to working most holidays in Washington, D.C., as a bartender and chauffeur. I addressed my father in French using the polite tense, which was practically unheard of in the 20th century. People who observed our infrequent interaction commented that we treated each other like formal strangers.

This estranged behavior had intensified during my days in Washington while Ahmed and I tried to save my father-in- law's consulting firm. After my father had received a *Washington Post* article about the company's impending liquidation, which had been sent by one of my board members, he called and announced, "I did not bring a child into this world to drag our good name into bankruptcy courts. You will resign your duties immediately and identify another position."

"That is impossible, Father. If I did that, the company will definitely go down the drain. My in-laws would be left penniless, with no hopes of a comfortable retirement. With Ahmed's help, I feel there is a good chance of pulling this thing out of its nosedive."

My father, who had known Ahmed since early childhood

answered,

"First of all, you both are too inexperienced to salvage such a mess. There is no one who will bail you out. If you end up without financial resources, do not think you can come to us for any assistance other than to find a place set at the dining room table to eat. Secondly, no businesspeople in America can take seriously anyone with an Arab name like Ahmed Yehia."

As Christi Heffner, Playboy's new successful CEO recently said: "If I knew then everything I know now, I would have failed." Like Ms. Heffner, my innocent beliefs in managing the crisis won, over a more experienced logic and led to success. But any furthering of a conversation based on differing views with my father was futile. In the next years, the fact that I disobeyed his order was not negated by the subsequent triumphant sale of the company to AMI. He certainly never stated or implied any regret for his gloomy forecast.

On the flight from London to Miami, I tried to prepare myself and my presentation to them about my homosexuality. I silently rehearsed sentences which would, hopefully, absolve them of any misguided feelings of guilt, both genetic and environmental. I reached Boca Raton that evening and, after many flattering comments about their new home, I began my speech.

"There are reasons for my recent divorce which you do not know. I apologize for not having been totally honest and up front with you. Please understand that what I have done is in no way because of any fault of yours, rather, it is about who I am. I hope you will understand why and forgive me."

Blank faces stared at me across the living room coffee table. I looked out a picture window at the ocean, took a deep breath and openly revealed my "fatal flaw," suspecting that I was merely confirming what my father already feared.

"I am gay and would like to explain myself by answering any questions or concerns you may have."

After an uncomfortable and prolonged silence, during which my sole focus was to disguise my inner terror of rejection, my father said,

"I will be retiring to my room now. Your mother will join me. I am in no mood, at this hour, to discuss such a thing and will meet with you, in my office, after breakfast tomorrow."

With that, they both rose. Favoring an arthritic hip, my father limped away. My mother turned off lights, and I was left sitting alone in near darkness.

After a sleepless night and a painfully uncomfortable breakfast, I met both parents in my father's den. They sat erect and created a mood similar to job interviews I'd had during my graduating semester at Business School. I broke the icy silence.

"I am sure this all comes as a shock, so please feel free to ask any question that may help explain things and hopefully put your minds at rest."

"We have no questions, René, and of course we realize that this tragedy is no fault of ours. Simply a statement," began my father. "We cannot see why you did not stay married and take occasional vacations to do whatever you like. If you decide to live an openly homosexual existence surrounded by hairdressers, that is your business. But understand you can *never* bring any — what am I supposed to call them, *boyfriends?* — home to us, unless you introduce them as your secretary."

Two decades earlier my father had lived on Cap Ferrat in the South of France near Monte Carlo. The villa was next door to the aging,

Somerset Maughan and his "secretary" Allan

well-known gay author Somerset Maugham. Every evening Maugham and his "secretary," Allan, would walk by my father's house. Everyone knew that Allan was the author's lover but went along with the ruse.

"If that did not work for Somerset Maugham in the 50s, it certainly will not work for me in the 80s. I cannot introduce a partner as 'my secretary,'" I said as forcefully as I knew how.

"I suppose this explains your divorce?" my mother questioned.

"In many ways, yes, mother," I replied, "but there were other mitigating factors caused by the strain of the difficult financial situation and the family's irrational behavior. It seemed to me that when AMI bought the business, the time was right for me to be honest."

"I just do not understand why you could not have stayed married and done whatever you wanted on the side from time to time," interjected my father. "Several of my French friends handled the problem that way," he concluded with an air of exasperation.

"Well, father," I tried to explain, "I'd hate to be on my death bed in several decades and look back at an adult life made up of one big lie."

"You know our rules about introducing your friends," he said. "I prefer to not discuss this subject any further."

And we never did.

I drove my rental car back to Miami airport, flew to Los Angeles, and immediately went to the one place I felt at home, unthreatened and in control: the 8709, Los Angeles' famous gay baths.

Chapter Five

1980

Lausanne, Switzerland

In the early part of 1980, I spent a lot of time in London working with Stanley. We became close friends and frequently traveled to Switzerland together where the old hotel, now Clinique Cecil, was undergoing major renovations. In French, the word "clinique" means private hospital, as opposed to government national health facilities that are called "hôpital." Jean-Claude Salamin had been hired to run our inaugural Swiss facility immediately after we met him at The President Hotel in Geneva. While in Lausanne working with Jean-Claude, we were actively involved in physician recruitment, to ascertain that upon completion of the construction, we would have an appropriate, qualified and diverse medical staff.

Jean-Claude had spent several months in the U.S. visiting numerous AMI hospitals and working with executives at the corporate office in Beverly Hills, to become familiar with the art of hospital management. From the beginning it was obvious that he quickly understood everything that we taught him. More importantly, he instinctively knew which American management practices would work in Switzerland, and which would not. Attempts to explain these subtle differences to the American senior executives, especially Wally Weisman, were usually not successful. Wally and most of his senior department heads believed we could run European hospitals like American facilities.

Stanley had "adjusted" Jean-Claude's thinking in London, explaining important differences between community hospitals in the United States and acute care private hospitals in Europe. The European strategy was to have high-end, luxurious facilities and services, to attract locals fortunate enough to afford relatively expensive supplementary hospital insurance to reimburse our costs. While the Harley Street Clinic was well appointed, Jean-Claude had higher aspirations for "his" Clinique Cecil, inspired in part from having run lavish hotels.

First and foremost was physician recruitment. In America that task is very regulated and, therefore, structured. U.S. hospitals cannot offer the types of incentives we could propose in Europe, such as free office space and even financial incentives, if a renowned specialist would see and admit patients at our facilities. We needed to improvise new methods to attract the quality of physicians we wanted. As with all start-up businesses, one big name was necessary to achieve industry recognition. In our case, we needed one famous physician, ideally a well-known professor of medicine. One summer day we had a lucky break.

Professor Léo Eckmann

During breakfast, at the Lausanne Palace Hotel, I read about a shakeup at The University Hospital in Bern, Switzerland's capitol. The paper mentioned a respected professor of medicine and surgery, Léo Eckmann, who was disenchanted with the city's major hospital's ability to fund new equipment. Jean-Claude walked — pranced, really — into the dining room to take us to a meeting in Geneva.

"Have you seen this article about trouble at the University Hospital in Bern?" I asked.

Jean-Claude took the paper and read the piece. "Let us try to reach Professor Eckmann from the car, we are late." We had one of the early car phones in Jean-Claude's prized BMW parked in front of the hotel. "You drive. I'll try to find the professor's number," he said.

Within minutes we were connected with Léo Eckmann, who was willing to discuss the problems with us, but preferred to do so in person. "Ask him when we can call on him," I told Jean-Claude, in what became our typically disjointed three-way conversation. "*Now!*" Salamin mouthed while still listening to the professor. I turned the car around and raced off in the opposite direction to Bern.

Travel between Switzerland's cities by train or on their modern highway system is both fast and pleasant. In an hour we were in Bern and, shortly thereafter, sitting with a tall white-haired gentleman who spoke more like a charming philosopher than any physician I knew. To make things even more pleasant, he had a sharp, dry, British-like sense of humor. Astonishingly, by the end of the day we had developed the basic terms for Professor Eckmann to leave Bern and occupy the ground floor of an attractive villa we had purchased adjacent to the hospital. We promised to reconfigure the space, creating both an office and a residential apartment. We also assured him that he would have all the modern equipment he needed, without dealing with any bureaucratic problems.

"I absolutely demand assurances that I will have the latest CT scanner at the clinique," he said.

"Guaranteed," I replied instantly.

"There are none yet in private hospitals in Switzerland," said Eckmann, still questioning our ability to purchase equipment that even the city had denied him.

"You'll have it *and* everything else we discussed," I assured him.

"By the way," he continued, "I am more interested now in a different specialty than surgery. Something I consider to be at the root of all medicine and an area that will be of increasing interest over the next decades. I'll be studying this subject carefully."

"And what might that be?" I inquired surprised.

"Immunology," responded Eckmann. "The topic fascinates me."

Princess Margaret Hospital, Harrow, England

London, England

In April, AMI opened its third hospital in England. The Princess Margaret Hospital in Harrow was our foray into expanding the concept of acute care private hospitals from London to secondary British cities. If the expensive experiment was successful, I would use a similar business model in Switzerland. Therefore, I was both very interested and more involved with the final preparations immediately before the hospital's opening.

Stanley had decided to name the hospital after Queen Elizabeth's younger sister, Princess Margaret. The unfortunate Royal had experienced a series of romantic disappointments, was always considered the "controversial Royal" and was struggling with alcohol abuse. As part of her Royal duties, Her Royal Highness was Grand President of the St. John Ambulance Brigade and later Colonel-in-Chief of Queen Alexandra's Royal Army Nursing Corp.

She was currently the subject of considerable gossip about her drinking and her romantic experiences in the Bahamas. We correctly believed that the combination of her activities with medical charities, as well as a need for a boost in her public image, might encourage her to lend her name and some of her time to our new hospital.

Stanley, Royce and I were to greet the Princess at the front door of the modern and recently completed facility, to take her on a tour, followed by cocktails and a luncheon. As is customary during the early days of a brand-new hospital, and especially at a highly publicized grand opening, only subacute patients are admitted. In this way, the dignitaries only see nursing units full of relatively happy patients.

Consequently, the rooms along the patient floor we were to visit were occupied by attractive mothers carrying their newborn babies and other sub-acute patients who were all well enough to try to look their best for the Princess.

As the long line of police vehicles approached, I noticed a baby-blue Rolls Royce in the middle of the cortège. The color was a small detail that surprised me, because at previous, somewhat similar events, I had always seen the guest of honor in specially designed large black cars. At 50, Her Royal Highness was still an attractive, albeit slightly heavy woman, with magnificent blue eyes. As the back door of her car was opened, I held out my hand to assist her.

"Welcome, Princess Margaret," I said. "I cannot help but notice that your beautiful eyes match the lovely blue color of your car."

The forward compliment momentarily took her aback and she responded with,

"This being a private occasioning, I was able to bring the blue Rolls Royce. Had it been a Royal occasion, I'd have been obliged to ride in a black Rolls Royce."

"Happily, for us!" I continued. "This car shows off your eyes," which filled with tears as she smiled and thanked me.

During the walk through the patient floors, the Princess commented,

"My, everyone looks so well and happy."

"Well, you know, we are from Los Angeles. So, I asked central casting to send us a selection of perfect-looking patients to place in the beds just for you!"

She hesitated, then got the joke and burst out laughing.

Thus, began an interesting relationship, which included many meetings with her. At one of our Christmas parties, which she always dutifully attended, I danced with her. When I brought her back to her seat, Stanley whispered in my ear,

"That's the first time the Princess danced with a queen."

Los Angeles, California

Only a few of the very largest domestic AMI hospitals had been allowed to order CT scanners in 1980. None had ever made any kind of agreement with a physician, regardless of fame, like we were proposing. I knew that my promises to Professor Eckmann were of critical importance to Clinique Cecil's future but could also cause jealousies among the regional managers back in America. I discussed this with Royce upon my return to Beverly Hills. As usual he questioned me carefully. After reviewing the costs and expected benefits of all the expenses Professor Eckmann's recruitment would involve, he allowed me to proceed and recommended we plan a major media event for the opening of Cecil's advanced surgery and radiology departments. He also advised me to overlook any jealousies as they are always present with successful people.

As I was leaving the Chief Executive-turned-father- figure's office, he said,

"You look drawn, Rick. Popping back and forth to Europe is taking a toll on you, even at 32 years old. Watch it. Why not get a physical?" The comment hit home. I felt drawn, and I decided to act on Royce's recommendation.

After work, I stopped by one of my usual watering spots, The Revolver bar, in West Hollywood. I picked up a gay newspaper that also had a classified section with advertisements from numerous professionals catering to a gay clientele, including physicians. The following day, I called Doctor Robert Davis and booked an appointment. After two visits and results of the then customary bloodwork, I met with "Bob," who had quickly become a friend.

"I see nothing unusual in your bloodwork. However, you *do* have enlarged lymph nodes."

"What does that mean, Bob?" I asked.

"Frankly, I'm not sure," he answered. "I feel confident it is not lymph cancer." The remark struck that same nerve anyone sitting in a physician's office feels when hearing the "C word" for the first time. "But I am seeing this symptom in several of my patients, particularly those with other ailments. In contrast, you have no other problems, right? No digestion problems, no white-colored growths in your mouth, no unusual fatigue?"

"No," I said awkwardly. "I mean, you know, I travel a lot."

"I have a meeting with two other physicians here in L.A. who also have seen these phenomena in their patients," he continued. "I tell ya what. I'll call you afterwards. We'll get together and discuss what Michael Gottlieb and Joel Weisman have to say. They have larger practices."

A few weeks later, my secretary announced that "a Doctor Davis" was on the line.

"Hi, Bob. What's up?" I asked joyfully. I had forgotten about the mysterious illnesses and was genuinely happy to speak with Bob.

"I have some information I'd like to talk to you about. How about a drink at The Revolver at seven o'clock?"

A few hours later, I met with my new friend. At first, we talked about Ronald Reagan's victory over Jimmy Carter, and how one of Reagan's greatest supporters, Jerry Fallwell, would like to see all gay men dead. We wondered if the civil liberties gay Americans had gained in the previous decade could be reversed. Then the topic switched from politics to medicine.

"René," he began, using my away-from-work-name. "Something very weird is going on. Serious, often fatal illnesses, which used to be rarely observed, are now being seen in both Joel's and Michael's practices."

"What kind of illnesses?" I asked.

"There are three really. A rare form of pneumonia..."

"Jesus," I interrupted. "I bumped into a French pulmonologist over a year ago who mentioned something like that."

"Well," continued Bob, "there are others. Have you ever heard of Toxoplasmosis?"

"No," I replied.

"It's a rare problem, previously only observed in elderly cat and bird owners, that now seems to be attacking brain cells in gay men . . ."

I thought of the young friend I had on Fire Island who had rapidly become demented.

"And the third?" I pushed on.

"A strange cancer called Kaposi's Sarcoma. It usually shows up as a smooth, painless skin lesion. Although it has been around forever, it used to only occur in middle-aged Mediterraneans, and was always slow progressing, usually not fatal. All that's different now."

Again, I cut in,

"Is it purple-like?"

"Exactly," he affirmed.

My heart skipped a few beats as I had noticed large purple blotches, what I thought were rashes, on a few friends both on Fire Island and in L.A.

"Joel suspects a correlation with low white blood cell counts. White cells help the body fend off illnesses, both viral and bacterial. Gottlieb, who has the huge resources of UCLA at his disposal, is counting something called T-Cells."

"What are T-Cells?" I asked, yet again learning new terminology.

"They are a lymphocyte, a type of white cell, and the main building block of the immune system."

I made a mental note to talk to Léo Eckmann about T-Cells when we were to meet right after the New Year. Bob continued,

"I was amazed to learn that these bizarre medical occurrences have now been observed on three continents. Here, mostly in L.A., New York and San Francisco, almost always in gay men, and in Europe and Zaire, Africa. Some have started calling this 'a gay plague.'"

"That does not make sense," I said. "We are no different genetically than straight men. We all drink coffee! Is this a virus or bacteria?"

"I have no idea, René. All I know is that Hepatitis B is rising at an alarming rate, as are all venereal diseases. I think the sexual revolution has gotten out of hand. Sadly, I have no advice, other than for you to come to me if you develop any of the symptoms I've mentioned."

"Sure thing. But what will you do if I develop one of these signs?"

"I have no idea," responded Bob, as a look of confusion and sadness came over his youthful face. "Just hope it does not happen. People are dying, René, and there seems little that anyone can do about it. That's all I know for sure."

Chapter Six

1981

Lausanne, Switzerland

Clinique Cecil's new surgery and radiology departments were completed in the spring of 1981. I had come to understand that Jean-Claude had a real flair for the dramatic during the planning of the grand opening party and looked forward to co-hosting what promised to be one of the city's major social events.

As usual, Jean-Claude picked me up at Geneva airport and we drove to the hospital. In the parking lot, by the entrance to the building, was a stretch Mercedes with a chauffeur and another gentleman in a dark blue suit standing near the car's door. Walking past them, Jean-Claude whispered to me,

"A limousine with chauffeur and bodyguard always means a foreign dignitary or royalty has come to see Professor Eckmann."

Living room Clinique Cecil

After two days of meetings, mostly with Jean-Claude and his new finance director, and on the day of the celebration, I met Professor Eckmann in the hospital's living-room, which Jean-Claude had made sure to restore to its earlier grandeur.

The lounge felt like the main drawing room of a historic luxury hotel. In one corner was a full bar, staffed by a uniformed waiter who served cappuccinos or drinks to guests and visitors. A great oval section in the middle of the far end of the room had large, beautifully etched windows with art glass details. Elegant, yet comfortable, furniture had been arranged so that the occupants of the room could look out over

Lake Geneva and see the French city of Evian in the distance, lying beneath snow-covered mountains.

Before the big event Léo, Jean-Claude and I sat in a quiet section of the room and discussed the Professor's activities at the hospital. His arrival as a primarily affiliated member of the medical staff had created the desired effect in the medical community, and several other prominent physicians were now also admitting their patients. Léo raised some administrative and medical staff issues, which Jean-Claude and I addressed point by point. When all the business matters had been covered, I directed the conversation to a more personal level.

"How do you like living in the villa?" I asked.

"It's very pleasant," he responded in his deliberate pronunciation. "It could be more so if I had a bit more cooperation from the architect. He insists that everything be painted white!" The gentle hint was noted.

"Please explain all the details." I said.

"Let's go over to my flat and I'll show you what I would like to have accomplished."

Clinique Cecil, Lausanne, Switzerland

Leaving Jean-Claude to attend to the caterers, we crossed the busy street to the villa and entered Leo's apartment, which was full of antiquities and exotic art collected during his many visits to Asia and Africa. After he described his design concerns, Léo poured two glasses of wine and invited me to sit in a large, brown leather chair. When we were both seated, I said,

"Léo, please tell me more about your interest in immunology."

"Well, my grandfather was an immunologist in Czarist Russia before the term was even used. My father followed in his footsteps.

They taught me that the strength of the immune system is at the basis of all medicine. I have made interesting observations ever since. For example, did you know the immune system weakens as one ages, which is principally responsible for the onset of many illnesses?"

Ignoring his rhetorical question, I proceeded,

"Have you been following the odd illnesses being observed in The States, largely in the homosexual community?"

"Of course, I have. But we have cases in Europe and even right here in Switzerland. I make a point of speaking with the physicians treating several of these patients."

"What are your conclusions?" I asked, hoping to finally hear some promising news.

"Many more questions than conclusions. But there definitely is a link between the cancer, pneumonia, digestive and nervous system problems. I'm sure there is an assault on the immune system. What we need are funds for research and *quickly*. This is not going away. More cases are being seen every week!"

"Sadly, our new President has cut the proposed Center for Disease Control's research budget from $320 million dollars to some $160 million," I said, quoting frightening statistics I had read on the recent overnight flight.

"I assume you have a personal interest in the subject," he asked, leading me to revealing more details.

"Yes, Léo, I do. I have friends who have exhibited many of the symptoms of what I have heard called "the gay plague" and my doctor pointed out that I have enlarged lymph nodes." The brilliant and intuitive Professor got the messages loud and clear.

"Believing that this is directly linked to homosexuality is idiocy. Note that I said 'directly.' There may be some behavior, drug or product consumed that is creating a battering to the immune system, in addition to the lack of necessary rest, which also weakens the body. I assume that these unknown causes are somehow linked to sex, but it's not what I'd call a typical sexually transmitted disease because there is no manifestation whatsoever on the genitals and, remember, sexually transmitted diseases are bacterial and easily treated."

"Is this not a bacterium?" I asked, using the commonly misused nomenclature of bacterium in the singular, and the same question that was being bounced around in many hospitals and research laboratories.

"That is not yet known for sure, but I'll place my bet on a virus.

We have to identify it!" he said raising his voice almost to a shout.

"Will you be my physician?" I asked bluntly.

"I'd be delighted, but remember, my theories are often controversial, and I make both medical and — let's call them — paramedical recommendations," he concluded in what began a 20-year relationship that often-made sense out of inexplicable facts.

"Now let's go to the party. I heard you will speak!"

"Do you not want to examine me?" I asked.

"Why? You said you have enlarged lymph nodes. That's enough for now." Over the following years, Léo never examined my body, but he certainly challenged my mind. "Let's go and see this spectacle!" he said as we both left his warm, inviting apartment.

The evening celebration certainly was a spectacle. Waiters wearing spotless white jackets served delicious hot and cold hors d'oeuvres and a selection of wines and Champagne. Small groups of dignitaries and physicians were individually escorted into the radiology and surgery departments. Reporters from Switzerland's three "sections" (French, German and Italian) were in attendance, as was a local television news crew. The *pièce de résistance* was waiting inside a new Mercedes ambulance with the hospital's name painted most prominently on the side and waiting in the parking lot.

Jean-Claude had arranged for the director of Lausanne's well-known museum to allow us to collect an Egyptian mummy, transport it to the hospital and place it in our new Siemens CT scanner, the first one in a private Swiss hospital. After the "examination," our proud new radiologist spoke to the group in the main lounge.

Lausanne Museum mummy at Clinique Cecil

"We have learned several things about the mummy many of us have seen at the museum. Now that we have looked *inside* this treasure, I will begin by referring to 'it' as 'she.' In addition, and to the amazement of the curator, there is a four-centimeter needle in the mummy's chest cavity which may explain the cause of death when the data is analyzed by an international team of experts."

The guests were all duly amazed as exhibited by many exclamations and muffled conversations. The newspaper and television reporters all gave the honest stunt great coverage which, in turn, brought our new hospital very much into the minds of most Swiss citizens.

Los Angeles, California

By the summer of 1981, what had been called "the gay plague" was being spoken about in many medical circles. A Center for Disease Control (CDC) task force had determined a link between the major illnesses of Pneumocystis Carinii, Kaposi's Sarcoma and Candida, and created a new term grouping them as Opportunistic Infections. OIs now defined the heretofore rare infirmities that attack the immune system. But sadly, since the problem was so largely prevalent in the homosexual community, the problem did not ignite much concern in the general public. A conservative wave was taking over in Washington, D.C., and it was clear that as long as "normal Americans" were not at risk, there was no reason to prioritize research programs.

The new name for the scourge did not help. GRID or Gay Related Immune Deficiency reinforced the belief that this was a problem which solely effected homosexuals and, therefore, was not to be taken very seriously. Worse, some ultra-conservative members of the Religious Right felt vindicated in their belief that God would eventually "get even" with the heathens. In their minds, it was perfectly all right if the problem eradicated all gay men as long as it stayed clear of the general population. Stories of deviant behavior abounded as a link to sexual activity emerged, and a theory about Patient Zero took root. The title was attributed to a handsome gay Air Canada flight attendant, Gaetan Ducas, who frequently visited the bath houses in Los Angeles, San Francisco and New York. It was wildly rumored that Gaetan, who had shown symptoms of KS for two years, engaged in unprotected sex with several thousand partners a year.

The Pines Harbor, Fire Island, New York

As the ferry from Sayville pulled into The Pines Harbor at Fire Island, I was eager to see all the sights I had missed. "Les Beaux" was moored on our port side, and the Ice Palace with its bar, restaurant and dance floor was on the starboard side. There was something that caught my eye as we disembarked. A booth was set up near the dock with a large sign that read: "Give to the Gay Cancer."

As I walked along the boardwalk to my boat, the excitement was again dampened as we passed a beautifully restored antique Chris Craft yacht belonging to a friend I had not seen all summer. At the boat's stern, I met the harbor master whom I knew well and inquired about the lovely old-fashioned boat's owner.

"He died in July, René, of the gay cancer which spread to his lungs. We are having a fund-raising drive this weekend."

That night, while eating a late dinner at an open-air rooftop restaurant, I talked with former acquaintances about "the gay plague," about whether my friend had died of KS or of pneumonia, and about patient zero. Everyone there knew someone who was ill, and everyone was all on the lookout for any signs of the gay cancer. Sleeping around was no longer a joking matter . . . the period when one measured success by numbers of conquests was over.

Part 2

TIM

1982 – 1989

René and Tim, Mykonos, Greece,

Chapter Seven

1982

Lausanne, Switzerland

By January 1982, The World Health Organization announced that there had been 36 reported cases of the illness in Europe, five in tiny Switzerland. The CDC had weighed in with their American tally of 108 and had requested funds for their "opportunistic infection and Kaposi's Sarcoma task force." The unanswered appeal for $830,000 represented an infinitesimal part of the multi-billion-dollar National Institute of Health (NIH) budget. There simply was no interest in studying, much less preparing any prevention, for a "gay cancer."

Back in Switzerland, I continued to enjoy building the physician and client base of Clinique Cecil, working closely with Jean-Claude and Léo Eckmann. Jean-Claude's flair for publicity never took a vacation as demonstrated on the first day of my January visit.

"Did you know that we have the oldest Great Sequoia in Switzerland on the property?" he asked out of the blue.

"I assume you mean that huge tree near the physician office building," I replied. "I love it but was unaware of its distinction."

"Well, it's sick. I see this as a great opportunity for good publicity. The expert we consulted said that it would slowly die and that the only hope was to use an expensive treatment developed in California."

"Okay," I said, wondering where this was leading. "Think about it! We are a California-based company often criticized as being insensitive to local concerns."

Still not quite getting it, I continued,

"You know perfectly well that you do not need my authority to incur that kind of expense. Just take care of it."

"Here *is* what I do need your authority for. I want to invite the best tree doctor in California to come *here* to treat 'Switzerland's oldest tree.' I'll have a huge coverage of the event in the press. Now do you understand?"

"Brilliant," I exclaimed, realizing that we would get some excellent publicity. "But while we are on the subject of approvals from 'corporate,' you must reread AMI's new Policy and Procedure Manual for hospital administrators and begin to comply. Wally Weisman, the Chief Operating Officer, has pointed out many areas of non-compliance."

"You know that the American and Swiss systems are fundamentally different, as are our strategies. You tell Wally that I wake up every morning and figure out how I can break one of those silly rules," Jean-Claude concluded.

Thus began a multi-year struggle I undertook to mediate Jean-Claude's contempt for the American side of the company, mostly as exhibited by Wally Weisman, and our instincts for what was needed to continue the now-evident success in Switzerland. Wally was not the only executive Jean-Claude teased. He had responded badly to Stanley's indignation that Queen Elizabeth had not been received with sufficient pomp during a recent visit to Geneva.

Jean-Claude, who was not *allowed* to call Stanley by his first name, seized the opportunity to provoke a violent reaction in anyone he felt had been illogical. "Look here, Doctor, we respect real work and accomplishments here in Switzerland. So, we feel that your Queen is really of no greater significance than my housekeeper!" That verbal recklessness had cost me a special trip to London to convince Stanley that Jean-Claude was doing his job and should not be "sacked" — the British term for fired.

In what was becoming my custom before I left Switzerland, I asked to have a personal conversation with my health advisor, Professor Eckmann.

"Léo, have you come closer to understanding the cause of the immune problems we have discussed?" I asked.

"No, but I am more and more convinced it is a virus. May I give you a quick course in virology?" he asked in his typical way of beginning conversations that would remain memorable for life.

"Please do," I urged.

"Well, virology has been studied for nearly 100 years, mostly in Europe, notably France. The Pasteur Institute, in collaboration with the ancestor of your friend, Doctor Mérieux, and another brilliant researcher named Roux, were sure of the destruction viruses cause, and differentiated this from bacterial illnesses. But it was not until the middle of the century, with the discovery of the electron microscope, that we could *see* viruses. Once we had the ability to watch them, we could much better understand their activity in the body. This led to the discovery of a sub-category called 'slow viruses.' If, indeed, we are dealing with a virus, I feel it is both slow and relatively difficult to contract."

Professor Léo Eckmann

"That's all good news," I said naively.

"Yes and no," he continued. "A slow virus can be in the system for years before manifesting itself. So, it can be spread unknowingly. Worse, it can 'mutate,' or transform itself, becoming a new virus with different characteristics. If a virus is easily transmitted from human to human, the world health authorities take action to avoid what is called 'a pandemic,' like we had here in Europe during the early part of the century. Immunology requires the identification of a virus in order to create a vaccine *from* it. In the history of virology, no serious viral condition has ever been solved by medications. It is useless to try to kill or to stop the virus, especially a mutating one. Rather we need to *change the host* so that the virus becomes ineffective. That is what a vaccine does. Think of the polio vaccine. The virus still exists, but it cannot hurt anyone who has been *immunized*. Back to the problem at hand," continued Léo. "There is a physician in Miami who believes that a transfusion caused his patient to develop pneumocystis pneumonia. Sad as this may be, if it is true, and *if* it is the same virus, the world may finally wake up to the fact that calling this a 'gay plague' is archaic and very dangerous. Once there is a spread to the general population, we may finally get much needed research funds! For now, we are at the mercy of some political radicals on both sides of the ocean. Extremists, like your Reagan and France's Le Pen, would like to turn their heads away from medicine and see you all disappear. It's outrageous to link a human behavior to a virus, but that is what is happening."

Like many of Léo's future lectures, delivered with consistent charm and knowledge, I never forgot his exact words and thought about how accurate this visionary man was.

Los Angeles, California

One Sunday afternoon, at a "tea dance" in West Hollywood, I saw a young man who took my breath away. He was the typical tall, dark and handsome wholesome boy. He had silky black hair, the same rich texture of a healthy young Native American brave, as well as sparkling blue eyes, and olive skin that looked like satin. I could not take my eyes off of him while he was speaking to a small gathering of other "real lookers." When he broke away from his friends and walked by me, I took hold of his arm in a bold attempt to start a conversation. This startled him and the first look that Tim shot at me was one of annoyance. But a conversation began and before long, I learned that Tim had only been in Los Angeles for six months and was very much enjoying being one of the hottest looking boys in town.

To my surprise, Tim agreed to accompany me to the beach in Santa Monica and watch the sun set. While there, he took off his shirt, revealing a very well-built lean athletic body revealing a perfect six-pack. As the sun fell into the Pacific, Tim did cartwheels on the beach, while the golden light made his blue eyes sparkle and his hair glisten. I watched his acrobatics, believing that I had seen the most perfect example of a healthy all-American young man. I was completely dazzled and invited him to join me on a weekend adventure to Catalina Island. There I discovered that Tim did, in fact, have the perfect body with one exception. He, too, had swollen lymph nodes on his neck and under his arms. It occurred to me that I was no longer waiting for something better to walk into my life.

From then on Tim and I saw as much of each other as possible. Tracy had graduated and left town, and I was enamored with Tim. I learned that he was from a typical Indiana family and had been the captain of his high school's basketball team, which made him something of a local celebrity. He was the first in his family to get a college education and, to his mother's dismay, the first to leave Indiana. He was living in a distant suburb of Los Angeles working at a job he hated at Kimberly-Clarke, mostly controlling inventory in a large warehouse. He was not "out" to his family and had no plans to have that conversation with them.

Tim was the first dedicated body builder I knew, and he quickly encouraged me to begin going to a gym with regularity. I joined West Hollywood's new large gym "Sports Connection," also referred to as the "Sports Erection" due to the many magnificent men who worked with weights, went to new aerobics classes and used the spa facilities. When I did not have a business lunch scheduled, I'd use my mid-day break to work out with a trainer at the nearby club. As I left, I always bought a protein shake and a salad and wolfed them down in my new Mercedes 500 SEC racing back to the office. I had never previously enjoyed clubs; had not even known about health clubs and I certainly loved this new experience.

By late winter, there were increasing hints that the new illness was not limited to the homosexual population. I read *The Wall Street Journal*, which one of my secretaries would place on my desk every morning. On February 25 I was struck by an article entitled "New, Often Fatal, Illness in Homosexuals Turns up in Women, Heterosexual Males." I faxed it to Léo, followed by an article in the *Los Angeles Times*, a month later, which basically said the same thing. I knew the new information would be the subject of a conversation with my sage advisor when we next met. In the meantime, the CDC reported the number of cases in the U.S. jumped to 285 in March. The illness' name was being altered routinely as the search for its origin and targets were being investigated. It went from GRID through several mutations of its own and was finally named AIDS for Acquired Immune Deficiency Syndrome by the CDC in July.

Unfortunately, two contradictory forces were at play. The CDC's efforts to inform the general population were countered by politicians who still believed it was an illness that only sought out certain "undesirable" minorities. The new members to join that group were Haitians, which created a pathetic nickname for the disease of "The Four H's": hemophiliacs, Haitians, heroin addicts and homosexuals, presumably in descending order of undesirability.

NIH's prejudice was made perfectly clear after the advent of a second mysterious illness called "Legionnaires Disease," so-named because of an outbreak of a sometimes fatal, respiratory problem during a Legionnaires convention in Pennsylvania. Perhaps because the latest illness only attacked "good Americans," NIH spent $34,000 on each fatal case of Legionnaires versus $3,200 per AIDS deaths.

In France, the right-wing Le Pen, mentioned by Léo, was relentless in his efforts to make his constituents believe that good Frenchmen were safe, because the illness was limited to the Four H's. It seemed that an international race for homophobia had begun when a slogan emerged during the gubernatorial campaign in New York between Mario Cuomo and Ed Koch, "Vote for Cuomo, not the homo."

By the end of 1982 Tim and I were seeing each other every weekend I was in Los Angeles. I was developing a deep affection for this youthful, energetic and naive young man. The number of Americans diagnosed with AIDS had risen to 691, of which 278 had died. There still was no ability to determine how many were infected. Léo's theory about slow viruses made sense when the term "pre-AIDS" emerged. This referred to the period from when an individual was exposed to the virus, showed some of the well-known symptoms, but had not developed any opportunistic infections (OI).

At a Christmas dinner I cooked in Santa Monica, with a guest list that included Bob Davis and several of his patients who were also friends, Tim asked Bob if our swollen lymph nodes could be considered "pre-AIDS."

"Since there is no way to know if you guys have been exposed, I'd have to say 'no.' None of my patients have had 'pre-AIDS' for long before progressing to an OI. The good news is that research is being well coordinated between the French at Pasteur, and NIH. Also, there is more evidence of a spread to the general population among hemophiliacs. It's also been reported in babies in New York. The government just can't stay quiet now. I'll bet there will be real progress soon, even if the majority of Americans hate and fear gay people."

Tim and I ended the year on that optimistic note and began talking about his moving into the Santa Monica condominium and his long-term goals.

Chapter Eight

1983

Europe

By 1983, we were further expanding our international activities into Spain and considering a move into Australia. Therefore, my monthly trips to Europe now always included visits to Spain and often on to Australia. Before leaving Switzerland, I never neglected a personal chat with Léo.

"There are small advances in understanding the mystery," he began one winter day. "Pasteur and one of their main scientists, Jean-Claude Chermann, believe it is a 'retrovirus' and not the prevailing thought that it is the virus that causes leukemia. Pasteur is also convinced that there is evidence it has been around for a number of years."

Professor Jean Claude Chermann

"What is a retrovirus?" I asked, readying myself for another brilliant lesson.

"I'll try to make this simple," began Léo. "A retrovirus not only attacks and kills its target, but it *invades* those cells. After destroying them, it explodes into the body, releasing *many more* 'killers.' Chermann has been studying retroviruses for years. I will make a special effort to meet with him soon. The illness has now been observed in 16 countries. I cannot understand why more efforts for research and education are not being made. But, I now believe that we are dealing with a blood disease and not a venereal disease."

On the flight to Barcelona, Spain, I read that the reported cases of AIDS in America had crossed the 1,000 mark. I looked around me in the first-class section of the plane. The usual variety of people was traveling:

male, female, old, young, handsome, unattractive, etc. Was I the only person on the plane with "contaminated blood," I wondered? And, if so, would I not happily change places with anyone else on the flight regardless of age, education or social condition?

Our first entry into the Spanish market was to acquire a 50 percent

Hospital Quiron, Barcelona, Spain

interest in the famous Clinica Quiron in Barcelona. For three generations, the well-respected private hospital had belonged to the Mestre family, which wrote the first book for medical students. Joaquin Mestre and his administrative team realized that the hospital needed an infusion of capital that was unrealistic for a family to meet. As a result, discussions with us lead to AMI becoming equal equity partners. I was particularly fond of the hospital administrator Antonio Vancells, and his young assistant Gabriel Massfurrol. Antonio was not only a competent manager and diplomat, but also a renowned sculptor, who had been commissioned by the Spanish Royal family to create busts of several of their loved ones.

My visits to "Quiron" were always rewarding. The people with whom I worked were more cultured and well-rounded than any other executives in my experience, with the exception of Royce. While challenging, our board meetings were productive and resulted in an unusual collaboration of differing experiences, resulting in successful efforts to renovate the hospital and return it to its earlier greatness. It always gave me a laugh when other members of the hospital's board referred to me as "Don Ricardo." Beginning with my first visits to Barcelona, I frequently met two of the hospital's regular famous local patients, Xavier Cugat and Salvador Dali. Later, I secretly made exceptions to our rule of only treating "acute cases" and allowed both artists to enjoy personalized long-term care in the facility. The hospital's dining room had a walled-off executive area where, in order to accommodate my schedule, we would meet after work at earlier hours than to which the Spaniards were accustomed. There we had many wonderful meals, often accompanied by famous patients and Catalonian friends.

In the spring of 1983, Pasteur was closely watching ten AIDS patients in an effort to isolate the virus. In America, Congressman Henry Waxman of California was trying to create greater awareness of the dangers AIDS posed. As a member of the House Subcommittee on Health, Waxman was the first to request federal funding specifically identified for AIDS research.

Los Angeles, California

Around this time, I received the first communication from my father since our discussion of my sexuality. In the interim, he had relied on my mother to relay all information to me. His communiqué actually was a copy of a letter he had sent to my brother. It explained that 1983 was a great year for our family because we all turned milestone ages. He would be 80, my mother 75, my brother 40 and I would turn 35. As a result, he was informing us that we were all to meet in Rotterdam, Holland in late summer, for a 12-day family cruise through the Norwegian Fjords and on to Leningrad. The letter was signed, "Your loving father, John Silvin."

I had *never* taken a two-week-long vacation. The prospect of spending my first, real holiday, longer than a three-day weekend, with my parents certainly was not what I had imagined. But, after considering the effort my father was making, I responded, also in writing. I explained that this would be my first prolonged absence from work, and I joked saying that, in a rapidly growing firm, anyone who left for two weeks ran the risk of returning to the office to find someone else sitting at his desk. Finally, I informed both parents that I was entering into a relationship, and I could only make such a "wonderful" long trip if my "friend" could join me.

After a period of silence, the second round of letters arrived. "Your mother and I have carefully considered your difficult request. We can accept you bringing this friend along but only if, as previously mentioned, he is introduced as your secretary." My brother was copied on the correspondence.

By return mail, I told him that this was unacceptable. I reminded him of how silly that game had sounded decades earlier with Somerset Maugham, and that I had no intention of humiliating Tim or the entire family in a like-fashion. Again, after a period of silence, I received a copy of a letter to my brother which included a check for $5,000 made out to me. The letter explained that "because René is being difficult," they had canceled the reservations for the cruise. The total cost of the vacation per couple, including the double cabins for my brother and his wife, was $10,000. The value of my brother's gift was enclosed in his letter. "As for René, since it was never intended that he be accompanied by anyone, I am sending him $5,000." It was signed "John Silvin." This must have hit a nerve in my brother who subsequently sent me $2,500 trying to "even things out."

I was crushed and asked my friend and physician, Bob Davis, to recommend a psychologist I could consult. He suggested a gay colleague who I began seeing regularly regarding my relationship with my father, my being gay in a hostile corporate environment (with the exception of my boss Royce), and about my serious insomnia and use of sleeping pills. I was using pills in the belief that they could lessen my frequent, horrible nightmares, but that proved not to be the case. In fact, with sleeping pills it took longer to wake up from a nightmare, resulting in more sleepless nights.

When I brought Doctor Bernard the letters regarding the proposed family meeting, I saw that he had a difficult time containing his laughter. But, over the ensuing two years, he was extremely professional in assisting me with the list of problematic subjects, including the unfolding of how to deal with what was not yet called HIV. One of his first recommendations was that I start attending meetings hosted by an enlightened psychologist who met with groups of gay men, mostly with health issues, at West Hollywood's Community Centre. Her name was Louise Hay, and she had just moved her rapidly growing gatherings from her back porch to a larger forum. Her classes and those of another forward- thinking psychologist, Marianne Williamson, were being called "A Course in Miracles!"

Melbourne, Australia

Stanley and I had already made several reconnaissance trips to

Australia. AMI had acquired its first hospital on the continent, in Melbourne. While we were the industry leader in developing hospitals outside the United States, we had entered the Australian market late. Hospital Corporation of America (HCA) had set up a subsidiary in Sydney and had acquired three small hospitals. We chose Melbourne, Australia's second city and the capital of Victoria Province, as our entry into this ripe new market, because we concluded we could become the dominant private health care provider more easily than taking on HCA in Sydney.

We were also studying building a new hospital in the rapidly growing affluent suburb of Melbourne. On this particular trip we met with a disconcerting piece of news. Our attorney advised us that our arch competitor, HCA, had acquired a piece of land in the same suburb, and had begun working with a local architect to design a community hospital. At first, it appeared that we would not be the only player in the province and that our strategy may have failed. By the next day, Stanley had developed a bold Machiavellian plan. We immediately made an unconditional offer on the property we had identified as optimal and hired a young architect. Before we left, we instructed the design firm to *immediately* erect a huge billboard on the site which read, "Coming Soon, New AMI Hospital."

"You must understand, gentlemen," began our architect, "it may take a year to finish the construction documents and to obtain the necessary permits."

"That may be," replied Stanley, "but how long will it take to arrange for two large bulldozers to start moving earth around in the center of the property?"

Our architect understood the plan and was willing to comply. As we left the office, Stanley turned at the door and said, "By the way, it won't take a year. It will take nine months. *It can be done.*"

Later we learned that HCA had abandoned its plans to build a hospital in Victoria. On the long Quantas flight back to London, I read an article in Sydney's newspaper that talked about AIDS, and which described several local occurrences. The reporter went on to say that the number of cases in the U.S. had gone from 1,000 at the beginning of the year to an estimated 3,000 by the end of 1983, and that approximately 650 Americans had already succumbed to the illness. He went on to extrapolate what a similar progression would yield in total number of Australian cases and fatalities within two years.

Lausanne, Switzerland

Before returning to California, I made my usual visit to Switzerland. Jean-Claude and I were evaluating the possibility of expanding the Swiss operations into other cities. Consequently, much of my time spent with him was driving around the country. On one road trip to Bern, we asked Léo to join us and the conversation quickly turned to AIDS and what Léo was learning.

Doctor Robert Gallo co-founder Institute of Human Virology

"Robert Gallo, at NIH, still believes that the virus which causes AIDS is the same as the Leukemia virus. The scientists at Pasteur do not agree. This debate is dragging on. But, fortunately, both research teams are now freely exchanging data. I'll attend a conference in Geneva in a few weeks at the World Health Organization on the subject, and I hope to obtain much more information. Apparently, representatives from more than 30 nations will attend! Of special interest to me is the fact that Pasteur will soon have an antibody test."

"What's that?" I asked.

"Once one has been exposed to any virus, the body develops what are called 'antibodies' in an attempt to fight the invader. The body may or may not be successful in this endeavor, but the antibodies are always present. We can detect their presence with something called 'ELISA' tests, which will be instrumental in determining if someone has the virus. I want to find out when the test will be commercially available and how accurate it is. Maybe we can finally begin testing large groups in order to inform people with national education programs of their status and to reduce cross infection."

"Who is Elisa?" asked Jean-Claude.

"It is not a person," laughed Léo. "It stands for Enzyme Linked Immuno Sorbent Assay. It is usually reliable, although there are more complicated tests which are even more reliable, such as RIPA tests or Radio Immuno Precipitation Assay. Let's hope Pasteur makes one available in early 1984. I am sure that there are many asymptomatic people who are, while the virus has not yet manifested itself. Given the history of the crisis, many people are infectious without being aware or even having any idea of the dangers they pose. Testing, along with education, will reduce, let us call them innocent transmissions by healthy carriers who have been exposed to the virus. Have you ever heard of Typhoid Mary?"

"All I know is that she lived in New York and was accused of spreading Typhoid Fever before the First World War," I answered.

"Yes, that's correct," continued Léo, "but she was a 'passive' carrier. She demonstrated no symptoms of the illness whatsoever, but the bacteria was continuously detected in her stool. It took health officials a long time to determine that her immune system was strong enough to prevent her from becoming sick. That did not mean she was not infectious. The concept of a 'healthy carrier' emerged from her tragic life, and also gave birth to the debate of balancing the rights of the sick versus the risk of contagion to the healthy. We are lucky that the virus that causes AIDS is relatively hard to transfer from human to human. If it were airborne or even transmitted though ingestion you would all be quarantined!"

"There has been some talk about that from the religious right extremists," I said.

"Yes, as usual, they speak from ignorance in order to spread their fears," said Léo, as he shrugged his shoulders.

The November 1983 meeting in Geneva would be the first of an ever-growing, hugely attended, international gathering of AIDS researchers and practitioners which Léo would always closely monitor. Unfortunately, national education programs were nowhere even *close* to the horizon. Equally as distressing was the fact that no antibody test was released to the public in 1984. Léo's delight at the collaboration between NIH and the Pasteur Institute would be short lived. Soon, both organizations would become enemies rather than scientific collaborators, which would further delay the progress of scientific and clinical knowledge.

Chapter Nine

1984

Los Angeles, California

At the beginning of the year, Tim moved into the condominium on Ocean Avenue in Santa Monica with me. I felt a deepening paternalistic affection for him and regretted that he was unhappy at his job with Kimberly-Clarke. One evening I asked him what he would like to do if he could choose any career or profession.

"That's easy!" he replied. "I'd like to be an interior designer."

"Okay," I said. "Why not look into LA's best design school and consider applying for admittance for their next semester?"

"I can't give up a job that pays me well and go to school," he said.

"I'll make you an offer you can't refuse," I continued. "If you get accepted to a program you want, I'll pay the tuition and take care of housing and entertainment expenses. All you have to do is find a part-time job for pocket money. I want to be your partner, not your parent, and giving you an allowance would make me feel very uncomfortable."

Tim was thrilled, and by spring he was admitted to the UCLA Extension Interior and Architectural Design program. We installed a drafting table in our guest room, which became Tim's workspace and the room quickly filled up with reference books, furniture catalogues, fabric samples and supplies. Tim's enthusiasm and obvious talent thrilled me, as did watching him at work behind the architect's table (almost always in a bathing suit). Tim was hired as a part-time assistant to a designer on trendy Melrose Avenue. She rearranged her street-front office to seat Tim at a desk in the showroom's window. I think she knew that more people would stop to look at Tim than at the furniture displays.

Our international operations were expanding rapidly, and I traveled constantly. In addition to Europe and Australia, I now made regular stops in Singapore, where we were building a new facility, as well as in Argentina and Ecuador, where we were studying the markets. Switzerland, however, was the focal point of my interest because of the relatively high capital investments and the corresponding returns. Jean- Claude was on the lookout for us to expand into other cities. Within 18 months we would own hospitals in five Swiss cities.

The King Khalid Eye Specialty Hospital, Riyadh,

Gstaad, Switzerland

Ahmed and I traveled together only on a few occasions. His focus was on securing a huge hospital management contract in Saudi Arabia, while I was developing facilities we would own and operate elsewhere. His long-term strategy to earn AMI a reputation of reliability and good performance in Kuwait had paid off, and he was negotiating a three-year $213 million contract to run The King Khalid Eye Specialty Hospital, which later became well-known as "KKESH." When AMI was awarded the contract, Ahmed embarked on a vast international recruiting effort to identify, hire and relocate every employee, from janitors to surgeons for the specialty medical center.

In March, we planned a long weekend together in Switzerland while on our separate ways, me to Singapore and Ahmed to Saudi Arabia. We had both attended Le Rosey boarding school in Switzerland, which was having a large alumni meeting in Gstaad to celebrate its one-hundred-year anniversary. We loved to ski and had many common friends and family members scheduled to be at the three-day event, including our respective brothers.

The Palace Hotel in Gstaad is a grand imposing, castle-like structure that dominates the small quaint alpine village. The hotel's owner, Ernst Scherz, was also a former "Rosey boy" and had made sure that we were all well received and pampered. There were gala dinners every night at the hotel, followed by speeches and awards. Ahmed and I ate lunch at mountaintop restaurants and skied as much as possible. While my brother, John, was among the participants, Ahmed's brother, Aziz, did not show up. Every

Palace Hotel, Gstaad, Switzerland

evening before dinner we would try to reach him at his apartment in Geneva — to no avail.

After the fantasy-fun-filled weekend, I left for Singapore. Ahmed decided to stop by Aziz's apartment on his way to the airport. There he discovered a horrible scene. Aziz, who had been plagued by serious depression, had committed suicide. I received the news upon my arrival in Singapore and promptly turned around and flew back to Switzerland, to attend my childhood friend's funeral and lend some small comfort to Ahmed and his mother.

....

Progress on understanding the virus, even giving it an accepted, international name, was slow. The Pasteur Institute called it LAV and made a patent application for its improved ELISA antibody test, while Gallo at the National Cancer Institute (NCI), still believed it was linked to leukemia, and named it HTLV III.

On March 30, the infamous "patient zero" died in Quebec, Canada. Those of us who had frequented some of his regular venues, wondered uselessly if we had met him years before. On April 23, the *New York Times* reported that the CDC felt Pasteur had isolated the virus. With all players now aspiring to win a Nobel Prize in medicine, any hopes of a tight trans- Atlantic cooperation were rapidly disappearing. In April, the number of reported cases in America rose to 4,100 with 1,807 deaths. Two months later, those figures were amended to 5,000 cases and 2,300 fatalities, while Secretary of Health and Human Services (HHS) Margaret Heckler, debated whether the Americans or the French were more advanced on their respective quests to understand the virus. Gallo, the CDC, NIH and the Pasteur Institute were consumed with winning, by being the first to clearly identify the virus and have an antibody test. Scientific advancement suffered as a result of the unfortunate competition, as the number of fatalities steadily climbed.

That spring a piece of news again gave us all some hope that AIDS would enter the mainstream of conversation and thinking.

One of America's most-famous male idols, Rock Hudson, was diagnosed with Kaposi's sarcoma. For months he tried in vain to conceal the news, which was rapidly spreading among anyone interested in the progression of the tragedy. But, he did fool one important friend: Nancy Reagan. In August at The White House, in response to the First Lady's question regarding his gaunt appearance, Hudson claimed he had contracted food poisoning while shooting a film on location in Israel. Once again, the gay world lost an opportunity to accelerate acceptance and research. This sad event coincided with the Democratic National Convention in San Francisco, where Jerry Falwell said we all "needed to return to moral sanity" and not to "favor homosexuals" in any medical research. At last, a few public protests began occurring in San Francisco and New York.

People afflicted with the illness, as well as their friends and family, pooled resources and raced off to Mexico, France and other countries, following reports of miracle drugs and bizarre treatments. One such weird action was an injection of ozone into the anus! Others talked of eliminating the virus by heating the patient's blood. Contradicting rumors of how the virus was transmitted flourished. Some believed it was easily transmitted through casual contact such as kissing or touching, while others believed it was not easily transmitted. Gallo even said that only one out of 100 people who were expo disease. This news was discredited when the CDC further revised its statistics, and the number of cases crossed the 6,000 mark.

Ronald Reagan's first term was drawing to a close, and it became painfully obvious that Reagan was oblivious to the fact that there was a pandemic developing. He had not once publicly uttered the word "AIDS" or made a single policy speech on the issue.

One bright spot was the advent of the Los Angeles Olympics. AMI was the official provider of medical and emergency services. Royce was presented with an Olympic torch as the flame carrying Olympiad ran past his house, and various executives were given well-located seats to numerous events. I had requested, and been granted, two seats to both the opening and closing ceremonies, which Tim and I regaled in using. This was made even more luxurious due to an AMI allocated parking space, which permitted us to avoid traffic jams and shuttle busses. Between the two book-end events, I went to Europe.

The opening ceremony of the Los Angeles Olympics, 1984

Switzerland

We had entered into an agreement to acquire an old, previously well-renowned hospital in the Capital city of Bern. The “Klinik” (the German word for private hospital) Beau Site had to be completely renovated, updated and re-equipped. Wally Weisman and I had an unpleasant discussion on the subject of whether we should run a radically scaled down hospital operation during construction or shut down the facility completely. I argued strongly for the former in order to create better acceptance of an American company taking over Béarnaise private health care. A local reporter had included a humorous cartoon in an article, which implied we would not run a hospital in keeping with the traditional, conservative norms of the citizens of Bern. The article was titled “McMedical?” and the drawing was of a patient in bed with an IV running into his arm from a Coca Cola bottle. Seizing the opportunity, I invited the reporter to dinner. I praised her humor, and we became friends. Subsequent articles were much more positive, and she often called me to get our opinion or explanation of an incident or decision.

In my argument with Weisman, I explained these events and considerations. I argued that terminating employees in Europe is much more difficult, costly and damaging to corporate reputations than in The States. At a dinner meeting, I pointed out that we would recoup the operating losses incurred during construction, from the good reputation we would gain by announcing we were not callously laying off employees in an "American fashion."

"I don't give a God damn! Blow 'em all out of the water!" he ordered.

Later in the meal, while being served by a somewhat- flamboyant waiter, Wally exclaimed, "I had better be nice to that fag or he'll spit in my food, and I'll get AIDS."

I could not contain myself any longer. "Wally, you are the Chief Operating Officer of a hospital corporation, not a trucking company. As a Jew, you, too, are part of a minority that has been the victim of ignorant prejudice throughout history. How does it feel when Jews are referred to with slurs? Please be more understanding."

His face turned red, and I knew that the rift between us had widened. It also did not help that when I asked Royce to weigh in on the

Klinik Beau Site, Bern, Switzerland

discussion of closing Klinik Beau Site, he ruled in my favor. When *that* meeting was over, I glimpsed inWally's eyes what he would do to me as soon as Royce retired and he became the Chief Executive.

While in Switzerland, I had my personal medical discussion with Léo Eckmann. I produced my list of questions for him to clarify.

"Are contaminated people infectious between couples?" I asked, wondering if Tim and I had to practice "safe sex" since I assumed we were both already infected.

"First of all, we call you 'sero-positives,' not contaminated," he corrected me. "I presume the answer is yes. You see, if the virus mutates there could be different strains. If so, you and Tim could cross infect yourselves which would further weaken the immune system."

Happy to use his new word, I continued.

"There are differing opinions about whether all 'sero-positives' will get AIDS. What is your opinion?"

"Again, allow me to correct the terminology. We call it 'progress' and refer to a 'latent period.' I assume that the vast majority of sero-positives will progress. The time spent in the latency period is, as of now, completely undetermined. Of equal importance are the various phases the illness takes after it has progressed, by gradually damaging the immune system. How old are you?"

"36," I replied.

"I assume we will have a therapeutic vaccine shortly. So, if you live to be 40, you'll live to be 80."

"What's a 'therapeutic' vaccine?" I asked, regaining my composure.

"All vaccines may not be beneficial to someone who already has the virus. A 'therapeutic' vaccine would specifically benefit sero-positive cases."

Once again, Léo proved to be way ahead of typically accepted medical thinking. Unfortunately, being an optimist, he was significantly off on the timing required to discover a vaccine, therapeutic or otherwise.

Barcelona, Spain

Before returning to California, I made my usual stop in Spain. Clinica Quiron was well on its way to profitability, and we acquired a controlling interest in a second facility in Barcelona. By now I had an increasing fear that my years, perhaps months were numbered. Bob Davis had recently said, "Face it, René, in two years, we'll all be pushing up daisies." After work, I asked Antonio, our hospital administrator turned respected sculptor, if he would carve my bust so that I could leave it to my parents upon my death.

"I'd be thrilled," he replied, "but it will take at least six sittings." While Antonio reviewed his technique and which medium he wanted to use, I calculated that it would take 18 months for me to visit Spain six times. I hoped that I could have a year and a half in order to complete the bust.

A year and a half later, a larger-than-life sculpture in extinct black Belgium marble, mounted on a Plexiglas base, was completed. Although I thought "it" looked more like Joaquin Mestre, Quiron's former owner, than me, I felt that another step in "getting one's affairs in order" had been accomplished.

On December 31, there were 7,699 reported cases of AIDS in America.

Chapter Ten

1985

Los Angeles, California

When the year began, I was faced with conflicting mental attitudes. Some friends had died, more were sick and there was a general consensus that anyone who had been sexually active in the gay community would soon follow. Offsetting this was the great satisfaction I was getting from my career and AMI's International Division's progress. We now owned and operated hospitals in England, France, Spain, Switzerland, Greece, Singapore, Ecuador and Australia. Most were successful and all presented many challenges, which I found invigorating.

Naturally there were difficulties, mostly caused by internal corporate politics. Stanley resigned and founded a company to own and operate extended care facilities in England. I hoped that the growing UK business would be turned over to me, but Wally Weisman had a different position. Wally felt comfortable in London, an opposite reaction to his experience in all other countries in which AMI was active. He wanted to be in control in England.

While discussing which airlines we preferred, I touted the comforts offered on Swissair. Wally responded with "I hate Swissair. Just give me a good hamburger on TWA." This attitude did not go unnoticed on the few trips he made with me, resulting in my managers being quite happy that our division was separate from London.

The poor fellow, albeit intelligent and diligent, was not in any way an "internationalist" and had no ability to develop the much-needed cultural flexibility all successful multi-national corporations must acquire. In a board room compromise, AMI's British operations were assigned to him, and all other owned facilities reported to me who, in turn, continued to report to Royce, the Chief Executive. Ahmed handled the large Saudi Arabian management contracts in addition to his responsibilities as AMI's chief marketing officer. While this was no ideal organizational chart, I had no choice but to accept it and to run "my" hospitals as best I could.

Over the years, a large corporate office had developed in London. After Stanley left, Wally appointed one of his young protégés, Gene Burleson from North Carolina. Within a short period of time, Gene developed spurious, sophisticated airs and attitudes. He went from an innocuous assistant hospital administrator, not having ever enjoyed a cup of tea, to talking about "the legs" on the Port he consumed nightly and the style of his chauffeur's uniform. He even developed a phony English accent, which many observers ridiculed. Wally regularly visited London, where he and Gene enjoyed extravagant luxuries. The sad overall organizational result was the odd fact that the company had two philosophically very different International Divisions.

I was building my international oversight office in Beverly Hills. It was lean and efficient, in large part because of my Chief Operating Officer, Marliese Mooney. I had recruited her from Humana, at the time a fierce competitor in the hospital business and she, in turn, recruited a number of excellent executives from Humana. Our International Division in Beverly Hills looked like a mini-Humana, staffed by a financial director, nursing director, hospital administrators and systems experts, many of whom were former Humana employees.

Both health care giants, AMI and Humana, had begun health insurance companies in the misguided belief that the two divisions (owned hospitals and health insurance) could be mutually supportive and reinforcing. In fact, it rapidly became apparent that they were anything but that. If efficient, the insurance group begrudged any profits the hospitals booked and vice versa. This resulted in a competitive and destructive environment.

....

During a mounting international concern, approaching hysteria, about the progression of AIDS, I buried myself in my work, perhaps in a form of denial. Every month I went around the world for board-of-directors and management meetings, as well as for discussions with influential political leaders. For many months I was away from Los

Angeles for two to three weeks at a time. This did not create ideal conditions to develop a strong partnership with Tim, who was hard at work in school.

Shortly after Ronald Reagan was sworn in for his second term, and as the number of AIDS cases in America reached 8,000, the Office of Management and Budget (OMB) actually *cut* AIDS spending from $96 million to $85 million. Equally disappointing was the fact that the usually forward-looking CDC did not fund a proposed unit, which was suggested to be called "Operations AIDS Control." These negligent decisions coincided with increasing documentation of heterosexual transmission of the virus, incidences of the disease in the U.S. Army, and a new awareness of the risk of sharing syringes among IV drug users.

One evening Tim returned home from a late class to find me trying to cook dinner blindfolded.

"What on earth are you doing, René?" he asked.

"Bob Davis told me that our friend, Don, is now blind because of CMV. I am practicing being able to cope if that happens to me."

"CMV" or "cytomegalovirus" was a much-feared untreatable opportunistic infection, which induced a rapid progression to blindness in AIDS patients.

With that we hugged each other, fell to the floor and had the first of many therapeutic cries.

The antibody test became available to the general population in March. Tim and I went to Bob Davis' office the very first day physicians were allowed to send blood samples to the approved central laboratory. The ensuing days were filled with anxiety as we both tried to carry on, as best as possible, with our respective routines. After all, we were regularly attending Louise Hay's positive lectures. Perhaps there were two miracles assigned to us. Eventually, mysecretary said that Doctor Davis was holding on the phone. In a rare act, I shut the door to my office and picked up an extension in the room's sitting area, near the picture windows, which overlooked the mountains behind Beverly Hills. I drew a deep breath.

Louise Hay

"Hi, Bob." I began. "How are we all doing?" "Two years, René. I'm sorry."

"What about Tim?"

"Same thing. I'm sorry, but we all knew the probable outcome."

"If Tim calls, please say you do not yet have the results. Promise? I want to tell him myself."

I looked out at the beautiful hills filled with stunning homes. Turning 90 degrees I could see the Pacific Ocean in the distance. I wondered how many people would be receiving this news today and over the next few days. At least, in one way, we were the lucky ones. There were many who had not lived long enough to experience this day. I left the office and went home to prepare a nice dinner for Tim and me. Why not?

When Tim arrived, I had a bottle of Champagne in a large ice bucket placed on the living room coffee table. His eyes sparkled as he saw it.

"Are we celebrating?" he asked.

"Actually, in one way, yes." I replied. "We are both positive . . ."

"That's good, right?" he interrupted.

"No, Tim, it's not good." The words tore out my heart as did the changed look on his face. "It means we have been exposed to the virus." I took his hands in mine as he began to cry.

"So, what's the Champagne all about?" he said, choking back tears.

"We both *knew* this was the expected outcome. The Champagne is to celebrate the fact that we are here today — *right now* — alive, feeling well, looking out at the ocean, with lots of time together and things to accomplish in life. Let's open this sucker, take our glasses across the street, sit on a park bench and look at the horizon knowing that we are not alone and that we are alive."

Tim and René after receiving HIV diagnoses

We sat in the park a long time. We cried and even laughed. We decided we would have a professional photographer take a picture of us in that very spot as soon as possible. We talked about Tim's graduation the following year and the possibilities of his creating a dual design office in L.A. and Gstaad, Switzerland. We contemplated following many wealthy Americans by going to Paris for an experimental treatment Jean-Claude Chermann was investigating called HPA 23, made well-known because Rock Hudson was trying it.

Although it represented little direct importance, we discussed the mounting feud between French and American researchers. The "two" viruses (LAV and HTLV) were too similar, and rumors mounted that Gallo had "stolen" the French virus. Congressman Waxman remained our lone voice in the desert trying to get Congress and the Administration to become actively involved in research and education. In contrast, Health and Human Services Secretary Margaret Heckler made a *faux-pas* and revealed her inner thoughts by saying that AIDS had to be addressed "before it reached the heterosexual population." Apparently, she did not know what everyone else did, namely, it already had! Altogether, the situation looked bleak and depressing. I felt we had no choice but to try as best we could to continue with our personal and professional lives.

The news did not improve all summer. In June, Mother Theresa was awarded the Medal of Freedom at a White House ceremony. While the word "AIDS" was not mentioned, she immediately proceeded to George Washington University Hospital, ten blocks away, to visit their AIDS ward and offer support and prayers to the patients. Finally, in July, increased gossip in Paris regarding Rock Hudson's diagnosis caused the American Hospital to ask him to leave. I was ashamed by the fact that I had run that facility nine years before.

One rainy July evening, I returned to our condominium to find Tim watching the news. "Rock Hudson just arrived back in Los Angeles, apparently near death," he said. "He chartered a 747 for the trip home."

"You must be mistaken," I said. "A 747 is a huge plane. It must have been a different aircraft."

Tim shrugged his shoulders as if to say "whatever." But, it was I who was mistaken. Consistent with a stream of bad advice, someone had recommended the stricken actor spend $250,000 to return to Los Angeles by private charter aboard a plane designed for several 100 people.

Rock Hudson, 1925-1985

<u>Zürich, Switzerland</u>

By mid-1985, AMI's success in Switzerland was known throughout the investor-owned hospital industry. The first competitor to get a share of the market was Humana, which acquired a hospital outside of Geneva on the border town of La Tour de Meyrin. The facility had been offered to us, but our feasibility study indicated that the price asked would not allow AMI to generate the returns we were used to in Switzerland.

Even so, considering the relative wealth of the Swiss population and the high percentage of people insured to cover the costs of private hospitals, Switzerland was Europe's most lucrative market. Zürich, the country's largest city, had one old out-of-date private hospital which belonged to UBS (Union Bank of Switzerland). Along with Humana and our other American competitors, HCA and NME (National Medical Enterprises), which were not yet in the international market, we were all trying to figure out how be the first to establish a hospital in Zürich, a hospital that we all knew would be destined to become Europe's finest.

Consequently, Jean-Claude and I spent a great deal of time in Zürich. The only requirement to build a hospital in Switzerland was to own a suitable site and obtain a building permit specifically identifying an advanced set of architectural drawings. These permits were awarded by the cities' mayors. Unlike Humana, which was operating in a suburb of Geneva, our strategy was to be located in the center of our target cities. Property values in Zürich were among the highest in the world, along with Tokyo, Japan. Therefore, a huge investment was required to reach the point at which a building permit might, or might not, be granted.

On each of my trips to Europe, Jean-Claude and I would look at possible though expensive sites in Zürich. More importantly, we would call on the city's powerful well- respected mayor, Thomas Wagner. We always told him of our activities, plans and properties we were currently studying. The mayor became both a friend and an advisor, explaining which neighborhoods were the most problematic and which were the most desirable.

On one trip, we were going to see a shut-down hotel in an upscale residential area within the city, Hotel Im Park in Zollikon. During breakfast with Jean-Claude at the Dolder Grand Hotel, we noticed both Humana's hospital administrator from Geneva *and* an HCA executive, seated at separate tables. We feared they were also aware of the Im Park site's desirability. As I walked past their tables I said, "Nice day here in Zürich, isn't it gentlemen? Is there a hospital

René and Jean Claude Salamin at Klinik Im Park

convention I was unaware of?" I said sarcastically.

After a few hours at the site with an architect and city planner, we were sure that it was *the* location for our goals. The land was both large enough and easily accessed from all parts of greater Zürich. The hotel was not on the national registry of historic structures and could, therefore, be demolished. On one corner of the property stood a magnificent-but-run-down villa, which had belonged to the Mussolini family prior to the end of the Second World War and was Mussolini's destination when he was apprehended and killed. It was a historic landmark, but, given its location, we were certain we could build an appropriately sized and designed hospital around it. As usual, we ended our day with a visit to the mayor's office. After the usual pleasantries about art and wine, we asked his opinion of the Im Park land and, more importantly, the likelihood of his granting us a building permit there. He was positive about the site's desirability and cautiously optimistic about our ability to obtain the necessary permits, *if* we owned the land and had a full set of working drawings.

Jean-Claude and I returned to the hotel and called Royce in Los Angeles. After describing "the find" and reviewing the various costs, notably the purchase price, Royce asked his usual, appropriate questions. "We have never spent that much on any site. Are you sure this is our best bet?"

"Not only the best, Royce, but possibly the only suitable site in Zürich," I responded.

"What is the likelihood of you getting a building permit?" he continued.

"Mayor Wagner was as positive as he could safely be, while still remaining impartial."

"Do you *feel* you can get the permits?" he insisted.

"Yes, I do," I said confidentially.

"You realize what will happen if you do not?" he said, more than ask.

"Yes, sir, I do."

We made an offer to acquire the property, which, in turn, was accepted. While both Jean-Claude and I knew that our jobs were at risk, we experienced a feeling of elation, even as we contemplated the huge amount of work and roadblocks ahead. We were correct about the former, we seriously underestimated the latter.

By fall, the number of AIDS cases in the United States had passed 10,000.

Chapter Eleven

1986

Switzerland

Because of the developing Zürich project, I was in Switzerland at least once a month. We hired a well-respected and politically-accepted architect, Karl Steiner, whose first challenge was to prepare a schematic plan of the proposed project. Before we even reached that point, the neighbors organized in an emotional, concerted effort to stop the project. Their primary complaint was that, while the old hotel could legally be demolished, any new structure should basically look similar. However, no efficient hospital could be planned in a configuration similar to the existing hotel.

Our architect suggested that the first schematic of the new hospital look similar to the hotel. The logic was to placate the neighbors and then to alter the plan once we had established a working dialogue with their representative. I explained the strategy to both Mayor Wagner and to Royce, who was very concerned about getting locked into an inefficient design which he constantly referred to as "three lumps." It was a gamble we were prepared to take and one that I had to frequently justify.

Even though I was spending more time in Zürich than in Lausanne, I never missed an opportunity to review the medical and political developments regarding AIDS with Professor Eckmann. The press in Europe contained almost daily articles about the origin, cause and future of the disease. I wanted to know Léo's opinion on how AIDS had developed.

"How does a new virus begin?" I asked him when we met for dinner.

"I rather doubt this is a 'new' virus," he said. "It certainly is a new illness and a different manifestation of the virus. But I believe the virus has been around for a long time."

"As you know," I continued, "I have seen clues for eight years."

"I believe it has been around a lot longer than that," continued Léo. "There have been sporadic, documented cases of the same series of opportunistic infections we now call AIDS. I'm sure there were pockets of immune-suppressed illnesses and I'd bet that the LAV virus was one virus that caused them. This theory could be easily proved *if* we had proper storage of blood samples prior to the 1960's. Sadly, that is not the case."

"Okay," I said, fascinated with this theory. "Then why did it suddenly blow up?"

"I don't think it was sudden," Léo explained. "I believe that something gradually upset a balance that coexisted between human beings and a silent virus. Fatigue created by all-night parties, promiscuous sex and already-unhealthy male prostitutes, notably in Haiti, were key elements which helped create a weakened host for a virus that was 'waiting' to attack. The *real* plague existed in rats for generations before conditions were ripe enough for it to jump into humans. The same set of conditions happened here. Unfortunately for you, the disease initially exploded in the international, homosexual community. But, as we already know for sure, AIDS will continue to spread to other groups. I'll guess malnourished, impoverished populations because, again, these are weakened potential hosts with inadequate hygiene, waiting to become ill."

"What is the future of treatment?" I asked.

"In the absence of a vaccine, there will be several levels of activity. The first is prevention, of course. Second is what I would call 'immune building,' in other words, taking advantage of products which are proven to strengthen the immune system. Products like the ones that are now used after serious surgeries or marrow transplants. Finally, anti-viral medications already exist, and will likely proliferate. But, remember what I have already told you, no serious viral condition has even been solved with anti-virals. You need to change the host through a vaccine."

Léo thought for what seemed to be an interminable period, and continued,

"The dilemma is that there is not much profit in vaccine research and production, but there are huge potential profits in the development and continual, long-term use of anti-viral therapy. Also, there is huge profit potential in developing medications to treat the *symptoms* of AIDS. There are already new treatments for the digestive and respiratory manifestations of LAV. You can expect to see many advances in treatment for sure. Think about it. It has been the same with cancer. We have improved chemotherapy regimens, as well as many new medications to make oncology more tolerable. But we have made little, if any, progress in understanding and treating the causes of cancer."

After my visit with Léo, I felt so grateful for the education but also felt quite depressed about what I, Tim and many friends would experience in the coming years. Most of them would not have the benefit of a wise physician who was also a historian and a philosopher.

By mid-year, the two viruses, HTLV III and LAV, were recognized as one and internationally renamed HIV (Human Immunodeficiency Virus). At the same time, it was becoming widely accepted that there were several strains of HIV, and that the easiest way to determine the virus' effect and damage on the immune system was to measure the CD-4 lymphocyte, also called the "T Helper Cell" and commonly referred to as the "T-Cell."

Los Angeles, California

Tim graduated in the spring and the ceremony was held and celebrated at UCLA. I bought him a silver-grey Corvette, which he had always wanted. It was parked on a lawn, near the building where the graduation took place; a huge red ribbon crisscrossed over the car and it had a big red bow on the roof. If we were only going to live a few years, I wanted Tim to have any material possessions I could afford. When we walked out of the building I said,

"Look, Tim! Some lucky fellow got a Corvette as a present! Let's go over and check it out!"

He walked all around the car until I held out a key and said:

"Hey, why not see if this works?"

Tim was so overcome that he had to sit down on the grass, because he was afraid he would faint, a condition that occurred twice during the spring. The second time, I had obtained tickets to the Academy Awards.

When I picked Tim up, he looked so handsome in his tuxedo and was so excited about

Tim in Mykonos summer 1986

going to the event he had always dreamed of attending. As we got out of a rented limousine and began to walk down the red carpet, we were sandwiched between Shirley MacLaine and Faye Dunaway. Tim grabbed my arm and said he was about to faint. I responded with, "Just take a deep breath, put one foot in front of the other and be grateful that everyone is wondering who *you* are. After all, you are the prettiest one here."

The following week, President Reagan bombed Libyan President Khadafi, killing several members of Khadafi's family. As I heard the news on my car radio, the phone rang. It was my secretary telling me that Stanley Balfour-Lynn had died. It was a rainy night in Los Angeles. I pulled over to the side of the road and thought about this amazing man and how very lucky I was to have known him.

....

AMI had completed a modern hospital in the city of Quito, Ecuador. Every time we opened a new facility, I would send a team from the corporate office to work with our newly recruited local hospital administration. The water and uncooked food in Quito was dangerous, resulting in several of my staff returning to California with amoebic dysentery. Eventually, we sent all the needed water, as well as many other supplies to the apartments we rented to house the team. After my first trip to Quito, I also developed severe intestinal problems. I followed several courses of treatment of an unpleasant arsenic-based pill called Flagyl. Time after time I would complete the required number of days on the medication only to have the symptoms return. After losing 25 pounds, I underwent several tests and met with Bob Davis.

"René, there is no current evidence of amoebas in your system. Although there is something called 'recurring amoebic dysentery,' I think you now have a yeast infection in your intestines, a sign of a weakened immune system."

He prescribed an antifungal medication and put me on a severe diet. Eventually, looking like skin and bones, the horrible symptoms subsided. I was sure I had experienced my first opportunistic infection, especially because many people commented on my appearance. Royce's concern was both comforting and alarming. I feared what Wally might be thinking.

Zürich, Switzerland

The story of the proposed new AMI hospital was of great interest throughout the city of Zürich. It was the topic of discussion everywhere we went, even when people did not know who we were. Our regular meetings with the neighbors of the Im Park site were difficult but did gradually result in a spirit of cooperation. Eventually the initial "three lump" plan was scrapped. Although the strategy of easing into the neighborhood was successful, the new plan was more

René with Jean Claude Salamin at a reception in Switzerland

expensive to construct. The site would have to be excavated to contain four underground levels at the highest part of the property, but by doing so we could prepare an efficient design. Finally, we had a completed set of detailed architectural plans which we presented to the city in order to be granted a building permit.

Jean-Claude and I waited outside the city council meeting the day of their vote on the project. I paced around the huge hallways, while Jean-Claude tried to joke about what our next career would be once the project was rejected and Wally made sure we were fired. After what seemed like an eternity, we were called into the meeting.

"We are willing to grant your company a building permit for the hospital project," began Mayor Wagner, "but with certain understandings."

"Thank you, sir, what are they?" I asked.

"First, you will have to construct a bomb shelter large enough to house all employees of the new hospital." I had been informed that this concession was being required of many large, new projects. We had already calculated the extravagant cost. The hospital could still become profitable after several years, but the "feasibility study" was less and less convincing. I feared the cost of further concessions.

"Yes, we accept the condition to include a bomb shelter of adequate size to protect 450 people in the event of a thermonuclear attack. What else, sir?" I asked.

"You have to add a new highly sophisticated energy conservation system." We had feared this also, due to the cost. It would require between nine and ten years of greatly reduced energy bills to recoup the investment.

"Very well," I said, hoping beyond all hope that was the last compromise.

"And finally," continued the mayor, "the Mussolini villa cannot move."

"I'm not quite sure I understand, sir," I began. "The plan calls for us to move the villa off the site, construct the underground areas of the hospital, replace the villa back to its *exact* current location and, finally, totally renovate it."

"That is what we do not accept," he said. Before I could further question him, he continued. "The villa must not move *at all* during construction. You will have to support it in place while you excavate underneath. Specific surveyor's sightings will be located to ascertain the villa does not move one centimeter during the construction phase. The city's architect assures us this can be done, but at great expense to you."

I was astounded and tried to imagine the price. I did understand that I had nothing to lose by accepting the condition. Any response other than an immediate acceptance would further delay our breaking ground. The financial studies would be recalculated after the price had been computed and then presented to Royce and AMIs full board of directors. I would also have to be fully prepared to be ridiculed and see the project, and my job, terminated.

"Granted," I said, hoping my knees would hold me up.

"Congratulations and good luck. We will have the lawyers draw up the agreement, and you will be required to submit monthly progress reports to the city building department," he concluded.

<u>**Los Angeles, California**</u>

At an Executive meeting in Los Angeles ten days later, I explained what occurred during the Zürich city council meeting. I had a new set of financial projections, which incorporated all the additional features. I had also increased the yet-to-be-built hospital's occupancy rates to slightly offset the added expenses. Obviously, I had reviewed the presentation with Royce the day before.

When it came to vote on whether to move forward or abort the effort, Wally spoke. "This will be the most expensive hospital AMI has ever built, both in the absolute and on a per- bed basis. The additional site preparation alone is over two million dollars. I also note that the projected initial occupancy rates are higher than that of any start-up facility we have experienced." Looking at me, he asked,

"How sure are you that there will be no further escalation of the construction costs and of these *very optimistic* occupancy rates?"

I responded, "There certainly will be many problems to address during construction over the next two years. I feel we have the best team to address them, and I will risk my reputation on the fact that we will achieve the financial results in the first three years as described in the report."

After the vote went in favor of proceeding, Wally closed the discussion with, "I want my concerns to go on record."

He looked me squarely in the eyes as if to say: *Another possible nail in your coffin, Silvin.*

Chapter Twelve

1987

Los Angeles, California

1987 began with conflicting emotions and information regarding any progress the world was making on AIDS research, education and acceptance. Religious leaders clearly had furthered their agenda in repressing any helpful conversation of the disaster. They had been successful in establishing the feeling among many of their followers that the "homos deserved what they got" even though there were adequate statistics to prove that the virus had no sexual preference.

AIDS activist Elizabeth Taylor

Albeit in a clumsy manner, President Reagan had finally uttered the term AIDS during a speech and, after an awkward joke about funding, he explained his position on the pandemic. He made no mention of education and chose to focus on testing. Sadly, no funding initiatives were proposed. These missed opportunities were partially offset by the huge attendance at the Third International Conference on AIDS in Washington, D.C. and Surgeon General Koop who emphasized education and acceptance.

Because AIDS was decimating the art world, including Hollywood, several celebrities, notably Liz Taylor, were speaking out. She was clear about her support for Rock Hudson and other friends, showing genuine emotion as she presented the Surgeon General with an award for his efforts. Civil rights leaders were beginning to make significant headway in organizing the collective voice of frustration including a controlled, but well-observed, protest when Vice President George Bush gave the opening remarks at the AIDS Conference.

I concluded that Tim and I needed to live our lives to the fullest: to prepare the worst and hope for the best.

Wally Weisman had been named "CEO Designate" and would assume the position of Chief Executive the following year, upon Royce's retirement. I was not the only member of the senior management group to be saddened, but not surprised, by the news. Many had hoped Royce would appoint an outsider to take the reins and lead the company out of new financial difficulties.

These difficulties were caused by the Reagan administration's new Medicare reimbursement program called "DRG" or "diagnosis-related group." Hospitals could no longer bill the government for services on a "cost-plus" basis. Instead, hospitals would be compensated by a fixed amount of money dependent on the patient's diagnoses. All health insurance carriers adopted the same standards, which put enormous pressure on the investor-owned hospital industry and rewarded low-cost providers.

Additionally, AMI had made a couple of significant investments which were drawing negative reactions from both individual and institutional shareholders. One of these investments was a failed foray into the health insurance business, and another was a corporate college, one of Wally's pet projects.

Wally decided to discontinue the insurance company's development and shut it down, taking a $100 million charge against 1987 earnings. Coinciding with the collapse of our stock price, a few substantial investors increased their positions in the company, in the hope of taking over with different leadership. The well-known Bass brothers from Texas and a wealthy Miami-based physician turned hospital and bank owner, Lee Pearce, had managed to put the company "in play," which meant that a takeover was possible. Tension in the executive offices at the Beverly Hills headquarters was palpable, and a most uncomfortable working environment emerged. The company's great growth era, which rewarded entrepreneurial spirit was replaced with a bureaucratic "cover your ass" approach to business. I found myself savoring the frequent trips to Zürich, even though it was detrimental to any personal life I had hoped for.

At Sea, Mid Atlantic

On numerous occasions I would begin my day in Beverly Hills, having made evening and weekend plans with Tim, only to be informed of one crisis or another at one of our Swiss hospital construction sites. By evening, I would be on a flight to Zürich after having apologized to Tim and the few social friends we had who were willing to cooperate with my schedule. My one huge thrill was to synchronize any emergency trips with an Eastbound crossing of the QE2, if it occurred over a weekend. I kept a sailing schedule in a drawer on my desk, which I consulted periodically.

One Wednesday I was informed of an unscheduled meeting at the mayor's office in Zürich to be held the following Tuesday. The QE2 was to set sail from New York the following day and, after five magnificent days at sea, dock in Europe in just enough time for me to prepare for, and attend, the meeting. As was often the case, I took a redeye flight to New York and went to the Cunard office to purchase a last-minute, best- available cabin for that day's departure. The popular trips were always heavily booked, especially in the best cabins and suits. However, some of these desirable accommodations routinely became available on the eve of the trip, due to passengers' unforeseen personal or business events. I was delighted to find such a situation upon my arrival in New York, which gave me just the right amount of time to buy the ticket, walk by the ship to admire the curve of its bow towering over the pier, catch a quick nap and board for the customary 4 PM sailing.

René on the QE2, 1987

My "Queen's Grill" cabin, so-named because of the special dining room to which passengers in these accommodations were assigned, was immediately adjacent to a suite occupied by a handsome young couple, whom I initially assumed were on their honeymoon. After dinner, on the first night at sea, the slender buxom blonde from the neighboring suite sat down next to me at the ship casino's bar. She began a rather forward and inquisitive conversation, which caused me to be evasive in my responses and to abort her obvious flirting as soon as possible. Two similar alleged chance encounters occurred the following day. Again, I terminated them prematurely.

During the subsequent two days, I had comparable meetings with her James Bond-like companion. One get- together was in the ship's gymnasium, followed by a steam room run-in, and meetings in several of the ship's bars over the next day and a half. Again, the conversation was intrusive and very forward, and again my reaction was to abbreviate each session. Over the weekend, I had several phone conversations with Jean-Claude, as well as a number of exchanges of telegrams relating to the construction in Zürich.

I became aware of just how odd the situation with the young British couple had become when, on the third day at sea, the handsome, but intrusive, couple's suite was vacated, and the striking pair vanished from sight. My cabin steward gave me an odd reason for the unusual mid-Atlantic occurrence. The day we disembarked in Southampton, England, I saw the duo enter an unmarked, yet official-looking, black Rover.

Los Angeles, California

Several months later, I ran into the mystery man at one of my favorite bars in Los Angeles and we began to chat.

"Fancy meeting you in a joint like this," I began. "Where is your beautiful friend?"

"She was a colleague, not a friend," he answered. "How is that hospital in Zürich coming along?" he asked to my amazement, as I had carefully avoided any mention of my business with either person.

After a hesitation, he continued,

"I used to work for the British Secret Service. We had a credible report of a terrorist threat on the QE2 to occur on that particular crossing. There were several teams aboard, lodged in cabins throughout the ship and posing as Cunard staff. At first, you met the profile, and we were primarily assigned to surveilling you."

"Why me?" I asked.

"You were alone in a high-end cabin, and you purchased the ticket the day of the trip. Then we reviewed a tape which showed you sitting on the pier several hours before embarkation. You didn't help matters by trying to slip away from us. When we concluded that the soft touch was not going to work, I made the move on you in the gym. I hate to tell you; we searched your cabin and monitored your calls and telegrams. When we discovered the nature of your business, we moved to a cabin adjacent to a second suspect."

It was an amazing tale, but one which fit the very odd events.

The following day, I had a meeting with Wally, and upon entering his office it was clear that a confrontation was going to happen.

"I'm not happy with the progress in Zürich and the occupancy rates in Bern and Lausanne," he began in an abrupt manner.

"Wally, we are ahead of the construction schedule in Zürich and on budget. The summer occupancy rates are cyclically below average in Switzerland, and I am perfectly confident we will meet our targets for the quarter and the year. I have kept Royce very closely aware of both facts and..."

"I am the Chief Executive-designate and Royce is on his way out!" he pointed out emphatically. "From now on, you will only report to me. If I tell you something different than Royce, you will follow my instructions! And I am telling you to improve the operations in Switzerland. So that you know, I will be firing Jean-Claude today!"

I felt under personal attack. Jean-Claude had been promoted to "country manager" with the various hospital administrators reporting to him. I had also appointed him to the position of Corporate Vice-President. When I was able to catch my breath and try to organize some thoughts, I answered:

"Wally, Switzerland's performance will be on or above target at each hospital. And, I'm sorry, but firing Jean- Claude will be a catastrophic error economically, politically and for the morale in all the hospitals. Whose side are you on?"

"Do you understand I have the power to blow anyone I like out of the water? Jean-Claude has mocked me, and everything we have tried to accomplish in bringing this company into a multi-billion-dollar league. I don't give a rat's ass about staff morale or the political implications, and I won't allow one more Swiss Franc to be spent than what has previously been approved. You can forget making any new capital expenditure requests."

"I'm sure you don't mean that," I continued. "There will be many essential investments required to achieve operating targets as we open the new hospitals. And, again, it's not in your interest to fire Jean-Claude before all five hospitals are opened. Then you can fire us both, if you wish. In the meantime, you may want to ask the Swiss holding company's board members what they think of losing Jean-Claude at this stage of the development."

"I don't need anyone's approval or consent. It's a done deal. Goodbye, Rick."

I knew very well that both Jean-Claude's and my days were numbered. I was completely committed to our employees and the politicians we had befriended in Switzerland, and I was determined to do my best to live up to our commitments, even if it meant my early departure from AMI.

I went to see Royce, fully aware of the rage that would elicit in Wally. As always, Royce heard me and solicited my opinions in significant detail. Royce then prevailed upon Wally not to alter our existing plans or to fire Jean-Claude, at least for now. But, I wondered what recourse would I have after Wally really was CEO and my boss?

Royce and I also agreed that an AMI with Wally as CEO would inevitably divest itself of the International Division, with the possible exception of the UK. The best strategy from a shareholder's perspective was to move the International Oversight Office to Switzerland, in order to establish it as a true Swiss company capable of operating independently from the corporate office in Beverly Hills; to open the three new hospitals that were coming online over the next months and, finally, to identify the best possible buyer for the entire International subsidiary. That would likely be a Swiss group, given the relatively high asset values of the Swiss properties.

"What do you think of *my* trying to buy the company?" I asked.

"All offers will be reviewed carefully. If you really feel you can embark on such an adventure, go right ahead. But, remember, Wally will become CEO and we will also have to pursue all options."

Athens, Greece

One market we had tested to determine if a hospital company with our strategy could be successful was Athens, Greece. We took a 35% interest in the capital city's largest, private hospital, the 350 bed Hygiea Hospital. We quickly learned that we had been duped into the acquisition and that we had little hope of controlling the rampant corruption which existed at all levels, starting with the Board of

Directors. Erroneously, and at great expense, Wally had insisted that we hire one of "his" domestic hospital administrators and move him and his family to Athens. While we were able to break-even at Hygiea, we never met any profit projections.

Hygiea Hospital, Athens,

My trips to Athens were extremely difficult and contentious as I sat through all-day board meetings, punctuated with arguments and accusations from the Greeks. On a few occasions, I received death threats because I represented the largest American employer of Greeks in Athens. When a threat seemed somewhat plausible, I would be met by a bodyguard at the airport. He would remain with me throughout the usual two-day visit and even sleep in front of my door at the Intercontinental Hotel.

On our fall visit to Greece, Marliese Mooney, my Chief Operating Officer, and I were met by the hospital's assistant administrator. His dour demeanor was quickly explained by his request to come up to my suite and tell us some disconcerting news.

"One of the hospital's ambulance drivers has been taking bribes," he began. "The butcher is his brother-in-law, and we are buying his inferior meat. We have hired other relatives of his, including mechanics and electricians, all of whom are sub-par."

"Have you told your boss, Ross the administrator?" I asked.

"Well, that's the problem," he began. "The driver is sleeping with Ross' daughter and has ingratiated himself with the family."

"I'll take it up with Ross," I said.

"Well, you need to know another problem as it relates to them. The driver also sleeps with Ross!" Marliese burst out laughing and I shook my head. Another one of Wally's decisions had ended in disaster. I would have to fire the administrator at the same time that we were trying to make changes to the physicians' remuneration package, which would reduce certain Board physician members' annual income. That difficult decision had been made and we were not about to alter our plan. Marliese and I agreed that I should lay low until the following day's shareholder meeting, when I would present the new doctors' pay package to the shareholders for a vote.

One of Athens's most powerful professors of medicine was also on the hospital's Board of Directors. In his usual arrogant fashion, he tried in vain to reach me to fend off our plan. However, he did reach Marliese.

"You must stop Rick from making an irresponsible and reckless proposals to the shareholders tomorrow," he told her. "You know, I am an old man and Rick is very young and reckless. If he does this, he is a fool."

Mykonos, Greece. Left to right: Marliese Mooney, Susan Harrison, René

"Well, Professor," Marliese answered, "no one can talk Rick out of what *we* plan to do. And, in America, we have an adage which says, 'there is no fool like an old fool.'"

The following day I conducted the shareholder meeting on the 17th floor of the tall hospital tower. Just as the contentiously debated issue was ready for the crucial vote, Athens experienced one of the worst earthquakes in its recent history. People jumped under desks, ran down stairwells and hid under door thresholds. Marliese and I were left alone on the dais. We looked at each other and burst out laughing. When the group reassembled, the motion passed by a slight majority, an important step to enable us to sell our holdings without taking a loss. As we left the meeting, Marliese told the professor:

"Now you know that Rick has special powers."

Los Angeles, California

As the year drew to a close, I continued to plan moving the key elements of the office, as well as Tim and me to Switzerland. AIDS had now attacked 36,000 Americans and caused 20,000 deaths. Tim and I were well into Bob Davis' predicted life expectancy of two years.

When I told Bob of my plans, he said, "Obviously, you can obtain excellent care at your facilities in Switzerland. The average is two hospitalizations before death. There are new treatments which you need to look into." His prediction of "excellent care" proved to not be quite accurate.

"Really, please tell me about these new treatments," I asked.

"A physician in Bethesda is studying a treatment using a product called 'Peptide T' and an old Burroughs Welcome medication called 'AZT,' These medications seem to have some effects in retarding the progression of the virus. AZT being renamed 'Retrovir' which is a clever name, but I doubt it is in any way a magic bullet."

Fortunately, I did not feel inclined to investigate either possibility until I could review the news with Léo. I'd be in Switzerland for much of the next months and would probably soon be living there. I'd also be 'living with AIDS,' which was the new expression used at the support groups conducted by Louise Hay and Marianne Williamson, as well as by many HIV -positive people. My usual evenings, previously spent at bars, were now used attending the meetings held by these two inspiring and brilliant ladies.

Chapter Thirteen

1988

Lausanne, Switzerland

During the early winter months of 1988, I spent more time in Switzerland than in California. At least once a week, I would meet Léo for a coffee in Clinique Cecil's opulent lounge. Like at the Palace Hotel, Jean-Claude had installed a trout tank there for guests to select a trout for a meal. The action had earned us an article on the front page of the Wall Street Journal in the left-hand column titled: "AMI's Swiss Hospitals Install Trout Tanks." On one occasion in the beautiful lounge, Wally had criticized us for not having a public address system throughout the hospitals. Jean-Claude proudly and defiantly said, "You see the cash register on the bar? That is the only noise I will allow in our hospitals. This is not LAX, Wally." The stress between them had obviously reached the boiling point.

"Léo," I began our conversation seated by the now-famous cash register, "please tell me about Peptide T and AZT."

"Well, Doctor Pert in Bethesda has an interesting theory about Peptide T. Although she is brilliant, her team focuses their work on the activity of oxidizing agents. I prefer the viral hypothesis. AZT is now being commonly prescribed, but it is very toxic, particularly in the high doses currently being administered. I strongly advise you to not start any such treatment in your current condition. I do recommend that you and Tim begin regular intravenous infusions of human immunoglobulin."

"What's that, Léo?" I inquired.

"It is a blood by-product which I use to boost the strength of elderly patients after surgery. The French use it on hemophiliacs, at least those who can afford it. I, myself, take it from time to time when I am run down. If it helps weakened surgical patients, I am confident it will strengthen you as well. Think about it. The more little soldiers we can put on the front line to fend off the virus the better. But, since the dose I would like you to take every month will require 14,000 blood donors to produce, you can imagine the cost. It has been observed in Paris that 50% of all hemophiliacs are HIV positive, and yet only a few progress to AIDS. I think immunoglobulin infusions are partially responsible for this good news."

Tim and I began to use this prophylactic treatment regularly. It was finally accepted as treatment for advanced AIDS patients in America five years later.

One morning, while looking over occupancy rates in Jean-Claude's office, he erupted while reading his mail. "Look at the kind of ridiculous complaints I receive!" he declared.

After I read the very angry letter from a dissatisfied client, I asked, "Who is Pierre Nussbaumer?"

"The Nussbaumer family has a major Swiss fortune. Pierre is our age and the son of the family's business empire's founder," he responded.

"Let's call him and ask him to please meet us for a drink at the hotel whenever it's convenient for him," I said.

That evening, I met a most charming and intelligent man who revealed some very valid criticisms about his lovely wife's treatment at the hospital. This first meeting set the basis for our becoming close friends.

I had been very secretive about my sexuality in business circles but, somehow Pierre's questioning allowed me to be honest when he asked me,

"How does your wife handle your constant traveling?"

"Well, Monsieur," I said, still being formal, "I have a partner, not a wife, and *he* finds my schedule challenging, to say the least."

Pierre's reaction was liberal, "un-Swiss" and refreshing.

"We'll be delighted to meet him and take you both to dinner the very first night he joins you in Switzerland," he said, with obvious honesty and enthusiasm. "I'll count on you to let me know when you come back."

"We plan on moving the company to Switzerland within a few months," I said. "There will be plenty of opportunity for us to get to know each other soon." Pierre then gave me useful advice on where to live in the area. Over the next months the four of us spent many wonderful evenings and a few weekends together in Gstaad and France.

Beverly Hills, California

The months before moving to Switzerland were spent preparing all necessary financial analyses. With my financial officer's assistance, I prepared a 200-page book that would become the prospectus we could use to interest buyers for the entire international division. The book value of the overseas facilities was approximately equal to the charge against earnings that AMI would declare at the close of our fiscal year in August. I felt the forecasts to reach profitability at the three new hospitals in Switzerland, and to improve other facilities' performance were optimistic, but achievable.

Determining the estimated variables of occupancy rates, uncollectible accounts and certain unpredictable start-up costs, became a frequent discussion among Wally, Royce and me. Although we did eventually reach an understanding on all estimates, the following conflict became apparent: overly optimistic forecasts would help both AMI and me identify financial backers, while reasonable projections would be easier for me to achieve as the executive ultimately in charge of operating results.

By late springtime the forecasts were all agreed upon, as was the desired sale price, net of debt, of $98 million. Several key members of my international team, as well as Tim and I, scheduled our phased move to Switzerland over the summer. I listed my Santa Monica condominium for sale. At my parting meeting with Wally, he said, "I'll give you a few months to come up with a buyer and I hope you have some idea of the magnitude of the venture and adventure you are embarking upon." That may have been the one profound statement he made to me during my brief tenure reporting to him. My emotional farewells to the loyal international staff remaining in Beverly Hills paled in comparison with leaving Royce, who was boss, mentor and beloved father figure.

I thought of something Tennessee Williams said: "I lived out in Santa Monica and had a ball until the money ran out." I lived "*out* in Santa Monica and had a ball" until Royce retired. It was time to leave, and I knew it.

As Tim and I prepared to move, we discussed the many obvious uncertainties about our careers, as well as a growing list of health issues. Several medications to restore immune system functioning were being considered. Among these were "Interleukin 2," Léo's

"Immunoglobulin Infusions," and "Imuthiol," also called "DTC," which was manufactured by the French pharmaceutical giant, The Mérieux Institute. The Mérieux family and my family had been close friends for three generations, and I planned to ask their advice.

During our initial months in Europe, Tim planned to master a working knowledge of French, while I focused on the leveraged buyout of the hospital group. We both followed whatever immune support therapies Léo recommended. We flew to Europe on the Concorde. However, it was difficult to have any conversation, because Tim was mesmerized by Diana Ross sitting across the narrow isle from him.

Switzerland

Tim and I rented a charming villa in the middle of the vineyards above Lausanne which my new friend, Pierre, had found. Like the hospital, it had a spectacular view across Lake Geneva at the French Alps in the distance. With the owner's consent, I allowed Tim to redecorate the rented house. We hoped this would establish him with an initial design project in Switzerland. We also rented an apartment in Gstaad, where Tim hoped to identify clients who were looking for interior design talent with a modern Californian flair. I spent most days away from Lausanne, in one Swiss city or another, as well as making quick trips to our other European hospitals.

Tim and René in Gstaad

It was imperative that I obtain permanent resident and working status in Switzerland. Léo warned me that an HIV test was now part of the mandatory physical exam to apply for the all-important documents. Upon questioning, we learned that there was still one canton (state) in the very decentralized Swiss Confederation which had not adopted the added blood test.

"We're going to Lugano in the morning," Jean Claude said one afternoon. "The Canton of Teccino is the only one which does not have HIV on the list of blood tests. You don't have syphilis, do you?" he joked. "I have spoken with the medical director of the Canton and told him that we hoped you would not have to wait in line in Lugano.

He was quite willing to have you go for the physical there without having to queue up. It will cost you a dinner at the best restaurant in Lugano for us with the doctor and his wife."

The plan worked perfectly. The Canton of Ticcino added the HIV test to its list of bloodwork the following month.

My friendship with Pierre took root and grew quickly. His attractive, liberal and sophisticated wife, Michèle, tried very hard to make us feel at home and to introduce us to their unusual trendy friends. Pierre took an interest in our efforts to find backers to acquire the company and gave us numerous excellent suggestions.

"If I was you," he said one night at dinner, "I'd resign my position at AMI and pursue the purchase as an outside independent party. I don't think you can serve two masters simultaneously. Up until now, you have represented AMI, but it will become increasingly difficult to do so and you will open yourself up to criticism." The difficulties I had encountered with Wally in coming to agreements on occupancy forecasts were a case in point. Unfortunately, I did not heed his sound advice.

....

While the rental house was torn apart, Tim and I lived at the Lausanne Palace Hotel. Late, on one of our first nights in Lausanne, I was awakened by a call from Wally who advised me that, consistent to what I had read in *The Wall Street Journal*, Lee Pearce was still trying to take over the entire company. He told me that Doctor Pearce was particularly interested in seeing all the European hospitals. I was to cancel any activities for the ensuing week and accompany Lee Pearce and an attorney with whom he was traveling throughout Europe. Wally proceeded to enumerate a list of important individuals associated with our activities that I was to introduce to the team arriving from Miami the following day.

I knew that when Doctor Pearce practiced medicine his partner, Doctor Brooks, had been imprisoned for hiring a hit man to kill his wife. Nevertheless, with an open mind, I met Doctor Pearce at Geneva airport and reviewed the travel plans I had made. I had hurriedly set up appointments with the hospital's administrations, select board members and local authorities in several cities. Within the first hour of our planned week together, it was clear that Doctor Pearce would present an image that was not at all in keeping with the

Doctor M. Lee Pearce

culturally adapted and politically correct stance we had worked so hard to achieve in each country. At restaurants he insisted on paying with 100-dollar bills, which created unnecessary attention to us as vulgar Americans. On the second day of the trip, and after having already heard many grotesque racial slurs and bad homophobic jokes, we entered the charming little Swiss city of Aarau where we were building a new hospital.

Doctor Pearce turned to his lawyer, who was sitting with him in the back of the company's Mercedes, and said, "Can you imagine what just five niggers from Miami let loose in this town could do to it in one year? It would look like Harlem!"

I instantly decided that I would cancel dinner planned that night in Zürich with my friend, Mayor Thomas Wagner, as well as several other appointments. There was no way I could introduce this hideous man, who was announcing his plan to take over the entire company, to certain individuals I had cultivated over the previous years. If such an acquisition were to occur, I would leave the company, but, until that time, I was willing to run the risk of creating any ruse necessary to save face. I called the mayor's office from the car and, in front of my American guests, but in French, simply told his assistant we had to change our plans and that I would explain at a later date.

"Mayor Wagner will not be joining us for dinner tonight," I told Pearce, hanging up the phone. "He had an emergency and left Zürich. But we will have a lovely evening and I'll take you through the new hospital tomorrow."

"But we *will* meet the producer of the TV station which is covering it in Switzerland's version of *60 Minutes*, right?" he asked.

"I'll confirm that in the morning. There was some doubt about their availability," I said, using what was to become a recurring phrase that week. Jean-Claude had managed to arrange for us to be featured on the well-respected weekly national program the following week.

At dinner that night, the four of us, including Jean- Claude, were seated in a corner table adjacent to an empty table for two. After ordering our meal, I gasped at the sight of Mayor Wagner and his wife being escorted to the neighboring table. I jumped up to meet him and quickly said in Swiss German, "Please trust me on this strange encounter. There is a good explanation, and I will call you tomorrow. For now, please understand that I am not going to introduce you to our guests."

Jean-Claude was hiding his face behind a dinner napkin, stifling laughter. There was no need for any lengthy explanation the next day. The mayor understood enough English to be totally shocked by what he overheard during the meal. Lee Pearce was talking about a trip to the African kingdom of Ghana, where the U.S. Ambassador said he would meet the country's queen that night. "Is she a real queen or just another fat nigger?" Pearce boasted he had asked the ambassador. I looked over at the mayor, whose expression and hand motions thanked me for sparing him the experience.

Barcelona, Spain

When our little group reached Barcelona, I explained that the two hospitals under our management had turned profitable and were the only acute-care private hospitals in Spain to enjoy that position. Antonio, the senior administrator and my sculptor, proudly spread out the two hospitals' financial statements on his desk for Pearce to examine.

"Let me understand this," Pearce said after looking over the documents. "Do you mean to tell me you have a total of 400 beds and only cleared a million dollars last year?"

"Doctor," began Antonio, "we have reversed a million- dollar *loss* into this profit and will be improving these results next year."

"Frankly, Antonio, I see no reason for you to get out of bed in the morning if it's to only make a million bucks," answered Pearce, as he got up and walked away.

My friend's face turned white with shock. He took me aside and said,

"Thank you for canceling lunch with Mestre, the hospital's previous owner. You know, I have nearly killed myself for AMI. But I beg of you, do not let me nor my staff fall into the hands of a man like this."

"All I can promise you, Antonio, is that I will do my best," I said putting my hands on this dear gentle man's shoulder, feeling his pain.

Switzerland

After the Miami delegation left Switzerland, I proceeded with the effort to identify a substantial backer for the leveraged buyout of the International Division. Since Union Bank of Switzerland (UBS) owned the only other private hospital in Zürich, it seemed likely they would be interested in fending off the huge competition our new well-staffed and equipped Klinik Im Park would present. I managed to set up an appointment with the three-member top management committee at the bank's headquarters in Zürich.

As Jean-Claude and I walked into the impressive building we chuckled at the well-known sign on the floor which simply read "BANK." We both knew that, in Swiss tradition, the executives we were about to meet would have detailed informational dossiers about us.

"What do you think these chaps will think about me being gay and living openly with another man in Switzerland?"

"Obviously their research has already revealed that," answered Jean-Claude. "If we pull this deal off, they will sweep the sidewalks in front of your faggy shoes as you walk down Zürich's main street, the Bahnhoffstrasse."

We had stopped laughing by the time we were formally ushered into a large board room where the three top Swiss bankers waited. Each had a file in front of them. After a few polite introductions, we took our seats across the table from our hosts and the Chief Executive officer asked, "Mr. Silvin, please tell me about your pre-college schooling. We Swiss like to know our future partners' backgrounds."

"Well, sir," I replied, "I attended Le Rosey boarding school in Gstaad from 1959 to 1966 when I graduated and…"

"But what about three earlier years at school in Villars," he interrupted as he thumbed through his file.

I answered this question as well as several others while his point was well-made: *We know all about you so let's not try to fool each other about anything.*

A copy of the thick prospectus we had prepared stood in front of each inquisitor. I easily responded to many questions because I knew every detail of our operations and how each Swiss Franc, Spanish Peseta, Greek Drachma, Singapore and Australian dollar were allocated. We also tactfully proposed a joint-venture between the UBS aging hospital, Hirslanden, and our new Im Park. Jean-Claude added many details about the famous medical professors we had housed in the beautifully remodeled Mussolini Villa, confidently adding that the transformed villa itself was to be written up in Zürich's paper, the *NZZ*. He also mentioned that he and I would be interviewed live on the Swiss *60 Minutes* program that week. He was now making *our* point: *Watch out fellas, we are about to blow you out of the water in your own backyard, if you don't team up with us.*

Completed Klinik Im Park, Zürich, with Mussolini Villa

At the end of the meeting, it was clear there was serious interest in our proposal. "As you may know, Switzerland's largest insurance company has two executives on our Board of Directors, and we are also represented on their board," said the bank's Chief Financial Officer. "Will you make a similar appearance as soon as possible with some executives at Zürich Assurances?"

The following day, we had an almost instant replay with the senior members of the large insurance group, as well as officers of Switzerland's largest electric company, EOS. Day after day we were introduced to a growing list of board members and corporate executives of each company. The original feeling of being grilled for information changed into an atmosphere of teamwork and culminated with a specific offer to loan us the Swiss Franc equivalent of $98 million to acquire the company. Five of the executives we dealt with were in Klinik Im Park's lobby while I discussed the hospital and its service on Swiss television that week.

Beverly Hills, California

I flew to Los Angeles after confirming a meeting with Wally. I went alone, of course, because there was no point in aggravating my new boss by bringing Jean-Claude to Beverly Hills. When I reached his office and reviewed the offer I was stunned at his reaction.

"Actually, Rick," he said, "the price has been raised to $114 million."

The elation I had experienced over the previous days evaporated as I answered.

"Wally, we had an agreement. You and I will both lose all credibility if we change the terms now. Even *if* UBS agrees to increase its loan package, I am not sure the group is viable with the added interest expense of $16 million."

"That's your problem, Silvin. I'm not concerned about credibility with UBS. Swiss Bank Corporation is *our* bank. Anyway, the company is worth more than we originally thought."

Switzerland

As feared, I had an embarrassing meeting with UBS which ended with a formal and permanent goodbye. I had the distinct and upsetting feeling that my likely partners believed that I had prior knowledge of the news I brought them and was involved in a corporate plot.

It took Jean-Claude and me less than a week to update the prospectus in order to justify the interest expense on $114 million, and to obtain a meeting with an infamous, Swiss Howard Hughes-type entrepreneur, Werner Ray.

Werner Ray

Jean-Claude and I met him at his heavily-guarded lakefront villa near Geneva. It was a luxurious property in front of which I had practiced competitive rowing when I was in boarding school nearby, two decades earlier. Mr. Ray was a dry, right-down-to-business type man who conducted discussions with no polite introductions or pleasantries. A much quicker and less detailed series of meetings followed which, again, resulted in a specific proposal to bring to California. Unlike the UBS proposal, where Jean-Claude and I would be the primary shareholders, in this second deal Werner

Ray would acquire the majority interest in the company. Jean-Claude and I would have minority positions in the proposed company, as well as be granted employment contracts.

Beverly Hills, California

Again, I immediately requested to meet with Wally. We decided that Mr. Ray's financial officer and a representative of their bank, SBC, would join us in Beverly Hills a day after my arrival. In a bizarre meeting, laced with *deja-vu*, Wally advised me that he decided to raise the purchase price to $126 million.

I took a deep breath and said as calmly as I knew how,

"Wally, two people are currently airborne on their way to meet with you regarding a deal you, yourself, suggested. How can we change the terms now?" I asked.

"You figure it out. It is evident that the price we are asking is inadequate, which is why you are able to raise commitments for this much money so quickly."

I was devastated when I met Mr. Ray's representatives at AMI's headquarters the following day and tried my best to explain the upsetting news. We spent the subsequent two days analyzing the new figures, resulting in a cold parting of ways and an agreement to meet again in Geneva the following Monday. Wally's parting words to me were:

"This is still a very good deal for this fellow Ray. It will elevate his reputation in Switzerland since he has a criminal record."

"No, Wally, he does not have a criminal record. He was indicted and cleared of all charges in a bank deal a few years back," I tried in vain to clarify. "To condemn him for that is like finding Lee Pearce guilty because his partner tried to kill his wife."

"Still, it is in his best interest to accept the new price. But if he does not, be advised we are raising the price to $135 million."

"That's outrageous," I said. "There is no way I can find a reputable buyer to undertake the risks associated with new start-up hospitals, carrying that much additional debt."

"Integrity is in the eye of the beholder, isn't it?" he continued. "In fact, feel free to talk to the devil himself as far as I am concerned."

The following day, completely exhausted, and on my way back to Geneva, I read the *Wall Street Journal*, which carried a front-page article explaining that another suitor had registered with the Securities and

W. Clement Stone

Exchange Commission announcing his intention to acquire AMI. He was another physician-become-hospital -investor named Roy Pesch, the son-in-law of Chicago's aging billionaire insurance king, W. Clement Stone. We were well aware of Dr Pesch because he had acquired two Swiss hospitals 24 months earlier. Jean-Claude had brilliantly undercut all their development plans, as well as recruited several cardiologists and cardiac surgeons whom they were trying to hire in order to inaugurate a major cardiac program. After this, Pesch had become somewhat of a joke in the hospital business in Switzerland. Nevertheless, I knew my days at AMI were fast drawing to a close and I thought I had just discovered the very "devil" Wally had referred to.

Switzerland

During this period of failing "shuttle negotiation," I would return to Switzerland by flying from L.A. to New York and connecting to Swissair's flight 111 to Geneva. I played a silly game with myself to see how long it would take from touchdown in Geneva to transit through the extremely efficient airport, exit the parking lot and be on the nearby highway to Lausanne. This morning it took only 11 minutes for what could take an hour in Los Angles or more in New York. Once on the autoroute speeding east, I phoned Tim.

A weary voice answered.

"What's wrong?" I asked.

"I was up all night, René," he said. "I have cramps in my stomach and can hardly stand up."

I called Léo who luckily was in Lausanne, picked up a doubled-over Tim and went straight to Clinique Cecil. A CT scan revealed nothing unusual, and an intravenous antibiotic and pain medication temporarily soothed Tim and relieved the symptoms. We went back to the villa in the vineyard early in the evening, where Tim and I went to bed, both worn out. In the middle of the night, Tim awoke in agony and, during a heavy late-fall snow storm, I slowly drove our Mercedes Puch truck down the mountain to the hospital. Léo met us and admitted Tim. Again, by morning, the symptoms subsided. Léo consulted an abdominal surgeon who saw no reason to operate, choosing instead to keep Tim on high doses of antibiotics and immunoglobulins.

"Would you consider this Tim's first AIDS-related hospitalization?" I asked Léo, thinking of Bob Davis' "two hospitalizations followed by death" prediction.

"Probably," he answered. "I think we need to keep a close eye on Tim and begin Retrovir and AL 721."

"I have never heard of that," I said.

"It's an Israeli drug made from egg yolks which may have some benefit. You have to understand, René, these are not cures, only possible temporary solutions."

My head was spinning. The divergence between the crazy-making process of selling the company, Wally's unpredictability and now, Tim's first hospitalization put me into a sort of trance I would come to know well over the next decade. I could only survive by operating with a personalized version of an auto pilot, trying to carry on as best I could. That day, I had to attend a Board of Directors meeting at the hospital in Bern. I went to Tim's room to tell him I was going to Bern but would be back that night. In front of his door stood a small table, atop of which was a breakfast tray. Carrying the untouched meal into his room I said,

"The nurse must have forgotten to bring this in to you."

"They are afraid of getting AIDS, René," he answered. "Only one nurse comes in. The rest drop supplies outside the door and run away," he said, his eyes filled with tears.

"You must be mistaken," I said, totally surprised. But I went to the nursing director's office and, with the administrator who replaced Jean-Claude when he became Swiss Country Manager, we discovered that, indeed, Tim was correct. The hospital had never had an HIV admission and the nursing staff's ignorance had paralyzed them. As I left for Bern, our director of nursing called the Canton's University Hospital and arranged for a team to come to Clinique Cecil to educate our nurses, aides and housekeepers as quickly as possible, explaining the risks and myths of HIV contagion. Bob Davis' thought that we would receive "excellent care" at our own hospital was only partially correct. The physicians were prepared to deal with Tim, but the nursing and housekeeping staff had never been trained in HIV care. Tim's admission changed that, but the experience further convinced Tim that he was uncomfortable in Switzerland and, faced with failing health, he wanted to return to the United States.

During the Board meeting in Bern my auto pilot took over as we discussed Klinik Beau-site's problems and achievements. The completed, totally renovated hospital had reached a high occupancy rate and achieved break-even way ahead of our projections. In the middle of a discussion, a secretary entered the room and whispered in my ear,

"Monsieur Weisman is on the phone, Monsieur."

"Please tell him I am in a meeting with the board and will call him back within an hour."

"I already told him that, Monsieur," she said. "He insists on speaking with you *now*."

I excused myself and went to an office where I picked up the phone.

"We need to sever and sever forthwith, Silvin," began Wally. "Meet me at the AMI office in London tomorrow." The phone went dead. I sat in stunned silence much of the rest of the board meeting and even attended a get-together with the medical staff afterward. When I got into the car to drive back to Lausanne to see Tim, I called my secretary.

"Please book me on an early flight to London tomorrow," I told her.

"I already have," she said.

"How did you know I need to be there?" I asked.

"I have received calls from many of your people in Spain, Greece, Singapore and even Australia telling me that Wally had ordered them to meet you both in London tomorrow. All your top people are on their way already, so I took the liberty of making your arrangements, since I did not want to interrupt the board meeting."

Sitting in Tim's room at the hospital, I held his hand and told him I had to be away over the next 24 hours.

"René, I'm frightened. Please take me back to America," he begged. "I feel like a leper here and I hate it."

"I think we'll be going home very shortly," I answered. "We'll make plans when I get back from England in a day or so. I promise. Hold on until then. You're still my big hunk, just remember that."

Jean-Claude drove me to Geneva airport for my flight to London. Once again, he proved his amazing ability to turn adversity into humor. He had stopped at our favorite sports equipment store to buy a thick piece of mountain climber's rope which he tied into the shape of a perfect hangman's noose. I appreciated the joke and, after the hectic and crazy events of the preceding six weeks, faced with Tim's mysterious sickness, I relished wearing it into the meeting with Wally.

"Your charming little *tête-à-tête* with Wally is the bad news," Jean-Claude said. "I have good news too."

"Oh, really? I'd love to hear some good news."

"Roy Pesch has agreed to meet with us the day after tomorrow in Geneva. He is on his way here from Chicago."

After a few moments of silence, I said, "It's worth a shot. Perhaps Pesch will save his Swiss hospitals, we will keep our jobs, and Wally will be rid of the nightmare of a hostile takeover by Pesch. It may just be a classical win-win-win. But it is far more likely that I will soon be unemployed *and uninsurable*. How much do you think it will cost me to pay for Tim's and my health care from now until the end?"

Jean-Claude could switch from buffoon to brilliant mathematician in a second.

"A million dollars," he answered.

"Get our attorney to prepare an indemnification letter stating that Pesch will pay us each a million dollars if we get fired for speaking with him? If he signs it and, *if* I still have any authority when I return from London, we'll meet with him and help him draft an offer."

"Wally may end up kissing your feet. Make sure you give him my warm regards," he said, laughing as we pulled up to the departure zone at Geneva's airport.

London, England

When I got to the AMI office in London the secretaries were visibly agitated. A few shot nervous looks at me and one whispered that the international executives were grouped in a meeting room, but that Mr. Weisman was waiting for me in Mr. Burleson's office. Sporting my hangman's noose and trying to be calm, I entered the same office where I had so many wonderful, amusing and productive meetings with the late Stanley Balfour-Lynn. The sad state of affairs our company had reached still had a way to go under the leadership of a man best categorized as the ordinary.

Wally looked more disheveled than usual. His few remaining strands of colored hair, usually combed from one ear across his bald head to the other side, were in disarray.

"Even you can't think this is amusing, Silvin," he said.

"Actually, Wally, I do," I began. "No one will comprehend the perverse self-sabotage inherent in our actions of the last weeks, nor will anyone understand why you yanked all these highly paid executives to London on an expensive whim. Is this your idea of how a 'low-cost provider' should behave?"

"None of that is any longer your concern. I want your people to be in the room when I officially terminate you. You have too tight a relationship with them. I do not believe any other situation can convey my intent and signal a clear transfer of power to Gene. Being there will be your last official duty at AMI. Your usefulness is over now that the Swiss hospitals are operational and, anyway, you would never be able to raise our new asking price of $140 million."

"That's where you are wrong, Wally," I said, playing my last card. "But I thought you were now asking $135 million."

"That's changed," he said flatly.

"I actually think there is only one chance for you to get that amount. I won't put my name on the line to justify the price because no rational person will pay it. However, there may be an emotional reason for a given party to do so."

"Who's that?" he barked.

"That's for me to know and you to find out. Give me a month." I correctly bet that Wally could never imagine turning a predator, as he perceived Roy Pesch to be, into an ally, finding common ground. Offering Pesch the International Division, even at Wally's outrageous asking price, was beyond his imagination.

Wally's face took on a blank stare and he answered, "Okay, two weeks."

Statements like that made Wally feel potent.

"Now let's go see *my* staff," I said. "I'm looking forward to what you are going to tell them about these unbudgeted travel expenses you just made them incur for no good reason."

We entered the adjacent conference room where more than a dozen worried faces, all close associates whom I had hired over the years, stared at me inquisitively. Wally made a clumsy explanation of the company's need to divest itself of the International Division, how sorry he was that the group was experiencing insecurities regarding their futures and, that he would have "further news" for them all "in the near term." Then, retreating into his comfort zone, he asked each administrator and country manager to give the assembly an update on their activities. Everyone complied amidst blank stares. Few listened and no one understood why they had traveled overseas for such a useless meeting.

My aborted public execution had been postponed at an estimated cost of $150,000.

Switzerland

Jean-Claude had André Kaploon, our personal attorney, draw up the document we had discussed for Dr. Pesch's possible signature. We went by the attorney's office to read it. André had been baffled by the recent events and said that Pesch would be in his office after lunch. We agreed that, if Pesch indemnified us for talking with him, we would meet to discuss the Swiss operations. We all knew that we were walking a fine line between high treason and pulling off a miracle. André said,

"You will either be heroes or zeros."

Before we even got back to Lausanne, André called to say that Pesch has signed the documents. We turned around at the next exit and went back to Geneva to meet the man we had heard so much about, and who had been seriously outmaneuvered by Jean-Claude and I, relative to his two Swiss hospitals. We gathered in the exact same suite Royce Diener occupied on several occasions at the Richmond Hotel.

The M.D. Who Would Be A Tycoon

Roy Pesch was a jovial-looking, blonde, overweight man with charm and social skills. He was the exact opposite of Lee Pearce, his arch enemy. While both physicians had become hospital owners and both had risen to great fame, one was a delight to meet, the other an embarrassing bigot. The two competitors now wanted to own all, or at least the International Division, of AMI. I had learned a lot about Doctor Pesch from an article which appeared on September 25 in the *New York Times* entitled, "The MD Who Would Be a Tycoon." Among other things we learned was that his late wife, Donna, had left him $250 million.

As we hoped, Doctor Pesch explained that he was primarily interested in the International hospitals, opening the door for our presentation.

“Frankly, Doctor Pesch,” I said, “why bother pursuing an acquisition of the whole company? Why not just buy AMIs international division for a fraction of the price and many less headaches? I’m sure Gary Winnick, your consultant at Drexel Burnham, can structure a stock swap deal that will satisfy everyone. We would like to manage the group for you and would be happy to help you and Drexel prepare an offer. You do know that you are considered to be a threat in the AMI board room, and this may be a way to capitalize on that?”

Pesch laughed out loud and voiced his contempt for what he alternatively called the “pathetic Weisman,” or the “not-so wise Weisman.” Pesch then handed us our indemnity letters and asked us for details about our proposed employment contracts. He appeared much more rational and civilized than Wally or Lee Pearce.

The following day, while taking him to see the Zürich and Bern hospitals, it was obvious that we were being followed by an amateurish detective. We even lost our tail while driving and then stopped to allow him to catch up with us.

When I got home, Wally called to say that Jean-Claude and I were to meet him at the Dolder Grand Hotel in Zürich. When our secretary made our reservations, the manager asked if we were having an AMI corporate meeting because eight other people were arriving from Los Angeles and London. I immediately understood that Wally, again, wanted to terminate us in front of a group. I asked André Kaploon to join us in Zürich.

My orders were to come to Wally’s suite at 9 AM. There I saw numerous executives from Beverly Hills, including in- house attorneys. Wally began the meeting with, “You both have behaved inexcusably by conspiring with an enemy of the company.” Then he repeated his overused cliché, “We have to sever and sever forthwith.”

Although I knew it was coming, the reality of being terminated from a career that had been much more than a job, was more than a professional blow. The personal relationships I had developed, the business successes we had achieved, both in start-up situations and in turning around hospitals in difficult markets, had become a personal avocation as well as a job. For Jean-Claude the moment of truth had arrived and he said, “Wally, you can save your ‘salad.’ Since you are incapable of saying ‘why,’ just tell us ‘how much.’ Our attorney can confer with yours, but you are wasting our time and yours.”

We left estimating that this latest corporate mismanagement

had cost shareholders another $100,000. I was shaken while Jean-Claude was thrilled he could finally walk away from Weisman. André negotiated with the in- house AMI lawyers and doubled the initial severance they offered, in return for me signing 27 resignations from various hospital boards and subsidiaries. I was worn out by both the business disappointments and Tim's poor health.

When I returned to Lausanne, Wally had seized my company car, which I had *no* intention of keeping. I went straight to the hillside villa to tell Tim his "good news," namely, we would sail home on the next westbound crossing of the QE2 shortly. We packed and stored our belongings and then flew to London, from where we continued on to Southampton and collapsed in a Queen's Grill suite on the ship. Preferring to have a cold meal in the suite, we did not go to the dining room the first night. We exchanged gifts. I gave Tim a Swiss watch he always wanted, and he gave me a Cartier money clip which matched my watch.

The presents commemorated our exit from Switzerland, the country of my childhood, a wonderful country with many distinctions, including the negative one of having Europe's highest incidence of HIV per capita, 7.6 cases for 100,000 residents.

Our restful six-day crossing was frenetically interrupted by Tim's newly developed coughing spells. When we reached New York, we flew to Key West, where we planned to take an extended two-month vacation, until after the Christmas holidays. Then we would return to California and pursue trying to pick up our shattered careers.

Key West, Florida

I had a childhood friend who lived and worked in Key West as a real estate broker. Richard "Dickey" Glassen lived in a house on a cute little lane off of Eaton Street, in the middle of Old Town Key West with his handsome young partner, Todd. On one side of their home

René and Tim

lived an up-and-coming real estate developer, Pridam Singh, with whom, along with his charming wife, I would become close friends. Pridam had just bought the entire Truman Annex Navy Base and had a clever plan to turn it into Key West's premier residential community. On the other side of Dickey's house was a small cottage, which belonged to the same landlord, and which Tim and I rented.

We had not been in Key West a full week when Tim's health started to deteriorate rapidly. One evening, while watching television from our bed, Tim said, "René, get that cat off the TV." There was no cat in the house. Tim's face was pale, and his nails were blue, signs of lack of oxygen to the brain. Since we had no car, I called a taxi and brought him to De Poo Hospital, where he was admitted and seen by a talented young pulmonologist, who had several HIV patients. Doctor John Calleja explained that Tim had Pneumocystis Carnii pneumonia and would be treated with the newly developed drug, "Pentemidine." After the nurse had started the intravenous treatment and Tim began to doze off, I met Doctor Calleja at the nurse's station and thanked him for his late-night care.

"I *think* he will be just fine in ten days or so," explained the physician.

"What do you mean 'think?'" I asked?

"Well, we have to be realistic, René. Tim's blood oxygen level is very low, and I have him on the maximum oxygen dose. I feel confident that the Pentemidine will work."

"But I don't understand," I said, bewildered. "Are you saying that Tim *could* die?"

"I'll give him better than a 50-50 chance of recovery," he said.

I sat down in a nearby chair and began to cry. Perhaps *because* we had more or less miraculously dealt with the issue of AIDS for several years, I was ill-prepared to enter a new level of danger and despair. I walked home in the middle of the night and wondered what would become of us. This was Tim's second hospitalization for an opportunistic infection. I thought what Bob Davis had told me about "two-and-one-half hospitalizations followed by death." That night I started to feel an annoying pain around my waist which rapidly flared up into a painful case of the shingles.

Tim's condition did gradually improve. Day after day I watched the level of prescribed oxygen diminish, but Tim's veins were collapsing and his IVs were becoming difficult to administer. Walking to and from the hospital with carry-out food for us both was my only recreation and exercise. One day, after the long walk, I entered Tim's room to see a new intravenous located high up on his still very muscular arm, near his shoulder. The odd sight made a huge and frightening impression on me. Tim had another visitor, Jay Harkow, a volunteer from a group which was forming called "AIDS Help." She was the first person who had raised both his spirits and his hopes of survival. When she left the room, after giving us both much needed down-to-earth advice, Tim said:

"René, I happily followed you to Switzerland where I was treated like a leper. I feel comfortable here. Jay was so caring and helpful. Now I am asking you to please arrange for us to stay here in Key West."

Cottage off Eaton Street
Key West

"Okay," I reassured him. "I'll figure it out. We'll stay right here."

I walked home and called our landlord.

"May I extend the lease for the cottage off of Eaton Street for six months," I asked.

"Of course," the owner answered, "but winter months are at a higher rate."

When that figure had been

agreed upon, I wanted to clear with my landlord the issue of Tim's health. The last thing I needed was complications with the proprietor, while an obviously ailing Tim lived in his house. To this end, I added,

"I must tell you that my partner has AIDS, and I will be caring for a very sick, young man at your house, including professional home-health care."

"I am so sorry to hear that," he said. "In that case, the rent will be significantly higher."

I had no intention of complying with this demand or to altering Tim's positive experience in Key West, but I needed a friend to consult. I walked next door and after telling Dickey how the pain in my sides was killing me, I told him about what had happened with the landlord.

"Well, René, you have a few choices," my friend answered. "You can pay the bastard; you can sue him or you can buy a home. I've known you all my life, so let's look at condominiums in the morning."

Within 48 hours I had an accepted offer to purchase a penthouse unit at Key West's recently completed Beach Club Condominium complex on Atlantic Boulevard. I proudly told Tim we would be homeowners and residents in Key West for as long as he liked. I balanced the good news I gave him with my request to get to know his parents. I suggested we explain to them that I was his life-partner and that he was very ill. I bought a Mercedes convertible which Tim picked out, and as soon as we moved into the condominium, we launched into studying what new AIDS treatments were available. NIH had set up an Office of AIDS Research and Clinical Trials. We sent them Tim's records and asked to be advised if he qualified for any trials, but never got a response.

While the FDA implemented new regulations designed to make promising therapies available sooner, we watched AIDS activists demonstrate at the FDA over the length of time new drug approvals were taking. The number of AIDS patients reported by the CDC had reached 86,000, half of whom had died. In November several new drugs were approved by the FDA for treating Kaposi's sarcoma and CMV, the cause of blindness in HIV patients. While Tim did not have those particular opportunistic infections, he began to rapidly lose weight and he became increasingly disoriented. After he backed our car into a neighbor's car, we had a difficult discussion about his ability to drive and decided to monitor it carefully.

One day, when I returned from Lighthouse Court's gym on my bicycle, I saw a lot of damage to the passenger side of the convertible. Tim admitted that he had hit a fence but had not stopped. After I found the house where the accident occurred and told the owner we would happily pay for the destroyed fence, I had to tell Tim he could not drive until his balance improved. It was a huge step for us both, but I emphasized how much more difficult our lives would be if "we" hurt or, worse, killed an innocent pedestrian.

We had bought Tim health insurance in Switzerland, but it was not valid in the U.S., which meant I had to pay for Tim's hospitalization, treatments and medications. While I budgeted for this unexpected expense and the cost of furnishing the apartment, Tim's joy at decorating the Beach Club condominium was short-lived. His strength deteriorated daily and there was little I could do to comfort, much less heal, him. When a hurricane was headed straight for Key West, my parents called. "There is a late season hurricane coming to the Keys. Why don't you stay at our house here in Boca Raton until the storm has passed?" my mother said.

The call was the catalyst for me to explain why I had not, and could not, see them.

"Mother," I began, "you need to know why I have not been to visit you since we arrived in Florida. Tim is very sick, and I do not want to leave him, even for two days."

After a nervous pause she continued.

"Is it . . . is it AIDS?"

"Yes, Mother," I said. "I'm sorry to worry you. But I am okay," I lied.

"Dear God," she shouted. "How long will this last?"

"I have no idea," I said, ending the conversation.

It was a question they began asking every few days during phone calls until my hurt turned into anger.

"Would you like me to go into the bedroom and put a pillow over his head?" I demanded sarcastically.

"Of course not," my mother said, "but your father and I cannot sleep. Is what killed Liberace the same pneumonia Tim has?"

"Yes, it was," I said as calmly as possible.

By late November, I had my second episode with shingles. Tim was passing out with some frequency and receiving regular blood transfusions at De Poo Hospital.

With Tim's parents' consent we decided to go to their home in

Indiana rather than have them travel to Key West. I called my parents to advise them that I would be away for an extended period of time. My father took the phone from my mother's hand.

"Do you know anything about these people?" he asked threateningly.

"Just that they are good parents; kind, generous and worried. They prefer we travel to their house instead of them coming here because they live in a family compound out in the country. Surrounded by relatives, they feel we are all better off caring for Tim in an environment with his family."

"Do they understand the gravity of the situation and exactly who you are? They have never even met you, correct?" he proceeded.

"No, Father, we have not met, and they only fear the gravity of *our* predicament." I said. "I intend to clarify this with Tim's father upon our arrival and to answer any questions he may have," I said, addressing the obligation I would soon have to undertake with great fear and trepidation.

"I urge you to go there with an attorney," he said, continuing to baffle me. Before I could answer he explained, "You are older and more fortunate than they. You brought their son to Switzerland and now are bringing him home to die. You need to protect yourself."

"It's out of the question, Father," I said emphatically. "I have no reason to believe that they are in any way hostile. The only emotion I have detected is overwhelming concern."

"And just when will this be over?" he demanded, repeating the absurd request for a time frame of the end of my partner's life.

"I have no idea," I answered as casually as possible.

"If you do not go in the company of an attorney, you are on your own," he said as he hung up. We did not speak again until "it was over."

Fort Wayne, Indiana

The day we flew to Fort Wayne, Tim had an early- morning transfusion to give him the strength to travel. His extraordinary parents were at the airport when we arrived. Gloria and Paul Bojrab were the perfect example of loving, wholesome, yet devastated parents. The look on these strangers' faces, when they saw the sad condition of their beloved son, was excruciating. They hugged and kissed Tim as they both cried. I stood some distance away, allowing the horrible reunion to be uninterrupted by an outsider. Eventually, one by one, his parents came over and welcomed me. When we reached their family farm-like group of houses, Paul asked me to talk with him in another room. The dreaded conversation was beginning.

"I'll get right to the point," he said. "Is Tim dying?"

"I'm afraid so, Paul," I said.

"But we have read about new treatments and medicines. We thought lots of progress was being made."

"I fear they are too late for us," I said, with the same effect as if I plunged a knife into this large, yet gentle, man's heart.

"I have all the available medications with us, and I recommend we go to a doctor in Fort Wayne who has other AIDS patients, as well as the local agency for home health care and AIDS support groups." Paul winced as the word "AIDS" was pronounced for the first time.

"I don't think you understand how our family works," he said. "Of course, we will consult our family doctor, but other than you, there will be no non-family people who will cross that doorway."

"But, Paul," I tried to make my point. "The day will soon come when Tim is bedridden. He may need diapers..."

"My son will never wear diapers," he interrupted in a calm but determined voice. "Aunt Mary lives across the street. She'll be assigned laundry. If she has to wash 100 sheets a day, she will. Grandma, down the road, will take turns with Gloria staying by his side at night and Aunt Judy, over there, will run all errands and do the cooking."

And with that, except for two brief hospitalizations, he described how the following eight weeks would unfold. It was the silk lining in a very gloomy sow's ear. I stayed at a nearby motel and spent the days at the family homestead with Tim. As the troubled year drew to an ominous close, a strange peace settled into the Bojrabs' warm house in the middle of a wind-blown, snow-covered farm field. I was as alien to my hosts as a Martian, and yet we all got along well as we devoted ourselves to a common cause.

The family did not celebrate the holidays this year.

Chapter Fourteen

January 1-February 9, 1989

Fort Wayne, Indiana

Tim ate less and less while he grew steadily weaker. Gradually, all he would eat were special sugar-coated popsicles that could only be found 50 miles away. Tim developed pneumonia in almost back-to-back episodes and was hospitalized in downtown Fort Wayne. His last lucid experience was watching the Super Bowl with his father and I. I knew his dad was contrasting his dying son to when he was the captain of the local high school's basketball team only a decade earlier. Two pictures of Tim hung in the middle of the living room wall. In one Tim was wearing his basketball uniform; in the other, a cap and gown at his graduation from Indiana University.

His dad and I started carrying him to the bathroom and back to his bed because his parents did not want him to be in a wheelchair.

I returned to Key West every few weeks for a long weekend. There, I rarely left the condo. I ordered food to be delivered and I sat on the balcony looking at the ocean in a trance.

In late January, Jean-Claude called to tell me that UBS had made a direct offer to AMI to acquire the Swiss hospitals for themselves. Our attorney recommended filing an immediate injunction to halt the transaction in what he believed would result in a payoff to us. I was too weary and told Jean-Claude I was not interested in pursuing what I considered to be a longshot, involving yet more stress and anxiety.

"My world has changed, Jean-Claude," I said, looking out the window at a bleak expanse of snow. "I am totally focused on helping Tim's parents the best I can and trying to add some quality and dignity to Tim's last days. Do whatever you like. I don't have it within me to focus on that right now. Please forgive me."

I was equally unenthused a few days later when a former AMI executive called to tell me that Wally had been fired. It seemed that several board members had become alert to the numerous errors in judgment their new Chief Executive had been making. They had chartered a plane and flew to all AMI regional offices to investigate the many stories they had heard. Upon their return to L.A., they immediately terminated the "not-so-wise Weisman." My friend finished his conversation by saying, "If you live by the sword, you die by the sword." Unfortunately, I was thinking of a different type of death: the real thing. As much as I was there for Tim and held a stoic façade with his wonderful family, I could sense great melancholy and depression within me. I felt as if in a vortex, helpless and increasingly self-absorbed in my black space.

In mid-January, we moved Tim's bed into the small house's living room. He was the center of our attention and lives, so why not locate him in the heart of the house? His conversation became more and more child-like, and his mother reassumed her earlier maternal role. Paul, Gloria and I developed a mutual affection, and I became very respectful of their basic instincts. The care Tim received during his gradual decline was reminiscent of the early days of pioneers, when families surrounded aging loved ones as they gently faded away.

By early February, we placed morphine drops under his tongue whenever he moaned. On February 3, I read that the FDA had approved a treatment for the prevention of Pneumocystis Carinii pneumonia. It would be of no help to Tim, who had endured the debilitating lung disease three times in as many months.

Then, quietly, in the early evening of February 9, at the age of 29, Tim's breathing slowed, and he slipped away surrounded by his loved ones. My once 180-pound "big hunk" now weighed 110 pounds.

We buried Tim two days later. The small funeral home was jammed full of family and friends. As I walked into the chapel where his coffin was placed, I noticed a small table carrying a phone which was off the hook. In front of it lay a sign which read "The Lord called." I found some humor in this charming rural ritual. The Bojrabs invited every attendee back to their house for a meal, which every female relative had begun to prepare the minute they were informed of Tim's death. Afterwards, in a blinding snowstorm, I returned to my motel for the last time. As I reflected on my time with Tim, I wondered if I had idealized our relationship. Now that he was gone, I felt strangely liberated in my solitude. The following day I flew back to Key West in great physical pain, as my third bout of shingles began.

For the next two days I stayed in bed, trying not to let my waist touch sheets or a T-shirt, because the pain was so severe. Finally, I called my parents to tell them I was back and that "it was over."

"Well, you'd better return to doing what you know best," said my father.

"What's that, Father," I asked weakly. "Making

money," he replied.

"I am barely able to get out of bed," I tried to explain. "I have just returned from burying my partner. I'm sure you can understand that it will take some time for me to get back on my feet."

His answer underscored his lack of comprehension that two men could ever have shared a life and make plans for a future with developing careers and experiences.

"No," he said, "we do not understand. We never did. But, if you need some time, I suggest you take a long ocean cruise and then get back to work. If you recall, I told you to put Tim in a nursing home last year. Had you followed my advice, you would not be in this position now."

This time, it was I who put down the phone first. I wondered how horrible it would be to live and die, if one had such an insensitive existence. I knew how my father had lived and the following year I would find out how one dies with that attitude of detachment. But, like Scarlet O'Hara in *Gone with The Wind*, I would worry about my parents another day. For now, I had to figure out how to survive alone, in a confused haze of mental and physical agony.

Part 3

BOB

1989 – 1998

René and Bob, Cassis, France

Chapter Fifteen

1989

Key West, Florida

The abandoned administration building in the Truman Annex

As soon as I was able to get out of bed, I called Jay Harkow at AIDS Help to tell her about Tim. I asked if I could drop by to see her at the organization's temporary offices, located in an old, abandoned building in the Truman Annex. The once-grand building had housed the former military base's administration when Key West was a vibrant deep-water navy harbor. The Administration Building was next to several other vacant structures, including the Truman White House, which was Harry and Bess Truman's home, both during and after his Presidency. My new local friend Pridam Singh had recently bought the entire complex at auction.

Jay expressed her condolences, recommended that I attend a bereavement group at Key West's hospice, and invited me to a gathering to be held the following weekend on the grounds of the Truman White House.

There I met many of the new organization's clients as well as a board member, Al McCarthy, and his partner, Ralph. Ralph was a radiology technician at Key West's hospital. We had met there previously, when I had taken Tim in for tests. I had been impressed with his kindness and compassion. At the gathering, the late-stage condition of several of the guests was obvious and frightening. A few were wheelchair bound, some were covered from head to foot with Kaposi's Sarcoma lesions, and most were emaciated.

Al told me how the struggling organization was planning to survive and what services he dreamed of being able to provide for its many indigent members. I offered my assistance in any way possible. That rapidly turned into a time-consuming positive and fulfilling job. I also signed up at Hospice to attend a six-week training program, which resulted in a Florida State license to make regular visits to AIDS patients who were registered for terminal care. There was no inpatient Hospice facility in town, so the dedicated staff worked with dying patients in their homes. In this way, I could work at both the grass roots level, by running errands for, and sitting with, bedridden patients, as well as with AIDS Help Incorporated's Board of Directors on policy and financial issues. The combination gave me a will to get out of bed and be of some assistance to those much less fortunate than I.

I also resumed going to the gym at the Light House Court guesthouse on Whitehead Street, across from the Hemingway House. The small gym, near the bed-and- breakfast's pool, had four regular morning clients, who quickly became friends as well as becoming my avenue for socialization. Mike Mulligan had a terrific sense of humor and would always cheer me up. He was also an aerobics instructor and an excellent local amateur actor.

While we lifted weights and kidded around, we also commented on the various new tourists' faces we noticed coming and going every few days at the inn. Michael, who like Time was a "Hoosier," had gotten to know and like Tim during his brief stay in Key West. After Tim's funeral I had told Michael that I "would never look at another man" and would prefer to castrate myself rather than date.

"Well, I don't think I'd castrate myself if there was a chance, I could have a date with that one," said Michael, pointing at a handsome well-built blonde sitting by the pool.

I looked through the window and agreed that the young man was amazingly good looking.

"That's funny, Michael," I said, "but I am too depressed to even think about it."

René and Bob when they met winter 1989

A few minutes later, Robert David Mann left his seat by the pool and entered both the gym and my life. As Michael left us alone in the small space, he shot me a look which said: "I guess you might reconsider."

Bob and I chatted. I learned that he had a Ph.D. in Clinical psychology and lived in Malibu, California. He was in Key West on vacation to recuperate from a recent break-up with a boyfriend. He had just changed jobs and taken a position with the Rader Institute, a well-known group that treated severe eating disorder victims as in-patients, usually for a 30 day stay.

"The Rader Institute!" I exclaimed. "Have you heard of AMI?"

"Well, yes, of course," answered Bob. "Didn't Rader just get kicked out of those hospitals?"

I explained what my position at AMI had been and that I was privy to discussions about the pros and cons of AMI's domestic hospitals housing eating disorder programs. We marveled at what a small world it was, as I became hypnotized by his strong yet sweet face, his soothing voice and gentle demeanor. After telling him that I had just lost my partner, I gathered up all my courage and asked Bob if he would have dinner with me that night, which was my last night in Key West. Early the following day I was going to New York to meet with the Chief Executive Officer of one of AMI's competitors, NME, National Medical Enterprises.

"I'm really sorry," he answered, "but I am in town with two friends, and we have already made plans."

The response did not surprise me, and I left the guest house unsure about whether or not I had been politely blown off. Shortly after I returned to the Beach Club the phone rang and it was Bob. "I hope you don't mind, but I got your number from the front desk. I spoke with my buddies, and they hoped that, perhaps, we could *all* have dinner together."

Quite nervous and not knowing why, I had inadvertently begun the process of dating. I picked Bob and his friends up in my two-seater convertible. It was a beautiful evening, the top was down, and Bob's friends sat on the trunk with their legs inside the car, while Bob sat next to me. He wore a pink and blue shirt and tight white pants, which showed off his beautiful figure and bubble butt. We drove up and down Duval Street and ended up at Louie's Back Yard restaurant, where we had a delightful dinner outside by the ocean. The conversation was animated, and Bob looked so handsome. He was obviously a genuinely kind and wise young man, with talents that were high on my list to find, given my recent experiences. After dinner, I took them all back to Lighthouse Court and went home mystified to realize that, so soon after losing Tim, I was falling in love with this man. I felt a deep connection within myself, paradoxically experiencing both pleasure and pain. I was unsure if I was totally crazy or the luckiest man alive. I soon understood that the latter case was the answer.

New York City, New York

Richard Eamer

Richard "Dick" Eamer, NME's Chief Executive Officer, had contacted me and asked to meet. Although the company was located in Santa Monica, California, we got together at the Plaza Hotel in New York. There he explained that NME was pursuing the construction of a $75 million hospital in Paris and wondered if I would review the plan and help him quantify the expected outcome. His Chief Operating Officer, Michael Focht, was also present.

"Frankly, Mr. Eamer," I said after hearing his plans, "I think the venture is extremely risky. In spite of my French heritage and love for the country, I spent a fair amount of time getting AMI *out* of France at a break-even. Their reimbursement rates are not at levels which can justify the large capital costs of the first-class private hospitals which you want to create."

"We are thinking of operating totally independent from the government and charging any rates we like," he said.

"Again, I think that strategy is also very risky for any hospital other than a small, highly specialized facility, which is not what I understand you are contemplating. There simply are not enough French people with adequate supplementary private health insurance to cover the rates you will have to charge."

When Mr. Eamer excused himself for a few minutes, Focht expanded,

"If I were you, I'd not be so pessimistic. Dick loves France and has his thoroughbred racehorses there to compete in Dauville and Paris. He really wants this project."

"That's all well and good," I answered, "but I think that your shareholders would prefer you not lose many tens of millions of dollars because you want to have an excuse to travel to France. You can have a small activity there to justify some trips or just pay for the *private* activity *privately*."

I could tell that Mike Focht and I would never see eye-to- eye. When Dick returned to the living room, he offered to pay me a hefty per-diem fee to go to France and look over the hospital's drawings at the architect's office. The mission would also include meeting several people, including a full-time representative, whom they had already housed in Paris.

"I'd be happy to," I answered, "but again, it's not the drawings that worry me. It's the project's *cost* and its ability to command the necessary revenues to turn a profit."

"But, will you go?" he asked.

"If you insist and understand where my focus will be, yes, I'll go."

As the day-long meeting drew to a close, all I could think about was going back to my room and calling Bob, who was in Chicago on his first mission for Rader. I was nervous as the phone rang in his hotel room, hoping, in part, that he would not answer so that I could retreat into my shell. Luckily, I was wrong. "Hello," I heard that deep, masculine voice say.

"Um . . . hi, Bob! It's René. How is it going in Chicago?"

Bob *never* complained and only gave detailed answers if specifically asked.

"It's a new job and my first time as clinical director at this program. I have a lot to learn, but it is going well, thanks." After a short pause he said, "I really enjoyed meeting you and hope we can get to know each other better."

"Come back to Key West any time you like. But I guess that's not feasible, eh?"

"To the contrary," he said. "I will be in a different East Coast city every week for a few months. I can easily route my weekends through Key West."

"How about this weekend?" I asked somewhat recklessly, partly hoping he would say "no," so my nerves could return to normal.

"I'll make the plans and let you know when I'll be there."

On the local news that day, in late March, I watched 3,000 protestors, organized by "Act-Up" picket New York's City Hall in protest of Mayor Koch's lack of progress in providing assistance to AIDS patients. 200 activists were arrested.

....

That first weekend Bob and I had a wonderful time. When I took Bob's small bag into the guest room, he appeared surprised and disappointed that I did not automatically put it in my room. We spent much of the weekend on my Boston Whaler, going to Sand Key, six miles from Key West during the day and cruising the harbor at sunset. As the sun slipped into the ocean, I cut the engine and took Bob's hand.

"You know that Tim just died from complications caused by AIDS," I began. "As you may have imagined, I am HIV positive. I think we have to be clear on the situation and discuss the risks. What is your status?"

"Well," he answered, "first of all, I appreciate the candor. I was tested about a year ago and I was negative. My last boyfriend said he, too, was negative. However, I am planning on making sure and I want to test again soon."

"How about Monday morning before you leave town?" I asked.

"Sure, if you know where to go."

The rest of the weekend we flirted and kissed. Bob's likely being HIV negative perplexed me. I feared I could never relax sexually around someone I cared for and who was HIV negative. After his blood was drawn, I dropped him off at the funky little Key West airport. We agreed to meet at that same spot, in two weeks, after I returned from Paris.

Paris, France

Jean-Claude Salamin met me in Paris and, as in years past, we had a fun time. I had not seen him since Tim and I left Switzerland, and his perspective on how I could get back on my feet after burying Tim was gratifying:

Clinique de Genolier, Genolier, Switzerland

"You need a new husband," he said. "And this time try to find a *husband*, not a wife."

While Jean-Claude had been generous with Tim, they did not have affinity with one another. I told Jean-Claude that I recently met an interesting man to which Jean-Claude responded:

"Good. Bring my new sister-in-law to Switzerland for my inspection."

Jean-Claude had been hired by Roy Pesch to run his two Swiss hospitals. He promptly closed the worst one and transferred their business to the better hospital, The Clinique de Genolier, near Geneva. Historically, the facility had been a horrible financial blunder, built by the aging mother of a childhood friend, the Duchess Serra de Cassano. After her death, the family had offered the hospital first to AMI and eventually found the gullible Doctor Pesch to buy it. He did not fare much better than the Duchess had until Jean-Claude took it over. It was hard for us to believe that, only six months before, we had frantically pursued the leveraged buy-out of AMI's international division.

"Do you remember when that silly ass, Wally, tried to impose a 30-mile zone around Lausanne where I could not work?" he giggled, reminding me of one of our many maneuvers during our termination process. Wally had told his lawyers to put a 30-mile "non-compete" clause in Jean- Claude's termination package. We already knew he might run the Genolier Hospital, which was about that distance from Lausanne. We had put a map on the bar at the Palace Hotel and drew a circle around Lausanne with a 48-kilometer (30-mile) radius. Genolier was one kilometer *inside* the no-work zone. Taking that into account we instructed Kaploon, our attorney, to tell Wally's lawyer that you could not use "miles" in a binding Swiss agreement. The 30 miles was changed to an adequate number of kilometers, which resulted in Genolier being one kilometer *outside* the forbidden zone. Jean-Claude assumed his new responsibilities, worry free of being sued by the very litigious Wally.

I informed Jean-Claude of NME's plan to build a major hospital in Paris and, not surprisingly to me, he agreed that it was pure folly. I told him about my visit to the proposed hospital's architect's office, to the selected site and about my discussions with NME's American representative in Paris.

"Oh, my God," he exclaimed. "Another American trying to impose a failed system on Europe! Let them build it, maybe we can sell it to Pesch." It was the first time I laughed in six months, and we howled until we feared we were annoying the other guests at the Palace bar.

I told Dick Eamer that I would report quickly and in person, to him after my review of the proposed Paris project. On my flight to Los Angeles, I drafted my verbal presentation but was distracted by a very chatty Joan Collins, sitting across the aisle, and my continuous thoughts about Bob, whom I would meet in Florida the following weekend.

Santa Monica, California

It was very strange being back in the city where Tim and I had lived. I deliberately did not drive by my former home or call Royce. My stay was planned to last one day, and I pretended I was a businessman quickly passing through L.A. NME had built a beautiful building on Santa Monica Boulevard and, of course, Dick Eamer's office was a grand Hollywood-like setting.

"I am convinced that you will lose your shirt if you build the mega-hospital in Paris," I said. "I have marked up your overly optimistic pro-forma with reasonable revenue levels and occupancy rates based on my experience in France. Obviously, it's your call, but I think you would be ill advised to move forward at this time in NME's history. How can you justify several years of certain losses in Paris when you are selling domestic facilities and while your growth has slowed significantly? Your shareholders will ask why are we losing money in Paris while adding to reserves for malpractice suits in the U.S. and uncollectible accounts in Saudi Arabia? It just seems like the wrong project at the wrong time."

"I guess we owe you a thank you," Eamer answered after a prolonged silence. "Would you consider working for me?"

"That is flattering," I answered, "but not right now. I have recently lost my partner and I have recurring debilitating bouts of shingles. This quick pop over to Paris was more tiring than my monthly round-the-world trips for AMI used to be. I feel it would not be honest to undertake an activity to which I cannot devote my full attention."

"That's the first time anyone has turned me down twice in one meeting," he said, laughing. "You torpedoed my pet project and now you refuse to work for me. Can we call on you for specific time limited projects?"

"Of course," I replied. "I'd be honored."

By mid-year, the FDA had approved numerous new treatments and medications for HIV disease. Among these were an aerosol Pentamidine; an initial treatment for CMV, the cause of blindness; a syrup form of AZT; as well as "ddI," a substitute for AZT for use by patients who were intolerant of the toxic AZT. Most importantly, the FDA created an AIDS Clinical Trial Information Service, so that people suffering from the disease could be informed of drug trials using medications in the late stages of their development.

Act-Up continued their effective protests at strategic locations, including the New York Stock Exchange and Burroughs Wellcome's corporate headquarters. The latter compelled AZT's manufacturer to reduce the price of AZT by 20 percent. In late July 300 protestors, organized by Act-Up, also demonstrated in Montreal, Canada. They achieved several major advances. Among these were putting a human face on HIV materials, promoting the slogan "Silence = Death," and drawing attention to the restrictive U.S. travel policies for HIV-positive visitors. All major news networks broadcast the protests which led to yet more displays of unrest at The Golden Gate Bridge. News networks also covered "A Day Without Art," which drew attention to the deaths of many artists, including Alvin Ailey, Robert Mapplethorpe and Amanda Blake, known as "Miss Kitty" from *Gunsmoke.*

Key West, Florida

Bob flew into Key West on Friday afternoon, and we proceeded straight to the Public Health office where, anonymously, he had his blood drawn ten days earlier. The receptionist told him that he would have to see a therapist before receiving the results.

"But I *am* a therapist," he said, hoping, in vain, to skip the step. While he was in an office with a psychologist, I walked around the block worried about what that requirement meant. Finally, strolling toward the building which housed the office, Bob emerged. Although I did not yet know him well, his face told the story. Bob, too, was HIV positive. We went back to the condominium and held each other for a very long time.

From that day on we spent every possible moment together in what became truly happy years. I was surrounded by both deep love and great competence, which I had never before experienced. I was 40 years old. If "life begins at 40," in spite of HIV, I was all for the program!

The following day, we went to the Key West hospital to visit my friend Dicky, who was being treated for PCP. We did not tell Dicky about Bob's diagnosis, but rather focused on his own health and planned recovery. Dicky had two major problems to contend with: his first hospitalization with an opportunistic infection, and the fact that his partner had left him. To add to his distress, Dicky was finding it increasingly difficult to keep his job at the new Truman Annex Real Estate Company. He asked Bob if he could consult him professionally, for free, on weekends, to which Bob generously agreed. I began to not only lust for, but also admire, this exceptional man with a surprisingly silent inner strength.

Bob and I spent every weekend together for the rest of the year. When he had to be in California for an extended period of time, I went there. Otherwise, he came to Key West, or we met somewhere on the East coast. One weekend in September, we got together at the Pines on Fire Island. I had never been there with anyone I loved, and I discovered that we had little desire to stay up late dancing. Instead, hand in hand, we took many hour-long walks along the beach to the neighboring towns and even ate several meals at restaurants in the "straight" villages on Fire Island. We walked around the Pines harbor once to see the slip where "Les Beaux" had been the venue for many wild parties. There, I learned that I was the only boat owner of the "gay side" of the harbor from the late 70's and early 80's who was known to be alive. Even the dock master had passed away.

A Mediterranean cruise

On the seaplane returning to Manhattan, we both agreed that we would not go back to Fire Island. The many memories were too painful and represented the past. We would try other vacation spots instead. Bob wanted to meet my family and friends in Switzerland, and we decided that we would sample Provincetown on Cape Cod. We would live life to the fullest.

"Let's squeeze 20 years into five," I said as we parted company at LaGuardia airport.

Toward the end of the year we decided that Bob would move to Key West, so I went to Los Angles to help him pack up what he referred to as "his gear."

Bob had grown up in a therapeutic community in Malibu. While he was the product of his mother's first marriage, Bob spent most of his formative years with her second husband, Garry Troy. Garry was a tough, but fair, former military man, who, in the 1960's, had allowed Bob and his brother to house their drug-addicted friends, providing that they underwent therapy and were drug-free while in his house. Over the following two decades, Garry bought several neighboring houses and, eventually, provided inpatient therapy for more than 30 recovering teenagers. The group was eventually named "Teamm House" and had its own school, recreational projects and therapists. Since it was located in Malibu, not far from the homes of many well-known Hollywood celebrities, donations kept the project alive. Bob explained that, as is often the case in similar environments, many of the graduates go on to become therapists themselves. He dreamed of running Teamm House as an adult, which he did after obtaining his Ph.D.

By the time we met, Garry was aging. The loyal supporters of the project were dwindling, and Los Angeles County had built numerous facilities for troubled teens. So, the group decided to close Teamm House, which is what caused Bob to look for a job and go to work for another well-known Malibu physician and businessman, Bill Rader, the founder of the Rader Institute. Bob became their clinical director and traveled to all their hospital-based programs, working with local psychiatrists to create a uniform standard of care. It was Doctor Rader who coined the still-used phrase, "It's not your fault, you are not alone, we care."

Even though Teamm House had closed by the time I got to know Garry and his wife, Nancy, their home was still run like a military academy. Approximately 20 remarkable former residents had remained fiercely loyal to the Troys and gathered in Malibu at least twice a week, both for ongoing group therapy sessions, as well as family-style meals. Although everyone was cordial toward me, I was aware that I was responsible for Bob's move away from the tightly knit group, and into a totally different environment and life. Bob was out to the understanding socially-liberal group. But, as the only gay member, he felt a bit isolated, and he welcomed both his professional and personal transition.

Teamm House had developed and practiced a unique psychological school called "Power of Mind" or "POM," which Bob taught me. This interesting version of "mind control" was very helpful in my recovery from Tim's death, as well as in having a healthier attitude towards my union with Bob and life in general. It prepared me for the challenge of 1990.

That first Christmas in Key West, I was totally enamored and mesmerized by my talented and kind partner. For the first time in my life, the term "lover" was a word of which I was proud and did not make me feel uncomfortable. We went to many Christmas parties given by the local gay set, and I watched everyone admire this newcomer to Key West society. One evening when I returned from bringing food to Dicky, who was again hospitalized, Bob said:

"There is a message on the answering machine you need to hear! Your fazzer called," imitating my dad's thick French accent.

I immediately returned the call.

"René, I am sick, and I demand your help at once. In fact, I need cardiac surgery. Set it up."

"Father," I said, "you don't just order cardiac surgery like carry-out food. You need a complete cardiac work-up before you can determine if you need or even qualify for surgery. After that you speak to a cardiac surgeon."

"Then get me an appointment with a cardiologist," he ordered in typical fashion. "And be here when I see him!"

Before he hung up, I asked to speak with my mother. After repeating what I had told my father I added:

"I speak with Tim's mother, Gloria, every week. She has not mentioned receiving a condolence letter from you. Have you written her yet?"

"I would have no idea of what to say to her," my mother replied to my surprise.

"Mother," I continued, "you have written dozens of sympathy letters. Say the same thing to Gloria that you would to anyone else. You may want to add something about the additional heartbreak a mother must feel when she loses a child."

"I cannot bring myself to do that," she said. "I'll send her a mass card."

The conversation troubled me for a long time, until Bob helped me understand that my parents were only able to deal with their anxiety about the tragedy through denial. Placing one's personal handwriting on a letter made Tim's death too real for my mother to handle. Of course, she also would never benefit from the healing that proper grieving creates.

Bob encouraged me to make an appointment with a cardiologist in Boca Raton and to be present at the meeting the first week of January. Before that occurred, however, my parents' long-term family physician called.

"René, I know your father is requesting cardiac surgery. You will find that is out of the question. I have ordered a CT scan. The results will be available right after New Year's. I recommend that you be here when we get the outcome. Please tell your brother to plan on a trip to The States." It was clear that Doctor Elkins already knew the prognosis and that it was not good.

During the closing days of 1989 I was overwhelmed at the knowledge that I had both buried a partner *and* found the big love of my life. Given my good fortune, I committed to be loyal to Bob, to support his career, and to care for both Dicky and my "fazzer."

On December 30, I received a call that my precious, ailing Nonnie had died. Bob held me on the balcony as I cried like never before. She was the same age as my father and had died peacefully in the very chair where she had sat as she told me her only concern for me being gay was who would cook and clean my house, and where she always said I "was as good as gold." Her last words to me, two days earlier, were, "I am tired, René. I've led a good, long life and have children, including you, who are safe and educated. I really am ready to meet my maker."

I would soon find out how rare, miraculous and important it was to leave the planet with such a serene attitude.

Chapter Sixteen

1990

Boca Raton, Florida

Right after New Year's, Bob and I left Key West. I dropped him off at Miami airport for his usual weekly trip to an eating disorder clinic and I waited for my brother, Jack, to arrive from Switzerland. After Jack's flight landed, we drove to Boca Raton where my father was hospitalized. My father had been one of the original founders of the local hospital 30 years previously, so he was given a suite at the end of a hall. My mother sat near his bed, holding his hand, as we awaited the family physician, Doctor Elkins.

"John," he began, "I have seen the results of all the tests we have run. I regret to inform you that you have cancer in every major organ. It is lung cancer that has metastasized to other areas of the body."

He paused to allow the news to sink in. Before he could continue, my father responded,

"That cannot be. I am not in pain. All I feel is a shortness of breath. I have not smoked in decades."

"I'm very sorry," continued Elkins, "but it is true. Sometimes cancer is not painful and there are many incidences of lung cancer in non-smokers."

"Is this treatable?" I asked.

"No, René," answered the physician. "In this advanced stage, it would not be helpful."

"So, what are we to do?" my mother asked, pleading for some direction.

"I recommend keeping Mr. Silvin as comfortable as possible at home."

"Doctor," I asked, trying to get a handle on the future, "How do you see this will unfold?"

"I expect that your father will not last two months," he said, almost as if he and I were alone in the room. My mother gasped.

I walked around the bed and put my arms around her as she cried.

"Do you promise you will keep him out of pain?" I asked, more to comfort my mother than anyone else.

"Of course! There is no reason for your father to experience pain. I'll sign the papers to discharge him in the morning and will add to his sleeping medication so that he gets some rest tonight."

With that, the brave physician left the room. The three of us sat silently by my father's bed for quite some time. When a nurse arrived with a dinner tray, she said:

"I have your dinner, Mr. Silvin."

"I don't want it. Get out!" he said, in the tone that he would keep for the rest of his life.

After my brother and I had taken my mother back to her condominium, we sat on each side of her on a living-room sofa. When she had stopped crying, she said in a weak voice:

"I am so worn out, boys. Two months of his bad temper will kill me. I want you both to know that."

"Mother," I said, "I have a suggested solution."

My brother and she stared at me.

"I'll set father up in a facility nearby, where he will be well taken care of and you can be with him as many hours a day as you have energy for."

"Oh, René!" she answered, crying again. "You know your father. There is no way he will agree to that."

"Mother," I said. "Remember the French adage, 'do not kill the living to help the dying.' If you truly feel there is no way to care for him at home, in spite of home health care nurses, I will put him in a nursing home."

We all discussed the option. It was my mother's clear wish, but one that she thought unavailable to her even in her declining health. She had been serious about fearing both their lives would end within two months. I left her and my brother and went into my father's office where I got on the phone to friends at NME in California. I got the name of the executive director of a skilled nursing facility in Boca Raton that, on occasion, took dying patients and worked with hospice. The lady was receptive to being called at home and asked me to meet her at the faculty the following morning at seven.

As we all retired for the evening, neither my mother nor my brother believed that the solution was possible. The following day,

I discovered a pleasant, new and well-run nursing home. The administrator and I made the financial arrangements, and then I met the Director of Nursing and the floor nurses who worked on the wing where my father would be housed in a single-bed room. I had not seen my brother or my mother that morning. Both of them were completely unaware of the specifics of what I was arranging.

I explained to the staff that my father was a difficult man.

"This is Boca Raton," answered a confident director of nursing. "We are used to spoiled and cranky people. We'll be able to deal with him."

"We'll see." I said as I left to get my father.

When I entered his room at the hospital, my father was dressed and sat in an armchair waving his cane.

"Where the hell have you been?" he demanded. "I have been waiting for you to take me home."

"I'm sorry I am late," I began taking a deep breath. "I was making arrangements for the best around-the-clock care I could find nearby, so that mother can be with you as long as her energy allows."

"The hell with that!" he bellowed. "I'm going home. Now!"

"I'm sorry to tell you, father, that I do not believe mother has the energy to supervise your care at home. I am taking you to a nursing facility where you will be well taken care of."

"That's bullshit" he screamed. "Home, now!"

"Father," I said, playing my trump card. "If you refuse, I will race home, grab mother and take her with me to Key West. You will never see either of us again. You know Jack has to return to Geneva. If you care anything about this woman who has been loyal to you for 55 years, you will go to the nursing home and be surrounded by competent people. Mother can come every day if she has the strength and I promise to be here half of each week."

Tracy, Dicky and René shortly before Dicky's death

I knew staying in Boca Raton full-time would be an exhausting experience. Also, my childhood friend, Dicky, was in a nursing home in Key West as his health worsened. It was the contrast of the two situations which made my very uncharacteristic strong action with my father possible. Dicky was less than half my father's age and was in a dilapidated county nursing home. The relatively luxurious surroundings, in a well- staffed facility in Boca, gave me the strength to make the case non-negotiable. I also decided to allocate some of my energy to be with Dicky, who had few friends, no money and was as frightened of dying as my father.

I was both astounded and relieved that the approach had worked. I rode in the ambulance with my father as we went to his last new home. When he was set up in his room, and after receiving his order to "buy a decent bed for me to die in," I returned to my parents' condominium to tell a very curious family what I had done. I was worried that after I would leave, my mother would change the arrangements and bring him home, which clearly would be a serious mistake. To give my mother some confidence I said:

"I will come back here every week for three days to relieve you from going to see him. You must understand that he will ask you to remove him from the nursing home and bring him back here. You will have to be strong on that point. My guess is that his condition will worsen quickly, and such a demand may only exist for a week or two."

Within a few days my brother and I had practiced our mother's driving to the nursing home to our satisfaction, and my father had accepted that he would not be returning to his apartment. On the second day he was at the nursing home he said:

"René, go into my office, bring a gun and shoot me."

"No, father," I answered. "That will cause me problems for years. I'll tell you what I *can* do, however. I'll take you home for a lunch break and you can jump off the balcony." Thankfully that trick elicited his reaction to never once ask to go back to his condominium for lunch.

Before leaving, I received a call from the director of nursing.

"René," she said, "we need to start around-the-clock private duty nurses for your father. The staff cannot handle him alone. Two nurses begged me to be reassigned to other wings in the building. I have some names for you to call."

"I'm not surprised," I said. "I'll schedule the nursing coverage."

I explained to the nursing agency that my father was indeed a difficult and challenging patient. The reaction I received was similar to the initial retort I always got:

"This is Palm Beach County. We are used to that."

The following day the first private-duty nurse arrived. I was reading in my father's room.

"Good morning, John. I am your nurse," she said cheerfully.

"Who the hell told you that you could call me John?" he growled.

"Well, what would you prefer I call you?" she asked sitting down.

"Mr. Silvin! And who gave you permission to be seated in my presence?"

Still willing, the nurse inquired,

"Where would you like me to stand, Mr. Silvin?"

"Take a chair into the hall and I'll call you if I need you."

I carried a large armchair into the hall for her. As the poor woman walked toward the door, my father said in a loud voice:

"I told you she wouldn't give a damn."

"To the contrary," she responded, as she turned around. "I care very much. Can I not please give you a back rub?"

"Fine," he snarled. "But warm up the lotion! It's too cold."

As the nurse put some lotion into her hands, I hoped beyond hope that we may, in fact, have found a woman who had the patience and ability to handle him. I watched my father turn over as the lady rubbed her hands together to warm them. When she touched his back, he screamed:

"Show me your hands!" The nurse complied.

"Just as I thought," said my father, as if he were Sherlock Holmes. "You're a peasant!"

"No, Mr. Silvin!" the now clearly exasperated professional answered. "I am not a peasant, but what's wrong with farmers?"

"Nothing," he answered, "but I'll be God damned if one will rub my back."

Looking at me the nurse said:

"Mr. Silvin, you were right. In fact, you understated the challenge. You'll have to find someone else to care for this man."

That was the first departure of a long stream of willing agency nurses.

The four-hour drive to Key West became my salvation. The beautiful blues of the ocean and the sky were so soothing and therapeutic. I drove slowly, with the top down, as I decompressed from the tension and readied myself to do what I could for Dicky, who was ending his life in a poorly furnished double room that smelled of urine, shared a bath and had no television.

My work with AIDS Help had also been beneficial. Their temporary offices at the Truman Annex had relocated to a more permanent site in a building owned by the Catholic Church. Monsignor Eugene Quinlan had rapidly become a friend and accompanied me to see Dicky at least once a week. He always brought a gift for both my friend and any other ailing AIDS patients he saw there and at the adjacent hospital. On several occasions, I would meet him with food baskets to distribute. If we visited a dying patient at their home, "Padre," as we all affectionately called him, would slip a 100-dollar bill in with the food packages.

After one such visit, it was clear that Padre was having a bad day. I asked him to be my guest for dinner at Antonia's restaurant on Duval Street. Without me asking what was bothering him he began:

"I am having problems dealing with the Toppinos, the leading Cuban Catholic family here. They all object to my asking 'who among you have reached out this week to an AIDS victim with assistance?' at each of my sermons. But I am not going to stop," he insisted. "I spoke to a mother in Ohio today," he went on. "I told her that if she wanted to see her young son again, it was time for her to come here. Do you know what she asked me?"

"No," I replied naturally. "Did repent yet?"

As I shrugged my shoulders, Padre continued:

"I told her: 'Lady, I'm trying to give you advance notice. Your son is going to die very shortly. I'd like you to come and see him, but only if you can find it in your heart to be loving and drop the *repent* crap.' She said that was not possible, to which I told her not to bother to use her broom stick to fly down here!"

My next weeks settled into a routine. I would spend the first three days trying to ease my mother's anguish. The second half was working with Padre in Key West, visiting patients, and setting up new policies at AIDS Help. By Friday evening, I was worn out. But standing by the chain-link fence at the small airport as I watched my handsome, compassionate and charming partner return to *our* home, was an immediate tonic. Our weekends were as blissful as anyone could imagine, and more than balanced out the horrors of the preceding week. One Sunday night, lying next to each other while we looked at the moon shine over the glittering ocean, Bob said:

"René, you have to put an end to your father's abuse."

"And how do you suggest I do that?" I asked laughing.

"Well, it is certain that he will say something cruel tomorrow. When that happens, just tell him that it's *not* acceptable."

"I'd love to have the power to do that. But I don't."

"Nonsense," said Bob. "Of course you do. If you feel too nervous at the moment of the insult, just spit out a few sentences. Let's practice them now. You'll be able to divorce yourself from the immediate tension and to end it forever. He'll never know the sentences were rehearsed."

Boca Raton, Florida

The following day, upon reaching the nursing home in Boca, my father demanded:

"Go to my favorite restaurant, Marcel's, and get me oysters for lunch."

I went to the restaurant, relieved I had an errand which would take me out of his room. Upon my return, I greeted my mother and a nurse, who had earned the great privilege to sit in his presence. I said:

"Father, Marcel had no oysters today. He did prepare a lovely tray of clams, which he said you also order frequently. He added that he would get fresh oysters at the market in Palm Beach for your lunch tomorrow."

As I placed the tray with ice and opened clams on the bed, my father threw them on me and the floor, spilling ice all over my shirt and giving me my golden opportunity to use Bob's brilliant sentences.

"That's the last time you will ever abuse me," I began my well-rehearsed lines.

"How dare you speak to me in that tone?" he yelled. "Actually, father, those were close to my next words."

Before I could continue, he looked at the two frightened women, my mother and the nurse, and yelled:

"Get out! Both of you!"

As they scurried into the hall, and before he had a chance to say another word, I continued reciting the script.

"I am very sorry that you are dying and that you are struggling with this. I have demonstrated that I am willing to put my life on its head to be here every week to help mother and to care for you, but I will not be the brunt of your rage. I know there is a polite gentleman in there," I said pointing at his head. "If you show *that* man to me, I will keep coming here. If not, you will see my back for the very last time. It's up to you."

He never answered. I sat silently for what seemed like an eternity, until I got up and went into the hall. My mother looked at me as if she were wondering who had been murdered in the duel.

"It's all right," I said, surprising myself. "Come back in now."

As usual, when I was about to go back to the Keys that week, and as I reached the door of my father's room, he said:

"René, did you notice I was polite? I was a gentleman!"

"Yes, father," I said compassionately. "You were polite and a gentleman. It was a delight to be able to care for you this week. I'll see you next Monday."

Many emotions raced through my mind on the restorative drive south. There were so many useless questions about what life would have been like if anyone had the ability to make my father realize he could not abuse those around him with abandon. Most importantly, I suddenly felt so secure that I lived with a wonderful man I deeply loved and being worthy of being loved. This was obviously the real thing, more important and better than ever before. I had finally found the one person who could understand me! I intuitively knew that he would have many more profound and helpful lessons for me over the years. I also *felt* loved and happy for the first time in my life. In a flash, I knew that the push-pull pattern I had always experienced with my father had been reversed. My father, who chronically had been so distant and so unavailable to me, thus damaging my self-esteem by reminding me of being unworthy, was now trying to gain my approval. Indeed, I was pushing, and *he* was trying to pull me in.

Bob's insight, advice and coaching were brilliant and timely. He had given me the key to my liberation and, presto, my inner feelings of shame disappeared. Indeed, I measured up to my father.

....

Dicky died on February 19, an hour after I'd left him in his sad room. He was 39 years old. My father followed the next day, February 20, in his nursing home with my mother by his side. He was 86. With typical humor, Padre said that my childhood friend stopped off in Boca to pick up my father and take him to heaven. I had selected a white, cashmere sweater for Dicky to wear in his coffin. Dicky's mother asked Padre if he was sure her son could go to heaven if he were not wearing a blue blazer. On February 21, after a mass at a crowded St. Mary, Star of the Sea Church on Truman Avenue, we buried him in a church plot donated by Padre.

From there I drove straight to Miami to meet the Swissair flight bringing my brother and his wife over from Geneva for our father's funeral.

When we got to my mother's condominium, she seemed weak, yet relieved. Then she said:

"I still have one concern. Although he never went to church, you know your father was a Catholic. You remember, he made you and me swear we would not have any—what he called— 'Tibetan rituals' when we buried him? I am so conflicted because I believe he needs to have a mass."

"Mother," I said, "we have discussed this concern before. I asked Padre about it, and he has a perfect solution. He will fly here tomorrow and will say some prayers at the funeral home. It is not technically a mass and is certainly not a Tibetan ritual. Padre assures me that father will, in fact, go to heaven, even though there is no mass, *and* he is being cremated."

My mother seemed relieved, so I almost broke out laughing at how easy that was, and how often Dicky and I had giggled over my father's words "Tibetan rituals" and "calcification," his term for cremation derived from his native French. I was not really sure about the "going to Heaven" part.

I met Padre at Fort Lauderdale airport and we drove to the funeral home in Boca. The only people present were my mother, my brother, his wife and I. Padre put on a religious robe and read several prayers and passages from the Bible. He then produced a small plastic bottle like I had seen at the drugstore and splashed holy water around the room and then on the coffin. There were no tears, just an odd sense of liberation. I had ordered a blanket of red roses to be placed on the casket. The only other flowers in the room were a huge arrangement from our friends, the Mérieux family, in Lyon, France. As we left the small room the only sadness I experienced was realizing that my father had died as he lived: alone, angry and frightened.

My brother left the funeral home with my mother, ahead of Padre and me. As we reached the front door, not being well-versed in Catholic tradition, I said:

"Oh, Padre, he never had his last rights. He was Catholic, after all. Shall we go back upstairs and do that now?"

"I was rather heavy handed with the holy water," said Padre. "Let's go have a good lunch."

I was overjoyed that I could leave that entire nightmare behind me and was very amused by padre's humor.

....

In spite of the difficulties of the year's first seven weeks, my home life and my love life were thriving. It was hard for me to believe that the world could hold such happiness, especially after enduring two difficult deaths. In an odd way, the trauma of my father's and Dicky's illnesses and deaths were a catalyst to deepen my love for Bob. I was able to see firsthand how competent and supportive he was in the face of adversity.

I spent much of my time working with AIDS Help in Key West, which proved both productive and curative. My main project was to identify and, hopefully, buy a housing unit for some of the less fortunate clients of our growing organization.

....

Ryan White

In April, the well-known Ryan White died at the young age of 18. His story and courage had done a great deal to bring awareness of the disease to a broader section of the American population. Ryan had become America's poster child for AIDS, and he was both HIV positive and a hemophiliac. He and his mother had fought hard to not only keep him in school, but also active in school activities. Their valiant efforts became the vehicle to educate middle America as to how HIV is and is *not* transmitted.

Shortly after Ryan died, Congress enacted the Ryan White Care Act, which still provides federal funds for the care of HIV-infected Americans. Three decades later, many have forgotten who this delightful young man was, but still derive significant benefits from the results of the law that honors his name and commemorates his battle.

Switzerland

Bob and I decided that it was time for us to go to Switzerland to meet my great friends, Jean-Claude, Léo and Pierre. Bob used his annual vacation to join me on a two-week trip. We stayed at the Palace Hotel in Gstaad and told our friends to schedule visits so that they and Bob could get to know each other.

At the first of many amusing dinners with Jean-Claude, it was clear

Hiking on the Eggli Mountain, Gstaad, Switzerland

that my former business associate was sizing up the man he knew I never wanted to be without. Jean-Claude loved to be provocative, using his humor to soften the points he was trying to make. During dinner at Gstaad's Olden Hotel in the middle of the village, Jean-Claude said:

"You used to bring boys to Switzerland who had an ass. This one may have a brain."

Bob seized the moment to not only amuse everyone at the dinner, but also to capture Jean-Claude's heart. He got up and turned around, showing his great physique from behind, and said:

"Jean-Claude, I have both!"

We spent our days hiking up the Eggli mountain and having wonderful mid-day meals at the restaurant beautifully situated at the top, where I had learned to ski over 30 years earlier.

My brother left his two sons with us for a long weekend so they could get to know Bob, especially since they had both been traumatized by Tim's death. Tim had played with them for hours when they were younger, throwing them onto their beds in what he called a "body slam." We had all laughed and enjoyed each other in what became the subtle teaching to young boys that their gay uncle was really quite normal and that I could bring a fun addition to their lives. Early on, Bob earned the respect and affection of "our" nephews also.

To complete Bob's introduction to my Swiss life, he met Pierre and Michèle Nussbaumer. In their typical generous, almost extravagant behavior, they invited Bob and me to join them at a luxurious "Château Hotel" in France. There they presented Bob and me with matching Hermès towels, which would forever symbolize our "wedding gift." Pierre does not snap to hasty decisions, but it was clear he too was impressed with Bob's quiet depth. I would soon learn that Pierre's support would come to mean a great deal to Bob.

Gstaad with Michèle

As usual, Léo was both enlightening and entertaining. Bob quickly had added Léo to the list of people who admired him and were relieved to see me in the company of an exceptional partner. I knew how much Léo enjoyed good red wines, so I brought a bottle of 1978 Vosne-Romanée, one of his favorites, to our room to drink before dinner.

"There are several new medications you both must become aware of," he said. "There is something called a 'reverse-transcriptase inhibitor,' which is helping patients who have progressed to AIDS."

Ever the statistician and student, Bob asked:

"What actually defines AIDS and differentiates it from HIV?"

"Each country defines AIDS differently," began the professor. "It is no surprise that the Americans have the most conservative definition, thus delaying the availability of practically non-existent government-sponsored relief programs. Here in Europe, one is considered as suffering from AIDS if he or she has a CD4 count under 500 and has had one life-threatening opportunistic infection.

There is another yardstick in which I am most interested called 'viral load testing.' Professor Chermann, who really is the man who isolated the virus at Pasteur eight years ago, has left Pasteur and opened an advanced research laboratory at the University of Luminy in Marseille, France. He is developing a measure of how present and active the virus is in its host. I assume that such a test, once made widely available, will be extremely useful in treating the illness. Chermann will be speaking on national television this Friday. I suggest you watch the program and go see him before you return to the States."

That Friday Bob and I were glued to the television in our room. Switzerland carries Italian, German and French networks as well as their own. We tuned into one of the French networks and listened to Chermann's illuminating description of how the HIV virus operates and mutates. A similar show on prime time in America would take another decade to air. After the program, I called my friend and pharmaceutical magnate, Doctor Allan Mérieux, to ask his opinion on what I had learned. The Mérieux Institute was the world's largest vaccine manufacturer in the 1990's and heavily involved in research. They had been kind enough to supply me for several years with their experimental HIV medication called DTC without cumbersome bureaucratic procedures. I had spent many wonderful weekends with Allan's sister, my life-long friend Nicole, at her house on the Lake of Annecy near Geneva. We would all water ski from her beautifully varnished Chris Craft speed boat named VIRUS.

Allan confirmed that he knew Jean-Claude Chermann well, and that his research was truly cutting edge.

"But you must understand, René, Chermann is testing a medication and working on measuring the virus' activity. But this is no magic bullet. The world is many years away from adequate treatment, much less a vaccine. Your Anthony Fauci at NIH is also trying to formalize the process of clinical trials for patients to access experimental treatments."

"I really want to meet Chermann," I said. "Would you please call him in Marseille and ask him if he would receive me there next week?"

By the following Monday, Allan's efficient secretary, who had kindly provided me with many favors, called saying that I had an appointment in Marseille with the legendary Jean- Claude Chermann.

Marseille, France

Bob's vacation was over, and he had to return to America. I took an extra few days to go to Marseille. Once I had found the research building at the University where Chermann had set up his laboratory and was ushered into his office, I received the first of many harsh lectures followed by affection, which was Chermann's signature, counter-balancing behavior.

"Before we begin," he said ominously, "I must tell you that I do not believe in medicine for the privileged. You did not have to ask a big shot like Mérieux to call for an appointment."

"I had no idea of who you do allow to visit and under what circumstances. I hope I did not offend you," I said sheepishly.

"No, you did not offend me, but you will be treated like any other person who walks through that door. Is that clear?" Thus began a relationship that constantly deepened.

Chermann's tone rapidly changed to include compassion and generous explanations. He confided that the weak link of his research was in compiling adequate statistics in a format acceptable to the scientific community. I volunteered Bob's services to help compile data and we agreed to meet frequently to that end.

When I returned to America, I was amazed that none of the physicians I consulted knew anything about viral load testing or Chermann's other research in geno- and pheno- typing analysis. These tests determine what mutations an HIV patient had developed to the virus. I quickly stopped even mentioning these terms when my descriptions drew blank faces, which indicated others thought I was crazy!

I gave up my inadequate quest to draw attention to European HIV developments, when a friend of mine in Washington, D.C., had *his* friend call me. Chris Wallace was an up-and-coming investigative reporter at that time and the son of the well-known CBS newsman Mike Wallace. We had a long conversation about the advances in HIV treatment research the Europeans were making, especially in France and Belgium. Chris said that he'd like to continue with follow-up conversations. But, it was apparent that *possible* future scientific developments in HIV did not present a subject for broad discussion in America.

As my emotion-charged year ended, it was clear that changes in the world of AIDS would be measured in baby steps resulting from hard work. There was no responsible promise of a cure or a vaccine. Unfortunately, progress was limited to providing assistance to the many victims of HIV disease who lost their life savings and their ability to remain productive members of society.

When Nelson Mandela was released from prison, one million South Africans had already been exposed to the virus, but the country's new liberal leader hardly talked about the crisis for the following five years. Other pressing issues kept his attention, as HIV gradually became South Africa's new Apartheid. AIDS would create the new under-class in Africa, dividing the more fortunate ones from those who could not afford treatment or comfortable surroundings in which to end their lives.

Chapter Seventeen

1991

Key West, Florida

As our time living together progressed, it was obvious that both Bob and I had each found a world of happiness we had not imagined existed. We told each other that often. During the work week, I missed him terribly and I kept busy at AIDS Help trying to raise enough money to acquire a housing unit for our clients. Having come from the for-profit health care industry, I had to adjust some of my thinking to adapt to a non-profit community organization. Even so, I became the sole voice of fiscal conservancy on the board of directors. This was driven by my obsession of being able to assure the long-term continuity of any new benefit we initiated.

During the week Bob worked hard at each of Rader's eating disorder units. Our perfect and peaceful weekends were action packed with social activities in Key West, daily visits to the new gym at Duval Square and romantic dinners, during which our non-stop conversation taught us more and more about each other. His descriptions of the patients he saw during the week, the gravity of their affliction, and his compassion for their plight was enlightening.

Shortly after the beginning of the year, we prepared a feasibility study to open an eating disorder clinic in Key West but decided against the endeavor. During this period, I got to know several of Bob's colleagues, all of whom respected his professional talent and personal charm. Bob's boss, the CEO of the company, believed that there was opportunity for the Rader Institute to expand into Europe. As a result, I made plans to spend the summer in Switzerland, while Bob and I looked into the possibility, and Bob traveled back and forth to existing clinics on the East coast.

On the eve of one trip to Europe, I went to my safe deposit box at a bank in Old Town, Key West, to get my passport, some travel money and a few other items. This included the Cartier money clip that Tim had given me when we moved back to America from Europe. I had placed the objects in a travel clutch and left them in the convertible in front of Lighthouse Court while I went in to pick up my work-out gloves. I was only inside for a few minutes, but when I emerged, I noticed my window had been broken and the small travel handbag was gone. I called the police who said that there was little they could do other than fill out a crime report, which we did. When I got back to my condominium, I called an infamous city councilman who represented "Bahama Village," the equivalent of a small inner city, situated on the blocks adjacent to Lighthouse Court. I knew Emory Majors because Padre and I wanted to set up an education program in the African-American churches about the risks of HIV. I was very surprised by the reluctance of the community leaders to acknowledge the problem and the relatively high incidence of bisexuality.

"Emory," I said, "my car was broken into in front of the Hemingway House less than an hour ago. I lost seven items of importance to me including an airplane ticket, my passport, a special pen and a money clip. The police indicated a lack of enthusiasm, and I wondered if you might help me recover them?"

"That's possible," he said.

"I'll offer $100 per item and will not ask any questions."

15 minutes later, Emory called with good news.

"I have six of your seven items. The money clip is not included."

That seemed obvious because my travel cash was attached. However, I had heard of a similar exchange when an acquaintance brought cash to retrieve a stolen car and got beaten up so badly, he ended up in the emergency room. "I'll be right there with 600 dollars to retrieve them. Will I be safe, or do I need to bring some protection?"

"Ain't no one here who'll hurt you," he said, laughing. "But if you feel more comfortable you can bring a cop."

15 minutes later, and in the presence of a police officer, I had my six items which allowed me to make my trip the following day. Even though I went to every pawn shop over the next months looking for it, Tim's money clip – like Tim — was gone forever.

Gstaad, Switzerland.

In Switzerland, I set up house in a rented chalet outside of Gstaad. I shared the lease with a close friend, Smith Richardson. I had met Smith when Tim and he were in design school together several years earlier, and we all had become close friends. Smith's partner, Rick, was HIV positive and one of the most fun people Bob and I knew. We loved being in their company and were thrilled that we would see a lot of them that summer. We also invited close friends from Key West to join us. Among them were Trip Hoffman and his partner, Alan Van Wieren. Both were active in the "gay social set" in Key West and had fallen on hard times with two failed business ventures: one in a start-up telephone company, the other a water filter product. We felt they needed the change of scenery and were happy to include them as our guests.

With Léo Eckmann's help, Bob and I interviewed hospital managers and owners, as well as psychiatrists, to determine if there was a need for a private-pay eating disorder clinic, as all European insurance companies had refused to cover hospitalization for the disease. In addition, we had difficulty translating the term "eating disorder" into German and French to create an understandable accurate description. While the incidence of eating disorders is high, its acceptance is lower in ultra conservative Switzerland. Most patients tried to treat the problem quietly in a psychiatrist's office. Hospitalization, if at all, was done under a different diagnosis, which further alienated the patients. At a decision-making meeting, we invited 20 well-to-do local people who either had, or were closely related to, someone with an advanced eating disorder.

In the Palace Hotel's main lounge one guest, a distant relative of Iran's deposed Shah, ordered pastries as we began the presentation. Trying to make his point and sensing a bad omen, Bob interrupted:

"I am sorry, Madam, but we will only be serving fruit juices."

Bob explained that in advanced cases of eating disorders, one's very life was at stake and that in less acute conditions, psychological well-being was almost always impaired. During a question-and-answer period, a waiter circulated among the guests with a silver tray containing several types of beautifully colored fruit juices. As the questions began, we realized our concept of an American-style eating disorder clinic was premature. Bob tried to diplomatically answer questions like, "Can I bring my chef to your clinic?" or worse, "Do you have a well-maintained barn nearby? I'd come if I could bring my horse."

After the gathering, Léo, Bob and I laughed at the naïveté of our plan. It had been a great learning experience about the cultural differences between continents, in relation to new medical thinking and beliefs.

"Don't you find it odd, Léo," I began, "that you are more advanced in discussing HIV in Europe than in America, but one still feels compelled to hide an eating disorder here?"

"It's actually easily understood," he answered. "AIDS is still considered a homosexual disease and you are much more homophobic in America. You can talk openly about alcoholism and psychiatric problems, but not homosexuality. Most Europeans have little or no problem with gay life but have not reached an acceptance of psychiatric problems. We don't have an Oprah! This experience today proves my point. Hopefully, as more heterosexual stars like Magic Johnson admit having the virus, you may evolve. But you are still a highly religious — even righteous — people."

We discussed the bizarre contradiction in America and our conservative President's lack of having adequately addressed AIDS in the early days of the pandemic.

"Now, René, you need to start anti-retroviral treatment. There are several new medications, including a good one made by Bristol-Myers Squibb."

"Which one do you recommend?" I asked.

"Several," he said. "We need to box the virus in. It is a complex and intelligent little devil that mutates quickly. You need a cocktail of drugs, not just one."

It would be more than a year before the term "cocktail" was adapted in the States to describe the multi-drug regimen which benefits most HIV positive patients.

"But I want you to see Chermann in Marseille before you start taking anything."

"Bob and I are going there next week," I said. "Won't you join us as our guest? There is a charming hotel on the coast in Cassis."

<u>Cassis, France</u>

All of us, including Smith and Rick, drove to the South of France the following week. It was their first meeting with the charismatic Professor Jean-Claude Chermann. Léo fell in love with the Roches Blanches hotel I had discovered and from then on always offered to

Hotel Roches Blanches, Cassis, France

meet us there when we visited Chermann's laboratory. The five of us, including Mrs. Chermann, became very close friends as we worked and traveled together several times a year. Bob had taken over helping Jean-Claude put his statistics in an acceptable format for publication in medical journals, and Léo balanced Jean-Claude's profound understanding of the virus with his own experience as a clinician and philosopher.

Like everyone else Bob met, Jean-Claude was wildly fond of my partner. Chermann spent hours describing how the virus operates and how to deal with it. In typical French tradition, he felt that we had gone overboard in America with an obsession for controlling the so called "co-factors."

"Don't get hysterical about diet and exercise," he advised. "Of course, a good balance is mandatory. But Americans are so extreme, and you need to have fun in life. Relax! Even *if* you are faced with a life-threatening illness, it will soon become manageable rather than a death sentence. Viral load testing will help clinicians recommend the timing to begin treatment. There again, I fear Americans will be overzealous in prescribing these very toxic drugs. And geno-typing will help competent physicians determine when a patient's virus has mutated so that medications can be altered as new drugs, and even new classes of drugs, are developed."

"We are going to Belgium when we leave here," Bob said, "to see the new lab there which processes the geno- and pheno-typing of HIV

Bob at Les Baux de Provence France

blood samples."

"Please call me when you have seen it," said Jean-Claude. "It is the wave of the future."

"Why is it," I began with a question which had tormented me for nearly a decade, "that I frequented all the places and had sexual relations with many HIV positive people who are all dead? Why am I here and relatively healthy?"

"You either were infected with a weak strain of the virus or, more likely, your system has the ability to 'plateau.' It finds a level at which your immune system can contain the virus from further damaging it. That's why viral load testing is an important component. But I go much further than simple viral load measurements. I measure the 'mood' of the virus in a 'co-culture' which takes 30 days, and it measures the types of antibodies the host produces. In your cases, at this point, I do not recommend treatment and I believe that you, René, may not benefit from traditional antiviral treatment over long periods. It's odd but there is also a mutant gene, called 'Delta 32,' which *prevents* infection! So, while you are lucky so far, there is an even more fortunate smaller minority who cannot become infected in the first place. I want to study them more in order to look into the possibility of a vaccine. Isn't it amazing that a genetic mistake can be life-saving?"

"Now," continued Chermann, "I want you to be interviewed on French television tomorrow. They will be in my office, and I need you to explain your case."

"But I am not French," I said.

"That's why I need you," he answered. "It would be of help to me and will show French people that, if some folks come from America for my tests, that more French should take advantage of what is at their disposal, especially non- progressors like you. We may even be able to locate some people with Delta 32."

"It's a good thing your father is dead, René," said Bob. "I don't think he'd be overjoyed to hear from his French relatives that you were coming out on national television."

The amusing comment made me realize how fortunate I was to not have those kinds of concerns any longer, and how much I hoped we could help others reach a similar position of freedom.

The following day, before the television interview, Chermann brought Bob, Rick, Léo and me into his office.

"We have received the results of your blood work and I have several pieces of news," he began. "Bob, you and René have a protective antibody called R7V."

Looking at Bob he said:

"Your counts are better than René's, so I definitely do not recommend you be treated at this time. Rick and René do require medication, but not with antivirals yet. I am convinced that the thymus is a key element in boosting the immune system. It is where CD4 T-Cells are made. I want you both to begin daily injections of a thymus extract, which I believe is the best available immune modulator. What do you think, Léo?"

"I have always maintained that strengthening the host while the patient still has an immune system to provide protection, is better than fighting the virus," answered Leo. "So, I whole-heartedly endorse the injectable thymus booster. I'll teach you both how to administer inter-muscular shots. You'll see that it is no big deal, and you will become comfortable with it within a few days."

For the following two years, Rick and I would have to go to Marseille every other month to get our two-month dose of the experimental medication, and to be monitored at Chermann's laboratory. We always hated coming through customs in Atlanta or New York with syringes and an unknown medication packaged in unmarked containers. Except for a few minor problems, when we were brought into a room to be questioned, letters explaining our condition and the medication sufficed to get us back into the country. All of my and Rick's blood counts improved significantly while we used the thymus extract.

Unfortunately, the product was purchased by Upjohn Pharmaceutical, which promptly discontinued it and did not honor the protocol agreements that had been entered into with all the voluntary experimental patients in France and the U.S. They refused to give us any explanation of their upsetting decision, or to allow

Professor Chermann and me to speak to their lead scientists or executives.

This was my second experimental medication, along with the Mérieux Institute's DTC, which had helped build my immune system, but which was cancelled before it became readily available to the public or to the trial patients. The experience, while devastating when it occurred, taught me the absolute need for flexibility and balance in dealing with the ever-changing world of HIV treatment. I learned that I had to control the usually brief euphoria associated with good medical news, so that the contrasting bad news was tolerable.

<u>Vevey, Switzerland</u>

Bob flew home from France, and I returned to Switzerland to admit my mother to a facility to address a prescription drug problem which had gradually worsened. Switzerland has always had various private specialty clinics where numerous conditions are discretely treated. Jean-Claude Salamin had recommended a clinic in Vevey, a charming flower-filled lakeside city, where Charlie Chaplin had lived and died, and Nestlé has its World Headquarters.

This particular clinic was located in one of the town's best hotels. Each patient enjoyed a lakefront room, on a dedicated floor of the

Left to right: Nancy, John Jacques and René Silvin
Vevey, Switzerland

hotel. A psychiatrist and psychologist were assigned to the case to wean my mother off of tranquilizers, anti-depressants and sleeping pills.

My mother was a willing patient because she had developed what is known as a "paradoxical reaction" to the tranquilizers. The more one takes, the more jitters one experiences, which is followed by yet more pills, and so on. Her physician in Boca Raton was dispensing 500 pills at a time. Bob called the doctor when we discovered the problem.

"Doctor, this is Doctor Mann speaking. I am calling on behalf of Mrs. Silvin and her son, René," he said. "We are both very concerned about her extreme agitation caused by excessive use of tranquilizers and anti-depressants."

"I wouldn't be overly disturbed about that," her physician answered.

"But we are, Doctor," he said in his calm yet determined manner. "In fact, we are taking Mrs. Silvin to a sanatorium overseas. The purpose of my call is to tell you that we fully expect you to only prescribe acceptable doses of such medication to her when she returns and *only* in consultation with me."

"Is that a threat?" he asked.

"No, Doctor," continued Bob. "I merely want you to know that if we find that you have allowed Mrs. Silvin to overuse prescription drugs again, I will call you up in front of a panel of your peers for review."

Unfortunately, Bob had to have a similar conversation with several physicians who preyed on elderly, lonely widows in Palm Beach County for the rest of my mother's life.

....

By the end of the year, several of my past associates had encountered serious legal problems. At National Medical Enterprises a class-action suit against the company and the two senior officers with whom I had been dealing began. Dick Eamer and Mike Focht were accused of a breach of fiduciary responsibility in handling company money and business.

Roy Pesch's Swiss hospital company was entering bankruptcy. Additionally, Emory Majors, the Key West town councilman who had been able to get my stolen possessions back to me, was sent to prison, and federal officers arrested several well-known local politicians.

All this news was overshadowed, and almost rendered irrelevant, by the fact that ten million people had been infected with HIV worldwide as 1991 drew to a close. I had lost hundreds of acquaintances, scores of friends and my partner, Tim. But I had a great life with Bob, and we were well on our way to "squeezing 25 into five."

Chapter Eighteen

1992

Key West, Florida

Bob in Key West, Florida

Stability and happiness would be the best way to describe 1992. While both Bob and I knew we had a life-threatening illness, we believed we were fortunate in being advised by a great infectious disease immunologist and the world's most advanced retrovirologist. Bob loved working on Jean-Claude Chermann's statistics, and we managed to make our frequent visits to France exciting. We tried not to focus on the dehumanizing time spent at the public health hospital in Marseille, every time I needed two more months of the experimental thymus injectable product.

Our friends, Trip and Alain, had a Jack Russell named Spanky, and Bob said that was the type of dog he would like. When Alain said that they had bred Spanky and would be happy to sell us one of his offspring, I was ecstatic and could hardly wait for the puppy to be old enough to adopt. We spent many fun moments thinking of an appropriate name and decided we wanted a female who would be called "T- Cell." That way, we could make light of the endless and tiresome conversations about "how many T-Cells you have?" and, after all, Jack Russells are strong, energetic and healthy, just like a real T-Cell should be.

My T-Cell count had begun to decline from 400 to 300 and Bob said:

"Think about it, René, we will always have at least one T-Cell!" Since I was the oldest, as well as the longest HIV positive one, we both assumed I'd be the first to go.

During the winter, I made two patches for the popular AIDS quilt project in San Francisco: one for Tim, the other for Dicky. I tried to design each one to match the character of the person it was meant to memorialize. The making of Tim's patch was a long-distance, joint venture because I included several of his childhood friends. We wanted it to be trendy, young, colorful and fun. We incorporated Tim's red high school basketball jersey and some mementoes from his all-too-brief career in interior design. Sadly, in Dicky's case, there was no one that I could enlist to assist me. I had several of Dicky's early dramatic black-and-white modeling photographs, which had been shot in New York, made into fabric patches. With them I created a quilt that was dramatic, handsome and stylish. The process was cathartic and necessary. I worked on the patches every day and, upon completion of the second one, decided I would never make another, but would continue to support the project financially. I felt that part of my healing process was over, and I was ready to move on.

Working with Al McCarthy in Key West, we identified several possible sites for a housing unit for those AIDS Help clients who qualified. The sites we could afford were either inadequate or required so much additional money to bring up to acceptable standards that the project appeared doomed. We finally found a compound on Bertha Street, near where Bob and I lived, which was ideal. Unfortunately, once again, the price was out of our reach.

One evening Al and I met with Jerry Hermann, the well-known song writer and lyricist, to tell him of our progress. Jerry had recently lost his partner, Marty Finkelstein, with whom I had worked out at the gym. We all called him "the best chest," and I was crushed when his illness got out of control, and he rapidly deteriorated and died.

"I'm afraid we will be abandoning the dream of having our own housing unit, at least for now." I began.

"What was the best one you saw?" asked Jerry.

"It is over near B's Restaurant and would be perfect for our needs, but we need $750,000 more than we can raise. Remember, Jerry, we have had over 15 local fund raisers. People here is Key West are pretty well tapped out."

Jerry asked for a few more details, got up, went into his study and came back with a check for the required $750,000. While Al and I sat speechless, Jerry said:

"I have two requirements you must agree to in accepting this donation. The first is that you not cash the check for ten days."

"That's hardly a problem," said Al, as we all chuckled.

"The second," continued Jerry "is that the project be named after Marty."

Al explained that we would bring the issue of the name to the full Board but that, again, the huge gift which would enable Key West to be a leader in housing for otherwise displaced AIDS patients would render his request moot. Within months the compound was acquired, several units were renovated, food was being routinely delivered each day from well-known local restaurants, and a beautiful gold-and-green sign sat at the entrance to the compound which read: "Marty's Place."

France

For my midwinter trip to France to collect my experimental medication, Bob was able to accompany me. He had never seen the great castles of the Loire Valley, which I had passionately told him about. In typical fashion, Bob researched several of them and we planned our holiday around visiting the châteaux with the most riveting histories and stayed in quaint local inns near each one.

Not surprisingly, my favorite, the Château de Chenonceau, also became Bob's. It was built over the river Cher, near the town of the same name, by Henry the Second for his mistress Diane de Poitiers, reputedly the most striking and inspiring woman of her time. We lingered in the perfectly planned gardens and absorbed every detail of the tour guide's explanations of the château. That night we saw a stunning production of *son et lumière* (sound and light) detailing the castle's history. Bob and I lay on a blanket and watched the dramatic show like two teenagers in love seeing the Nutcracker at Christmas for the first time.

Nephew Johnny and Bob at the Château de Chenonceau

Highlands, North Carolina

During the summer, together with our friends Smith and Rick, we rented a house in Highlands, North Carolina. Smith and Rick lived in Atlanta and could easily escape the hot city to reach the mountain resort that, at 5,000 feet, was almost always cool. The plan was perfect, especially since neighbors at the Key West Beach Club also rented mountain cabins in the area.

Since my years of working in Washington, D.C., I had owned a cabin near Charlottesville, Virginia in the neighboring county of Louisa. Bob pointed out that as we never used the little house, I should look for a similarly valued property in the Highlands area and swap the Virginia cabin for something that we could frequently use during summers. I was invariably very excited when I picked Bob up at the Asheville airport. On our way back up the mountain, Bob would tell me about his nameless, yet fascinating, eating disorder patients and I'd show Bob the cabins I had seen. We would also drive around various other neighborhoods. One evening we drove past a contemporary home, built across a stream.

Bob had never before expressed a passion for any material item and surprised me when he said he thought the house was the most beautiful home he had ever seen, and he wanted us "to live and die there."

René and Bob in North Carolina

"It's hardly a cabin, Bob," I said, "but I have seen this house listed for sale in a real estate broker's window in Highlands. Let's go speak with him tomorrow."

The following day we went into the John Shiffli office on Main Street. My thoughts that the realtor's name was Swiss were confirmed by the décor in the office, which included several Swiss artifacts like a cowbell and yoke. However, any resemblance to a Swiss *personality* vanished when we met the gentleman. From the start, dealing with Mr. Shiffli was strained, a strain which increased when he was reluctant to show us the listed property. Day after day, I would return to the office trying to schedule a showing. Each time there was another excuse. Finally, the standoffish broker gave me a key and told me to "go see it on your own."

I drove the eight miles to the property only to find that the key did not work. After a repeated experience, I concluded that Mr. Shiffli, decidedly, did not want to show me the property. Undeterred, I wrote the owner and eventually received a call from a sweet elderly lady who was surprised by my letter and the information it contained.

"I have been away, but I am here now, and you may come by any time you like," said Mrs. Asbury.

After our second meeting, she and I sat on the deck overlooking the scenic private pond. We had an immediate affinity for one another, which was proven by her statement:

"Mr. Silvin, I am sorry you had such a difficult time with old Shiffli."

"Do you know why he would not show me the house when he has the listing?" I asked.

"It is embarrassing," she began, "but he told me that he was a friend of my late husband's and Jack would 'roll over in his grave' if he knew I might sell the house to 'two fags.' You must know that, if you do move here, there will be others who are stupid, old bigots, even in this

Chenoncette, home to Bob and René in North Carolina

neighborhood, and who may try to make life unpleasant for you."

"That won't bother Bob and me," I replied naïvely. "The world is changing. Imagine! An AIDS patient named Mary Fischer even spoke at the Republican National convention! Also, the gay community hopes that if Bill Clinton is elected in November we'll enter a period of greater acceptance, understanding and medical research."

"I want you to have this house, which brought Jack and me great happiness, but I want to warn you that there are other Shifflis around here."

That Saturday, when Bob returned for the weekend, we spent over an hour touring the house and the property. Even though the house had been badly maintained and needed extensive renovation, Bob's delight at the thought of moving there was apparent. "Let's make this our retirement home, René," he said. "There are 200,000 HIV infected people in America, one and a half million worldwide. Who knows how long *we* have?"

"Since it crosses a river, let's name it something to do with Chenonceau," I added, as our excitement turned into exuberance. "Instead of Henry the Second building it for the most beautiful woman in the world, I'll *remodel* it for the most handsome *man* in the world."

Within a few days we were under contract to buy the house of our dreams, which we would name "Chenoncette" (baby Chenonceau) and close the transaction nine months later. This would allow Mrs. Asbury the time she wanted, and also offer us time to sell our condominium in Key West. We pledged to each other to make it into a small island of tranquility and love, and for us to end our days there.

Key West, Florida

Bob never ceased to amaze me with his unwavering devotion, absolute emotional presence, and authentic attention to my feelings. It was a common occurrence that gay men would blatantly "cruise" Bob, on occasion even placing their telephone numbers in his hand or trying to lure him into another room to talk, hoping I would not notice. Invariably, Bob would say:

"Excuse me, but I guess you have not met my partner, René," and he would put his arm around my shoulder and smile at me.

That fall, I developed pains in my esophagus and went to see one of the local Key West physicians. He told me that it was indigestion which could be handled with antacids. When the problem persisted, I decided to call Léo Eckmann.

"What is your current T-Cell count?" he asked.

"200," I replied.

"Tell your local doctor you want a prescription for an anti-fungal. I recommend 100 milligrams of Diflucan per day. You will see that the symptoms will end in a week."

"But he is sure it is indigestion."

"Tell him two things. The first is that he must start reading the New England Journal of Medicine, and the second is that you need another doctor!" concluded Léo with his usual clever humor.

By the end of the year, Bill Clinton had been elected President, and hopes for a more liberal and understanding life in America flourished among most of our friends. His wife, Hillary, had pledged to overhaul the nation's healthcare system as soon as they took office, and there were rumblings that life for gay military men and women might also, finally, be able to be undertaken without fear of reprisals and dishonorable discharge.

As Léo predicted, other anti-viral drugs were in various phases of research. The FDA approved "ddC" or "Hivid," the first drug to be used in combination with AZT.

There definitely was reason for optimism to fuel my hopes to live many healthy years with Bob at the house of his dreams.

Chapter Nineteen

1993

The year began with great excitement about moving to North Carolina, and possible significant improvements for the AIDS community. Bob and I enjoyed Key West, but we both felt the gay set was limiting and somewhat self-serving. Wearing a new silk shirt to an AIDS fundraiser at a local restaurant became trite, and we both preferred to actually *do* something. Our communication with Professor Chermann increased, even as his ability to spend full-time in his research laboratory at the University was made more difficult. His newly acquired international fame kept him traveling for several weeks a month.

Marseille, a major French city on the Mediterranean, had both a liberal and an extreme right political element. The National Front (Le Front National) was led by Jean-Marie Le Pen, France's equivalent of Jerry Falwell. The opposition was led by the liberal senator (Deputé) Bernard Tapie, who had been under intense pressure from his political opponent and was forced to resign amid charges of improprieties while running his sports apparel giant Adidas. Under the French system, a Senator who resigns is allowed to pick his or her successor to serve during the balance of the elected term. Bernard Tapie selected Jean-Claude Chermann to be his replacement (Suppléant).

Both Jean-Claude and his intelligent activist wife, Dani, sprang into action to combat Le Pen's extremist views of cracking down on immigration, encouraging women to stay home and have babies, and reinstituting the death penalty. It was a strange political movement in an otherwise socially liberal France, and one the Chermanns were determined to combat. We were all particularly outraged at Le Pen's pronouncements that the Nazi gas chambers were a "detail of history" and that his position was "neither left nor right" — a slogan he used in his repeated efforts to be elected to the French Presidency.

V. Duane Rath

We had also become close friends with an unusual couple who had recently bought President Eisenhower's former house, a historic building in the Truman Annex in Key West. Their names were Duane Rath and Fredrick "Ted" Hurdman. Pridam Singh, the neighborhood's developer, needed a strong vote of confidence to prove that the property could, indeed, become the exclusive area he had in mind. Several abandoned former Navy buildings were scattered throughout the 19 acres. These included a hospital, an administration building, two red brick foundry buildings, some admiral quarters, Harry Truman's Little White House and President Eisenhower's former home.

Duane Rath bought 51 Front Street and beautifully landscaped and remodeled it, in a style consistent with the home's design and reminiscent of where the vacationing President would relax. 50-foot-tall royal palms were brought in as this largest single piece of property in the area was professionally landscaped. The abandoned and dilapidated house, overlooking the harbor, was rebuilt and splendidly decorated and furnished. The living room featured one of the island's few beautiful fireplaces in front of which sat a tea table, one of a set of two. The other belonged to Elizabeth Taylor. A huge Venetian glass chandelier hung above a contemporary custom-made dining-room table and chairs. Adjacent to the living room was a warm, elegant library decorated with rare Indian chief pictures, which Duane acquired from the Curtis Elephant portfolio. The library furniture was upholstered with Clarence House fabric, with additional rolls stored nearby in case the dog soiled a seat. This expensive endeavor gave the Truman Annex the vote of confidence it indeed needed. The remaining lots along Front Street sold in rapid succession, and new large duplications of historic homes in Old Town were planned and erected.

Duane and Ted had been together for 15 years and were envied among the gay set because Duane had great wealth and added a totally new, and superior dimension to the level of possible charitable contributions. It was odd to us that their arrival in town did not create a sense of comfort amongst our friends, but rather jealously and envy. I suppose that Duane and Ted spent more and more time with Bob and me, because we were not jealous of these two amazing philanthropists. We felt lucky to be able to offer our thoughts on how Duane could position himself as a leader of the gay community. The more good that Duane did, including offering friends like Trip and Alan a much-needed mortgage on their home at 313 William Street, the more the slightly-veiled resentment from the gay set grew.

Duane was a true entrepreneur, even at a very young age. At four years old, he bought candy bars from a local store in his hometown of Council Bluffs, Iowa, and sold them from his little red wagon for a profitable ten cents each. Later, after graduating from the University of Wisconsin, Duane went to work for his father, who manufactured stainless-steel tubing. When Duane eventually took over the company, he developed the business and the technology which brought the newly named "Rath Corporation" to international fame for superior quality stainless steel tubing for the food industry. Their development of a "mirror-finish" greatly reduced to the point of virtually eliminating, the possibility for bacteria to form and contaminate food, especially in industrial kitchens. I had seen his products installed in hospitals in Europe.

Duane had recently sold the business and created a charitable foundation with the bulk of his vast fortune. While the initial charter of the foundation was to fund education, Duane set a plan in motion to change the Rath foundation's charter and instead to focus on gay issues. Most importantly he wanted to implement education for underprivileged inner-city gay Adolescents, whose suicide rates were ten times higher than that of their straight peers.

Duane took a shine to us, especially to Bob. In working with Pridam Singh, a plan was conceived to carry out Duane's dream on a national scale. Initially, Bob and Duane worked with police departments in both small and large American cities to develop an information data base on crime and suicide, especially in the gay subculture. In later phases of the master plan, a staff of teachers and psychologists would operate at each site to promote self-esteem and pride to the targeted group. Duane planned to also start an all-gay television network, as well as radio stations.

Duane spoke with Bob about turning the passionate part- time activity into a full-time project and began plans to do so as we prepared to leave Key West. The four of us became inseparable friends. Since we all rarely gave large parties or even attended the constant, shallow cocktail gatherings of the set, the four of us became both an oddity and a subject of considerable gossip and invented intrigue. This would quickly magnify.

Ted was a sexy, handsome former Green Beret and defined the expression "tall, dark and handsome." He had been Duane's loyal partner during the years of Duane's hard work and had assisted him in their rise to fame and fortune as the company expanded. When Duane sold the Rath Corporation he had allowed Ted to indulge his several hobbies, including automobiles, horses and fox hunting. Ted bought world-class horses and hunted at all the well-known fox hunting clubs. He had his beautiful hunting clothes made on Savile Row in London and generously gave many sets of "pinks," saddles, bridles and other expensive equipment to friends, including Trip, who fancied himself as a great hunter but did not have the means to indulge in the expensive sport. The adage of "no good deed goes unpunished" became evident as Ted's generosity was accepted by increasingly jealous sycophants.

I resigned from the AIDS Help board. Bob and I sold our condominium and we moved to Cashiers, North Carolina. There I loved working with Jim Fox, the architect who had originally designed Chenoncette. Together we had removed a poorly added wing and restored the house to its original design. Smith and I went to many furniture stores in Atlanta to try to find furniture that would match the Frank Lloyd Wright design of the house, but we finally decided that I should ask Jim if he would design our home's furniture. Thinking that my request was a parallel to asking Michelangelo to paint my bathroom ceiling, I put the request to Jim, who was delighted to comply in what would be a two-year project.

My brother owned a small house in the new Truman Annex, near the mansion at 51 Front Street, which he agreed to sell us the following winter. This would allow us the affordable luxury of spending winters in Key West, albeit much less of the year than previously, and to be near Duane.

This became all the more logical and achievable because the Rader Institute had been experiencing financial difficulties and was restructuring. Bob was let go and his position was assumed by Doctor Rader's son, Jonathan. Bob's unemployment coincided with our move to North Carolina, and our first months there were spent both renovating the house, searching for a new position for Bob, and deciding if his working for our friend Duane at the Rath Foundation was wise.

By late summer, I was experiencing intestinal discomfort, which steadily continued to worsen. In consultation with Léo and Chermann, I had begun my first combination therapy using the available anti-viral drugs of AZT and Hivid. I had found these medications extremely hard to tolerate and assumed that they were greatly responsible for my stomach problems.

One night, after dinner, while reading with Bob in our den, I felt as if I had been shot in the stomach. Bob had to help me to bed. Against his advice, I spent the next two days in near agony in our bed, terrified to go to a hospital.

"René, we have to get you to a hospital," he said.

"It will be better in the morning," I replied, preferring to die in my own bed than be treated in a hospital.

Bob was so surprised that, for someone who had spent his entire career in hospitals, I was terrified to access one. I explained to him that it was *because* I had worked and lived in many hospitals, some of the most famous in the world, that I was anxious. On the third day, when Bob tried to help me to the bathroom, I passed out and he decided to take matters in his own hands, regardless of my protests. He asked a neighbor to help him carry me to the car and take me to Atlanta. They reclined the passenger seat to the maximum and padded it with several comforters, as even the slightest movement was agonizing. As we drove out of our property, two of our many curious neighbors, who wondered about the mysterious gay couple, happened to be walking by. Michael Jackson had just been accused in his first child molestation case. As I waved at the nosy neighbors from my apparently, absurdly, luxurious car-bed, I said:

"You know, Bob, these people may think this is how we go to the supermarket every day, and that we are as nutty as Michael Jackson."

The humor ended there because after an examination and a CT scan at Emory Hospital in Atlanta, I was told that my intestines had ruptured.

"You are a very lucky man," began a surgical intern, "most people die within a few hours of an intestinal rupture. Your body was able to 'wall off' the area by encapsulating it. We will operate in the morning."

I was exceedingly anxious that night in the typically austere hospital room. Bob stayed by my bed the entire time. When I had anxiety attacks, and felt as if I could not breathe, he would gently put his hand on my chest and speak in his soothing voice:

"Take deep, slow breaths, René. You'll be fine, this is just anxiety. Everything will be fine."

The following morning, a team of surgical students, parading behind the chief of surgery, all crowded into my room. I was expecting to be prepped and brought to an operating room, but instead, after a lengthy discussion in my presence, they felt that I should be treated with intravenous antibiotics in the hope of reducing the infection before an operation. Could the HIV issue complicate the decision and the operation, they asked one another? An infectious disease specialist was brought in for consultation, a delay which left Bob and me baffled.

Day after day, similar "classes" on walled-off HIV-related ruptured intestines took place in my room. Day after day surgery was postponed. I had been given no food, of course, and the weakness that it created, combined with a morphine drip, began to cause bizarre hallucinations. Thankfully, each time I awakened, Bob and Smith and/or Rick were in my room, ready to comfort and orient me. On the fifth day during the daily medical team discussion, Bob said:

"Look doctor, René has had no food in six days. He is shaking

Bob and René's mother shortly before her stroke

from weakness. Either you operate today or feed him, but I will not stand by and see him starve to death."

The team still considered surgery too risky, so I was given some soft foods. After several days, the chief of surgery said that the infection was reduced, but that it would be best to operate in six to eight weeks, during which time more antibiotics would further reduce the threat of a possibly fatal sepsis infection during surgery.

The day I was released from the hospital, we stayed at Smith's and Rick's lovely home in Atlanta's residential neighborhood of Buckhead. Bob sat on the floor next to the couch on which I was lying on while we had dinner. Even though surgery would eventually follow, the relief I experienced from being out of the hospital was enormous. I was never happier than the following day when we were back in our home in Cashiers. The joy of spreading out in our bed, with Bob by my side, and in relative comfort, was equivalent to the greatest feeling of relaxation I had ever experienced. In the middle of the night, the phone rang.

"This is Sophie," began my mother's companion. "Your mother is lying on the floor, and I cannot revive her."

"Call 911, go to the hospital in the ambulance and call me back when a physician has been assigned," I said.

Bob and I noticed that I could make sane health decisions for others, but not for myself.

We had several conversations that night with the staff at the Boca Raton hospital. My mother had suffered a stroke, fallen and ruptured her spleen, which had to be removed. It seemed so odd that our two medical crises had converged. Unfortunately, my mother appeared to have had another stroke on the operating table and then lingered, for ten days, on a ventilator in a state called conscious but non-responsive. After two weeks of being in this condition a decision had to be made, and I asked my surgeon at Emory if I could travel to Florida to monitor my mother's care.

"It's a bit risky," he said, "but as long as you do not exercise, lift anything or strain yourself in any way, it should be safe. We will need to operate in a month, though."

Bob and I drove the 800 miles to South Florida. I was so happy to have him with me to help with this otherwise-overwhelming predicament. We even spoke about how fortunate the timing of his being unemployed was. Otherwise, he might not have been able to be with me during the two concurrent life-threatening medical emergencies. I wondered how hard-working single people could cope with numerous disasters by themselves, and we pledged that, regardless of cost or employment, we would never leave the other when similar challenges occurred.

Bob and I met with the primary doctor caring for my mother in an office at the Boca Raton Hospital. The physician recommended removing my mother from the ventilator. Since she had both a living will and a DNR (do not resuscitate,) he explained that she would probably die within a few hours of removing the ventilator. We called my brother in Switzerland and told him he had to come back to Florida immediately. We decided that, upon his arrival, we would do as the physician recommended.

My brother, his wife, Bob and I sat with her for three days, not hours as predicted, after the respirator was removed and we watched her slip away. Several nurses asked me why I clutched my stomach constantly, but I pretended that my pain was not worsening. Following my mother's death and funeral in late December, we decided to go to Key West for a few days to recuperate, after which, my brother would return to Switzerland, and I would be operated on in Atlanta.

Bob and I discussed what a sad life my mother had experienced, living with a tyrant, not having been appreciated, and always putting on "a good face" to outsiders, regardless of humiliating psychological pain. She was the sad victim of a generation of women who were raised to believe that they had to obey their husbands, regardless of how illogical or even cruel the situation became.

On New Year's Eve, Bob and I dined with Duane and Ted in the recently completed former home of President Eisenhower. Instead of a formal meal in the dining room, we ate in a family area off the kitchen so we could feel at ease. We marveled at the beautiful landscaping and furnishings, which included elaborate Chihuly chandeliers. At midnight we drank a bottle of champagne and we all retired, after making ambitious and exciting plans for the gay mission of the transformed Rath Foundation. The new year held so much promise. Duane had met with President-elect Clinton to discuss his dream, and other meetings were scheduled with the new administration. Duane had pledged to fund a gay wing of the Holocaust Museum on the Mall in Washington, D.C., and wanted Bob to serve on the museum's board. The possibilities of great progress for AIDS patients and for the greater gay world seemed endless. Although it embarrassed Duane, we told him that, finally, there was the possibility for the American gay community to have its own Martin Luther King. Duane laughed modestly.

We spoke of the many friends we had lost during the year, as well as the famous AIDS-related deaths of tennis star Arthur Ashe and ballet legend Rudolf Nureyev. Duane relied heavily on our knowledge of HIV, because it was a world he had not been exposed to. He planned to send Ted to visit Jean-Claude Chermann and express his intent to support Chermann's vaccine research. I was impressed to hear how delighted Duane was that the CDC had revised its definition of AIDS. He hoped that would result in greater benefits being provided to organizations, like our local AIDS Help. He was encouraged that opportunistic infections were now included in CDC language relating to HIV disease.

Duane believed strongly in Key West and wanted to upgrade the town. To this end he offered details of his generous donations to create a park adjacent to the historic Key West library and a kidney dialysis unit.

I followed one sad story in the closing days of 1993, namely that Jacqueline Kennedy Onassis was diagnosed with large-cell Non-Hodgkin's lymphoma. Since I admired her and had seen her several times in both Paris and Gstaad, I felt particular compassion and concern for what the distant idol must be enduring. I would soon learn more about her suffering than I had planned or wanted to.

Chapter Twenty

1994

Key West, Florida

My Swiss friends, the Nussbaumers, visited Key West in the opening days of January. Pierre was alarmed about my posture, always clutching my stomach, and said I looked terrible. I was scheduled to return to Atlanta a few days after Pierre left town, but my plans were abruptly aborted. After returning from taking Pierre to the airport, I told Bob I felt like going to bed. I took one call from France telling me about Alain Mérieux's brother, Jean, who had been killed in a car accident, ate some soup and tried to sleep.

Around 2 AM the same acute and agonizing stomach pain I had experienced five weeks earlier reoccurred. There was no doubt that my intestines had ruptured a second time. Stupidly, I tried to stay still and let Bob sleep. At 6 AM I told him we had to go to the hospital.

The Key West hospital was not where one wants to be treated for any serious condition. It was badly maintained, dirtier than most hospitals in developing countries, and overcrowded. It was designed to treat less acute patients than it currently served, which resulted in congested corridors, sloppy storage areas and stressed staff. To make things worse, there were no medical teaching programs or up-to-date medical committees which resulted in ego maniacal physicians who practiced bad medicine.

An emergency room physician, who was not only asleep on a cot but also reeked of alcohol met us. We begged "Doctor" Bermudez to examine me gently, as even the slightest pressure on my abdomen was excruciating. After his initial palpation, which was more like a punch, Bob told him that he was not to touch me again, and that we demanded another physician. The new doctor ordered a CT scan. Bob stayed by my gurney hour after hour. When he asked why it was taking so long to get me to radiology, he was told:

"They have an emergency case there."

"What would you call ruptured intestines?" Bob asked.

It was mid-afternoon when I was scanned and received the confirmation that my intestines had, indeed, ruptured and that I needed immediate surgery. I waved at Bob to avoid his commenting on the "immediacy" issue, as I had already been lying around for eight hours. At 6 PM I was rolled into surgery after having met the surgeon, Michael Klitnick. He asked me to sign a release for a possible colostomy, which I did. As the anesthetic was about to be administered, Roger Mills, a nurse I knew well and who was to assist the surgeon, said:

"You know who is going to perform the operation, don't you?"

"Yes, Doctor Klitnick," I said. "No, I'll

perform the surgery."

With that horrible joke, the lights went out.

When I woke up in the middle of the night, Bob was sitting by my bedside in the recovery area.

"Do I have a colostomy?" were my first words.

"No," he answered. Later he confessed that he had wanted to add that I would not need new shoes to match my bag.

Around midday, Klitnick came into our dirty room. All morning I had been listening to a patient moan across the hall and screaming for a nurse, while Bob was dozing in a chair. The only time he ever left me was to walk our dog, T-Cell.

"Well, I have good news and bad news," began the surgeon, inappropriately. "I have cleaned up the abdomen. It was a mess! As you may know, I have not sutured you as there is a risk of infection. But, if all goes well, I will do so in two days. You really are lucky you did not die from peritonitis."

"So what's the bad news?" asked Bob.

"The pathology indicates René has lymphoma. Given his HIV status, there is no way he can survive chemotherapy. Dan Gill will be here shortly to tell you the same thing."

Dan Gill was the hospital's pathologist, chief of staff and a close friend.

Bob cried for the second time in our lives together, which hurt me as much as the news we had received. Dan delivered the same prognosis along with his partner, Fran, another close friend. Fran sat on my bed and held my hand as the death sentence was delivered,

"Large cell Non-Hodgkin's lymphoma. No hope for treatment, given the diminished strength of your immune system — four months." The same diagnosis as Jackie Onassis, but, hopefully, she had been given her prognosis in a more humane manner.

After Dan and Fran left the room, a prolonged silence mercifully came to an end when Bob said:

"René, these clowns are not oncologists. Let's get on the phone and do some research."

I tried to ignore both the physical and psychological pain and retain some element of humor which always energized Bob.

"If, in the future I croak in an ambulance going to Miami," I began, "I will not damn you. But, if I *ever* wake up in this dump again, I *will* damn you!"

Bob called several oncologists over the subsequent two days. The first one essentially confirmed what we had heard from the local staff. Undaunted, Bob found a young oncologist at the University of Miami who said there was a ten percent chance of survival, but the next year would be rough, and I would have to start chemotherapy in two weeks, regardless of how I felt.

"Can you both accept this prognosis?" asked Doctor Levy.

I listened through a morphine haze.

"Doctor, you are telling us that René will be shot at dawn. But, there is a ten percent chance he can escape. Of course, we will try to escape."

My friend Pierre, called from Geneva to express his surprise and alarm. He had told my brother we had eaten together in Florida the previous day.

"He had surgery and is in the hospital," my brother answered.

After we told Pierre our interim prognosis, he related several stories about friends who had been given death sentences only to go on to a lead a normal life. His encouraging words added power to our belief that I could survive HIV, cancer and *even* the Key West hospital.

The worst part of the next days was cleaning my open wound. It was simply agonizing. No matter how careful the nurse was, the previous bandages were stuck to the raw flesh and had to be pulled off. I screamed and bit my sheets to not overly disturb other patients. The day Klitnick told me I would be discharged, I reminded him I needed to be closed up.

"Mr. Silvin," he said in his detached way, "I have told you. You will be dead in four months. Why not just go home and get your affairs in order?"

Bob responded, uncharacteristically, showing his anger.

"Doctor, even if René will die in four months, we want him sutured. By the way, René's 'affairs' *are* in order. And, may I suggest you check your bedside manners when you address your patients?"

Klitnick was too busy to close my open abdomen, and I left the hospital never having been sutured, stapled or even taped. Bob changed my dressings every two hours to avoid the pain of removing a bandage stuck to coagulating blood and flesh. He gave me courage to persevere and stayed on our bed, with T-Cell nestled between us, most of the day.

René and Jean Claude Salamin transiting the Panama Canal

When Jean-Claude Salamin saw my scar several months later he said:

"That idiot did not operate; he gave you an autopsy!"

Ten days later we went to Miami to meet our oncologist and have a marrow tap. There was a Boston Chicken restaurant nearby, which became our usual stop before chemotherapy treatments. To this day, I get nauseous if I think of Boston Kitchen, as the chain was later renamed.

As always, Bob insisted on staying by my side for the unpleasant marrow exam. At the start of my first chemotherapy session, I had one of my panic attacks and started gasping for air. Again, Bob calmed me down and told the nurse not to be alarmed. He patiently dealt with my fears and bad mood, buying books like *How to Survive Chemotherapy* and carefully editing medical news relevant to my condition, so as to deliver any available, small piece of optimism. He had read that my hair would fall out about ten days after my first round of chemo, so he brought me to a barber before then to shave my head.

"This will be less traumatic than seeing large patches of hair on your pillow or in your hands. Anyway, bald is in vogue and stylish now," he said.

Every three weeks we would return to Miami for treatment, and I gradually grew thinner and weaker. We had discussed with Doctor

Levy my having the second half of my treatments at or near home in North Carolina. Young Isaac Levy had become a friend and did not typify the hardened attitude of many oncologists. He was very grateful when Bob bought his office a case of each of the most informative and positive books on chemotherapy to distribute to other patients. Eventually, to my great delight, I was allowed to return to North Carolina. The last evening in Key West, accompanied only by Duane because Ted was out of town, we ate at our favorite restaurant, Antonia's. Bob joined us later because he had been working at the Key West Police Department collecting data for use as a baseline when Duane implemented their inner-city self-esteem program for adolescent gays.

It was obvious that the many friendly waiters and the owners, Antonia and Philip, all expected not to see me return the following season. Who could blame them? I was gray, wore a wool beret and begged to have the temperature repeatedly moved higher.

Before Bob arrived, Duane urged me to verbalize my greatest fears. I looked around at the charming space and focused on the Dade County pine woodwork, adorned with art from local artist friends, to collect my thoughts. I stared at the kitsch and fun bust of Caesar by the front door, grateful for the opportunity to delve deeply into my heart and reveal the thoughts most lovers have when facing possible death.

"I worry about Bob," I said. "If I die, I wonder how he will be able to manage Chenoncette. I worry about his future. He wants to work and is so good at what he does."

"Let's hope that will not happen," Duane answered instantly, understanding the specifics of my general statements. "But, if it does, I promise I will have my handyman at the property the next day and I will assume all expenses immediately."

While I tried to formulate words of appreciation, Duane continued,

"René, I care deeply for Bob. I want to work with him and build the new foundation with him. Are you aware of local gossip about an inappropriate relationship between Bob and me?"

"Yes, Duane," I said. In an attempt to lighten the moment, I added, "Some 'well-meaning' jerks have already given me their condolences. In fact, I was naughty and said something to Luccio which may have fueled the gossip."

Luccio was an unhappy, overweight, former looker, who was

partnered with a wealthy and educated man, a descendant of the Weyerhouser Company's founder. Instead of enjoying his position, Luccio was bitterly jealous of Duane, like so many other so-called leaders of the gay community in Key West.

"What did you say?" asked Duane.

"Understand, I was angry when Lou pretended to be doing me a great favor. I told him I would give him the real inside story. I whispered in his ear that we could not afford our two homes, trips to Europe on the Concorde and nice cars. So, I had an arrangement with you to give me $10,000 every time you popped Bob. Lou swallowed it, swore to never repeat my confidence and probably told the whole town by nightfall."

"You are wonderfully wicked," Duane said, smiling briefly. His jovial look quickly disappeared, and Duane returned to serious words, which were his trademark.

"You know that Ted and I have had some problems and I won't deny lusting for Bob, but I swear to you, Bob has never given me the slightest encouragement and nothing unfaithful to you has ever happened."

"Duane, I questioned Bob when the first 'friend' brought the cheery rumor back to me. You will learn that Bob is incapable of lying. His denial was enough for me. Anyway, we know you are more of a prude than a predator!"

"Would I have your blessing to pursue Bob *if* he was left alone without you?"

Some people may have been offended at such a question posed during a perilous, life-threatening time. But, I was flattered and even honored to be so close to such a profound gentleman.

"Duane, you don't need my permission," I said pleasantly. "I love Bob and want the very best for him. I'm realistic about my chances. If, as the French say, I 'break my pipe,' I can't imagine a better life for Bob than being with a man of your kindness, generosity and talents. Speaking of generosity, I know you will be very generous to Ted."

Duane affirmed that he had given thoughts to the specifics of a separation agreement with Ted and that, indeed, Ted would remain very comfortable, with horses, cars and houses.

"He'll be happier than with a boring workaholic like me," he added.

The following day Bob and I drove out of Key West for what I knew might well be my last time. I was greatly relieved by my extraordinary conversation with Duane as, well as how amusing we must look with an intravenous drip pinned to the convertible top of the car, while Bob drove, and T-Cell sat on my lap.

I told Bob about my conversation with Duane, and Bob repeated the question:

"What are you most frightened of?"

"Dying alone and being cold," I said. "I have heard that brain cells remain alive for ten minutes after the last breath is taken. I have a huge fear of being thrown into a morgue's refrigerator before then and being cold."

Cashiers, North Carolina

It was a great relief to be back in our home. The serenity and beauty were like a tonic to me, even as my strength deteriorated. Bob had told me that I had to walk one hour each day, even if that was the only time I got off the couch. I believe that daily walk was an important element in my mental and physical well-being. Adjacent to Chenoncette there is a park with paths that wander through hills, which are thick with old oak trees, wild azaleas and native rhododendrons. I walked this path every day. The only annoying experience I encountered during these pensive walks was running into Doug Smith, a deacon in the local Episcopal Church and a hysterical homophobe. He had called me a liar by saying that there was no way I could have served on the Washington National Cathedral's board, because I was going to hell. As my appearance worsened, he added,

"The only thing that can save you now is to repent and pray."

The rest of my days consisted of lying on a couch in our den, often with a roaring fire, even during that summer as I could not get warm. When Bob traveled with Duane, I missed him terribly, and did my best to keep my mind off of my likely plight.

Two neighbors started bringing me food on a regular basis. It taught me that food, especially when delivered in disposable containers, is the very best gift a caring neighbor can give. Virginia Smith, the hypocritical doomsday announcer's wife, was one of the generous providers of meals. She would sneak into my property when her husband was away and asked me to not let "Doug know that we have a relationship."

In sharp contrast, the other angel was Bennie Addison. She and her husband, Ed, had retired to the neighborhood after a brilliant career which had culminated in Ed's tenure as Chief Executive Officer of the Southern Company. The Southern Company is one of the world's largest utility companies and the largest investor-owned electric utility holding company in the United States. The Addisons were considered the neighborhood's royalty, and Bennie's endorsement of Bob and me provided us with a protective shield from the homophobes. If Bennie accepted us, the rest had "better watch out" was clearly how she positioned her affection for, and attention on, us.

Ed and Bennie Addison

Bennie was one of those ladies who did everything perfectly and, like Jackie Onassis, with style and beauty. Her posture was erect, her hazel green eyes always sparkled, and they revealed her loving nature. She delivered her meals on beautiful trays and included pretty linen napkins and, usually, a sweet note. I always admired her unique yet tasteful clothes during her brief but frequent visits, which became all I longed for aside from Bob's return. On one such visit she said:

"Ed and I never knew that a gay couple could be responsible neighbors, lead a constructive life in a well-run home and love each other deeply. I hope you will forgive me for my ignorance." That day we sobbed in each other's arms.

Even my eyesight was affected by the chemotherapy, and I found reading very difficult and painful. So, I indulged into mindless television and watched every word of the O.J. Simpson pre-trial hearings. It even provided me with some humor when the testimony of OJ's house guest, Kato Kaelin, was more like a comedy soap opera. My only serious subjects of interest were Jackie Onassis' progress with her treatments for the same type of cancer I had, and searching out single mothers in chemotherapy. Some days when I hardly had the energy to make a sandwich, my thoughts turned to single moms with cancer. Consequently, my condition took on a different perspective as my plight was relatively easy. The only responsibility I had which required any physical effort, was to open the door for T-Cell. How could a mother prepare food, clean house, work and cope with similar aches, pains and fears, I wondered? I soon identified an organization that worked with women living such nightmares and became a contributor.

In May, on my birthday, I heard that Jackie O had been taken to a hospital in New York. I left the television news networks on all day, hoping for some information. I thought of her amazing life as First Lady and later as Mrs. Onassis. I recalled with affection the few times I had laid eyes on her. I always marveled at how graceful she was, and I chuckled remembering how she had said that she never wanted to be called First Lady because it "sounded like a saddle horse." She had also made many profound statements that stuck in my mind; notably, "I want to live my life — not record it."

Her death on May 19 hit me harder than my own diagnosis, probably because it brought to the fore the very real possibility that I would soon follow her. The following morning, when her son John addressed reporters in front of her Fifth Avenue home, he used words which meant a lot to me. He said something like:

"My mother died last night around 10 PM, surrounded by her friends, family and books." He went on to utter a phrase I will never forget, "She did it on her own terms." I took this as a clear signal that she had decided not to pursue treatment for her relapsed lymphoma and chose to end her life. I admired that decision. If I relapsed immediately after treatment, as Jackie did, Duane would take care of Bob, his handyman would care for T-Cell and I would do things on my own terms, rather than being tortured by aggressive treatments in dehumanizing hospitals.

My treatments ended in September. Both Jean-Claude Chermann and Léo had urged me to come to Europe right after my last chemotherapy treatment, so that they could take baseline statistics and prescribe paramedical immune system boosters. Bob walked beside me in my wheelchair as we boarded a Swissair flight. I had lost 30 pounds and shook like a Parkinson's patient. In the middle of the overnight flight, I overheard a flight attendant say to her colleague:

"I sure hope he does not die before we get to Zürich." I was acutely aware of my appearance, so the comment was more amusing than offensive. My T-cell count had dropped to single digits and Bob and I joked that we could now assign names to each of them. Our medical team decided I should begin Bristol-Meyers Squibb's new drug "d4T" as soon as I got home.

When we returned to the States, Bob had to catch up on his work with Duane's foundation, which had become a passionate, full-time activity. While they traveled to inner city projects in New York and California, Bob kept close tabs on my condition while Duane worried about his mother, Marjorie, who was in poor health with congestive heart failure. Bob was alarmed that the World Health Organization had reduced its staff assigned to the AIDS desk to four. He lamented that, only three years earlier, more than 200 people worked on the crisis. Perhaps this was something that Duane would ask President Clinton to review, along with the loss of a strong voice for pediatric AIDS due to Elizabeth Glaser's death.

On October 4, Bob called me with the news that they were shortening their trip to San Francisco because Marjorie's condition had worsened, and Duane wanted to be with her. Duane flew to his home in Janesville, Wisconsin, and I picked Bob up in Asheville, as I had just begun feeling comfortable driving again. On October 5, we both spoke with Ted and Duane at their farmhouse outside Janesville, mostly about Marjorie. Duane repeated his offer that if I wanted to go to Key West his new chef, Michael Pelke, would be bringing food each day and looking after me until I was stronger. He also spoke of his new project of creating another residential community with Pridam at the Key West Golf Course, concluding with specifics about the progress on three units he was building in the Truman Annex's historic foundry building. His intention was to give one to Ted, one to his parents and the third to us. Ted gave me details concerning what he was preparing for them to eat that evening, and our only concern as we spoke with them for the last time was Duane's mother. Ted and Duane appeared to be entering a new and mature space, even while a friendly separation was being considered.

The following morning in Bob's home office, as I was reading and Bob was working, David Mixner called. David was a Washington, D.C. insider who had been a key fundraiser for the Clinton campaign and had become an advisor to Duane and the President. We had all sat together by the pool in Key West lamenting over President Clinton's compromise concerning gays in the military, the unacceptable "don't ask, don't tell" solution.

Shortly after Bob had greeted David, I heard a huge crash and saw that Bob had fainted. After checking on Bob and reviving him, David, still on the phone, continued relating early reports of the devastating news. Both Ted and Duane were dead! Duane was found in their bed with multiple knife wounds while Ted had been asphyxiated in their garage with two car engines running.

"It appears to be a murder-suicide," said David.

"Who found the bodies?" I asked.

"Schultz, the handyman," he answered. "Did he stay until the police arrived?"

"Actually, he called Jim Sanger, a foundation trustee, not the police," concluded David, with a statement that was more like a lingering question.

A few moments later I spoke with Duane's exceptional sister, Beverly, who confirmed the disaster as clearly as possible through her grief. To compound her misery, her mother had passed away the same morning and a dual funeral was being planned for Duane and his mother. Ted's body would not be honored along with them, she explained. She asked us to meet her in Janesville as soon as possible. Bob and I were as close to being physically numb as I can recall. Not only had we lost our dearest friends, but also the dreams of bringing significant benefits to underprivileged adolescent gay men, and huge supplemental relief programs to AIDS organizations had vanished. Although the paperwork for changing the foundation's charter had been prepared, it was unsigned as Duane had not yet given the bad news to his existing trustees, who were to be replaced. We spent much of the rest of that sad day taking calls from gossip seekers in Key West as the news spread like wildfire.

"I guess we'll see you at the funeral," I told several recipients of Duane's largesse. I was repeatedly disappointed at their negative response, hearing statements like "we are too busy" or "there is nothing we can do to help anyone."

Janesville, Wisconsin

On October 7, Beverly met us at Duane's office on the top floor of what had been the Parker Pen Company building in Janesville, before Duane bought it. She was controlled but clearly devastated with compounded grief. Duane's flair for design, which had been executed by the best interior decorators, had produced a large, comfortable and dramatic suite of offices. One of Duane's trustees, Jim Dodson, was sitting behind Duane's desk. Dodson's wife was there also and the both of them were smoking and had their feet propped up on the furniture. Two shredders were humming, and numerous large, full, black plastic trash bags were being stuffed and placed in the foyer. A copy of *The Janesville Gazette* was on a coffee table and read in part,

"Rath's body was lying face-up on his bed in a front bedroom on the main floor. Rath had suffered 12 stab wounds or a few more and he had put up a fight."

The article made reference to a suicide note left by Ted. I asked if a handwriting analysis was being performed on the note. Dodson did not answer my question.

Another article read: "Rath was stabbed to death after an argument that police surmise was over either Rath's new lover or money."

Bob and I read the articles in astonishment as we knew beyond a doubt that there was no new lover, that the environment in the farmhouse on the night of the deaths was cordial, and that Ted had no reason to be suicidal.

Between outbursts of tears, Beverly and Bob drafted Duane's obituary, and I overheard Bob tell Beverly that Duane had frequently referred to her as his best friend.

"There are several people in Key West who you do not know and who Duane was caring for," I said to Dodson. "I'm sure you will want to honor Duane's wishes and treat them compassionately."

As Dodson looked at me with skeptical eyes, I removed a piece of paper from my pocket and proceeded to describe the various charity cases.

"Jeremy, the gardener, is uninsured and has AIDS. Duanc has sent him to our physician in Switzerland and pays for all his medications in Key West. I'd like to tell him that you will continue that commitment."

"What do other indigent AIDS patients do in Key West?" he asked.

"There is an organization called AIDS Help, which tries their best to provide necessary benefits but…"

"Tell Jeremy to go there," he interrupted.

Initially, I thought the man had a personal vendetta against poor

Jeremy, so I persisted as more documents were put in the shredder.

"There is a young medical student who Duane has committed to send through school. Duane pays the tuition from a personal account in Key West. I'd like to tell him that the foundation will pay his last year's tuition."

"Tell him to get a grant somewhere else," I heard and wondered if I was confused by the insensitive words.

I had to finish my list, regardless of the unreasonable responses.

"Duane hired a cook away from a gay friend. His name is Pelke. Duane sent him to Italy for a vacation before he would begin working at the Front Street home. The poor chap will soon discover that his job does not exist. He may find getting back on his feet difficult. Can we give him a very generous severance?"

"But he has not begun his duties and Duane bought him a house and was ripped off by his brother, Walter."

"Jim, I am talking about incidental expenses, which a responsible trustee will surely want brought to his attention. I urge you to carry through with what Duane would have asked us to do."

"They can all screw themselves. The party is over, and you can tell them that."

I wondered if I was dreaming or living through an outlandish hallucination. As I sat by Duane's desk, now occupied by a silly tyrant trying to exercise newly found power, I heard Jim take a call regarding Ted's horses.

"Tell Mrs. Hurdman that she must move the horses, which now belong to her. We want them moved by tomorrow or we will turn them out of the barn. That's what she gets for having them registered in Ted's name."

"Jim, I beg of you! Be human!" I said, raising my voice. "These poor animals are innocent. I'm sure Ted's mother will sell them as soon as she can. I think it's cruel of you to further offend her in her grief. You can charge her for boarding the horses until she figures out what to do with them." That was the only concession I was granted that rainy Sunday afternoon on the top floor of a once vibrant and forward-looking foundation office.

The following day, the day of the funerals, *The Janesville Gazette* wrote,

"Police said Thursday that the deaths are suspicious and are being investigated as homicides."

Beverly, Bob and I drove to the funeral home with Patches,

Duane's Jack Russell terrier. We both fantasized about what the sweet little dog would say if she could speak. Beverly told us that as long as Patches lived, as long as her little heartbeat, she would feel Duane's heart beating. What happened in that house on October 5, we wondered? I was certain it was either a dual murder or a hit on Duane which had gone wrong so that Ted had to be killed also. Continuing the surreal experience, another trustee, the man Schultz had called before calling the police, met us at the door of the funeral home and said,

"Be sure to look at Duane's neck. They did a good job, but you can see the slash. And, fear not, we will take that platinum Patek Philippe watch off Duane before we close the casket."

I looked around the room and noticed we were the only gay people there. Not one friend or beneficiary of Duane's largesse from Key West had bothered to come. Several Pinkerton security guards were making themselves very obvious. I wondered who had ordered them and why had that person not protected Duane while he was alive? Two identical silver open caskets were placed near each other, forming a V in the far end of the room. I glanced over at Marjorie's coffin and stood by Duane's for a very long time. They looked more like brother and sister than mother and son. Eventually someone led Bob and me to seats where I started to shiver, which did not stop for several days.

On our way to the airport we studied yet another baffling article which read,

"Recently, Rath found a new lover," and "Rath had become so afraid of Hurdman that he discussed the possibility of hiring a bodyguard with a friend."

"Did Duane mention anything to you about hiring a bodyguard?" I asked Bob.

"No!" he replied empathically. "This is so bizarre and makes no sense whatsoever."

Key West, Florida

A month later, Bob and I returned to the Truman Annex, once a residential paradise which Duane had been so instrumental in creating. It was among the dreariest days of my life, and I spent most of the time on a couch. I got up only to walk T-Cell and our new rescue dog, Silly. All of Duane's properties were for sale. Walking the dogs past them was too difficult, and I deliberately went the other way regardless of the inconvenience.

T-Cell and Silly

Bob recommended that I start taking an antidepressant, which deadened my feelings, but I wanted them deadened. I so liked the effect. Our sadness was worsened because no other acquaintances showed much, if any, grief or sadness at our community's indescribable loss. The more Duane had given to people, the less they wanted to express sorrow at his disappearance or discuss the murders. No one had called to offer condolences to Beverly or Duane's father, Virgil — not *one* of the beneficiaries of Duane's great generosity in Key West or the foundation trustees.

I had kept one of our cars in Duane's garage, next to one of Ted's classic antique Mercedes. The tires of the Mercedes gradually lost pressure and eventually went flat, just like our emotions in the last days of the horrific year.

Chapter Twenty-One

1995

If staying in bed for excessive periods of time is a symptom of depression, Bob and I certainly were depressed at the beginning of the year. We amused ourselves by scheduling some redecorating of our Truman Annex house and by going to the local gym. Chemotherapy had taken all my strength away, so I also hired a trainer at the gym who carefully and diligently worked with me to gain some weight and energy. He treated me like an octogenarian who had just begun to visit a gym. He started me off with walking on a treadmill, and he persuaded me to drink protein shakes nearly all day long. Gradually, some weight and vigor began to return.

Numerous nasty rumors swarmed around town. One described the murders as a murder-suicide, claiming Ted could not accept that Bob and Duane were lovers. An even more hurtful rumor promoted by Pelke, the very man we had tried to help, actually accused Bob of doing the killings. He nicknamed Bob "the murderess," which we overheard on several occasions. I loved Bob more than I could ever have previously imagined and hearing such cruelty focused on him, while he was grieving the loss of our friends, was excruciating. The result was that we completely disassociated from society in town and became reclusive. I even retreated from social gatherings with former fellow board members of AIDS Help.

The popular Gay magazine *The Advocate*, had a cover story written by Jorge Morales called "Sleeping With The Enemy, The Life and Death of Duane Rath" with a drawing of a jagged, bloody knife on the cover.

Referring to this article, *The Janesville Gazette* wrote,

"Janesville businessman and philanthropist Duane Rath donated millions to gay rights and AIDS-related charities in the last few years, and his death is a loss of profound proportions to the national gay community. This is according to an article that appeared in *The Advocate* . . ." That article in *The Advocate* said:

"He (Rath) was a gay man who had it all: money, power, influence, a friendship with Elizabeth Taylor, and ties to England's royal family. He gave millions to gay organizations and even put the children of his company's employees through college. But a tempestuous love triangle changed everything."

The gossip among the phony Key West gay set went wild and the very sight of several people with whom we used to associate became distasteful and counterproductive to my physical rehabilitation. We deliberately accelerated our isolation from the hypocrites.

I amused myself by throwing tennis balls for my dogs and taking them swimming in the harbor. Gradually, after accepting no more invitations to the nightly, purely social cocktail parties, the calls mercifully stopped. On several occasions when we ate at Square One or Antonia's, people would point at us and whisper. As a result, we even stopped frequenting our former preferred restaurants. These experiences were some of the worst I had ever endured, and I challenged myself to not pay too much attention to them and to focus on recovering from chemotherapy.

It had been futile to even ask Duane's trustees about Bob's employment with the foundation. We assumed that he had seen his last paycheck the second Duane died, so we knew he needed to find a new career. The foundation's trustees discontinued any donations to gay charities almost immediately and continued a shockingly aggressive attitude toward anyone Duane had previously assisted, including his dear sister, Beverly. They refused to allow her to keep a car that Duane had provided her, or for her children to receive sentimental gifts of relatively little value, such as Duane's leather jacket collection. It was a dark, sad period.

We converted a bedroom in our house into an office and added matching, side-by-side desks made of distressed pine. We then spent a lot of time exploring what job opportunities existed for

Bob. Like our furniture, we too were indeed distressed as we searched for a new life away from the painful memories of Duane and how Key West was dealing with it.

Our physician was an infectious disease doctor in Miami named Corky Steinhardt. Corky had recently sold his practice to a clever, hard-charging entrepreneur named Ray Mirra. Ray embarked on a buying spree of HIV-related physician practices in a new industry called PPM, or physician practice management. The amount required to buy a physician practice varied greatly but went as high as two million dollars per doctor. Ray gradually bought some 70 doctors' practices on both coasts.

We were fond of Corky Steinhardt, who had recently gone through a costly and messy divorce. By selling his practice to Ray, he hoped to get back on his financial feet. He was also considering other options, including moving to Europe. We explained that, even if appropriate permits could be obtained and the language barrier properly addressed, physicians in most West European countries made even less than their well-known American counterparts.

Bob on the QE2

To prove the point, we invited Corky and his new wife to accompany us to France on one of our regularly scheduled trips to visit and work with Jean-Claude Chermann. Corky was eager to hear Jean-Claude's explanations and theories. We also scheduled several meetings with physicians with whom I had remained in contact since my days with AMI. During the trip, we learned more about Ray Mirra and his clever business strategy to become a major player on a national level in HIV medicine.

It became clear to us and, eventually to Corky, that Ray's deal was as good as it was going to get. It became increasingly difficult to earn a living consistent to what physicians had become accustomed to. Furthermore, it was obvious that Corky, and his typically American wife, would never be able to adapt culturally in France or Switzerland. Bob and I would roll our eyes when Mrs. Steinhardt would screech, "I want my American coffee!" after each meal.

Bob and I returned to the States aboard the QE2 accompanied by Jean-Claude Salamin, his girlfriend and the Nussbaumers. We had planned the celebratory trip a year in advance and booked the Queen Elizabeth suite for us and, across the hall, the Queen Mary suite for Jean-Claude. Crossing the Atlantic by ship was one of my passions, and Bob and the others had never done it. So, I decided to splurge and treat Bob to an extravagant trip. It was the only time Bob questioned any expense I undertook.

"Are you sure we can afford this?" he asked.

"No, we can't," I replied, "but we are going to do it anyway. I want you to experience this the right way."

One night after a great dinner, Jean-Claude and I stopped at the Cunard travel bureau on the ship and asked the agent when our suites would both be available at the same time again. The agent told us that it would be several years but that another Cunard ship, the Sagafjord, had recently added similar suites and those two were available the following spring in Southeast Asia. Since Bob had never been to Asia, we recklessly booked both apartments for what we hoped would be Bob's introduction to the Orient.

Dressed for dinner on the

....

HIV medicine was changing quickly. President Clinton conducted a first conference on HIV/AIDS. The treatments, albeit costly and replete with side effects, were improving. Medicare reimbursement rates were based on the number of minutes a physician spent with their patients, often regardless of their specialty. Naturally, the vast majority of insurance carriers followed Medicare's rate structures, and many physicians were reimbursed on a ten-minute-per-patient visit. While that amount of time with a patient is restrictive in most specialties, it is absurd for HIV. Most AIDS patients cannot even describe their numerous symptoms in ten minutes, much less get any feedback and information from their doctor. Infectious disease physicians, in turn, were becoming specialists in all disciplines because long-term survivors were developing problems in dermatology, cardiology, orthopedics, neurology, and ear-nose-throat, in addition to the original AIDS problems of oncology and pulmonology. Patients began expecting these dedicated, often overworked men and women to be pharmacists, researchers, psychologists and physicians.

The FDA approved the new category of anti-retroviral medications, which were called protease inhibitors. Swiss pharmaceutical giant, Roche, was given permission to sell their equally expensive "PI" called "Saquinivir." Glaxo Wellcome's "Epivir," a nucleocide, also became widely prescribed. Since many of the newly approved medications, or others still in trials, ended with "vir" (Sequinivir, Epivir, Ritonavir and Norvir), the joke was that the next breakthrough would be called "save-a-queer."

We shortened our winter in Key West and decided that Chenoncette, our little paradise in the mountains, was preferable, even in the cold. At least that cold was physical and not psychological.

By the end of the year, AIDS was still mainly thought of as a gay disease, even though the incidence of the illness was spreading rapidly into the heterosexual community, mainly in poorer inner-city neighborhoods. Numerous, well known gay celebrities' disclosures of their positive HIV status fueled the unfortunate view in the broader American public's eye. The admission by Greg Louganis, Olympic gold medal winner, that he had been diagnosed prior to the 1988 Olympic Games in Seoul, Korea, was a case in point.

Bob said he wanted to have a traditional Christmas and he launched into a major plan to decorate the house. We bought floating lighted stars, like the ones we had seen at Mangoes in Key West and placed them all along our balconies. Before long, tourists and residents were driving by the house just to see the wonderful decorations at night. Bob went into the woods and chopped down a 25-foot-tall spruce tree, which we placed in the living room and decorated beautifully. Visiting gay friends watched him cut down the tree marveling,

"My God! He is so butch!"

Each night we lay on the floor in front of a roaring fire in one room or another, happy to have each other and to have survived Duane's tragic murder, as we began to plan for a world without the gay community's most qualified philanthropist to date.

Chapter Twenty-Two

1996

We hardly went to Key West during the winter. After our wonderful Christmas at home in North Carolina, Bob suggested we further improve Chenoncette by buying an adjacent cabin and adding a fireplace to the master bedroom. The owner of the cabin was reluctant to sell, and this began a several-year discussion with him. As much as Bob loved nesting, he was a worker, and his need to be actively employed became our priority. We decided to meet Ray Mirra, the man we had heard so much about from Corky.

Ray was a fascinating man who embodied a series of interesting contradictions. He was bright and street-wise, but not organizationally trained or motivated. He was short but had a sweetness about him which made him handsome. He was kind, but subject to fairly violent outbreaks of rage. Finally, he was frugal in many aspects, but lived in grand residences in New York's Columbus Circle and on the beach in Fort Lauderdale.

Gigi Jordan

His sexy and beautiful long-term partner, Gigi, was equally bright and hard charging. Together they conceived the clever plan to own HIV physician practices, as well as regional reference laboratories and a mail-order pharmacy. While the physicians could not encourage, much less compel, patients to use these sister businesses, one arm of the business eventually fed the others. The result was that the lucrative laboratories and pharmacies more than compensated for the relatively unprofitable physician practices.

Since Bob and I had met the owners of the patents for both HIV viral load testing and geno/phenol HIV typing in Europe, we recommended that Ray acquire as many of these rights as possible.

While he ultimately declined to do so, the due diligence undertaken to reach that decision led to a mutual respect and friendship.

Ray hired Bob to become his company's Chief Operating Officer in charge of the physician practice side of the emerging empire. He also asked me to advise him on preparing the joint company to study the possibilities of going public through an initial public offering, or IPO. Bob was very effective at understanding the ins and outs of the various physician offices and, through his determined yet non-threatening manner, was able to maximize any possible efficiencies. He traveled weekly, as before when he had been working for the Rader Institute or the Rath Foundation, but mostly to doctors' offices in South Florida and throughout California.

The new company was named Quest Medical and by the end of the year it "owned" physicians as famous as Joel Weisman and Robert Smith in California. Both men had been pioneers in the initial discovery and treatment of HIV 14 years previously. Bob also recruited and hired several younger physicians to assist the lead doctors in the South Florida offices. Among these recruits was Donna Jacobsen for Steinhardt's group at Mercy Hospital in Miami, and Peter Englehard in Fort Lauderdale.

One day, shortly before we were preparing to leave for our vacation, I received a call from our travel agent. She told us that the Sagafjord, which we were to have boarded a week later, had burned up the previous day in the South China Sea. Bob was relieved. because he had just started working with Quest and even though we had told Ray about our previously reserved trip, Bob was uncomfortable taking ten days off so close to having begun a new job. Cunard offered us two identical suites aboard the sister ship, the Vistafjord, the following year.

"How about we celebrate your 40th birthday next year and take advantage of Cunard's offer?" I asked him.

With that, we happily booked the suggested trip. In addition, Jean-Claude Salamin and his new girlfriend planned to join us. We now had another entire year to look forward to a grand adventure.

In July, we read that Roy Pesch, the "physician who would be a billionaire" and had tried, in vain, to acquire AMI, was arrested for fraud. In a rarely used agreement between the U.S. and Switzerland, he was extradited in August to Switzerland where he was imprisoned.

1996 saw a huge increase in the use of protease inhibitors, the new class of anti-retroviral medications. Among these were: "Norvir" from Abbott Labs and "Crixivan" from Merck. "Viramune," a nonnucleocide from Roxane Labs, joined the other two medications in receiving FDA approvals during the year. As a result, a fundamental change emerged in the HIV/AIDS community, which had far-reaching implications. The new combination of drugs instantly became known as "the cocktail," a term Professor Eckmann had coined in 1991, years before the drugs were invented.

Interestingly, many severely ill patients began to improve and return to some sort of normal energy levels. However, this development was not without great costs, both literally and figuratively. The new cocktails typically cost in excess of $1,200 a month. As one could imagine, many HIV patients could not afford these expensive breakthroughs. Some others, like me, found the cocktails very hard to tolerate, while yet other group developed what became known as the Lazarus complex.

Lazarus was the biblical figure who returned from the dead. The new term referred to relatively young, ill patients who had budgeted their resources to hopefully carry them through a shortened life to a premature death. Suddenly, many found themselves financially and emotionally challenged with aborted careers.

At the same time, AIDS organizations scrambled to address both the financial and psychological repercussions of the changing times. *The New York Times Sunday Magazine* offered the first insights to this on November 10, in the article by Andrew Sullivan: "When AIDS Ends." It discussed the unprecedented experience of the end of a plague, during which victims would have contemplated their deaths and adjusted their lives accordingly, but would then, later, have to reassess their possible survival.

50 years ago, in his book *La Peste* (The Plague), the father of Existentialism, Albert Camus, brilliantly described the mindset of a population as it evolves to face death. Now, Sullivan had studied what occurs when that condition is, at least partially, reversed.

Patients' adherence to the new cocktails was also an interesting sociological study. Some became excessively focused on the strict protocols and resulting daily schedules, while others were unable or unwilling to comply.

My "triple-therapy" cocktail included both Crixivan and Norvir. The former had to be taken three times a day on an empty stomach, or two hours after eating, and one hour before a meal. This rigid program led those of us using this very popular medication to get up in the night and to adjust our mealtimes to a strict routine. The physical side effects of Crixivan are also significant, as illustrated by the new term "Crix belly" to accompany "AZT butt," because many patients on Crixivan develop abnormally large stomachs, while AZT users tend to lose muscle in their rear end. The worst physical side effect for me was from Norvir, which led to the rebirth of the term "lypodystrophy," which means a redistribution of fat, usually from the face to the upper neck. The hollow, sunken cheeks became a sign, like a scarlet-letter arm band, to many HIV patients, as did the "buffalo bump" on their necks.

Personally, I managed to adjust to the daily routine surrounding the use of Crixivan, even during travels to France, but I hated the advent of the physical side effects, which also included constant stomach discomfort, indigestion, headaches and reduced energy levels.

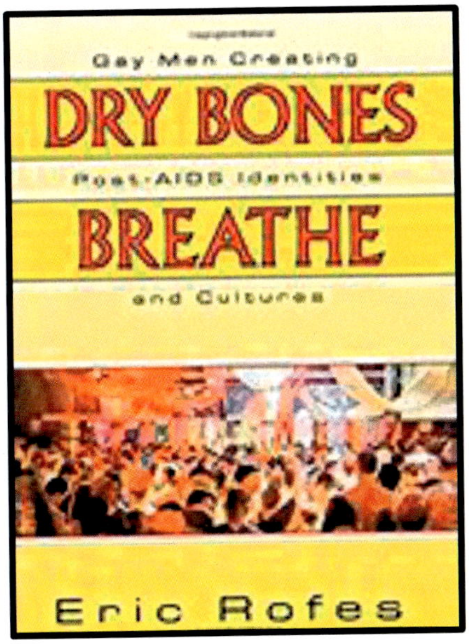

In his profound book, *Dry Bones Breathe*, the late Eric Rofes analyzes these conditions in a chapter entitled, "The Protease Moment Takes Hold." He points out how, suddenly, national marketing campaigns for the new medications showed very healthy smiling faces, boasting which drug they were using. Fortunately, yet not without some physiological and psychological side effects, many AIDS patients were facing and planning for a life beyond AIDS, a life that was no longer solely defined by *having* AIDS. Rofes concludes his chapter on PI's with:

"As men construct new identities for themselves in a post-AIDS period, finding new language that captures our experience will be a critically important activity."

It was clear that these people also had to add new behaviors and thinking to the "new language."

Although my lymphoma diagnosis was, even by the most conservative definitions, an "AIDS defining diagnosis," and I was learning how to cope with the cocktail, Bob and I were not significantly affected by these problems. Bob was too healthy mentally to allow either of us to wallow in self-pity or senseless blame. Bob was more focused on getting to know the major players in American HIV treatment and research, including HIV researcher David Ho, who became *Time Magazine's* 1996 Man of The Year. He also met the head of the World Health Organization's HIV team, Doctor Jonathan Mann, who was often confused with Bob due to the similarity of their names.

Bob's new career during an era of evolving HIV medicine and science was our avenue to maintain a balanced, somewhat positive and productive outlook.

Chapter Twenty-Three

1997

Since Quest had several large HIV physician practices in California, Bob traveled there regularly. On most trips he made time to visit his stepfather, Gary Troy, who had been instrumental in bringing life to Bob's career in psychology. Gary had recently been diagnosed with cancer and his prognosis was poor. In midwinter, Bob and I went to Gary's home in Malibu to see him for what we knew would be the last time. Many of Teamm House's "graduates" had gone on to become clinical psychologists, and many of those loving and devoted former protégées surrounded Gary and his lovely wife, Nancy, while Gary deteriorated in his own bed. Although I had seen numerous friends die, my presence at Gary's bedside was a new, constructive experience that would serve me well during my biggest challenge, which would happen the following year — the saddest period of my life.

Later that winter, Bob developed a severe headache, which gradually worsened over several days. When we went to the emergency room, a spinal tap revealed that he had meningitis and was hospitalized. During the week he spent at the Key West hospital we discovered that Bob's blood counts had deteriorated significantly and, after consultation with Jean-Claude Chermann and Corky Steinhardt, Bob began his first HIV cocktail.

In early April, Bob and I met with Ray and Gigi in Fort Lauderdale. Ray had recently acquired a beautiful piece of property on the beach in Lauderdale and had remodeled the previously unassuming house into what Bob and I called "Miami Vice." During the meetings with Ray and Gigi, we made progress on the plans to launch the IPO the following year. One of the decisions to maximize the chances of success was to move Quest's headquarters from Ray's building in Philadelphia to a yet-to-be-determined office in Lauderdale. That evening I told Bob it seemed silly for us to have a house in Key West from which Bob would have to travel weekly, only to stay in a hotel in Lauderdale. We decided that our Key West experience would end. We would sell the little house in the Truman Annex and buy a home in Fort Lauderdale. This was an easy decision for several reasons, the most fundamental being that Duane's murder had definitely changed our pleasure of being in "The Conch Republic."

....

Jean-Claude Salamin and his girlfriend "du jour" joined us in Florida for our scheduled crossing on the Vistafjord, which had been in the planning stages for two years and had been aborted a year earlier due to the fire aboard its sister ship the Sagfjord. The trip was to be a crossing of the Atlantic from Fort Lauderdale with several stops, and ultimately ending in Malta, 14 days later. Ray and Gigi gave us an old-fashioned "bon voyage party" at their beautiful beachfront home, and we all proceeded to a grand finale on the ship. The two adjacent suites' living rooms could be opened into one large room facing forward, looking out over the ship's bow. An impressive semicircular bar dominated the back of the room, while picture windows surrounded the front. One of the guests who came to the party was the head of the U.S. Coast Guard for South Florida.

Vistafjord

We sailed at dusk on April 5 and, after a great dinner, we four sat out on the large terrace in front of our suite. Tired from flying over to the States, our shipmates retired, and Bob and I enjoyed a Jacuzzi outside our bedroom under a clear sky full of brilliant stars. Shortly after midnight, I awoke aware that the usual vibrations from the ship's engines had stopped. I went up our private stairs to the living room above and out on the balcony. The ship had definitely stopped and,

Jean Claude, René, Bob and the girlfriend du jour boarding the Vistafjord

as I looked aft at the great funnel, I saw sparks and a flame flying out. Looking down, I saw several sailors frantically unwrapping tarpaulins from lifeboats.

I ran into our bedroom and told Bob to grab his passport and wallet just as the fire alarms began ringing. Then I crossed the hall to wake up Jean-Claude and told him the same thing.

"It's not a joke," I added, since we habitually teased each other with elaborate plots.

"Oh, I fully realize that," he said, as we all preceded to our assigned evacuation spots adjacent to life boats. The lifeboats were lowered, ready for us to board and we all stayed in that position, wearing life jackets, for five hours as the ship's staff fought the fire in an attempt to save her. Before long, U.S. Coast Guard planes were over-flying the ship and my new Coast Guard friend, from the previous evening's party, later told me that he personally supervised the possible rescue at sea if the fire worsened during the night. Bob comforted several elderly passengers who were visibly nearly panicked, using his soothing voice and smart psychology to reassure as many as possible. Seeing that a few of our fellow lifeboat colleagues needed medical attention, he found a doctor and assisted him in attending to them.

By dawn, huddled together under blankets, we were told that we would not have to abandon ship. Instead, we would be towed into Freeport in the Bahamas, where we would disembark and be flown either back to Lauderdale or to London, England. Sadly, we learned that one young sailor had been killed in the fire. During the day that we stayed aboard in Freeport awaiting charter flights to arrive, Jean- Claude and I raised a relief fund for the poor German sailor's family.

We listed our house in Key West for sale at a high price which Trip Hoffman said we would never get. When it sold at full asking price in a week, we decided to stay at Chenoncette through the end of the year, after which we would go to Fort Lauderdale. The plan was for Bob to open the new Quest office and for me to identify and buy a home nearby.

In mid-December, we went to New York. We stayed at the Waldorf Astoria and were to attend a dinner-dance party atop Rockefeller Center. Gigi and Ray had recently sold their company's home health care division to a New York Stock Exchange medical conglomerate, Integrated Health Services, Inc. IHS's well-known flamboyant Chairman, Doctor Robert Elkins, a psychiatrist, had founded the company a decade earlier. He led a successful IPO in 1991 as he aggressively bought up nursing homes in a strategy of "bigger is better" in sub-acute inpatient care. I had seen this strategy, or rather lack thereof, fail during my career in publicly traded hospital companies as it related to chemical dependency and psychiatric hospitals, and was very skeptical about IHS's long-term future, even though its revenues had gone from $195 million to $3 billion in just five years.

I begged Ray to bail out of the company stock as quickly as possible. This advice proved helpful as IHS's stock plummeted from $40 a share to just pennies 18 months later. This was caused by the company defaulting on loans and it was de-listed from the stock exchange. Lawsuits initiated by family members alleging inadequate care soon followed.

Bob had never seen New York at Christmas time, so we walked up and down Fifth and Madison Avenues, admiring all the dazzling windows. The night of the black-tie event, I brought out the two dinner jackets I had packed before we left North Carolina. To my shock, and Bob's disappointment, I had correctly packed mine but had mistakenly included an old one that Bob had outgrown, as his chest and shoulder muscles had developed as a result of our workouts. We only had a few hours before the party, and we decided to go to the concierge to ask where we might be able to rent a tuxedo at the last minute. When the elevator door opened and we entered, Imelda Marcos, the Philippines' former First Lady, was inside accompanied by several male companions. I had met her in Manila some 20 years earlier.

"Good evening Mrs. Marcos," I said. "You may not remember me, but I was standing near you at the opening of the Philippine Heart Center when you endured that unpleasant experience many years ago." In fact, she had been stabbed while we stood on the receiving line with several world-famous cardiologists and cardiac surgeons. Using quick reaction, Mrs. Marcos had raised her hand and deflected the would-be assassin's knife, which only badly cut her hand. I never heard about the aggressor's fate.

"Of course, I remember you," she said rather unconvincingly, but with charm. "What are you up to?"

After introducing Bob, I continued,

"We are going to a black-tie event tonight and I did not bring the correct tuxedo for Bob. So, we are in a panic looking for a substitute."

Mercifully, one of her associates gave us directions to a place where they rented tuxedoes for last-minute dress events. As we walked away, Bob whispered

"Why didn't you ask for some shoes while you were at it?" referring to Imelda's well-publicized huge shoe collection.

"I didn't think they would fit your big feet," I joked back.

Bob looked so very handsome as we walked past the great Christmas tree at Rockefeller Center, and passed the long line at the public elevator to ride an express elevator that only goes to the roof top restaurant. Once inside the restaurant we noticed a large collection of Chuhuly glass sculptures placed along the top of the walls. Bob and I had met Dale Chuhuly with Duane when he had ordered a chandelier and garden sculptures for the Key West house, and I saw a flash of sadness on Bob's face as we were reminded of our loss.

I could not help but compare IHS's executives to AMI's domestic staff under Wally Weisman. They were a similar group of overconfident under-experienced upstarts. The only difference was that Wally's herd emulated their boss' total lack of style while this group, one decade later, obviously overly indulged in expensive clothes consistent with their leader's *nouveau riche* look. They seemed uncomfortable in their newly found arrogance, and it was evident that a shock was soon to come as thousands were fired when the company collapsed.

The only rewarding part of mixing with them, was how very clear it was just how respected and admired Bob had quickly become among a group of people with which he had little in common.

After the exciting weekend, we returned to Chenoncette where Bob put on his usual big Christmas decorating showcase.

By year end, it was discovered that HIV both "hides" in reservoirs of the body and learns how to "mutate" in order to render parts of the cocktail inefficient to many patients. These discoveries underscored the need for geno/pheno HIV testing to specifically define which medications had become useless. Unfortunately, those patents had been acquired by LabCorp after Ray and Gigi had rejected buying them a year earlier.

The "triple therapy cocktails" had reduced HIV-related deaths in the United States by 40%, which gave Bob and me some hope that our mutual relative health could be sustained. Globally the HIV news was not good, as the virus thrived with the advent of globalization and the collapse of the Soviet Union. It was estimated by year end that 30 million people had been infected with the HIV virus worldwide.

During the last ten days of the year there were several mountain storms, including a serious ice storm. We built large fires, played with our dogs and enjoyed each other's company. We also invited several couples to spend a few days each with us during that very festive last Christmas we had together.

René with T-Cell and Silly, Whiteside Mountain, NC

Chapter Twenty-Four

1998

Fort Lauderdale, Florida

In the opening days of January, Bob and I loaded up two cars and drove to Fort Lauderdale, along with our dogs Silly and T-Cell. I had rented a house for six weeks in the hope that we would be under contract for our own home by then. The first night we were there, Bob had some indigestion that reoccurred every day for a week.

After consulting both Corky Steinhardt and Peter Engelhard, we made an appointment with a gastro-enterologist to scope Bob's stomach. While I waited in a room nearby, I watched breaking news on television about Linda Tripp and Monica Lewinsky as the most famous blow job in history began to be discussed worldwide.

Mercy Hospital, Miami, Florida

Bob's first investigations revealed nothing, and a CT scan was performed. Since the report said that a certain mass in the pancreas was "consistent with lymphoma," Corky scheduled a biopsy to be performed, in surgery, at Mercy Hospital in Miami. When Bob was rolled into the operating room at 3 PM, the surgeon told me that the procedure would take 30 minutes and that he would speak with me as soon as it was over. I sat in a huge, crowded waiting room, which was more like a boarding area for an overbooked 747 flight to Havana. Mercy Hospital is predominantly Cuban, and English is definitely the second language. It appeared that each patient had his entire family waiting.

I sat alone trying my best to stay calm. Family after family was called up for news of their loved one. I heard calls for the Sanchez, Ramirez, Gutierrez and Garcia families as the room gradually emptied out. My inquiries at the information desk were met with, "We have not heard anything yet." At around 6 PM, the lights were dimmed, and the cleaning crew arrived.

Corky had not answered my calls, so I phoned Bob Smith in San Diego and begged him to help me. Within a few minutes, after speaking with people in the OR, he returned my call.

"René, it's unbelievable," he said, "but the surgeon left without speaking with you and left no word for anyone else either. Bob is in recovery, and you can see him there."

Trying to control my anger, I spoke with a resident in the recovery area who said that the tissue "looked like lymphoma," but that it needed to be confirmed by pathology the following day.

Dejected, I returned to our rental house and cuddled up with our dogs. When I went to Bob's room at Mercy Hospital the following morning, Donna Jacobsen, a physician Bob had recruited to work in Corky's office, was sitting in his room. As I entered, they stopped speaking and Bob tapped the sheets next to him, indicating that I should sit on his bed. He then took my hand and gave me the news with the same compassion as if it were I who had the cancer diagnosis. He had large cell non-Hodgkin's lymphoma, just like I had four years before. Donna explained that Bob would have a bone marrow tap to determine the staging, but that it was doubtful they would find marrow involvement. By late afternoon, after the marrow exam and an initial consultation with Corky's recommended oncologist, Manuel Guerra, we returned to our house and dogs.

"Bob," I began sincerely, "I beat this, and you are stronger and younger than I. We will get through this together. Consider me caring for you for the next nine months as payback for all you did for me. And you will, once again, be the biggest ox back at the gym in a year."

Early the following morning, Corky called to say that, contrary to what they had assumed, the marrow, too, was positive for lymphoma and that we needed to meet as quickly as possible. Two hours later, Bob and I sat in his office along with Donna.

"I don't like it at all," began Corky, in a surprisingly negative tone. "All the choices will be bad."

"Neither do we like it, Corky," I said, holding Bob's hand, "but we need to define where we go from here?"

"You'll have to speak to Manny again, but the treatment you

discussed yesterday will not be adequate. I have no idea what he'll say."

Thankfully, Manny was much more compassionate and professional than Corky. He explained that Bob would have CHOP, the same chemotherapy regimen as I had received. In addition, he would have three chemo injections directly into the spine. Those treatments would have to take place as an inpatient and begin as soon as possible.

When we got back to Lauderdale, I returned numerous phone calls from concerned friends and loved ones, including Jean-Claude Salamin in Switzerland.

"Bob has lymphoma," I said.

"Where was it discovered?" asked Jean Claude. "In the pancreas," I answered.

"René, you'd better ready yourself. Pancreatic cancer is always fatal."

We then called Ray with the news. After reassuring Bob that we could work around his treatments, Ray spoke with me.

"What are you going to do?" he asked.

"I guess I'll see if we can extend our lease here and stay all winter."

"Don't do that, René," said Ray. "We won't be using our house in Fort Lauderdale this year so just move in there."

"Why won't you be using 'Miami Vice' this winter? There is much to be done here and it's miserable in New York."

"I, too, received a cancer diagnosis this week," he said to my shock. "Mine is in the thyroid and will require several operations in Boston. Gigi and I feel more comfortable not wandering far from Boston and New York. You and the dogs are most welcome at our house. Just do it."

"What will this mean for the IPO?" I asked.

"I'll decide in a few days, but with both Bob and I laid up most of the time, I think we will alter course."

On the first day of Bob's initial hospitalization, Ray informed us that he had made a deal with IHS to sell some additional ancillary units of his company, and that he had decided to shut down the physician practices. There would be no IPO.

"How do you want to handle the doctors?" asked Bob.

"You know that most of them are goof balls," said Ray. "I gave them a ton of money and now they'll be whining about small shit. Just do the best you can but dump them all. As far as I'm concerned, they can buy the office equipment for peanuts."

"Ray," I interjected, "the fight will be over the receivables."

Medicare and the insurance companies take up to 90 days to reimburse physicians. I knew that all the doctors would not be able to self-finance 90 days of operations under their ownership and would want Ray to concede the delayed revenues from their practices while they were salaried by Ray.

"Do the very best you can," he said.

Unfortunately, we had to interact once again with Corky's surgeon to place a port in Bob's chest for safer administration of the chemotherapy. This time he kept Bob waiting on a stretcher in front of the operating room for six hours and then did not implant the device properly. It had to be replaced by another surgeon two days later, so Bob and I made sure to report the arrogant quack to every possible agency and review board. He did not practice surgery for long, but no apologies were forthcoming.

Our lives set into a new routine. When Bob was at home, we played in the surf in front of Miami Vice with the dogs and I cooked dinners at home every night. When Bob felt well, we negotiated separate deals with each physician, and when he did not feel up to it, I would field the calls. Only two doctors were intolerant of Bob's bad days. Of course, Corky was one of them. On one occasion, Corky came to Bob's room in the hospital after a painful spinal treatment. He wanted to discuss shaving a bit more out of the deal to help him cover the 90 days of new receivables in the pipeline. When he ignored my plea to defer his concerns until Bob felt better, I literally took his arm, escorted him to the door and pushed him out of our room.

We started to rely more on Peter Engelhard when we were in Lauderdale, and exclusively on Donna when Bob was hospitalized in Miami. Both were professional and compassionate, and they always made themselves available to us. Peter came to our rescue when, after a failed spinal injection, Bob developed a debilitating and painful spinal leak. On his day off, Peter concocted and administered a "blood patch" made from Bob's blood, which sealed the leak and ended the pain.

Miami Vice's housekeeper also cleaned several of the local physician offices. Gradually, I had spread the numerous syringes, medications and assorted paraphernalia I used to boost both Bob's red and white blood cell count out on a table in Gigi's dressing room. The first day she was scheduled to work and saw the medical supplies, I explained to her what they were. When she did not come to work the next scheduled day, I called her to inquire why, and she said that her religion would not allow her to work in a house where there was AIDS.

"But you clean Doctor Engelhard's office," I said confused.

"That's a business and it's different. This ain't right," she replied.

When one is under the type of stress such as I was going through, a small slap in the face can take on huge proportions. The discussion with the cleaning lady broke my dam of tears, and I dreaded telling Ray as much as I had dreaded speaking with Corky about "all the bad choices."

I knew I loved Ray when, after composing myself, I called him to explain.

"Do you think Bob might limp out to the pool and cough on the pool man," he said. "Gigi hates him, too. So maybe he will quit as well. Also, Gigi hopes you will not wear out any of her pretty clothes in her closet!"

"Not a chance," I said, so relieved. "They don't fit either of us."

Cashiers, North Carolina

Immediately after Bob's last hospitalized five-day spinal chemotherapy infusion, we folded camp at Miami Vice, loaded the cars and dogs and drove back to North Carolina. During the previous weeks, we made arrangements with a home health care agency recommended by IHS to handle Bob's next three chemotherapy sessions, and to liaise with Doctor Manny in Miami.

In very much the same way as when I had returned to Chenoncette to complete my treatments, we were nearly ecstatic to be going home to our island of peace and hope. The typical lymphoma treatment of CHOP had advanced in the years since I had endured it, mostly because a gradual continuous five-day infusion had been determined less toxic and more effective. Bob wore a belt containing a pump which delivered the mixture 24 hours a day. He was able to work, take walks and even accompany me on errands, where only a few people wondered what the waist belt was. I'd lay awake at night trying to keep him as comfortable as possible, in spite of the tubing and the noise from the pump.

One day, I received a call from my friend Pierre Nussbaumer in Switzerland.

"What are you both doing this Saturday and Sunday?" he asked.

"As you know, Pierre, we are pretty well homebound now."

"We were wondering if we may come by for the weekend."

"I know Bob would be delighted, Pierre. Where in the States are you coming from or traveling to?"

"Nowhere," he said. "We'd like to come over just to spend an evening with Bob."

This extraordinary gesture from a busy friend who, with his wife, was prepared to fly round trip to Atlanta, and then drive three more hours to the North Carolina Mountains meant so much to us both. Bob lit up and enjoyed the evening. He even cooked his famous chocolate soufflé dessert. I will never forget it.

We routinely saw our internist, Doctor Patti Wheeler, at the nearby Highlands-Cashiers hospital. She also prescribed medication for nausea, pain and anxiety, if needed. For my 50th birthday in mid-May, Bob gave me some lovely Frank Lloyd Wright items to match the décor of the house, as well as a wonderful, adoring letter, expressing his appreciation for my care and his never-ending love.

Shortly before Bob's last treatment, I asked him what he wanted to do after to celebrate. His response was:

"Go to Switzerland and take walks up the Eggli Mountain for lunch."

Happy to oblige, I made the necessary reservations. The only remaining issue was removing the subcutaneous port. Bob wanted it out as soon as possible and for us to leave for Europe immediately afterwards.

Just prior to the end of treatment, we had a CT scan which was e-mailed to our friend, Doctor Manny, in Miami. Upon receiving it, he called immediately.

"Congratulations," he began in his jovial voice, "you both deserve champagne. Bob's scan was clear, and you are good to go to Switzerland."

On June 13 we said good-by to the home health care agency, which removed all the equipment and supplies from our bedroom, returning it to a more intimate and less therapeutic atmosphere. When Bob started complaining of stomach pains the following day, I was certain it was only the destructive effects of the chemotherapy. But, I became alarmed the day after that, when his stomach appeared distended. We went directly to Doctor Wheeler, who palpated his abdomen and said:

"I think you need a CT scan."

"He just had one last week," I interjected in her examination room.

"I think he needs another," she repeated.

"When?" I asked.

"Right now. Let's walk across to the hospital now."

The small-town local hospital was well-equipped and, without any wait, Bob was on a table having a scan while Patti and I were in the control room with a technician.

"René, it's everywhere," said the alarmed physician.

"What do you mean?" I said, hoping for a miracle in her next statement.

"There is evidence tumors in every organ I am looking at. This is serious."

In retrospect, I realized that I almost broke Patti's arm as I squeezed it during her brave delivery of that horrific news. We told Bob right there in the Radiology Department, and then we walked back to Patti's office, where she made an appointment for us to see an oncologist in Asheville the following day.

The overcrowded oncology office had grudgingly decided to squeeze us in. As a result, we sat for two and a half hours waiting to see the oncologist, a tough lady with a thick East European accent.

"There is nothing I can do other than to prescribe morphine and refer you to hospice," she said after examining Bob, and looking at several frames from the CT scan. She filled out the prescriptions and added nonchalantly,

"He will be dead in ten days."

In total silence, we got back in our car to drive the hour and a half to Cashiers.

"Doctor Milosevic is not the last word," I said after a prolonged period, referring to Slobodan Milosevic, Serbia's tyrannical strongman. "Let's call Doctor Levine."

Alexandra Levine was a revered, self-described "lymphomaniac," who practiced at the Kenneth Norris Cancer Research Center at the University of Southern California. We had tried to see her when I was diagnosed with lymphoma and again, six months earlier, when Bob received the same news. I had never even been able to speak with anyone other than her secretarial staff, and both earlier attempts at being treated by her had been unsuccessful. This time, however, I reached her.

"I will take Bob as a patient," she began in her long stream of confidence-building statements. "But if, and only if, he is here, in L.A. tomorrow. The ten-day prognosis you received is generous. That tumor is likely doubling in size daily and Bob will not live out the week, unless we begin some aggressive experimental drugs immediately."

"We'll be there," I said.

We made all the necessary calls from the car in the following hour. We scheduled flights for the following day from Asheville to Los Angeles and begged a sweet lady, whom we had previously hired, to sit with our dogs while we were gone. As we drove into Stillmont, the residential community where Chenoncette was located, Ed Addison was collecting his mail at a community mailbox, which we had erected for the neighborhood at a pull-off on our property. Ed's miraculous wife, Bennie, had been monitoring the crisis with several calls each day and delivered her loving signature frequent nightly meals. Ed took one look at us both and, without either of us uttering a single word, burst into tears.

After a restless and, for Bob painful, night, when we cuddled together in bed with our dogs, I packed a few things, including cash and passports. While I was running around doing these chores, Bob sat outside on our deck, overlooking the pond we had rebuilt. It was dried up when we had bought the house, as the retaining dam had been broken. The new pond was totally lined and symbolized the peacefulness of our home, as did the large Koi living in it. The Koi swam around the Lily pads, seemingly in a dancing circle, whenever we played music outside on the deck.

I knew what Bob was thinking, and watching his ashen bald head look over the railing at the fish was heartbreaking.

<u>USC Medical Center, Los Angeles, California</u>

Bob nearly died in the plane from Atlanta to L.A. He began throwing up and we stayed huddled in a bathroom for most of the last half of the flight. Although Bob's real and adopted families live in the Los Angeles area, we had not asked, nor expected anyone to pick us up at the airport. I almost carried Bob to a taxi, and we made the long ride to East L.A. where the USC medical center is located.

Though I had lived in L.A. for several years, I had never been to this part of town. While doing field work, during his Ph.D. in psychology, Bob had worked at a juvenile detention center located

USC Medical Center Los Angeles, California

adjacent to the medical complex. Otherwise, there would be no reason to visit this area. The compound itself was pleasant and, during the day, full of busy students and family members who walked between the several hospital buildings, dormitories and classrooms. The area surrounding the medical center, however, is one of the worst and most dangerous parts of the city. At night it was empty, dark, dangerous and austere.

Doctor Levine and several of her colleagues received us immediately. She was eccentric, yet stylish in her dress and appearance, a tall, brilliant, compassionate lady, full of energy and enthusiasm. We both adored her from the second we laid our tired, frightened eyes on her. Bob and I, and Doctor Levine and three of her associates were cramped into a windowless room, sitting around a central square table. An easel and flip chart were tightly squeezed into a corner. Dr. Levine reconfirmed that a rapid relapse after the regimen Bob had received was usually immediately fatal. The tumor, which now looked like the worst "crix belly" we had ever seen, was crowding his organs and creating the pain and the dry heaving. She explained several experimental procedures and medications to which she had access, and carefully reviewed all pertinent details. There was little room for questions because we had no options. We were traumatized and terrified. Furthermore, the experts' explanations were so complete that we had no need for queries. Finally, I only asked,

"When do we start, and do you really believe we have a chance of success?"

Alexandra went back to the easel and, with a red magic marker wrote: "Now and YES."

We had experienced so many ups and downs, beginning with the initial cancer diagnosis. We then had to go through Corky's pessimism, when the marrow test results were unfavorable, then a successful clean scan at the end of the treatments, which was rapidly followed by a relapse. Now, contrary to what Doctor Milosevic had told us, this legendary lady, whom we had so recently met, was telling us that Bob would live, and she would personally see to it. I could see in Bob's eyes that he not only believed her, but he was fearless about the medications she was proposing.

Alexandra's team was equally impressive. One physician's assistant, Lisa, knew more about oncology than ten physicians combined. The floor nurses were competent and efficient. What a difference from Mercy Hospital, much less the pest hole in Key West, we thought.

Although I took a room at a nearby Omni Hotel, I stayed at the hospital all day and many nights. Bob's mother, sister and brother visited, as did the exceptional "graduates" from Teamm House.

The summer was a hot one in Los Angeles history, with temperatures hovering at 100 degrees most days. The students ate at a nearby cafeteria, located in the main medical center, which had been acquired by NME and endowed by my former client, Richard Eamer, NME's Chief Executive Officer. I passed by a huge painting of him, which hung in the lobby, on my way to one of the cafeterias which I frequented daily. I brought Bob our breakfast and lunches. At four o'clock each day, I bought ten iced cappuccinos and handed them out to tired employees in the hospital. I also bought our dinners at that time, as the cafeterias, as well as the entire neighborhood all shut down in the late afternoon.

Days turned into weeks and there was significant hope of recovery during an entire month. After our first week at Norris, Alexandra flew to Geneva to lecture at the World AIDS Conference. Jean-Claude Salamin put a chauffeur-driven Mercedes at her disposal and met her at the airport with one of his typically classic and blatant statements,

"If you can save our Bob, we will all be forever in your debt."

Some weekends we were allowed to leave the hospital. Even though Bob was weak, and we never left our room except to get carry-out food, we enjoyed these furloughs. Several of them were spent in a hotel on Ocean Avenue in Santa Monica, three blocks from where Tim and I had lived, and several others at our friend Smith Richardson's guest cottage in Venice. One of Bob's former Teamm House associates, a beautiful, competent woman, Melanie Kassman, was a production assistant at a movie studio. She brought us a large suitcase full of videos containing all the films which had been nominated for academy awards in 1998.

Even with an ever-increasing number of intravenous pumps on his rolling pole, I walked Bob around the hospital's floor several times a day. A second double-access IV port was surgically placed to allow for more and more medications. To amuse Bob, I would talk about the architectural design flaws at Norris, as well as the managerial discrepancies between American and private European hospitals. On our frequent daily walks, we saw many patients and some family visitors come and go. Some patients left alive, others didn't. Eventually, every nurse and hospital worker knew us and marveled at our dedication to each other. The more fortunate patients had visitors for a few hours every day. Some sad cases had few or no family and friends sitting by their beds at all, but I lived there. Bob used his new laptop computer and watched the business channel on television. We talked about the various interviews that were on the business channel, as well as interviews focusing on several IPO's, thinking that if things had been different, we could have been talking about Ray's IPO on CNBC.

Bob monitored the beginnings of discussions regarding human trials for an AIDS vaccine on the Internet and tried to educate me on how to surf the web. He reminded me that we had all been told 15 years earlier that vaccine trials would begin within two years and a cure would be available within five years. We learned that, for the first time since the beginning of the pandemic, the crisis in Africa was beginning to be discussed in some progressive circles, thanks, in part, to Congresswoman Maxine Waters. We were interested that a few European pharmaceutical companies were making generic anti-retrovirals to distribute in Africa's most devastated areas in defiance of American patent law.

I did not want Bob to wear a hospital gown and, for most of his stay, he was allowed to wear a sweat suit. There was no laundromat nearby, but I noticed washing machines in the basement of a locked dormitory. I would gather up our clothes and take a small paper cup used for salad dressing from the cafeteria. Then I would go to the only bathroom which had liquid soap and fill my makeshift detergent container. Necessity definitely became the mother of invention and, shamelessly, I managed to jimmy a basement window in the dorm in order to get inside and wash our clothes there every few days. The only time I recall leaving East L.A. was to have a Sunday lunch with my childhood friend, Ahmed, and his family at their country club on the west side of town. His lovely wife, Laurie, made sure the club packed a beautiful dinner for Bob.

Gradually, the sense of optimism began to disappear as one experimental drug after yet another was tried. After five weeks, I told Bob's father that he had better come from Minnesota. We spent that weekend aboard the Queen Mary in Long Beach, but Bob was barely able to get out of bed. The following week, Bob began having two IV poles with three and then four pumps on each. Finally, I could see despair on the faces of all the doctors, except Alexandra's. I attended a meeting with her entire team to assess what should be done, and we decided to tell Bob that everything possible had been tried but that, now, they recommended discontinuing treatments. Five of us walked into his room as he watched the business channel. For some reason, everyone lined up on one side of his bed, except Alexandra, who stood along the opposite wall. I stood at the foot of the bed. Before anyone had a chance to speak, Bob did.

"You all are bears," he said, pointing at the team and making reference to business analysts who took a negative view of the economy. "You, Alexandra are the only bull. I'm sticking with the bull."

We all walked out of the room without having delivered our prepared speech.

"I just couldn't say it, René," said Alexandra. "I'll try one more experimental drug, but it is highly toxic and is not well tested. I just can't tell that man I'm done. I just cannot."

For that new regimen, during the seventh week of our stay at Norris, Bob was moved into the "BMT" or "bone marrow transplant" unit, which is equivalent to a super-sterile intensive care unit. Everything deteriorated, from the nurse's abilities and compassion to Bob's condition. We clearly were just another hopeless case versus the friendly survivors who had become close to the staff on the regular hospital's floor. Bob began sleeping more and more in a state of semi- consciousness.

One day, the phone rang. It was our neighbor in Cashiers who owned the cottage we had tried to buy for two years. He offered to meet our last price. I responded with:

"I am not in a position to respond or to think clearly. Thank you anyway," and I hung up.

"Who was that?" mumbled Bob.

"Letchworth. He wants to meet our last offer."

"And you said no? Call him right back and say you will buy it. If something happens to me, you will put a caretaker in there that can maintain the property and make your life easier. Do it, René!" Bob's wish became my command.

After a long day, August 5th, I decided to go to the hotel to sleep. As I left Bob's room, a physician who worked in the BMT said,

"You know we are at the edge of physiology."

"Doctor, if you mean that Bob is dying, yes, I know."

I turned to the nurse's station and told them to call me if there was any change in Bob's condition during the night.

When I returned at 7 AM the following morning Bob was mumbling, gasping for air and not alert. I raced back to the nurse's station to tell them.

"It's shift change time and you'll have to wait until the new team gets up to speed. We are reviewing all the charts now," said a nurse, who looked amazingly like a human pig.

I had remained controlled for as long as possible. My nerves were frayed, and my patience was exhausted. With one huge sweep of my arm, I threw all the charts on the floor. I yelled,

"You come in there with me now!" pointing at the doctor who had said "he is on the edge of physiology." The pig-like nurse franticly picked up the phone and asked for hospital security as I returned to Bob's room with the physician.

After the doctor examined Bob, I said,

"Remove everything and let this man be in peace." I pointed to eight IVs with an air of disgust as a security guard came into the room. The doctor shoved the officer back into the hall.

"That is the right decision," he said looking at me, "but you need to leave one line in for morphine."

"Thank you, doctor," I said, "but do it now! No crap about shift changes."

Five minutes later I climbed into the bed next to Bob, who had one remaining IV tube going into his body. I called Bob's friend Melanie and told her that she had to come to the hospital immediately, as did any other Teamm House member who wanted to be with Bob on his last day.

"I have a very full day," she said.

"That's fine," I said, "just remember I called."

The phone was not back in its cradle for even a full minute before Melanie called back, "I've told my associates I have to leave, and I'll also call everyone else. We'll all be there as quickly as possible."

I lay next to Bob whispering sweet words into his ear. I told him many things, including that he imagine that we were in bed at Chenoncette, looking out at the lake with our dog, T- Cell, tucked in beside his tummy. I also told him how valiantly he had fought, that our partnership had brought out the best in me so that I felt anchored in myself, how much I loved him and that it was "okay to let go now."

When Melanie and many friends arrived, I got out of the bed and went out into the hall.

"This is how we are going to do this," I said with a strength that appeared from some unknown source deep inside me.

"You all wait in the family room over there. Then, one at a time, you come into the room for five minutes each. You are to say nice things in a gentle voice. This is not a time for unfinished business. It is to help Bob leave us peacefully. Okay?"

For the next two hours, Bob's friends and loving colleagues did exactly that. Nancy Troy, Garry's widow, sang a song. Others rubbed Bob's feet or freshened a washcloth and put it on his head. I stayed in bed with him, hugging him. As I embraced him, I sensed within me a new level of emotional sensitivity and depth that Bob helped me reach.

At 10:25 AM pacific time on August 6, alone with Bob in bed, he drew his last breath and died in my arms. I respected our "ten-minute rule" and chose to hold him for 20 more minutes and until I was certain his brain waves had ceased. This was my way of staying with the deeply felt connection between us, purposefully transferring Bob's essence as we merged into one.

I have a spotty recollection of signing papers and speaking with Alexandra afterwards, and there are differing reports about how I got to LAX airport. I left everything I had brought to the hotel and somehow, in complete darkness, I flew to Asheville via Atlanta. I have boarding passes to prove that I changed planes but all I remember is "waking up" in the Asheville airport parking lot looking for a car I had left there weeks earlier.

<u>Chenoncette, Cashiers, North Carolina</u>

For the first month after Bob died, I rarely left the house. Bennie delivered my meals. Donny, the same friend who drove one car back from Fort Lauderdale, came for a few days. He was a clever former insurance actuary, and he worked on reversing the sale of Bob's life insurance. Shortly before, in an effort to cover some of the expenses of the previous months, Bob had sold his policy to a viatical company. I could not go near Bob's dressing area in our bedroom and only went into his office to help Donny find documents.

Ten days after I had returned from California, our neighborhood held its annual property owners' meeting. It was a custom to stand and pay respects to current and past owners who had died. Ed called and urged me to "emerge from my hole" and attend the meeting. Doug Smith, the self-righteous Christian, who would not pay for his cancer-stricken wife's medications, presided. Not a word was mentioned about Bob, his struggle or how much the neighborhood had lost. As a result, I retreated further into the secure darkness of Chenoncette.

At the end of August, I went to the same lawyer's office where Bob and I had signed the papers to close on the purchase of the house five and half years earlier. The attorney had two sets of documents ready for execution. One set opened Bob's estate so we could process his will, and the other set was to acquire the small house adjacent to Chenoncette, which we had tried so hard to buy together. I only recall the attorney explaining that there would be taxes to be paid on our home.

"That can't be," I said naively. "We own it as joint-tenants with right of survivorship."

"Sadly, that applies only to husband and wife in North Carolina," she began. "The tax will be less than if you had not recorded the deed in that manner, but there still will be a tax liability. With right of survivor there is no tax for a spouse, a small tax for a blood relative and a higher rate for joint tenants who are not related," she said.

One day Bennie arrived carrying a small box. The lady post office manager had called her to let her know that Bob's ashes had arrived and that she hoped a friend could pick them up and bring them to me, rather than for me to find them in the mail. That generous, perhaps even illegal gesture more than made up for the news of the estate tax law. I would have to work hard to overcome my emerging revulsion for the few neighborhood homophobes who had used my weakened condition to make nasty statements. I recalled my first and only real boss, Royce Diener, saying that "the oppressed become the oppressors and can kick you when you are down."

On September 3, I heard that Swissair Flight 111, traveling from New York to Geneva, had crashed the previous evening near Halifax, Nova Scotia, killing everyone aboard. I had taken that same flight literally dozens of times and had three acquaintances aboard that day, including Doctor Jonathan Mann, who Bob and I had met on several occasions.

Bennie called me that afternoon to inquire what plans I had for Bob's memorial service.

"I have not even thought about it," I replied. "Nothing I guess."

"I think that's a mistake, René," she said in her gentle voice. "Think about it and let's discuss it again tomorrow."

Together, we decided to have a small, non-religious gathering on Chenoncette's deck and place Bob's ashes in the pond he so loved.

"Just a few intimate, local friends," I said.

In the ensuing few days, several friends who lived in different parts of the country called to inquire about me. To my surprise, when I mentioned the emergence of a plan for a ceremony, one after the other asked for dates and offered to travel in order to be included. Gradually, the group grew and, while still intimate, was made up of many life-long friends.

One sunny September day, we all sat around in a circle on the deck. I had placed a special item of Bob's on each chair, along with a card I had printed to send to acknowledge the huge number of sympathy letters I was receiving each day. The front of the card had a black-and-white picture of our house in the snow with the pond frozen over. The back read,

"Winter came early to Chenoncette. Please keep Bob alive in your hearts."

I delivered a brief acknowledgement of my appreciation for the attendees' presence and asked each guest to read a statement received from friends of Bob's who could not be with us. I had placed them in a deliberate sequence which resulted in a history of Bob's 42 years, beginning with his kindergarten teacher and ending with recent friends' accounts of his incredible character. When the testimonials were read, each guest put some of Bob's ashes in "his lake."

One guest had catered a beautiful lunch to be held at a cliff-side house nearby. There, a few poems were read, and each guest threw a rose over the cliff. Local guests then drove the out-of-town friends to airports. As I left, Ed said,

"In all my experience, reading the statement was the hardest thing I ever did and that was the most beautiful memorial service I ever attended."

By the end of the year AIDS had killed an estimated 20 million people worldwide. 20 years before, there were only vague hints of a killer virus brewing and little attention had been attributed to this "gay plague." By December 1998, one quarter of African-Americans in some inner-city communities were HIV positive, while black churches still resisted confronting the crisis, much less hosting open discussions on safe sex and HIV transmission. This was in spite of the new statistics which showed that 80% of new American infections were among minorities.

Bob and I had been told that the Koi would never reproduce in our pond and, in the five years we watched them grow, they had not. Mysteriously, however, the following spring there were literally several hundred baby Koi swimming around in the lake.

EPILOGUE

René and Robert, Provincetown, Massachusetts, 2019

As I wrote in the Foreword, it occurred to me that, many of you gentle readers might be interested in finding out what happened to those characters described in the book, who survived beyond 2008.

Allow me to begin with myself, after which everyone's lives will be updated in the order they appear in the book.

After Bob died, I entered into a prolonged, dark period, which meandered through several gloomy phases. The first two years were spent being a recluse at Chenoncette. During this period, I was nearly comatose, relying on the kindness of a few friends to survive, even to eat. I drank too much, didn't socialize enough, and generally tread water, while leading a life with no direction.

I can't say I made bad financial decisions. Perhaps worse, I made *no* financial decisions. I had no motivation to make or monitor my investments. I took no steps to seize financial opportunities my directionless, meandering life accidentally fell upon. Without a plan, I was a rudderless ship; waiting for the time I would join Bob. I endured this lackluster existence, waiting for my time to die; not fearing death, but terrified of being hospitalized.

Like during my 18 months caring for Tim and, later Bob, my one healthy salvation was going to a gym. I began referring to the gym as "gay church" and I became a very devout churchgoer!

I eventually decided to sell Chenoncette. Probably because I really didn't care, the property lingered on the market for two years with no offers, so I ended up selling it at auction for a very low price. The day of the auction and the ensuing few weeks, moving out were a particularly sad, low-point in my life.

The currents pushed my powerless ship to move into the guesthouse of loving, generous friend in nearby Highlands. A few months later, I rented a duplex in Key West.

In October of 2005 the duplex in Key West was heavily damaged by hurricane Wilma. I spent the closing months of 2005 and the winter of 2006 in a tiny, rental house on Eaton Street in Old Town, Key West. The first night there, sitting alone with my ever-faithful dog, T-Cell, I decided to try writing

In Key West with T-Cell Beach Club in the background

a book. In spite of being depressed, dejected and lonely, that accidental decision was my first small step to taking some charge of my life.

I had never written anything other than business reports, and I immersed myself into documenting my childhood. *I Survived Swiss Boarding Schools,* easily spilled out of me, 3 months later.

After I finished writing the book, I decided it was time to draw a line under my Key West life and I moved to Palm Beach, where I had some roots since my early childhood. I recall driving out of the town in which I had once been blissfully happy, cared for two dying lovers, survived a ruptured appendix, endured a late-stage cancer and the murders of two dear friends, thinking I was living in the Twilight Zone.

My brother took great offense at my first book. There is a very simple explanation: John had spent his life as a Swiss banker. Swiss bankers *never* talk about their families or reveal inner demons. Also, for his own sanity, he had adopted an idealized memory of our childhood. Fortunately, with the help of his French second wife, Christine, we eventually bridged that abyss.

My beloved T-Cell died in my arms in 2007. She had lived half her long life with Bob and me. From the time of Bob's death, nine years earlier, T-Cell never stopped looking for him. My heart ached every time she looked in his closet or the empty passenger seat in my car. When her own little heart stopped beating, the floodgates of tears and grief opened up all over again.

Although excruciatingly painful, T-Cell's death was cathartic and a necessary, final chapter of my acute mourning phase. A butterfly flew by as I brought her motionless body to the veterinarian's car. I will always think of that powerful yet sweet dog every time I see a butterfly.

Recovering from near physical and psychological death was not a straight line up for me. It required a series of baby steps, mixed in with some setbacks. However, I gradually realized that I was no longer a businessman, nor was I just a directionless widower. A new *raison d'être* had to develop. Gradually, I stumbled into new careers: That of a bodybuilder and author.

One day in 2008, my trainer commented on how, at 60, he thought I had reached a point where I could compete in body building events. Naïvely, I accepted the challenge and allowed him to sign me up for an "over 60s class" at a regional body building competition. A year later I won a gold medal in

The finalists during a "pose down" at the Gay Games
Cologne, Germany

New York. It was indeed naïve, because I had no idea of how dedicated one must become to prepare for major body building competitions. I quickly learned to live with a very rigorous physical schedule and to lead a life totally focused on my training. Health and strength became my beacon.

After repeating my performance, the following year, my trainer convinced me to sign up for the Gay Games, also referred to as the Gay Olympics. With great coaching and hard work, at 62, in front of a 1,000 spectators, I won the gold medal in Cologne, Germany in 2010. I chose *I Feel Pretty* from *Westside Story* as my theme song.

Other books flowed out every two years. Following the Work, you have just completed, I wrote about my experiences with the Duchess of Windsor in the 1970's. *Noblesse Oblige*, as I named it, using one of the duchess' favorite expressions, gave birth to my love for lecturing on the subjects of my writings.

Speaking about the iconic woman, at ever larger and more important venues, became my passion. Like the duchess who created a brand centered on her style, my brand was to write and, more importantly, lecture about glamorous subjects.

My next book was about Palm Beach's legendary architect, Addison Mizner and his wealthy, fascinating clients. Researching, writing and lecturing about it was exhilarating.

2013 was a transformational year. My brother, whom I always assumed would out-live me, developed a serious cancer. That summer, I shuttled back and forth to Switzerland where he was going through the horrors of chemotherapy, as I had done nearly 20 years earlier. Sadly, his outcome was less happy than mine and, with his wife holding one hand, and I his other, he drew his last breath in Geneva on October 6.

....

A few months earlier and after having been single for 15 years, I met a handsome, fit Dutchman, 20 years my junior. Robert Versteeg was a social worker who, at the time, worked in nursing homes and for hospice in South Florida. He tried and always succeeded in making dying patients as happy and comfortable as possible. Robert loved his job, which is contrary to what most people guessed. That was one of the many traits that endeared me to him. Whether it was his support during my brother's illness or his positive, happy nature, we became lovers and, within a few months of our seeing each other, Robert moved to Palm Beach.

That first year we were together, I told Robert about one of my passions: the great ocean liners which survived the Second World War, and which I had been fortunate enough to know during the 1950s and 1960s. One beautiful summer evening, having dinner on a terrace overlooking the ocean on Cape Cod, I told Robert about what I believed to be the greatest of all liners, but which had been tragically lost before I was born. This was the seed that germinated into my fifth book about the grand, 1930's, French flagship *SS Normandie.*

Robert has since gotten his doctorate in social work and has livened up my "third age" as the French charmingly refer to senior citizens. In the 6 years we have been together, he has ably inspired my writing and taken over creating our lectures, which, thanks to him, present more like glamorous shows than typical speeches. I have gone from delivering a handful of rather bland presentations per year to limiting our vibrant appearances to 25 joyous ones each winter.

We happily summer in Provincetown, Massachusetts on the tip of Cape Cod, where I write, and we prepare the subsequent winter's lectures.

Oh, I nearly forgot. I assume some of you may wonder about my health. After all, you just finished a book on HIV/AIDS, which took place during the worst part of the scourge, when everyone around me succumbed to horrible deaths.

I certainly do not want to be flippant about it, but I hardly ever think about my health. To be honest, the subject bores me. At 71, I am as vigorous and energetic as any of my contemporaries. I still go to "gay church" every day and I ride a bicycle as much as possible. Of course, I have many of the aches and pains other septuagenarians have and I religiously swallow some two-dozen pills a day, made up of anti-retrovirals and various vitamins and supplements. But, life is good and as Napoleon's mother is reputed to have often said in early 19th century Paris: "Let's hope it lasts!"

I have also gotten involved with the business of my adopted hometown of Palm Beach. I put my love of historic buildings to work and currently have the honor of serving as vice-chairman of Palm Beach's Landmarks Preservation Commission. I love the work, which has become a passion and I travel back to Palm Beach every summer month to attend the mandatory meetings.

So now, allow me to bring you up to date on the other people who survived *Walking the Rainbow*.

ROYCE DIENER

99th birthday party for Royce Diener (Left), René standing

Royce and I grew apart after I left AMI. Even today, I am unable to properly explain why. I regret he never met Bob and that I did not see him during the horrid seven weeks Bob and I stayed at the USC Hospital in East Los Angeles.

One day around ten years ago, I sent him a copy of *Walking the Rainbow*, with a cover letter telling him, he was one of the best things that ever happened to me. He answered lovingly, of course, and was very supportive of

René and Royce Diener,

my writing avocation, sharing with me some thoughts about *Walking* and a memoir he was writing.

Reestablishing communication with him and his lovely, loyal wife, Jennifer, was enormously gratifying. It made me realize that, even though my life had totally changed, my former relationships need not do so.

In 2016 Robert and I were honored to be invited to join a small group to celebrate his 98th birthday at his and Jennifer's Santa Monica home. The same home where I had spent many wonderful Sundays during my long tenure working for the best father figure anyone could ever have hoped for.

The following year we repeated the pilgrimage for Royce's 99th birthday. He sat at the head of the beautifully set table and served some of his legendary wines to accompany a most masterfully presented and served gourmet dinner. Royce eloquently told each guest how important he or she had been to him. He then asked us each to make a statement describing our relationship with him. It was a hugely moving event, totally appropriate for the great man, sensing his end near.

The amazing Royce Diener passed away at 99 and a half, six months later. Shortly before his death, I told him I would carry him in my heart for the rest of my life and I revere his memory every single day.

AHMED YEHIA

Ahmed and René, 2017

My childhood friend, Ahmed, and I have remained close. We have been so for 61 years and most assuredly will remain so as long as we both are alive.

Shortly after I left AMI, Ahmed married for the third time. His new wife, Laurie, was one of the attorneys who worked on my severance package at AMI. She was an able lawyer and drove a hard bargain, which did not alter our mutual respect. Since retiring from corporate law, she has become a notable Los Angeles artist.

After leaving AMI, Ahmed founded Quantum Leadership Solutions, a nationally recognized company, which provides management-consulting services to a variety of senior corporate executives. He lives in Santa Monica, California where he and Laurie have raised three wonderful children.

The only time I left Bob during our long stay at USC, was to have lunch with Ahmed and Laurie. I returned to the hospital carrying a lovely care package of food, which was one of Bob's last pleasures on the planet.

Ahmed and I speak routinely and make a point to see each other as often as our geographical separation allows. We refer to each other as "my brother."

STANLEY BALFOUR-LYNN

Even though the book mentions that Stanley died in 1986, I feel a need to describe how that still young, uniquely charming, talented man passed away.

After Stanley left AMI, he created a British chain of extended care facilities. Like many of us who began working with Royce during AMI's grand expansion period, he lamented that the pioneering days of the company were over. He found surviving in a large, bureaucratic organization difficult. It was not his cup of tea, so he took his wooden sign "It Can Be Done" and began a successful, second entrepreneurial career.

Stanley was a vegetarian who was fanatic about his health. In spite of this, he developed a leaky heart valve, while still in his 50's. As one of the pioneers of open-heart surgery in the UK, he was well placed to have one of Britain's premier thoracic surgeons replace the defective valve.

A then-new procedure of using a porcine device (pig valve) was recommended because it was, and still is, less likely to be rejected by the patient's body. The surgery was successful but a few days later, while recuperating in his London home, the valve's sutures ripped. Stanley knew exactly what was happening and he told his wife to call an ambulance.

Stanley and his clinics had owned many ambulances and he was proud of being able to reach emergency patients in record time. Unfortunately, on this sad night in mid-March of 1986, it took nearly an hour for one to get to his home. His last words were: "It is not fair."

JEAN CLAUDE SALAMIN

René and Jean Claude in Abu Dhabi 2018

Shortly after leaving AMI, Jean-Claude and his Swiss wife divorced. It is always risky to find simplistic solutions to complex problems, but he and I both felt that his wife was comfortable leading a low-key life in her native Switzerland. Jean-Claude, on the other, hand had become an internationalist while working with Royce and me. This was, at the very least, an important contributing factor to the couple growing apart and separating.

After their divorce, Jean-Claude partnered and ultimately married Regine Naqui, an extraordinary French lady who worked for the royal family in Abu Dhabi. They have lived happily together in that advanced Emirate for 25 years.

In 2009, during one of my visits to Abu Dhabi, the Salamins sponsored a lecture on the Duchess of Windsor. The grand event took place in a stunningly beautiful, torch lit garden. Many of the west European ambassadors, serving in the Emirates attended.

LÉO ECKMANN

René and Léo Eckmann, 2007

The brilliant and one-of-a-kind professor Léo Eckmann and I remained friends well after this Work was originally published.

When I was treating a serious cancer in 1994, Léo was in constant contact with me and my Miami based oncologist. After my last chemotherapy infusion, he urged me to come back to Switzerland for hospitalization, during which he prescribed numerous immune system boosters not approved in the US at that time.

Léo retired in 2002 and he moved to Geneva, where he continued to write articles published in numerous scientific journals. Ever erudite, he also wrote three novels and appeared in two movies.

I'm convinced the professor saved my life on many occasions while the world searched for viable AIDS treatments and medications. I will always revere him and honor his memory.

The great Léo Eckmann passed away in July 2011.

JEAN-CLAUDE CHERMANN

After Bob died, I stopped making my quarterly visits to Professor Chermann's laboratory. Initially, I did not have the energy or the motivation to cross the Atlantic. Afterwards, my zeal for monitoring all the latest research and developments in HIV lessened. Once HIV viral load testing became commonly accepted in the US, there was no need for me visit Marseille or for the laboratory to keep storing and studying my blood.

In the ensuing quarter of a century, Jean Claude has written an excellent book: *Tout Le Monde Doit Connaitre Cette Histoire* (Everyone Should Know This Story) and has secured numerous patents pertaining to his many discoveries related to virology. He has also appeared in countless televised interviews.

It has always been felt by many of us that he deserved the Nobel Prize in Medicine. The honor was never awarded to either Professor Chermann or any member of the French or American teams responsible for identifying the Human Immunodeficiency Virus.

Instead, the 1984 Nobel Prize in medicine was awarded to four scientists, a Dane, a German, an Argentine and a Brit, for their work in controlling the immune system. To this day, many believe this was an unfortunate and weak decision, motivated by the acrimonious competition that developed between NIH and the Pasteur Institute during the final stages of isolating the virus in 1983 and 1984.

WALTER (WALLY) L. WEISMAN

Every complex story has a villain. However, I could not have survived a four-decade-long, terminal illness by focusing on this story's villain.

I hope the now-85-year-old Wally has matured over time, and that his socially liberal, charming wife has been able to soften his earlier bigoted views.

PIERRE & MICHÈLE NUSSBAUMER

René and Pierre in Provincetown, 2018

I will never forget what the Nussbaumers' two trips from Switzerland to the mountains of North Carolina meant to Bob. That gesture will always stand out in my mind as one of the best gifts anyone could ever give me, because of the joy it brought to the ailing Bob.

The Nussbaumers phoned frequently during my dark period, and we met on both sides of the Atlantic with some frequency.

Pierre's patriarchal father passed away three years ago, and Pierre has assumed the role as the dynastic family's benevolent leader. He is generous, kind and wise. A true renaissance man who loves to travel, whether it be on a luxury-chartered aircraft or riding a bus across a region of a country he does not know.

A few years ago, Pierre decided to make a pilgrimage to Selma, Alabama. He wanted to walk across the Edmund Pettus Bridge. Talking with local people who still remembered the "bloody Sunday march" in 1965 exhilarated him.

It took both Pierre and Robert some time to adjust to each other. Robert was different from Bob and Robert had never met anyone like Pierre. But good people with good common motives always overcome such well-meaning protectiveness, and the four of us are now very close.

As I look back on the 30 years I have known the Nussbaumers, I realize they are the closest things I have to "family" in this story.

René and Michèle in Provincetown, 2017

LEROY "ROY" PESCH

After Doctor Pesch's failed bid to acquire AMI, his Swiss hospital corporation declared bankruptcy.

In March of 1987, in an attempt to salvage some of his Swiss investments, he illegally moved several assets from Switzerland to the US. This included a $5 million transfer, which was contested by his Kuwaiti investors. Doctor Pesch lost the suit, was arrested and extradited to Switzerland. After he served out his sentence, he retired to Idaho.

LeRoy Pesch had lost almost all of his $250M inheritance from his wife, Donna, the only daughter of Chicago billionaire W. Clement Stone.

He died in Boise, Idaho on June 19, 2010, at the age of 78.

RICHARD "DICK" EAMER

Dick Eamer and NME never built their huge, proposed hospital in Paris. NME's meteoritic rise to fame and extraordinary wealth came to an abrupt end.

The company that was once thought by NY Stock Exchange analysis as being unable to do wrong, fell victim to numerous lawsuits, alleging hundreds of millions of dollars in fraudulent charges. The company's stock collapsed and Eamer was forced to resign in disgrace.

Dick Eamer passed away on May 2, 2016, at the age of 88.

BEVERLY ZOLTE

Duane Rath's lovely sister, Beverly, never contested what she and I are certain was not a murder suicide in Janesville, Wisconsin on October 5, 1994.

Jim Sanger and Jim Dodson, the Rath Foundation's trustees, have, enjoyed a life of great luxury.

Jim Sanger lives in Madison, Wisconsin, while Jim Dodson recently died following a highly publicized romance. Dodson's children now control the Rath Foundation.

BENNIE AND ED ADDISON

Bennie and Ed Addison remained kind, supportive friends after Bennie engineered Bob's memorial service.

On one occasion I was put on an HIV medication, which has, as a known side effects in some patients, hallucinogenic reactions. The night after I began taking the drug, I had dinner at a neighbors' house along with the Addisons.

As my visual and mental impairment progressed that evening, I asked Bennie to pass me the salad and, as I reached into the salad, said:

"I need to take a napkin out of that bowl."

Bennie knew about my having started the medication, took my arm, and led me home. She never told the guests why I left, other than to say I did not feel well. No one questioned Bennie Addison, who was regarded as the social leader of the community. I am very grateful for her *savoir faire* and kindness, especially that night, which could have been very embarrassing.

Bennie choked eating in her bed in 2003 on my birthday, May 16. Ed and I, along with a devoted couple who worked for the Addisons, stayed with her in the local hospital. She was breathing but was unconscious. She was transferred to Asheville, North Carolina by helicopter where she died the following day.

Her funeral in Walterboro, a small community in South Carolina where both Addisons were from, was the most moving funeral I have ever seen. The local women had prepared an unequalled feast, simply served in the local church.

I still think about this amazing lady every day. I will never forget how her support kept the insulting homophobes at bay when Bob and I first moved into the neighborhood. After Bob's death, I might have starved to death had it not been for Bennie's kindness and generosity delivering food to my door daily.

RAY MIRRA and GIGI JORDAN

After Bob died, I remained in contact with Ray until he had divested himself of his unrestricted IHS stock.

Ray and Gigi married in 1998 and divorced in 2001. During their marriage, Gigi had an affair with her yoga instructor, Emil Tzekov, and had a son, Jude. Immediately after her divorce from Ray, Gigi married Emil.

Jude was legally adopted by Ray and never took the name of his biological father. By the age of 2, Jude was diagnosed as severely autistic. Within a few years, Gigi made numerous serious allegations about both Ray and Emil's alleged mistreatment of Jude.

Gigi killed Jude on February 4, 2010, calling it a mercy killing. She was sentenced to 18 years in prison and is currently serving out the sentence.

ALEXANDRA LEVINE

I stayed in close touch with Doctor Alexandra Levine for several years after Bob passed away. During the first year, I wrote her every month expressing my appreciation for how she had cared for Bob.

Although my frequent contact has faded away, I will always recall how she made Bob's failing, last seven weeks as pleasant as possible. Her compassionate treatment stands out in my mind still today and is in stark contrast to his earlier, disastrous hospitalizations at Mercy Hospital in Miami.

In 2000, Alexandra left USC's Norris Cancer Center and was appointed Chief Medical Officer of the City of Hope Medical Center in Duarte, California.

An internationally acclaimed Lymphoma expert, she is also Professor at City of Hope's Hematologic Malignancies and Stem Cell Transplantation Institute.

Most recently, she holds the newly endowed Chair at the City of Hope, which honors her epic achievements.

ABOUT THE AUTHOR

Born in New York, Richard René Silvin grew up in Switzerland. He spent 25 years in the investor-owned hospital industry and rose to the head of the international division of American Medical International, Inc. which owned and operated hospitals in 10 countries.

Since retiring after surviving a late-stage cancer, René published five books. Although his writing began as a retirement hobby, it quickly morphed into a second career. He lectures widely on the historical subjects of his books and has become recognized as a leading authority on the Duchess of Windsor, Addison Mizner, the SS Normandie, and Mar-a-Lago in Palm Beach. He also lectures on the lives of some famous women he has met throughout his life, like Audrey Hepburn, Jacqueline Kennedy Onassis, and Marlene Dietrich.

Silvin is the former Chairman of the Palm Beach Landmarks Preservation Commission, and he is listed in Who's Who in the World and Who's Who in Health Care.

ALSO BY RICHARD RENÉ SILVIN:

Villa Mizner - The House That Changed Palm Beach, 2014
Star Group International

Normandie - The Tragic Story of the Most Majestic Ocean Liner, 2016
Silvin Books LLC

Noblesse Oblige - The Duchess of Windsor as I knew her, 2nd edition 2017
Silvin Books LLC

I Survived Swiss Boarding Schools - All That Glitters Is Not Gold, 2nd edition 2018 Silvin Books LLC

Walking the Rainbow – All That Glitters Is Not Gold, 2nd edition 2021 Silvin Books LLC

To purchase books or for information about lectures visit:

www.rrsilvin.com

Made in the USA
Columbia, SC
25 February 2023

da6a42ff-6f10-4be9-b4f5-bf8742e8f125R12